Kurt Vonnegut in the USSR

Literatures, Cultures, Translation

Literatures, Cultures, Translation presents books that engage central issues in translation studies such as history, politics, and gender in and of literary translation, as well as books that open new avenues for study. Volumes in the series follow two main strands of inquiry: one strand brings a wider context to translation through an interdisciplinary interrogation, while the other hones in on the history and politics of the translation of seminal works in literary and intellectual history.

Series Editors

Brian James Baer, Kent State University, USA
Michelle Woods, The State University of New York, New Paltz, USA

Editorial Board

Paul Bandia, Professeur titulaire, Concordia University, Canada, and Senior Fellow, the W.E.B. Du Bois Institute for African American Research, Harvard University, USA
Susan Bassnett, Professor of Comparative Literature, Warwick University, UK
Leo Tak-hung Chan, Guangxi University, Hong Kong, China
Michael Cronin, Dublin City University, Republic of Ireland
Edwin Gentzler, University of Massachusetts Amherst, USA
Denise Merkle, Moncton University, Canada
Michaela Wolf, University of Graz, Austria

Volumes in the Series

Translation and the Making of Modern Russian Literature
Brian James Baer
Interpreting in Nazi Concentration Camps
Edited by Michaela Wolf

Exorcising Translation: Towards an Intercivilizational Turn
Douglas Robinson

Literary Translation and the Making of Originals
Karen Emmerich

The Translator on Stage
Geraldine Brodie

Transgender, Translation, Translingual Address
Douglas Robinson

Western Theory in East Asian Contexts: Translation and Translingual Writing
Leo Tak-hung Chan

The Translator's Visibility: Scenes from Contemporary Latin American Fiction
Heather Cleary

The Relocation of Culture: Translations, Migrations, Borders
Simona Bertacco and Nicoletta Vallorani

The Art of Translation in Light of Bakhtin's Re-accentuation
Edited by Slav Gratchev and Margarita Marinova

Migration and Mutation: New Perspectives on the Sonnet in Translation
Edited by Carole Birkan-Berz, Oriane Monthéard, and Erin Cunningham

This Is a Classic: Translators on Making Writers Global
Edited by Regina Galasso

Language Smugglers: Postlingual Literatures and Translation within the Canadian Context
Arianne Des Rochers

Translating Warhol
Edited by Reva Wolf

Cold War Women: Female Translators of Russian and Soviet Literature in the Twentieth Century
Cathy McAteer

Invading the American Canon: Translators of Russian Literary Fiction, 1863-1984
Muireann Maguire
Kurt Vonnegut in the USSR
Sarah D. Phillips
Interpreting the Amistad *Trials: How Interpreters and Translators Make and Shape History*
Jeanette Zaragoza-De León

Kurt Vonnegut in the USSR

Sarah D. Phillips

BLOOMSBURY ACADEMIC
NEW YORK • LONDON • OXFORD • NEW DELHI • SYDNEY

BLOOMSBURY ACADEMIC

Bloomsbury Publishing Inc, 1359 Broadway, New York, NY 10018, USA
Bloomsbury Publishing Plc, 50 Bedford Square, London, WC1B 3DP, UK
Bloomsbury Publishing Ireland, 29 Earlsfort Terrace, Dublin 2, D02 AY28, Ireland

BLOOMSBURY, BLOOMSBURY ACADEMIC and the Diana logo are trademarks of Bloomsbury Publishing Plc

First published in the United States of America 2026

Copyright © Sarah D. Phillips, 2026

For legal purposes the Acknowledgements on p. xiii and List of Illustrations on p. x constitute an extension of this copyright page.

Cover design by Daniel Benneworth-Grey
Cover photograph courtesy of Konstantin Azadovsky

All rights reserved. No part of this publication may be: i) reproduced or transmitted in any form, electronic or mechanical, including photocopying, recording or by means of any information storage or retrieval system without prior permission in writing from the publishers; or ii) used or reproduced in any way for the training, development or operation of artificial intelligence (AI) technologies, including generative AI technologies. The rights holders expressly reserve this publication from the text and data mining exception as per Article 4(3) of the Digital Single Market Directive (EU) 2019/790.

Bloomsbury Publishing Inc does not have any control over, or responsibility for, any third-party websites referred to or in this book. All internet addresses given in this book were correct at the time of going to press. The author and publisher regret any inconvenience caused if addresses have changed or sites have ceased to exist, but can accept no responsibility for any such changes.

Whilst every effort has been made to locate copyright holders the publishers would be grateful to hear from any person(s) not here acknowledged.

A catalogue record for this book is available from the British Library.

A catalog record for this book is available from the Library of Congress.

ISBN: HB: 979-8-7651-3220-3
PB: 979-8-7651-3221-0
ePDF: 979-8-7651-3219-7
eBook: 979-8-7651-3222-7

Series: Literatures, Cultures, Translation

Typeset by Deanta Global Publishing Services, Chennai, India
Printed and bound in the United States of America

For product safety related questions contact productsafety@bloomsbury.com.

To find out more about our authors and books visit www.bloomsbury.com and sign up for our newsletters.

For William ("Billy") Hamilton, who started it all

Contents

List of Figures	x
Acknowledgments	xiii
Note on Translation and Transliteration	xvi
List of Abbreviations	xvii
Soviet and Russian Journals and Publishing Houses in English	xviii

1	Introduction	1
2	Interlude: Forty-eight Hours in Leningrad, 1967	19
3	The Translator	25
4	Interlude: Rendezvous in Paris, 1972	89
5	Vonnegut and Soviet Readers	101
6	Interlude: Five Days in Moscow, 1974	143
7	The Wanderings of Billy Pilgrim, or Cinderella in the Concentration Camp	159
8	Finding Comrade Vonnegut: Vonnegut and His Soviet Critics	187
9	Interlude: No Free Breakfast in the Land of Lenin, 1977	219
10	Vonnegut and the Dissidents	231
11	Conclusion: Back to the Future:	259

Bibliography	267
Index	280

Illustrations

Figures

2.1 Kurt Vonnegut's transit visa for the Soviet Union, 1967. Courtesy Lilly Library, Indiana University, Bloomington, Indiana.   20
3.1 Donald M. Fiene, Louisville, Kentucky, 1975. Courtesy of Judith Fiene.   29
4.1 Kurt Vonnegut photographed with Rita Rait by Jill Krementz in Paris on October 28, 1972. All rights reserved. Photograph by Jill Krementz. Used with permission. Courtesy Lilly Library, Indiana University, Bloomington, Indiana.   94
6.1 Candlestick presented to Kurt Vonnegut in Moscow in 1974 by Rita Rait-Kovaleva. Photograph by Nanette Vonnegut. Used with permission.   152
6.2 Kurt Vonnegut's inscription on a candlestick presented to him in Moscow in 1974 by Rita Rait-Kovaleva. Photograph by Nanette Vonnegut. Used with permission.   153
6.3 Kurt Vonnegut photographed with Konstantin Simonov by Jill Krementz in Moscow, October 1974. All rights reserved. Photograph by Jill Krementz, used with permission. Courtesy Russian State Archive of Literature and Art, Fond 2871, opus 3, item 354, document 17.   155
7.1 Imaginary playbill for *The Wanderings of Billy Pilgrim*, Moscow, 1975–6. By Jenny El-Shamy. Used with permission.   160
7.2 Entrance to the Soviet Army Theater, Moscow, with the billboard of the stage play *The Wanderings of Billy Pilgrim* after Kurt Vonnegut, directed by Mikhail Levitin, March 19, 1976. Courtesy of Sputnik.   163
7.3 Soviet Army Theater, Moscow, October 2019. Photograph by Sarah D. Phillips.   164
7.4 Scene from *The Wanderings of Billy Pilgrim*, staged at the Soviet Army Theater, Moscow, May 1976. Courtesy of the Russian State Documentary Film and Photo Archive, Private Collection of N.N. Bobrov (0-356381).   183
7.5 Scene from *The Wanderings of Billy Pilgrim*, staged at the Soviet Army Theater, Moscow, May 1976. Courtesy of the Russian State Documentary Film and Photo Archive, Private Collection of N.N. Bobrov (0-356382).   184
7.6 Theater director Mikhail Levitin in his office at the Hermitage Theater, Moscow, October 18, 2019. Photograph by Sarah D. Phillips.   185

9.1	Konstantin Azadovsky (far left, fur hat), Rita Rait-Kovaleva (center, white hat), Kurt Vonnegut (second from right), and unknown colleagues, Finland Station, Leningrad, 1977. Courtesy Konstantin Azadovsky.	228
10.1	Writers Sergei Dovlatov and Kurt Vonnegut at Vonnegut's New York apartment, 1982. Photograph by Nina Alovert. Used with permission.	241
10.2	Kurt Vonnegut near the headquarters of the Soviet Mission to the United Nations in New York, protesting the trials of dissidents Anatoly Shcharansky and Alexander Ginzburg, July 11, 1978. Courtesy of Getty Images.	247
11.1	Nataliya Shulga (left) and Eri Shulga (right) with Kurt Vonnegut, Rochester, NY, 1995. Courtesy of Nataliya Shulga.	260
11.2	Sasha with the new Ukrainian translation of *Slaughterhouse-Five*, Kyiv, 2017. Photograph by Sarah D. Phillips.	262
11.3	Anti-war protester near Red Square, Moscow, March 13, 2022. Courtesy of Sota Vision.	265

Plates

5.1 A scene from *Breakfast of Champions*. "[The driver told Kilgore Trout], 'I was arrested for speeding down there [in Libertyville, Georgia] . . . I had some words with the policeman, and he put me in jail.'" By Nataliya Shulga and Oleksandr Kotlyarevskyy. Courtesy Lilly Library, Indiana University, Bloomington, Indiana.

5.2 A scene from *Slaughterhouse-Five*. "Billy was working on this letter in the basement rumpus room of his empty house . . ." By Nataliya Shulga and Oleksandr Kotlyarevskyy. Courtesy Lilly Library, Indiana University, Bloomington, Indiana.

5.3 A scene from *Slaughterhouse-Five*. "One time on maneuvers Billy was playing 'A Mighty Fortress Is Our God,' with music by Johann Sebastian Bach and words by Martin Luther . . ." By Nataliya Shulga and Oleksandr Kotlyarevskyy. Courtesy Lilly Library, Indiana University, Bloomington, Indiana.

5.4 A scene from *Breakfast of Champions*. "The words in the book, incidentally, were about life on a dying planet named Lingo-Three, whose inhabitants resembled American automobiles . . ." By Nataliya Shulga and Oleksandr Kotlyarevskyy. Courtesy Lilly Library, Indiana University, Bloomington, Indiana.

5.5 A scene from *Breakfast of Champions*. " . . . Kilgore Trout found himself standing on the shoulder of the Interstate . . . There were no bridges across the creek. He would have to wade."

By Nataliya Shulga and Oleksandr Kotlyarevskyy. Courtesy Lilly Library, Indiana University, Bloomington, Indiana.
5.6 A scene from *God Bless You, Mr. Rosewater*. "Trout, the author of eighty-seven paperback books, was a very poor man and unknown outside the science fiction field." By Nataliya Shulga and Oleksandr Kotlyarevskyy. Courtesy Lilly Library, Indiana University, Bloomington, Indiana.
5.7 A samizdat Russian-language "Book of Bokonon" that synthesizes all references to Bokononism across Vonnegut's novels. Leningrad, 1973. Used with permission.
5.8 Viktor Shklovskii and Rita Rait, Yalta, 1963. Courtesy Russian State Archive of Literature and Art, Fond 3112, opus 1, item 270, document 3.

Acknowledgments

I was able to research and write this book thanks to support from many institutions and individuals. Research and travel funds from Indiana University's Office of the Vice President for International Affairs, the College Arts and Humanities Institute, the Robert F. Byrnes Russian and East European Institute, and the Hamilton Lugar School of Global and International Studies facilitated archival and interview research in Russia and Ukraine. This work was partially funded by the IU Presidential Arts and Humanities Program. An Eastman Residency for the Arts and Humanities provided invaluable time, space, and inspiration just when I needed it most. Long live the humanities.

I got the idea for this project thanks to "Salo University," a 2017 Indiana University Bloomington Public Humanities Project. Salo University convened several IUB faculty members from different fields to ponder together the significance of Hoosier author Kurt Vonnegut's fiction. I am grateful to Ed Comentale for that opportunity, which sparked my interest in Vonnegut's "Soviet chapter."

That spark grew into a steady, sometimes unrelenting flame, thanks to the work of outstanding scholars who blazed a trail for my own investigations. Primary among these trailblazers are Yana Skorobogatov and Donald M. Fiene. Don, whom I unfortunately never met, is in many ways a coauthor of this project. I hope in some small measure this book does his vision justice. One unexpected pleasure of the research was being in touch with Don's wife Judith Fiene, his daughter Karen, and his son Bruce. I thank the entire Fiene family for their enthusiasm and generosity. Getting to know Nannette Vonnegut has been a treasure, too. Thank you, Nanny, for your support and contributions to this zany project.

Yana and Don are at the top of a long list of colleagues and friends who contributed to and supported this project from start to finish. Janet Rabinowitch's friendship and editorial expertise were invaluable, as was feedback from two anonymous readers for Bloomsbury Academic. I thank the fates that put Frederick H. White and me in the foyer of the Russian State Archive of Literature and Art on the same day and time. Fred, your guidance has been priceless, and I look forward to continuing our "Vonnegut and Hemingway in the USSR" road show.

From day one of the project, Zhanna Chernova was my constant companion and master troubleshooter, the project's greatest on-the-ground facilitator and source of moral support. Zhanna, your friendship means the world, especially in these times. Fellow scholars Konstantin Azadovsky, Gardner Bovingdon, Peter Budrin, Wookjin Cheun, Rossen Diagalov, Olga Filippova, Elena Gapova, Dmitrii Kharitonov, Neringa Klumbyte, Ivan Kurilla, Barbara Lönnqvist, Olga Panova, Tatiana Saburova, Olga Shevchenko, Francesca Silano, Lev Sobolev, and Ilya Utekhin provided generous guidance and feedback on the project in its various stages. I am grateful to Yulia Kleiman, Ilya Utekhin, and Natalia Uvarova, who facilitated my interviews with theater director Mikhail Levitin and poet-bard-composer Yulii Kim.

The generous scholars and Vonnegut fans who agreed to be interviewed for this project enriched the research enormously. I am happy to be able to thank some by name, including Olia Bueva, Elena Gapova, Roman Malynovsky, Nataliya Shulga, Lev Sobolev, Ilya Utekhin, and Lynn Visson. Other interviewees go by pseudonyms in the book, but their contributions to the story are no less valuable. Natalka Yasko in Kyiv, the first "real live Ukrainian" I ever met (in Urbana-Champaign, Illinois in 1994), cheered me and the project on through the years. She also recruited interviewees in Ukraine. Thank you, Natalka, for always having my back. Natalka's daughter Sasha also inspired the project, just by being herself. Stateside, Mark Trotter's enthusiasm for the project often kept me going.

I am grateful beyond words to artists Nataliya Shulga and Oleksandr Kotlyarevskyy, who allowed me to reproduce their beautiful illustrations inspired by scenes in Vonnegut's books. Our broken world needs to see these treasures. Thanks to Nataliya, Oleksandr, and the Lilly Library at Indiana University, now it will. Warm gratitude also extends to Nanette Vonnegut, Nina Alovert, and Jill Krementz for permission to feature their beautiful photographs in the book, and to Konstantin Azadovsky for generously sharing his personal archives of photographs and letters. Jeremy Hogan provided invaluable technical assistance in preparing the book's photographs. Viva *The Bloomingtonian*! Jenny El Shamy generously lent her design talents to create the "playbill" for Chapter Seven, and Kate Wiegele's magical editing greatly improved parts of the text.

I offer warm thanks to the many librarians and archivists who patiently fielded my queries and dealt so cheerfully and efficiently with my repeated requests for materials at the Lilly Library at Indiana University, the Ekstrom Library at the University of Louisville, the Bakhmeteff Archive in the Rare Book and Manuscript Library at Columbia University, the University of Delaware Library Special Collection, the Russian State Archive of Literature and Art, the Lenin Library in Moscow, the National Library of Russia in St. Petersburg, and the Russian State Documentary Film and Photo Archive. Julia Whitehead and Chris Lafave at the Kurt Vonnegut Museum and Library in Indianapolis continue to cheer on the project and its many twists and turns. Y'all are part of my karass! I thank series editors Brian James Baer and Michelle Wood for believing in the project, and Hali Han for being the most organized, responsive, and supportive editor an author could hope for. Hali, working with you has been a gift.

The greatest gratitude of all goes to my family—William R. Morris, Jr., Roman Savytskyy, and Micah Savytskyy. Dear hearts, I apologize for all the time I spent on this book, away from the three of you. Maybe someone will think it was worth it.

Note on Translation and Transliteration

In this text I usually use the Library of Congress system of transliteration for Russian and Ukrainian. For purposes of simplification, I transcribe the Russian letter "ё" as "e" and the Ukrainian letter "ï" as "yi." In the text, Notes, and Bibliography I refer to Russian and Ukrainian cultural figures, published authors, and interviewees according to how they write their names in English or how their names are usually rendered in scholarship and the press (e.g., Aksyonov, Azadovsky, Chukovsky, Efimov). I use common spellings of Soviet, Russian, and Ukrainian newspapers and other publications (e.g., *Literaturnaia gazeta*). All translations are my own, except where otherwise noted.

Abbreviations

BA-RRK	Rita Rait-Kovaleva Correspondence, Bakhmeteff Archive, Rare Book and Manuscript Library, Columbia University
DMF	Donald M. Fiene
DMFC	Donald M. Fiene Archive (Correspondence) at the University of Louisville
FIEN	Donald M. Fiene Manuscripts, Lilly Library, Indiana University, Bloomington, Indiana
Glavlit	Chief Directorate for the Protection of State Secrets in the Press
JK	Jerome Klinkowitz
KMA	Konstantin Markovich Azadovsky
KMAC	Personal archives of Konstantin Markovich Azadovsky, Correspondence
KV	Kurt Vonnegut
KVM	Kurt Vonnegut Manuscripts, Lilly Library, Indiana University, Bloomington, Indiana
LGL	Lauren G. Leighton
LitFond	Literary Foundation
LV	Dr. Lynn Visson, United Nations (retired)
RGALI	Russian State Archive of Literature and Art
RRK	Rita Rait-Kovaleva
SG	Sara Ginsburg
UCC	Universal Copyright Convention
VOA	Voice of America

Soviet and Russian Journals and Publishing Houses in English

Artistic Literature	Khudozhestvennaia literatura
Foreign Literature	Inostrannaia literatura
Herald of Foreign Literature	Vestnik inostrannoi literatury
International Literature	Internatsional'naia literatura
Komsomol Truth	Komsomol'skaia Pravda
Literary Armenia	Literaturnaia Armeniia
Literary Gazette	Literaturnaia gazeta
Literature of the World Revolution	Literatura mirovoi revolutsii
New American	Novyi Amerikanets
New Literature Review	Novoe literaturnoe obozrenie (NLO)
New World	Novyi Mir (sometimes also Novy Mir)
Problems of Literature	Voprosy literatury
Soviet Culture	Sovetskaia kul'tura
Soviet Writer	Sovetskii pisatel'

1

Introduction

In September 1978, Donald M. Fiene, a professor of Russian at the University of Tennessee, Knoxville, wrote a letter to his friend and colleague, the writer Kurt Vonnegut. He related a grim story about an acquaintance, a Soviet dissident, who had been subjected to severe interrogation at the infamous Lubyanka Prison in Moscow. "It was his intention to answer none of the questions—yet he had to endure the hours-long process just the same. He was advised by friends to take an infinitely absorbing book along to read." The harrowing experience had a silver lining, one that no doubt pleased Kurt Vonnegut. The dissident "pondered a long time about which book to take." Finally, wrote Fiene, "he settled on *Cat's Cradle*," Vonnegut's 1963 novel, which he read in Russian translation. "He made it through just fine without cracking."[1]

This book tells the story of one unusual American author—Kurt Vonnegut—and his unusual love affair with the Soviet Union. To be precise, it tells the story—multiple versions of it in fact—of that country's unusual love affair with Kurt Vonnegut. It is not widely known that Vonnegut's most famous novels and many of his short stories were translated into Russian in the 1970s and early 1980s by one of the Soviet Union's preeminent literary translators, the great Rita Rait. Also called Rait-Kovaleva, Rait had for decades translated foreign authors such as Salinger and Faulkner to great acclaim. Even fewer Westerners know that Vonnegut was immensely popular in the Soviet Union. The Soviet reading public fell in love with Vonnegut's books, his heroes and antiheroes, and with the author himself. "Comrade Vonnegut" had many lives in the Soviet Union during the political era that many inaccurately call "Stagnation."

Today, mentioning Kurt Vonnegut, his book titles, his key characters, or linguistic "Vonnegutisms" in the company of people who grew up in the Soviet Union elicits a host of recollections: memories of one's high school and university years, experiments with fashion to achieve a "Western and

---

[1] Donald M. Fiene (hereafter DMF) to Kurt Vonnegut (hereafter KV), September 16, 1978, p. 11. Fiene MSS, Lilly Library, Indiana University, Bloomington, Indiana (hereafter FIEN), Folder 4, "1978."

contemporary" look (e.g., blue jeans), listening to rock and jazz music, and tuning the radio to the Voice of America (VOA) and the BBC. But Vonnegut also calls up the dashed hopes of the Prague Spring, the heartless repression of dissident writers and scientists, and the stultifying sense among these former Soviets that nothing would ever change. These people initially read translated Vonnegut novels in serialized form in the sanctioned literary "thick journals." They think of Vonnegut alongside authors like Alexander Solzhenitsyn, Mikhail Bulgakov, and Sergei Dovlatov, who, unlike Vonnegut, were not approved by the state for consumption. Many readers remember the colors, textures, feel, and smell of the decent-quality paper the Soviet state publishing houses used to issue the collected editions of Vonnegut's novels in the late 1970s and early 1980s. And they recall the tattered pages of samizdat—the illegal self-published booklets and gazettes by dissident writers and human rights defenders—that were furtively passed around alongside the "allowed" books.

Anthropologists believe that when an object or a phenomenon elicits a rich array of narratives and associations, it means the thing is "good to think with." Kurt Vonnegut's books traveled to the Soviet Union where they were translated, published, and devoured by readers. The Soviet state used his writing to critique the West, especially the United States and its war in Vietnam. Soviet readers understood his work in a multitude of ways. Vonnegut himself even reflected on his "Soviet chapter." Having spent more than six years tracking these narratives and associations, I am more than convinced that "comrade Vonnegut" is good to think with, especially when it comes to understanding what was bubbling beneath the so-called Stagnation. This is because during this particularly fraught period of US-Soviet relations, Vonnegut—at times without knowing it, at times fully aware—was doing the vital and often unheralded work of literary cultural diplomacy.

But the American author didn't do this work alone. This work required the active participation of an entire cast of translators, scholars, publishers, literary critics, journalists, editors, censors, theater directors, composers, actors, librarians, political dissidents, and most of all, readers. The voices of these characters echo through this book. Through the lens of engagement with "comrade Vonnegut," they relate in chorus a complex story about how the Cold War looked and felt to Soviet citizens. Indeed, although the period we have learned to call "stagnation" was saturated with boredom and ennui, dynamism and hope for change boiled just below the surface.

In this book I tell the story of how that undercurrent of possibility was kindled in part by the avid consumption of foreign literature in translation, particularly the work of Kurt Vonnegut. I use the tools of my trade: cultural anthropology, history, and literary and translation studies to reveal an unfolding story of cultural transformation, ideological refusal, and literary friendship between Americans and Soviet citizens during the Cold War.

The "other side" of the Cold War

Quite a bit has been written about "Cold War culture" at the level of domestic life in the United States. In *The Culture of the Cold War*, Stephen Whitfield introduced the notion of "American Cold War culture," a culture deeply rooted in militant anti-communism that dominated all aspects of American life.[2] Paul Boyer, in *By the Bomb's Early Light*, explored the nuclear bomb as a prominent obsession of American Cold War culture, a fixation recently confirmed by the popularity of the blockbuster film, "Oppenheimer."[3] The rise of American consumer culture as a Cold War cultural-political phenomenon has also been explored in Cold War studies such as Lary May's volume of essays *Recasting America: Culture and Politics in the Age of the Cold War*.[4] Together, these works provide a chilling commentary on the key cultural touchpoints for a generation of baby boomers reared in post-Second World War America: anti-communism, fears of nuclear annihilation, and powerful mass media and advertising that shaped Americans' desires, values, and notions of success.[5]

On the other hand, we don't know very much about Cold War culture in the Soviet Union. One of the main sources that examines Cold War cultures in the Soviet bloc focuses almost exclusively on the "satellite states" in East-Central Europe, not the Soviet Union.[6] Recent scholarship concentrates on the cultural exchanges and confrontations between the United States and the USSR in sports, the space race, and music and the arts that permeated Cold

---

[2] Stephen J. Whitfield, *The Culture of the Cold War* (Second edition) (Johns Hopkins University Press, 1996).
[3] Paul Boyer, *By the Bomb's Early Light: American Thought and Culture at the Dawn of the Atomic Age* (University of North Carolina Press, 1985).
[4] Lary May, *Recasting America: Culture and Politics in the Age of Cold War* (University of Chicago Press, 1988.)
[5] This work on American Cold War culture has been enriched by additional interventions, including Douglas Field, ed., *American Cold War Culture* (Edinburgh University Press, 2005), and George Lipsitz, *Class and Culture in Cold War America: Rainbow at Midnight*, (Praeger Scientific, 1981). Both volumes incorporated neglected issues of race, gender, and class into analyses of Cold War cultures in the United States.
[6] Annette Vowinckel, Marcus M. Payk, and Thomas Lindenberger, eds., *Cold War Cultures: Perspectives on Eastern and Western European Societies* (Berghahn Books, 2012).

War cultures in both locales.[7] Consumption and "consumer politics" were key features of both Cold War cultures, as evidenced by the famous "kitchen debate" in 1959 between Nixon and Khrushchev at the American National Exhibit in Moscow. One episode of the narrative exchange took place during a joint visit to the model American kitchen featured in the exhibition. The leaders debated the respective merits of capitalist and socialist economic systems for generating innovations in technology and manufacturing, including the design, manufacture, accessibility, and affordability of color televisions, automated washing machines, and other consumer goods.[8] Another key feature of Cold War consumer politics was the consumption of books.

Scholars of post-World-War-II Soviet culture have argued persuasively that Soviet citizens were much more interested in the United States—and in the West in general—than Americans were in the Soviet Union. Just as the Russian Empire had, Soviet internationalism encouraged citizens to be interested in the rest of the world. American historian Eleonory Gilburd writes, "the capitalist West was the standard of development and a challenge to be overtaken."[9] Americans as a rule, were more insular and less interested in life outside the boundaries of the United States.[10] By contrast, the Soviet people, especially youth, were quite fixated on life in the West, particularly life in the United States. This is one reason Western literature in translation was so sought after in the USSR: it offered a window to the mysterious, elusive West. Likewise, exploring the Soviets' fascination with this literature offers a window into the Cold War from Soviet perspectives. While Americans worried about the communist threat, the bomb, and keeping up with the Joneses, what kept their Soviet counterparts up at night? Believe it or not, Soviet people were not hunkered down in bomb shelters, cut off from the world and clueless about foreign affairs. They were listening to international news broadcasts, dreaming about Paris, London, and New York City, and reading the novels of Hemingway, Faulkner, and Kurt Vonnegut.

---

[7] Robert Edelman and Christopher Young, eds., *The Whole World Was Watching: Sport in the Cold War* (Stanford University Press, 2019); James T. Andrews and Asif A. Siddiqi, eds., *Into the Cosmos: Space Exploration and Soviet Culture* (Pittsburgh University Press, 2011); Danielle Fosler-Lussier, *Music in America's Cold War Diplomacy* (University of California Press, 2015).

[8] Ruth Oldenziel and Karin Zachmann, *Cold War Kitchen: Americanization, Technology, and European Users* (MIT Press, 2009).

[9] Eleonory Gilburd, *To See Paris and Die: The Soviet Lives of Western Culture* (The Belknap Press of Harvard University Press, 2018), 8.

[10] Dina Fainberg, "Radio Moscow, Decolonization, and the Cold War," discussant comments presented at the fifty-third convention of the Association for Slavic, East European and Eurasian Studies (virtual), December 2, 2021.

Vonnegut-mania and the paradoxes of Stagnation

Under the brutal totalitarian regime of Joseph Stalin, who ruled the USSR with an iron fist from 1924 until 1953, the Soviet regime controlled every aspect of life. Stalin presided over extensive purges, the forced collectivization of agriculture, industrialization campaigns, and widespread human rights abuses, resulting in millions of deaths and a tightly controlled society. His rule solidified the USSR's role as a global power while imposing immense suffering and repression on its citizens. In the world of literature in the 1930s, Soviet translators had some room for direct contact with Western authors and cultural figures. Translators' individual efforts were crucial in acquiring foreign literature, choosing pieces for translation, and presenting the completed translations to publishers and other distribution channels.[11] However, the Great Terror under Stalin (1937–8) had a chilling effect on cultural collaboration with the West, especially on foreign literary imports. Literary exchanges, which were once a natural consequence of large-scale cultural collaboration when representatives of the Soviet and Western intelligentsia actively traveled back and forth between countries and continents, were all but frozen.

On February 25, 1956, Nikita Khrushchev denounced the excesses of his predecessor Stalin's reign of terror in his infamous "secret speech" to the 20th Party Congress. He subsequently pursued a policy of de-Stalinization and ushered in the "Thaw," a period of internal easing of political reins and repression in the Soviet Union, and the concomitant détente in foreign relations with other countries, especially the United States. The Thaw lasted from 1953 to 1964. In addition to a relaxed political atmosphere and the release of millions of political prisoners from labor camps, the Thaw loosened the "cultural shackles," with major implications for the Soviet literary scene.[12] The Thaw was an "epoch of reforms, vibrant polemics, and tectonic sociocultural transformations . . . a moment when literature remained culturally and politically significant for the authorities and for readers, while at the same time the literary environment once again came to enjoy a considerable degree of autonomy."[13]

---

[11] Nailya Safiullina and Rachel Platonov, "Literary Translation and Soviet Cultural Politics in the 1930s: The Role of the Journal Internacional'naja Literatura," *Russian Literature* 72 (2012): 239–69.
[12] Jekaterina Young, *Sergei Dovlatov and His Narrative Masks* (Northwestern University Press, 2009), 4.
[13] Denis Kozlov, *The Readers of Novyi Mir: Coming to Terms with the Stalinist Past* (Harvard University Press, 2013), 6.

The post-war and Thaw periods were about "coming to terms" with Stalin's purges, the devastating loss of human life borne by the Soviet Union during the Second World War, and other collective traumas, according to Denis Kozlov in his book on "literature-centrism" of the era:

> At the turn of the second half of the century, thousands of people sought to comprehend the first half, rethinking and actively debating the experiences of the Revolution, the Civil War, the forced collectivization of agriculture, World War II, and, principally, the historic tragedy that would later come to be known as the Stalin terror. Literature became the principal medium for these reflections and conversations.[14]

Previously banned authors could now be read by Soviet citizens, and a veritable deluge of Western writers in translation saturated the literary milieu. In her brilliant book, *To See Paris and Die*, Eleonory Gilburd tracked how imported Western novels, films, paintings, and other cultural products influenced Soviet culture and became "an intimate part of Soviet cities and biographies."[15] "American literature in translation played a particularly important role in the literary process" in the 1960s USSR,[16] with the publication of authors such as Salinger, Faulkner, and Hemingway, the latter being a particular favorite of Soviet readers and a huge influence on an entire generation of writers. J. D. Salinger's *Catcher in the Rye* was serialized in Russian translation in the journal *Foreign Literature* (*Inostrannaia literatura*) in 1960 with a whopping print run of 350,000 that still did not satiate readers' demand. It was reissued in book form in 1965 and again in 1967.[17]

By 1964, the year Khrushchev was ousted from power, the tide had shifted and the relative liberalism of the Thaw period came to an end. Destalinization had resulted in critiques not only of Stalin but of the entire Soviet system that made Stalin and his brutal tactics possible. Khrushchev's successors prioritized squelching the burgeoning dissident movement that destalinization and the Thaw had incubated. They invaded Czechoslovakia in 1968 (the "Prague Spring") and subsequently clamped down on dissent, officially ushering in the period of Stagnation under Leonid Brezhnev,

---

[14] Kozlov, *Readers of Novyi Mir*, 6–7.
[15] Gilburd, *To See Paris*, 1.
[16] Young, *Sergei Dovlatov*, 5.
[17] The Salinger translations were by Rita Rait, who would later translate Kurt Vonnegut's books into Russian. The 1965 and 1967 book-form publications of *Catcher in the Rye* were both from Young Guard publishing house, with print runs of 115,000 and 100,000, respectively. Source: Archival Inquiry re: Raisa Iakovlevna Rait provided to the author by the Russian State Archive of Literature and Art, September 25, 2019 (No. 655/5–4).

which lasted from 1964 to 1985. Brezhnev's "ideological turn of the screw"[18] narrowed the pipeline of Western cultural products entering the USSR, including (and at times, especially) translated literature. It also put a tight squeeze on what Soviet authors could publish in official outlets. Repression of dissent had a dramatically chilling effect on creative expression, including writing. Ideological assessment of the pre-published word was the primary task of Glavlit, shorthand for "Chief Directorate for the Protection of State Secrets in the Press."[19] Glavlit, the foremost arm of the Soviet institution of censorship, operated "with unremitting diligence" during Stagnation.[20] The result was a burgeoning underground circulation of samizdat writing, including fiction (e.g., Bulgakov's *Heart of a Dog*) and non-fiction (e.g., the human rights publication *Chronicle of Current Events*, and Aleksandr Solzhenitsyn's *Gulag Archipelago*).[21]

It is curious that Vonnegut broke onto the Soviet literary scene when he did—1970 to 1981—a decade marked by cultural (and economic) stagnation and tightened ideological reins. Throughout that decade, translations of Vonnegut's novels and stories were published across a diverse spread of publications. These include the literary "thick journals" such as *Foreign Literature, New World* (*Novyi Mir*), and *Literary Gazette* (*Literaturnaia gazeta*). His novels also appeared in periodicals targeting youth, young adults, and their parents, as well as periodicals and anthologies dealing with popular mechanics and popular science.[22] Vonnegut in translation appeared not only in publications in the "center" of the Soviet Union—Moscow and Leningrad—but also in the various Soviet republics—Estonia and Latvia,

---

[18] Anne Lange, Daniele Monticelli, and Christopher Rundle, "Translation and the History of European Communism," in *Translation Under Communism*, ed. Christopher Rundle, Anne Lange, and Daniele Monticelli (Routledge, 2022), 28.
[19] Leonid Vladimirov, "Soviet Censorship: A View from the Inside," in *The Red Pencil: Artists, Scholars, and Censors in the USSR*, ed. Marianna Tax Choldin and Maurice Friedberg (Unwin Hyman, 1989), 18.
[20] Young, *Sergei Dovlatov*, 21.
[21] On samizdat, see Liudmila Alekseeva, *Soviet Dissent: Contemporary Movements for National, Religious, and Human Rights*, trans. Carol Pearce and John Glad (Wesleyan University Press, 1985); Ann Komaromi, "The Material Existence of Soviet Samizdat," *Slavic Review* 63, no. 3 (2004): 597–618.
[22] Michael Khmelnitsky, "Sex, Lies, and Red Tape: Ideological and Political Barriers in Soviet Translation of Cold War American Satire, 1964-1988" (PhD diss, University of Calgary, 2015), 64–5 (doi:10.11575/PRISM/27766).

for instance—and in rural settings (e.g., the periodical *Rural youth* [*Sel'skaia molodezh'*]).[23]

What should we make of this seeming contradiction? If Stagnation in the Soviet Union was a time of economic sluggishness and cultural boredom borne of ideological constraints, if Stagnation marked a period of "bureaucratic 'prosperity and peace' during which the role of Glavlit in the political system of the state practically did not budge at all,"[24] how did Kurt Vonnegut and his "fabulations"[25] make it through the cracks in the Iron Curtain, past the desks of the Glavlit censors, and into the homes and hearts of millions of Soviet readers?

Stagnation is important for our story not only for the tight ideological restrictions imposed on the literary scene during Vonnegut's "Soviet chapter," but also because it was the context of everyday life for Vonnegut's Soviet readers. The Soviet 1970s were "boring, utterly boring," a woman who grew up in Kyiv told me. It was easy for Soviet citizens—especially young people—to feel stuck, hopeless that the system would ever change, especially after the dashed hopes of the Prague Spring. But some people I talked to challenged taken-for-granted stereotypes of a stultified, bland society during the period of so-called Stagnation. Children of intelligentsia families described the towers and rows of books—many of them translations of foreign literature, or the originals—lining the walls of the apartments they grew up in, creating a kind of litero-centric nest where they escaped the humdrum life outside. Others spoke of explorations with their friends of anything and everything "Western," by any means available. "We knew the music (not only the Beatles and the Rolling Stones, but also Led Zeppelin, Queen, etc.)," said Nadia, "and we knew American classics: *Catcher in the Rye* . . . *The Great Gatsby, Tender is the Night* . . . Hemingway . . ." Nadia (a pseudonym) was born in Moscow in 1959. "We loved everything American, including faded blue jeans and Wrigley's chewing gum." Much of what she and her "gang" learned about America came from movies, she told me.

The scholar Alexander Burak explains the unique appeal of anything Western to Nadia's generation at the time.

---

[23] The Estonian translation by Valda Raud of *Slaughterhouse-Five* was published in 1971, and a Latvian translation of *Cat's Cradle* (by A. Bauga) appeared in 1973. See Donald M. Fiene, "Kurt Vonnegut as an American Dissident: His Popularity in the Soviet Union and His Affinities with Russian Literature," in *Vonnegut in America: An Introduction to the Life and Work of Kurt Vonnegut*, ed. Jerome Klinkowitz and Donald L. Lawler (Delacorte Press/Seymour Lawrence, 1977), 285.
[24] T.M. Goriaeva, *Politicheskaia tsenzura v SSSR 1917–1991* [Political censorship in the USSR 1917–1991] (ROSSPEN, 2022), 15.
[25] Robert Scholes, *The Fabulators* (Oxford University Press, 1967).

Beginning with the Khrushchev Thaw, a number of coincidences collided, and, thanks to translators, the Soviet logocentric readership received a Russian version of Hemingway that perfectly fit and reinforced the mindset of the new Soviet "lost generations" of the 1960s and 1970s, the generations that had become disillusioned with the remnants of Bolshevik values and the idea of "socialism with a human face."[26]

It was precisely this so-called "lost generation" of young people who devoured Vonnegut in translation beginning in 1970. Some of these readers, whom historian Donald Raleigh calls "Soviet baby boomers," were broad-minded and widely read folks locked into certain "safe" professions in the hard sciences and engineering. In another socio-political context, these people may have studied social sciences or gone into politics or social work. Reading Western literature in translation, especially Vonnegut—whose work bordered on science fiction and who ruminated on the moral-ethical considerations of technical progress—enabled the Soviet "technical intelligentsia" to safely sublimate their interest in social issues without engaging in dissident activities. These themes are explored in Chapter 5.

The Vonnegut fans I talked to shed light on what it meant that Vonnegut hit the Soviet scene in the early 1970s. Leonid, who discovered Vonnegut as a student in Leningrad, told me he received Vonnegut's works in "the style of the Prague Spring." "We were still living on the fumes of Khrushchev's Thaw and the [1968] Prague Spring." Reading Vonnegut spoke to—if not entirely satisfied—his and his friends' pressing desire to preserve channels between the East and West. Nadia (mentioned above), who read Vonnegut as a high school student in Moscow, said, "He was popular because it was the time of the Cold War, the confrontation between the USSR and the United States. And he connected the two countries with his books." In other words, Vonnegut gave Soviet citizens hope that real, sustainable, human-to-human connections between the United States and the Soviet Union were possible. At a time when there was little else to sustain hope—the Soviets' 1968 invasion of Czechoslovakia after the Prague Spring shattered hopes for freer speech, media, and travel—this mattered a great deal to them. This is Vonnegut's little-known legacy as a literary cultural diplomat, a legacy this book is about to explore.

[26] Alexander Burak, *"The Other" in Translation: A Case for Comparative Translation Studies* (Slavica, 2013), 28.

Kurt Vonnegut's literary cultural diplomacy

During the Cold War era, the United States "sent American performing artists and athletes around the world to improve the image of the United States."[27] This "Cultural Presentations" program, sponsored by the U.S. Department of State from 1954 to the early 1970s, is described in Danielle Fosler-Lussier's groundbreaking study, *Music in America's Cold War Diplomacy*. Fosler-Lussier explains that the musicians who traveled to perform in the Soviet bloc, Latin America, Southeast Asia, and elsewhere were "unlikely diplomats." They were little concerned with the political aspects of their mission and received no diplomatic training.[28] Nevertheless, thanks to informal personal interactions baked into the encounters—especially for amateur and collegiate groups and small professional ensembles—these musicians-cum-unwitting cultural diplomats managed to create "memorable human connections" and even a feeling of community among those involved. American musicians (especially jazz musicians) would play in jam sessions with musicians from the host countries.[29] Fosler-Lussier's insights about U.S. musical diplomacy inspired me to think about literature as another form of cultural diplomacy during the Cold War.

Cultural diplomacy is often discussed as a form of soft power practiced by states, in which countries (such as the United States) seek to mobilize cultural resources to achieve foreign policy goals. In foreign relations studies, cultural diplomacy, "the use of creative expression and exchanges of ideas, information, and people to increase mutual understanding," is thought to supply much of the content for public diplomacy, which "consists of all a nation does to explain itself to the world."[30] When I speak of Kurt Vonnegut's literary cultural diplomacy, I am not thinking in terms of official foreign policy and high-level state strategy. Instead, as an anthropologist interested in history, lived experience, and Cold War divisions and bridges at the level of everyday life, I discuss it as a phenomenon that unfolded on the ground, in experience-near ways, quite detached from formal foreign policy goals or state priorities. I center relationships—between author and translator, between translator and editor, and between readers themselves—as the key mechanism for cultural diplomacy in the 1970s. Vonnegut's literary cultural diplomacy unfolded through relationships as his texts moved (in Donald

---

[27] Fosler-Lussier, *Music in America's*, 2.
[28] Fosler-Lussier, *Music in America's*, 14.
[29] Fosler-Lussier, *Music in America's*, 18.
[30] Cynthia P. Schneider, "Cultural Diplomacy: Hard to Define, but You'd Know It If You Saw It," *The Brown Journal of World Affairs* 13, no. 1 (2006): 191.

Fiene's suitcase!) from Bloomington, Indiana, to Moscow; as his masterful American-language prose was transformed into equally masterful Russian by "his" translator, the legendary Rita Rait-Kovaleva; and as Vonnegut-in-translation made its way into the hands and socio-literary networks of hungry Soviet readers, who imagined themselves in dialogue with Vonnegut's characters, with the country they came from (the United States), and with Vonnegut himself.

Literary cultural diplomacy, at least of the kind I follow in this book, was not usually an official, top-down, highly choreographed affair, as many forms of U.S. cultural diplomacy directed at Soviet citizens were. Think, for instance, about US-Soviet space cooperation, or U.S. government-sponsored cultural festivals in the USSR, such as the American National Exhibition in Moscow in summer of 1959 that engendered the "kitchen debate" between Nixon and Khrushchev. In Kurt Vonnegut's case, it was most certainly a bottom-up, uncoordinated, and rather happenstance undertaking. In fact, Vonnegut initially accomplished great feats of literary cultural diplomacy in the Soviet Union without even knowing it. *Slaughterhouse-Five* and *Cat's Cradle* were both published in Russian in the USSR in 1970, making Vonnegut a rock star of American literature for Soviet readers. Vonnegut learned of this fact only in 1972.

Clearly, others besides Vonnegut were pulling the strings. In reality, the heavy lifting of what I call literary cultural diplomacy often fell not to authors like Vonnegut, Hemingway, or Fitzgerald, but to their translators. It is no wonder that literary translators in the 1960s and 1970s Soviet Union have been aptly called the "quiet heroes of revolution."[31] Again, we face a contradiction: as Lauren G. Leighton describes in *Two Worlds, One Art: Literary Translation in Russia and America*, the Soviet state devoted enormous material and moral support to translation, while it was simultaneously subject to severe censorship.[32] To explain how translation was thoroughly "implicated in the project of remaking Soviet citizens" in such a complicated context, Brian James Baer argues that translation (and translators) were "*reauthorized*" in the 1920s and 30s, the most repressive period.[33] Others

---

[31] Vadim Mikhailin, "Perevedi menia zherez made in: neslol'ko zamechanii o khudozhestvennom perevedi i o poiskakh kanonov" ["Translate me through made in: a few remarks on artistic translation and on searching for canons"], *Novoe literaturnoe obozrenie* [New Literature Survey] 1 (2002).

[32] Lauren G. Leighton, *Two Worlds, One Art: Literary Translation in Russia and America* (Northern Illinois University Press, 1991), 19.

[33] Brian James Baer, *Translation and the Making of Modern Russian Literature* (Bloomsbury Academic, 2016), 116, 119.

have written about the "death of the author" in the early Soviet Union, when writers who challenged the system were "de-authorized" and "just" given translation work to do—Mikhail Bulgakov, Anna Akhmatova, and Osip Mandelstam come to mind. It is easy to interpret this role change from author to translator as a demotion, as pure punishment. But Baer argues that translation in this context was a process with productive potential despite its repressive character—a "reauthorization," or re-authoring. After all, the Soviet Union devoted robust state resources to the translation industry, which became a key site of ideological reformation of Soviet citizens. Baer's notion of reauthorization, although it predates the Stagnation era, highlights the creative power of literary translators and their importance for literary cultural diplomacy.

Though he does not use the term re-authoring, Alexander Burak notes some important examples of it in the Soviet 1970s when literary translators such as Rita Rait "collectively invented Hemingway's, Salinger's, and Vonnegut's styles in Russian." They established what Burak calls the "Russian Amerikanskii substyle" within Soviet Russian literature. It was a "'Russian American language . . .' that to Soviets, sounded 'cooler . . .' compared to mainstream Soviet literature."[34]

At least two moments are important here. First, the appeal of this "Russian American language" led many Soviet readers and literati to profess: "Vonnegut writes better in Russian" (see Chapter 5). Second, if we take seriously Baer's insights about Soviet translators as creative re-authoring agents with productive potential, we begin to see translators' tweaks and embellishments to the original texts not as evidence of censorship, but as instances of enrichment. They are the building blocks of the new Russian-American language. As the anthropologist Ilya Utekhin told me, "Rita Rait didn't 'domesticate' or 'censor' Vonnegut for the Soviet reader. She translated Vonnegut in a way that enriched the Russian language."

Soviet translators, in another example of creative re-authoring, "smuggled the cultural 'other' into Russia under the guise of 'unacceptability.'"[35] Thus, Rita Rait introduced Vonnegut's oeuvre to Soviet readers in translation as examples of the "perils of the decadent West," knowing full well that readers would ignore this official ideological framing and sympathetically identify with Vonnegut's characters. Additionally, Michael Khmelnitsky points out that Rait "was instrumental in the attempt to resynchronize the U.S.S.R. with the West (and the rest of the world) with the aid of Vonnegut's most influential

---

[34] Burak, "The Other," 19.
[35] Burak, "The Other," 19.

works."³⁶ This "resynchronizing" of East and West, an important element of literary cultural diplomacy, was accomplished at least in part through the Russian-American language that Rait and other translators created and that Soviet readers eagerly learned to speak.

Readers, too, played a large part in literary cultural diplomacy. Reading was an escape from the socialist world—an example of what some historians call "socialist escapes"—and a very important one for cultural diplomacy.³⁷ Readers developed an affinity for Vonnegut and his characters. By extension, they felt a connection and compassion for the mixed-up America he was writing about. Thanks to Vonnegut in translation, Soviet readers glimpsed the "imaginary West," a place most of them could only dream about visiting in person.³⁸ Reading Vonnegut enabled a kind of East-West dialogue at the "micro-level" of Soviet readers, who unexpectedly experienced "pleasures of recognition" when they encountered Vonnegut's characters and their challenges.³⁹ I describe in Chapter 5 how some fans were inspired to creatively "co-produce" with Vonnegut. Their Vonnegut-inspired drawings, notes, "encyclopedias," and other curiosities linked the worlds he described and the worlds they inhabited. These creations are tangible artifacts of 1970s Soviet-American literary cultural diplomacy.

In addition to imagining relationships with Western authors and their characters, Soviet fans forged relations with one another, forming interpretive communities of readers.⁴⁰ To explore Vonnegut's ideas and debate them with friends was a thoroughly social and interactive experience and a way to define oneself to oneself and others. Entire social groups formed around practices like reading Vonnegut and other Western authors, listening to certain kinds of music, and dressing in a particular way (yes, the blue jeans): all of these were generative practices for Soviet young people to reimagine potential futures.

This book explores the multifaceted connections that made Vonnegut's literary cultural diplomacy in the Soviet Union possible. As much as this book is about literature, translation, and the Cold War, it is also about relationships—between Vonnegut and his translator Rita Rait, between

---

³⁶ Khmelnitsky, "Sex, Lies, and Red Tape," 63.
³⁷ Cathleen M. Giustino, Catherine J. Plum, and Alexander Vari, eds., *Socialist Escapes: Breaking Away from Ideology and Everyday Routine in Eastern Europe, 1945–1989* (Berghahn, 2013); Juliane Fürst and Josie McLellan, eds., *Dropping Out of Socialism: The Creation of Alternate Spheres in the Soviet Bloc* (Lexington Books, 2017).
³⁸ Alexei Yurchak, *Everything Was Forever, Until it Was No More: The Last Soviet Generation* (Princeton University Press, 2005).
³⁹ Gilburd, *To See Paris*, 2.
⁴⁰ Stanley Fish, *Is There a Text in This Class? The Authority of Interpretive Communities* (Harvard University Press, 1980).

Vonnegut and the Soviet reading public, between Vonnegut and the Soviet literary establishment, between Rita Rait and the Soviet censors and publishing houses, and between Vonnegut and dissident Soviet writers. By centering the relationships between writers, translators, readers, and critics across geographical and ideological divides, we get glimpses of important US-Soviet affinities made possible by literary cultural diplomacy in the 1970s.

Sources, methods, and outline of the book

For this book, I have used primarily original source materials, most of them previously untouched. In 2019, I explored archival sources in Moscow at the Russian State Archive of Literature and Art and the Lenin Library, and in St. Petersburg at the Russian State Library ("Publichka"). I scoured the Vonnegut papers and the Donald Fiene papers at Indiana University's Lilly Library. I worked in the Donald Fiene archive at the Ekstrom Library of the University of Louisville. Colleagues in Russia who knew Rita Rait generously offered me access to their personal archives of letters from her. I also mined the Rita Rait-Kovaleva Correspondence at the Bakhmeteff Archive in the Rare Book and Manuscript Library at Columbia University, and I tapped relevant materials in the Seymour Lawrence Publishing Files related to Kurt Vonnegut at the University of Delaware Library's Special Collections. In 2022, I traveled to Bremen, Germany, to study recorded oral history interviews that scholar Barbara Lönnqvist conducted with Rita Rait in the late 1970s.

A cultural anthropologist by training who speaks fluent Russian and Ukrainian, I also conducted personal interviews for the project, including with cultural and literary figures who knew Rita Rait and who met Vonnegut when he visited the USSR in 1974 and 1977. The Moscow theater director Mikhail Levitin, who staged a play based on Vonnegut's *Slaughterhouse-Five* at the Soviet Army Theater in 1975–6 was one of my key interviewees. Other prominent cultural and intellectual figures I interviewed about Rita Rait and Kurt Vonnegut were the literary scholar Konstantin Azadovsky and the bard, poet, librettist, and dramatist Yulii Kim. I also interviewed fifteen members of the Soviet interpretive community of readers devoted to Vonnegut—individuals who came of age in the 1970s and fell in love with Vonnegut, his prose, his characters, and his ideas. These interviewees were not systematically chosen for the study to serve as representative readers of Vonnegut during the Soviet 1970s but were largely referred to me as Vonnegut super fans by colleagues and friends. Most of these fifteen interviewees still live in the former Soviet Union. They hail from Moscow, St. Petersburg, Saratov, Novosibirsk, Arkhangelsk, Minsk, and Kyiv.[41]

Besides yielding insights about how Soviet citizens interpreted Vonnegut, these interviews unearthed additional priceless material, including a magnificent set of original colored pencil drawings that a couple of Soviet Ukrainian teenagers produced to illustrate Vonnegut's novels, and a unique samizdat Russian-language "Book of Bokonon" (see Chapter 5).

The book comprises five thematic chapters with short personalistic "interludes" between each chapter. Chapter 3, "The Translator," uses the example of Vonnegut to track the process by which foreign—especially American—authors were chosen for translation in the USSR, and how the translation, publishing, and censorship process worked. We learn of the balancing act translators like Rita Rait performed trying to channel Vonnegut and other authors from Western capitalist countries to a Soviet readership in a politically correct manner. The chapter pulls back the curtain on "Vonnegut in translation" to reveal the complicated political and literary milieu in which Vonnegut's work made such a splash during the 1970s Stagnation period in the Soviet Union. It is rather a miracle, we find, that Vonnegut in Russian translation ever saw the light of day. And we learn how, in Rita Rait's masterful hands, Vonnegut and other American writers spoke to Soviet readers in a new and unique Russian-American language.

Chapter 5, "Vonnegut and Soviet Readers," explores Vonnegut's appeal to readers in the USSR. Through personal interviews with Vonnegut devotees who, I argue, formed a specific interpretive community, the chapter unpacks the elements of Vonnegut's writing that appealed to certain kinds of Soviet citizens—especially university students and members of the technical intelligentsia (the "engineering class")—and how these themes resonated in the specific context of Stagnation in the Soviet Union. We explore how reading Vonnegut helped some Soviet citizens, especially young people, imagine a different society, inhabit an alternate reality, and form a kind of loose, underground community. On the lighter side, this chapter offers playful examples of the extreme lengths to which Vonnegut fans would go to acquire hard-to-find copies of his books in translation.

Chapter 7, "The Wanderings of Billy Pilgrim, or Cinderella in the Concentration Camp," takes readers on a raucous excursion to the Soviet Army Theater where a theater adaptation of *Slaughterhouse-Five* was staged in 1975–6. Featuring rare interview material with librettist and dissident Yulii Kim, as well as the play's director, Mikhail Levitin, the chapter tracks

---

[41] With permission to do so, I use the real names of several interviewees who are prominent literary and scholarly figures. Other interviewees I have assigned pseudonyms.

the adventures and mishaps involved in bringing the stage play to life, and the play's significance as an artifact of US-Soviet cultural diplomacy. I reflect on the incongruities of staging a play based on an "anti-war" book by an American author, in a carnivalesque/grotesque style, at a military theater, and in the very heart of the Soviet state's mythology of the glory of the "Great Patriotic War" (the Second World War).

Chapter 8, "Finding Comrade Vonnegut," examines Vonnegut through the eyes of the Soviet state apparatus and Soviet literary criticism. These entities were two sides of the same coin, since official, published literary criticism in the 1970s Soviet Union, while often insightful, was nevertheless an extension of the Communist Party line. I use published reflections and critiques of Vonnegut in Soviet literary journals and newspapers to understand what Vonnegut "meant" for the Soviet authorities; for instance, how and why Vonnegut was a convenient and sanctioned anti-American American author in the 1970s. I use archival documents to show how Soviet authorities absolved Vonnegut of the sin of "pacifism" and instead awkwardly squeezed him into the more correct Soviet category of engaging in the "struggle for peace" (*borba za mir*).

In "Vonnegut and the Dissidents," Chapter 10, the story comes home, so to speak, with Vonnegut's relationships with Soviet dissident writers and intellectuals, including emigres to the United States like Sergei Dovlatov. I explore Vonnegut's literary cultural diplomacy and the afterlife of Vonnegut's love affair with the Soviet Union through the lens of international politics and the international community of writers. The book concludes with reflections on what lessons we might learn about socio-political division and hope for reconciliation from Vonnegut's legacy of literary cultural diplomacy in the 1970s Soviet Union.

Four shorter chapters are sandwiched between the thematic ones. Titled "Interludes," they describe Vonnegut's travels to the USSR chronologically to provide an even more personal view of Vonnegut's engagements with the Soviet Union. The Interludes quote liberally from Rait's and Vonnegut's letters and draw on the recollections of various Russian cultural figures who met Vonnegut during his trips to Paris and the USSR.[42]

---

[42] Many of Vonnegut's letters archived in the Kurt Vonnegut Papers at Indiana University's Lilly Library are published in Dan Wakefield, *Kurt Vonnegut—Letters* (Dial Press Trade Paperbacks, 2014). I retrieved many of these letters from the archive, but when quoting letters that also appear in *Kurt Vonnegut—Letters*, I cite from Wakefield's volume to make the source material more accessible to readers.

The most impressive proof

In late 1976, Vonnegut wrote a letter asking Professor Nikolai Fedorenko, chair of the Soviet Writers' Union, to grant permission to Rita Rait to join Vonnegut in a seminar on translation at the University of Tennessee. Vonnegut averred that, "our appearance on the same stage will be the most impressive proof that the American people have seen so far that détente is in certain areas indeed working well."[43] Permission was not granted, calling into question Vonnegut's optimistic evaluation of literary cultural diplomacy as proof of détente's success. The Soviet publishing establishment was prepared to allow translation and publication of most of Vonnegut's oeuvre for Soviet readers to enjoy, but allowing renowned literary translator Rita Rait, aged seventy-seven, to visit the United States was a bridge too far. In this light, the feats of literary cultural diplomacy accomplished by Kurt Vonnegut, Rita Rait, and Soviet readers in the 1970s Soviet Union are even more remarkable. It is a story that needs to be told.

Listen:

---

[43] KV to Professor Nikolai Fedorenko, December 3, 1976, Donald M. Fiene Archive at the University of Louisville, Correspondence (hereafter DMFC), Box 4, Folder 4, "Rita Rait-Kovaleva . . . invitation to her from U.S. 1976–1977."

2

Interlude

Forty-eight Hours in Leningrad, 1967

Kurt Vonnegut's engagement with the Soviet Union was tightly knotted with his breakout novel *Slaughterhouse-Five*, the book he wrote for twenty-three years. In the first chapter, Vonnegut described his 1967 trip to Dresden with his Second World War battalion mate Bernard O'Hare. He fervently wished that returning to Dresden, where he and O'Hare had, as German POWs, survived the firebombing of that city by British and American forces, would shake something loose and allow him to finally bring the "Dresden story" to completion. His wish was granted.

On the way to Dresden, Vonnegut and O'Hare stopped off in Leningrad to witness the fiftieth anniversary celebrations of the Russian Revolution. They aimed to signal gratitude to the Red Army soldiers who had liberated them from Nazi captors.[1] But the pair arrived in Leningrad two days behind schedule, having been "flimflammed by a travel agency behind the Iron Curtain."[2] Their papers weren't in order. They were turned back at the Soviet border and had to regroup. By the time they arrived in Leningrad, the two American vets had missed the big parade. Adding insult to injury, they were unceremoniously kicked out of their hotel and out of the country, forty-eight hours after arriving.

Vonnegut described the 1967 Leningrad misadventure to fellow writer Alexander Minchin in a 1986 interview:

> First my friend and I flew to Helsinki, where we got on a train to cross the border. We crossed it no problem. We stayed in the Hotel Astoria, a fine one, for foreigners... Forty-eight hours later the hotel presented us with return tickets to Helsinki. They said they needed our room. But we had time to see the Hermitage...

---

[1] Charles J. Shields, *And So it Goes. Kurt Vonnegut: A Life* (St. Martin's Griffin, 2011), 225.
[2] Shields, *So it Goes*, 225.

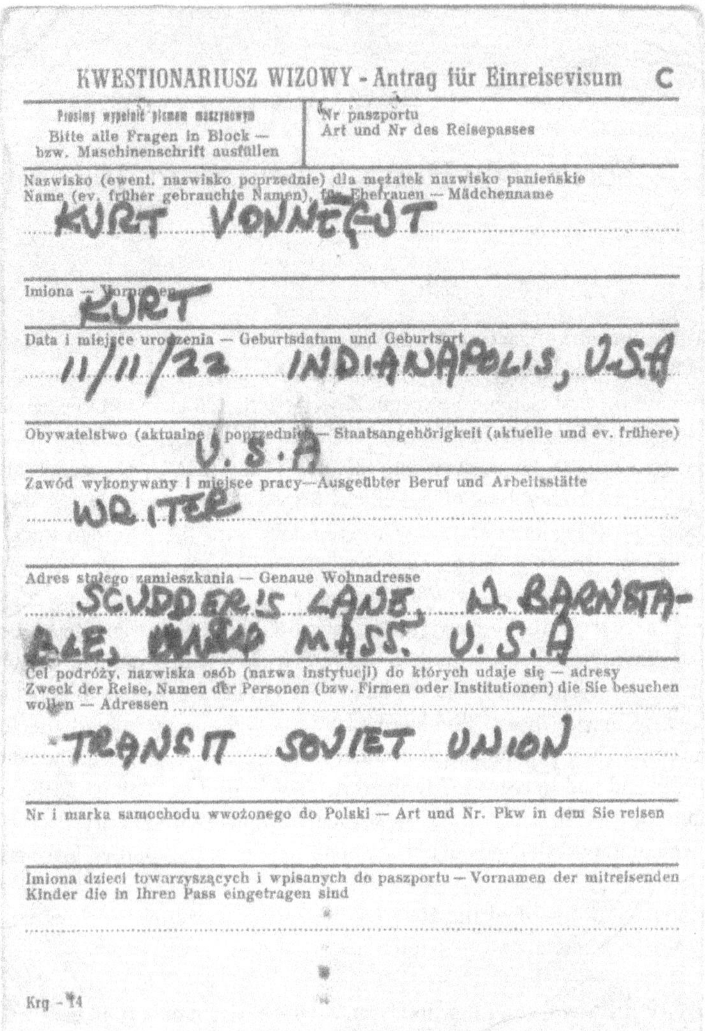

KWESTIONARIUSZ WIZOWY - Antrag für Einreisevisum C

Prosimy wypełnić pismem maszynowym
Bitte alle Fragen in Block — bzw. Maschinenschrift ausfüllen

Nr paszportu
Art und Nr des Reisepasses

Nazwisko (ewent. nazwisko poprzednie) dla mężatek nazwisko panieńskie
Name (ev. früher gebrauchte Namen), für Ehefrauen — Mädchenname
KURT VONNEGUT

Imiona — Vornamen
KURT

Data i miejsce urodzenia — Geburtsdatum und Geburtsort
11/11/22 INDIANAPOLIS, U.S.A

Obywatelstwo (aktualne i poprzednie) — Staatsangehörigkeit (aktuelle und ev. frühere)
U.S.A

Zawód wykonywany i miejsce pracy — Ausgeübter Beruf und Arbeitsstätte
WRITER

Adres stałego zamieszkania — Genaue Wohnadresse
SCUDDER'S LANE, W. BARNSTABLE, MASS. U.S.A

Cel podróży, nazwiska osób (nazwa instytucji) do których udaje się — adresy
Zweck der Reise, Namen der Personen (bzw. Firmen oder Institutionen) die Sie besuchen wollen — Adressen
TRANSIT SOVIET UNION

Nr i marka samochodu wwożonego do Polski — Art und Nr. Pkw in dem Sie reisen

Imiona dzieci towarzyszących i wpisanych do paszportu — Vornamen der mitreisenden Kinder die in Ihren Pass eingetragen sind

Krg - 14

Figure 2.1 Kurt Vonnegut's transit visa for the Soviet Union, 1967. Courtesy Lilly Library, Indiana University, Bloomington, Indiana.

So we were sent back to Helsinki. That was in 1967. A few years later in New York I met [the poet Evgenii] Evtushenko, at a banquet in his honor I'd been invited to. He knew my work and said: "You have to visit my country." I said: "The last time I tried to do that, they kicked me out of the country." He said he'd find out why. A few years later he returned to America to give a poetry reading. I asked him if he'd found anything out. He told me: "Yes, it's really funny. They thought you were homosexuals!"[3]

I spent a month in Moscow and St. Petersburg (formerly Leningrad) in autumn 2019 doing archival and interview research for this book. Hoping to find traces of Vonnegut and O'Hare's short 1967 Leningrad stopover, one sunny afternoon I decided to stop by the Hotel Astoria. It's an imposing brown Art Nouveau building shaped like a huge triangular wedge. The Astoria is conveniently situated near the city's main avenue, Nevsky Prospekt, right across the street from the famed St. Isaac's Cathedral with its huge golden dome.

I approached Reception and made my request. I sought evidence of a short stay in the storied hotel by the famous American writer Kurt Vonnegut, in October 1967. A smartly dressed young woman—starched, tight-fitting bright-white shirt with pert lapels, black pencil skirt, and impossibly high-heeled black stilettos—blinked with sympathy. "We keep information about our guests confidential and private," she efficiently explained. She tapped bright-red inch-long nails on the shiny reception desk and continued, "But let me get a manager."

Waiting for the next step in my investigation, I explored the hotel lobby. I ascended the dramatic white marble staircase that wound its way in a spiral to the hotel's second floor. My explorations were cut short by the polite but unhelpful manager who found me and said what I already knew she would say: hotels like the Astoria don't keep records of their guests. "Well, I'm pretty sure they did in the 1960s, especially when foreigners visited," I wanted to say, but didn't. The manager led me back down the stairs to the hotel's main elevator, its cabins flanked by rows of small, polished, gold-colored "name plates," a bragging list of prominent guests who'd stayed at the Astoria. "So much for not keeping records of guests," I thought. "See if your writer's name is here," said the manager.

---

[3] Aleksandr Minchin, "Kurt Vonnegut," in *21 Interviews* (Prometei, 2013), 50. Minchin published the same interview with Vonnegut earlier in a dissident journal under a pseudonym: A. Mirchev, "Inter'viu s Kurtom Vonnegutom" ["Interview with Kurt Vonnegut"], *Kontinent* 51 (1987): 437–46.

I scanned the list of vaunted hotel guests. A jumble of names, writers, politicians, and entertainers from across the world, over the last 100-odd years. The Russians got their names listed twice—first in Russian, then in English. (A law stipulates that non-Russian language words may not be used in advertising without translation or transliteration. Are these name plates considered "advertising?") Margaret Thatcher. H.G. Wells. Placido Domingo. Jack Nicholson. Pierre Cardin. Hugh Grant. Hillary Rodham Clinton. Robert Michael Gates. Vladimir Lenin. Woody Allen. Truman Capote. Mikhail Bulgakov. Maxim Gorky. Sergey Yesenin. Naomi Campbell.

About 100 names in all, but no Kurt Vonnegut, no Bernard O'Hare. I left the Astoria with a sigh, wondering what Sean Lennon (whose name was listed) had on Vonnegut, whose name was not. At least Vonnegut got forty-eight hours in the Hotel Astoria; I got about four minutes and eight seconds.

I did learn more about Vonnegut's abbreviated 1967 trip to Leningrad, thanks to a telegram he sent to Donald Fiene in May 1972. Rita Rait had heard that Vonnegut would be part of a delegation that U.S. President Richard Nixon had invited to accompany him on a trip that month to the USSR. In excited anticipation, Rait, whose blockbuster translations of *Slaughterhouse-Five* and *Cat's Cradle* had been published in Soviet editions in 1970, wrote to Fiene. "They say MY Vonnegut is coming? I really want to see him—after all, everyone here knows him THROUGH MY TRANSLATIONS . . . and in the last five years no American [writer] has enjoyed this much SUCCESS, except for Salinger (Faulkner was earlier, and Hemingway—so long ago. . .)."[4]

Rait asked Fiene to write to Vonnegut, whom she very much hoped to meet. "And you tell Vonnegut, TODAY, that HIS FIRST AND THUS FAR ONLY TRANSLATOR wants to see him."[5] Fiene subsequently wrote his first of many letters to Kurt Vonnegut. He included details about Rita Rait and her translations and asked Vonnegut to confirm or deny the rumors that he would soon travel to Moscow with the Nixon delegation.

> I just received a letter from your Russian translator, Rita Rait-Kovalyova. . . . I introduced her to your books in 1967 and have sent her copies of the recent ones. I insisted she read them all, and she did, and she got turned on. I'm glad I got used by the universe for that one small task (which, by the way, already makes me more influential on world history than Nixon and Agnew together, doesn't it? Let's hope so.) . . .

---

[4] Rita Rait-Kovaleva (hereafter RRK) to DMF, May 1972 (no date), p. 1, DMFC, Box 4, Folder 3, "Rait Kovaleva 1963–1976."
[5] RRK to DMF, May 1972 (no date), p. 2, DMFC, Box 4, Folder 3, "Rait Kovaleva 1963–1976."

She is under the impression, which could be true for all I know, that you are shortly going to visit Russia (like, as part of the cultural entourage of Nixon or something; can that really be true?). And she wants very much to meet you. She admires you very much. She's worried that maybe she won't be on the official list of people for you to meet.[6]

Five days later, Fiene received the following short telegram from Vonnegut: "PROBABLY NEVER GONE [SIC.] TO RUSSIA. HAVEN'T BEEN INITED [SIC.] WAS ASKED TO LEAVE IN 1967 THE ONLY TIME I WENT THERE. YOUR EXCELLENT LETTER MADE ME FALL IN LOVE WITH RITA. KURT VONNEGUT."[7] Thus began a friendship and correspondence between Fiene and Vonnegut that would last for nearly two decades. The result was hundreds of typed and handwritten pages exchanged by Vonnegut and the enthusiastic literary scholar Fiene, who taught at the University of Louisville, Franklin College, and the University of Tennessee. So, too, did that first, flurried triangle of correspondence ignite a long-lasting comradery between Vonnegut and "his" Russian translator, Rita Rait. Rait's claim that she was Vonnegut's "first and only" translator in the Soviet Union was hyperbolic, but the credit she took for having "made him famous" there was eminently well-deserved.

In my mind's eye, I imagine a grey day in October 1967, when Kurt Vonnegut and Bernard O'Hare were unceremoniously ushered out of the Hotel Astoria, and out of the Soviet Union. Vonnegut could never have dreamed that just five years later readers across the Soviet Union would regard him as one of the most celebrated American writers of a generation.

It happened like this:

---

[6] DMF to KV, May 12, 1972, FIEN, Folder 1, "1972–1974."
[7] KV to DMF, May 17, 1972, FIEN, Folder 1, "1972–1974."

3

The Translator

Kurt Vonnegut got lucky, and so did Soviet readers. Thanks to an Indiana University graduate student's obsession with J. D. Salinger, dirty words, Dostoevsky, and communism, in the late 1960s and early 1970s Vonnegut's novels *Cat's Cradle* and *Slaughterhouse-Five* ended up in the hands of Russian translator extraordinaire, Rita Rait. In 1959, Donald M. Fiene, a middle school teacher in Louisville, Kentucky, was fired for having his composition students read J. D. Salinger's *Catcher in the Rye*. The school's principal considered the book's dirty language inappropriate. Fiene then enrolled for a master's degree in English at the University of Louisville. He wrote his thesis on Salinger. Deeply interested in Soviet communism and Russian literature, and studying the Russian language in his spare time, Fiene wondered about Salinger's reception in the Soviet Union. He learned that *Catcher in the Rye* had been translated into Russian with great success by a woman named Rita Rait. He decided to contact her.[1]

There is an irony that is hard to miss. For assigning *Catcher in the Rye* to students, Fiene lost his teaching job at an American middle school. Rait's experience in the Soviet Union was the opposite. Her 1957 Russian translation of *Catcher* was a sensation with readers and critics in the Soviet Union. It established her position as a preeminent Soviet translator of foreign literature.

Fiene addressed his first letter, dated July 13, 1961, to "Miss Wright-Kovaleva." He sent it care of the journal *Foreign Literature* in Moscow, which had published Rait's translation of *Catcher in the Rye* over two issues in 1957. Fiene asked Rait to write a statement about Salinger he could cite in his book about Salinger's life and work. Would Rait please state her opinion of his talent, and "any special problems you might have had in translating modern American slang and taboo words into idiomatic Russian?" Fiene did not discuss political minutiae but stated his belief that "the two countries [America and Russia] have more in common than any other two countries in

---

[1] Biographical details are taken from Fiene's Russian-language "Answers to Questionnaire" (May 1983) that Fiene prepared for an interview by Sergei Dovlatov. DMFC, Box 1, "Dovlatov, Sergei Donatovich, 1982–1984."

the world." Fiene was thoroughly disillusioned with American capitalism and the US government, especially racial segregation and discrimination. He had begun to consider himself a communist. Reflecting on Salinger's reception in the United States and the USSR, he noted that "it seems impossible ever to divorce literature from politics."[2]

Rait replied, in English, to Fiene's letter in late October, but her response touched only lightly on the questions he had posed. Rait did promise Fiene "full cooperation" in his work on Salinger. She asked him to send her "a cheap edition of the new Salinger novel *Franny and Zooey*." She would, she pledged, start translating *Franny and Zooey* "pronto," if she liked it "as much as the *Catcher*." In her signature line, Rait informed Fiene how he should address her: "Rita Wright-Kovaleva (Mrs.)."[3]

These letters sparked a prolific correspondence on literature, translation, culture, and politics that continued for over two decades. Fiene was an American leftist and self-professed communist. Rait was a Russian-Jewish doctor and scientist turned translator who never joined the Communist Party of the Soviet Union. Their written discussions initially focused on Salinger's novels and Rait's Russian translations. In spring 1962, Rait was unable to supply Fiene with a copy of her translation of *Catcher in the Rye* as he requested. All 350,000 copies of the two issues of *Foreign Literature* where *Catcher* was published in 1957 were sold out.

In 1962 Rait was still waiting for Young Guard (*Molodaia Gvardia*) publishing house to publish her translation of *Catcher* in book form. (The book appeared only in 1965, with a print run of 115,000. Another 100,000 copies were printed in 1967.) But she implored Fiene to keep writing her. "Your letters are a great treat for me and my friends. Do write more about the Holden Caulfields of your University."[4] Fiene later referred to his and Rita's "friendship birthday" in 1961, the date of Fiene's "first letter to Rita, about her translation of the dirty words in Catcher in the Rye, which began it all."[5]

Fiene did not complete the book he had hoped to publish on Salinger's life and work, in part due to Salinger's refusal to cooperate with the project. However, in 1963 he did publish the first comprehensive bibliography of works by and about Salinger. It ran to forty pages and included some 1,500 items in

---

[2] DMF to RRK, July 13, 1961, DMFC, Box 4, "Rait-Kovaleva, Rita, 1961–1989."
[3] RRK to DMF, October 29, 1961, DMFC, Box 4, "Rait-Kovaleva, Rita, 1961–1989."
[4] RRK to DMF, April 2, 1962, DMFC, Box 4, "Rait-Kovaleva, Rita, 1961–1989."
[5] DMF to Lauren Gray Leighton (hereafter LGL), December 21, 1978, DMFC, Box 4, "Leighton, Lauren Gray, 1978–1979."

twenty languages.⁶ In the mid-1960s Fiene enrolled in the PhD program in Slavic Languages and Literatures at Indiana University, and wrote a nearly 1,000-page dissertation on the exiled Russian author Mikhail Osorgin. It was during his PhD studies that Fiene made his first of many trips to the Soviet Union, where in Moscow in 1966 he met Rita Rait in person for the first time. Rait's "dear Salingerist," as she called Fiene, wondered if Rita might like the work of another hot American writer: Kurt Vonnegut.⁷ Fiene gave Rait copies of *Cat's Cradle* and several other of Vonnegut's books. She was immediately smitten by the books and their author, talked constantly about her "now-favorite, Kurt Vonnegat," (*sic.*) and vowed to translate his work into Russian.⁸ She wrote to Fiene in September 1967, "I loved the Vonnegut books! How does he stand in USA?"⁹

Rait went on to translate *Cat's Cradle* (1970) and *Slaughterhouse-Five* (1970), as well as *Happy Birthday, Wanda June* (1973); *Breakfast of Champions* (1975); *God Bless You, Mr. Rosewater* (1978); and several short stories. Her translation of *Slaughterhouse-Five* was the basis of a stage adaptation, "The Wanderings of Billy Pilgrim," which had a terrifically successful run of eighty-five shows at the Moscow Soviet Army Theater in 1975-6. *Happy Birthday, Wanda June* was also staged in the Soviet Union, in Tallinn, in an Estonian translation.¹⁰

It is quite impossible to understand Vonnegut's immense popularity in the Soviet Union without foregrounding Rita Rait's key role in introducing Soviet readers and critics to Vonnegut's writing. But it is equally impossible to talk about Vonnegut's "Soviet chapter," or Kurt and Rita's extraordinary friendship, without acknowledging the pivotal role played by that erstwhile "Salingerist" and eventual Slavicist, Donald Fiene. As Fiene reflected in a 1974 letter to Rita, "I'm proud that I helped introduce the two of you:

---

⁶ Donald M. Fiene, "J. D. Salinger: A Bibliography," *Wisconsin Studies in Contemporary Literature* 4, no. 1 (Winter, 1963). Fiene maintained a collection of Salinger first editions and first appearance in print, in many languages; this collection is now housed at the University of Louisville Ekstrom Library's Rare Books, Archives and Special Collections, as is the correspondence between Fiene and J. D. Salinger, 1957-1962 (DMFC, Box 6).
⁷ RRK to Sara Ginsburg (hereafter SG), April 21, 1967, Rita Rait-Kovaleva Correspondence, Bakhmeteff Archive, Rare Book and Manuscript Library, Columbia University Library (hereafter BA-RRK).
⁸ RRK to Lili Brik, December 29, 1969, Russian State Archive of Literature and Art (hereafter RGALI) fond 2577, opus 1, item 417, page 29 (hereafter 2577/1/417/29).
⁹ RRK to DMF, September 6, 1967, DMFC, Box 4, Folder 3, "Rait-Kovaleva, Rita, 1963-1976."
¹⁰ In a letter to Donald Fiene, Rita Rait noted that the theater in Tallin had requested the text of her Russian translation of *Wanda June* for use in headsets for theatergoers needing Russian interpretation. RRK to DMF, November 5, 1976, p. 1, DMFC, Box 4, Folder 2, "Rait-Kovaleva, Rita, 1968-1978."

America's best writer and Russia's best translator."[11] Fiene himself became a dear friend of Vonnegut's, who in 1976 asked Fiene to be his literary executor. (Vonnegut gently retracted this request in 1982.) By the time Fiene first wrote to Vonnegut at Rita's urging, he had known her for nearly eleven years.

For his part, Fiene gave Rita full credit for her role in bringing him into contact and friendship with Vonnegut. In a 1977 letter to Rita, he mused, "I am convinced he [Kurt] is a great man. I feel lucky (and honored) to be his friend. If it hadn't been for you, I would never have got to know him. We both helped each other immeasurably in this: that each of us became friends with Kurt."[12] It was in no small part thanks to Rita and her encouragement that Fiene committed himself to becoming a Slavicist focused on Russian literature and the Russian translation of American literature.

The connection was lucky for Rita as well. Translation work was hard to come by, especially for Rita, who at the age of sixty-eight had earned a reputation as an exceptional translator but a saucy, sometimes difficult, colleague. Among the top editors and publishing houses, it was said, "Rita was not a favorite." Plus, translation work never paid all that well in the Soviet Union, and Rita had debts to pay. She was looking for a new project, and it was a leap of faith to propose translating Vonnegut for Soviet publishing houses.

Rait finally met Vonnegut in person in Paris in 1972, and she entertained him twice in the Soviet Union—in Moscow in 1974, and in Leningrad in 1977. Vonnegut wanted to host Rita in America, and he supported several unsuccessful attempts to bring her to the United States for a lecture tour. Although she was one of the USSR's preeminent translators of American and British letters, the Union of Soviet Writers, an organ of the Soviet state, never allowed Rita Rait to visit the United States.

Rait and Vonnegut met in person only three times. But they maintained a lively correspondence through letters, telegrams, and telephone calls throughout the 1970s and into the 1980s. Both were frustrated by the terribly slow and inefficient international postal system. They frequently suspected their letters had been confiscated. Vonnegut and Rait also regularly sent greetings and messages to one another through mutual friends and acquaintances who traveled between the USSR, Europe, and the United States. Professor Lauren G. Leighton once wrote, "The close relationship between

---

[11] DMF to RRK, August 5, 1974, p. 1, DMFC, Box 4, Folder 3, "Rait-Kovaleva, Rita, 1963–1976."
[12] DMF to RRK, April 5, 1977, p. 2, DMFC, Box 4, Folder 5, "Rait-Kovaleva, Rita, 1976–1982."

Figure 3.1 Donald M. Fiene, Louisville, Kentucky, 1975. Courtesy of Judith Fiene.

this Russian translator and her American subject is the most important Russian-American friendship since the Nabokov-Wilson collaboration."[13]

This comparison to the long-time correspondence, literary debate, friendship, and rivalry between the great writers Vladimir Nabokov and Edmund Wilson was rather hyperbolic. Kurt Vonnegut and Rita Rait indeed

[13] Leighton, *Two Worlds*, 98.

enjoyed a long-term collaboration, and their friendship was deep. But unlike Nabokov and Wilson, they were not two literary figures (albeit "frenemies") meeting on a common footing. Although Rita herself was a published writer, her original publications were mainly memoirs about her life in the 1920s. Her biography of French Resistance writer and activist Boris Vilde, which included substantial translations of Vilde's writings, was a respectable but mostly overlooked book. Rita aspired to write more, but she usually self-identified as "just" a translator, albeit one of the best translators in the Soviet Union. Her stature never approached that of Vonnegut's, for reasons having to do more with Cold War politics and Soviet political structures than with talent.

Rita Rait's relationship with Vonnegut and her role in translating his work shed significant light on the political and cultural context of the US-Soviet Cold War. To understand who Kurt Vonnegut was for Soviet readers, and for the Soviet state, we must first understand who Kurt Vonnegut was for Rita Rait. She was a cultural conduit and a gatekeeper of Kurt Vonnegut's prose for a Soviet readership. Understanding Rait's translation process, the challenges she faced, and the choices she made illuminates key aspects of Cold War life in the Soviet Union. These include literary censorship, freedom of speech and the press, possibilities for cultural creativity in repressive conditions, freedom of movement and its limits, cultural divisions in Soviet society, and even the precarious material conditions of the literary intelligentsia. Understanding Rait's relationship with Vonnegut, in turn, brings into focus US-USSR power dynamics during the Cold War. We can track the trickle-down effect on citizens of both countries.

Rait and Vonnegut approached one another with fundamentally different philosophies about the role of the artist in society. They also held different economic philosophes and came from very disparate positions of power. Vonnegut possessed critical amounts of economic, political, and cultural capital. Rait, in contrast, in addition to her enormous talent, survived thanks to an abundance of cultural capital and social capital—relations and networks which she carefully and aggressively cultivated. She possessed incredible will power, too.

Rita Rait was not the only translator of Vonnegut in the Soviet Union in the late 1960s and the 1970s. But she was the most successful and most published, and by nearly all accounts, the most capable. At one point, Donald Fiene planned to conduct a comparison "of various translations of Vonnegut (Rita vs. non-Rita), to see what makes Rita so good." (Unfortunately, he did not complete this project.)[14] What made Rita "so good" was her mastery of

[14] DMF to LGL, September 5, 1984, DMFC, Box 4, "Leighton, Lauren Gray, 1980–1991."

the technical skills of translation, combined with her extraordinary "feel" for interpretation and genre. She layered technical mastery of translation with superb interpretation. Rait's translations involved both virtuosity and artistry.[15] Several other Western scholars of Russian and Soviet culture, literature, and translation, have singled out Rait's translations of Vonnegut for analysis. They point out her virtuosity,[16] but also the obvious censorship of parts of the text.[17] As discussed below, Rait's "systematic enlivenment" of her translated texts compensated for the obligatory erasure of political jabs and "vulgar" material.[18] In other words, thanks to Rita Rait, Vonnegut fans in the Soviet Union may have been correct to claim that "Vonnegut is better in Russian" than in English.

Vonnegut's first novel to appear in Russian was *Player Piano*. It was published in a science fiction series in 1967, under the title *Utopia 14*. The translation was by Marat Brukhnov. The edition featured a critical foreword by scholar Igor Bestuzhev-Lada, a "futurologist," a specific kind of sociologist. The book had a healthy print run of 200,000 copies but attracted little critical attention. Fiene surmised this was due to the poor quality of Brukhnov's translation. Fiene called it "mediocre."[19]

Irina Razumovskaia and Svetlana Samostrelova undertook the first Russian translation of *God Bless You, Mr. Rosewater*. This much condensed version of Vonnegut's book was serialized across three issues of the journal *Avrora*. By the next year, however, Rita Rait was working on her own translation of *Rosewater*. It was part of the first collected volume of Vonnegut translations to appear in the Soviet Union. (It included *Cat's Cradle*, *Rosewater*, *Slaughterhouse Five*, and *Breakfast of Champions*.) Rita explained in a January 1977 letter, "The publisher is INSISTING that I RE-translate "Rosewater," since the translation published in "Avrora" is trash (*gadost'*) and incorrect."[20] Indeed, Fiene assessed Rait's *Rosewater* translation as "a

---

[15] My ideas here are influenced by the anthropologist Anya Peterson Royce: "Virtuosity is great technical skill; mastery of the technique of a genre; incorporation of . . . extra-technical elements . . . Artistry comes from the foundation of a certain level of virtuosity—technical mastery—and involves an interpretation (based on the elements of style) that is so harmonious with the genre and with the piece that it seems inevitable." Anya Peterson Royce, *Anthropology of the Performing Arts: Artistry, Virtuosity, and Interpretation in a Cross-Cultural Perspective* (AltaMira Press, 2004), 24.
[16] Lauren G. Leighton, "Rita Rajt-Kovaleva's Vonnegut: A Review Article," *Slavic and East European Journal* 24, no. 4 (1980): 412–19; Leighton, *Two Worlds*, 97–107.
[17] Khmelnitsky, "Sex, Lies, and Red Tape"; Ann C. Vinograde, "A Soviet Translation of Slaughterhouse-Five," *Russian Language Journal* 26, no. 93 (1972), 14–18.
[18] Burak, "The Other," 26.
[19] Fiene, "American Dissident," 260.
[20] RRK to Lynn Visson (hereafter LV), January 13, 1977. DMFC, Box 4, Folder 5, "Rait-Kovaleva, Rita, 1976–1982."

much-improved rendering of the novel in Russian" over Razumovskaia and Samostrelova's version.[21] Without question, it was Rita Rait's translations that established Vonnegut as required reading for a wide swath of Soviet readers, especially young adults and the so-called "technical intelligentsia."

Rait was a "jealous" translator, in the positive sense of the word. She was possessive of "her" authors. When she dedicated herself to translating an author's works, it was an all-consuming, head-long process. Rait's philosophy of translation, her approach to the craft, necessitated full immersion with mind, soul, and body into the universe of the text. There was no room for competition, and certainly no room for others' "mediocre," "incorrect," "trashy" translations.

How did Rita Rait access novels and stories by Kurt Vonnegut? Although it was not always easy for Soviet citizens in the 1960s and 1970s to obtain literature from abroad, it was by no means impossible. Rait and members of her social circles—the elite intelligentsia interested in literature, theater, and the visual arts—were extremely well read in literature of all genres and national origins. Rait was part of an international network of the "literati" class. These producers and consumers of "high" literature spanned not only throughout the Soviet Union, but across Europe and America as well.

Rita was constantly on the look-out for interesting books from abroad and she leveraged her international literary networks to obtain them. She corresponded with her fellow literati in Europe—mostly in the UK, Sweden, and France—and in the United States. She received books from abroad through the international post, sometimes through official book provision services. Friends and acquaintances also couriered books over international borders for Rait during tourist and business trips to the Soviet Union. Fluent in English, German, and French, Rait devoured literature in all three languages. Like others of her circle, Rait had access to critical literary periodicals from Europe and the U.S., including the *Times Literary Supplement*.[22] Fiene sponsored a subscription to *The New York Review of Books* for Rait during the early 1970s.[23] Rait also traveled abroad several times herself in the 1960s and 1970s, to England, Scotland, France, Czechoslovakia, and Sweden. She undoubtedly utilized these opportunities to stock up on new books by foreign authors.

---

[21] DMF to LGL, October 17, 1978, DMFC, Box 4, "Leighton, Lauren Gray, 1978–1979."
[22] RRK to DMF, February 18, 1967, DMFC, Box 4, Folder 3, "Rait-Kovaleva, Rita, 1963–1976."
[23] Ethel Schroeder to DMF, March 17, 1972, FEIN, Box 2, "List of donations of books to the USSR; titles were changed often; ca. 1966–75."

Between 1966 and 1975, Fiene sent innumerable books to Rita Rait and his other friends in the Soviet Union. He used programs designed to send free books to individuals in the Soviet Bloc and the USSR, including the International Advisory Council Planning and Management, Inc., and Bedford Publications, Inc.[24] During 1966–7, Fiene sent Rait books by S. S. Van Dine, Bernard Malamud, John Updike, and Lawrence Ferlinghetti.[25] In 1974–5 another of Rita's American friends, Lynn Visson, sent her books by Joyce Carol Oates, Sylvia Plath, John Barth, Jimmy Breslin, Joseph Heller, and Lois Gould.[26] During this time Fiene and others continued to send Vonnegut's books to the USSR via international post. They also couriered them over during trips to the USSR.[27]

Rait's acclaim did not begin or end with her translations of Kurt Vonnegut. By the time her first Vonnegut translations appeared in 1970, she was already a *grande dame* of Soviet translation. She began her long and storied translation career at the age of twenty-three when she translated Vladimir Mayakovsky's play "Mystery-Bouffe" into German for a performance at the Moscow meeting of the Third Communist International in 1921.[28] Her translations of Franz Kafka and Heinrich Böll in the 1960s were major literary events. Rita's "post-Vonnegut" phase was likewise productive. She "dumped" (or, as she put it, "cheated on") Vonnegut for the Austrian author Thomas Bernhard in the early 1980s.[29]

This book centers the vital role that Rita Rait played in introducing a broad Soviet readership to Vonnegut's writing, a role she recognized and relished. Rita bragged to Fiene, "He [Vonnegut] wrote for me in a book: 'Cat's Cradle: So many different people in the same device. You are the only person

---

[24] FEIN, Box 2, "List of donations of books to the USSR; titles were changed often; ca. 1966–75." The Bedford Publishing Company was the brainchild of Radio Liberty employees Isaac ("Ike") Patch and Betty Carter. It was established as a private venture, but funded by the CIA, to publish Russian translations of Western works and distribute them to Soviet visitors to the West and Western visitors to the Soviet Union. See Yale Richmond, *Cultural Exchange and the Cold War: Raising the Iron Curtain* (The Pennsylvania State University Press, 2004), 137.

[25] RRK to DMF, February 18, 1967; 3 March, 1967; 30 September, 1967, DMFC, Box 4, Folder 3, "Rait-Kovaleva, Rita, 1963–1976."

[26] RRK to LV and Vova, November 18, 1973, BA-RRK; RRK to LV, 28 January, 1974, BA-RRK.

[27] FEIN, Box 2, "List of donations of books to the USSR; titles were changed often; ca. 1966–75."

[28] Rita Rait-Kovaleva, "Tol'ko vospominaniia" ["Just remembrances"], in *Vladimir Mayakovsky: V vospominaniiakh sovremennikov* [Vladimir Mayakovsky: In the recollections of his contemporaries], ed. A. Kozlovskii (GIXL, 1963), 259–67.

[29] RRK to LV, September 2, 1981, BA-RRK.

I have ever acknowledged as a member of my karass.'"[30] Rita wrote Fiene in January 1974, "I think of him [Vonnegut] as if he were my own son: after all, I am the one giving him a 'second birth' here [in the USSR]."[31] Who, then, was Rita Rait?

Raisa (Rita) Iakovlevna Chernomordik Wright (Rait) Kovaleva, aka Rita Rait

All historical personages, whether "small" or "great," roll out biographical details piecemeal. A person's own account of their life, their past, their "origin story," changes over time. Details depend on one's interlocutor, the political winds, and an individual's own continuous reassessment of events and their significance. For this biographical sketch of Rita Rait, I have relied on a range of sources. These include Rait's own accounts of her life, which appeared in letters to Donald Fiene and other correspondents. I utilize Rait's published memoirs of the 1920s–1940s.[32] The archivists at the Russian State Archive of Literature and Art (RGALI) generously prepared an archival "spravka" (biographical inquiry) about Rait. An unpublished article Rait wrote about her relationship with the great man of letters Kornei Chukovsky was also helpful.[33] I additionally draw on descriptions of Rita from letters in the Kurt Vonnegut Manuscripts (Lilly Library, Indiana University) and the Donald Fiene Papers (Lilly Library, Indiana University, and Ekstrom

---

[30] Rita Rait, "Reflections on Kurt Vonnegut," in *Happy Birthday, Kurt Vonnegut: A Festschrift for Kurt Vonnegut on His Sixtieth Birthday*, ed. Jill Krementz (Delacorte Press, 1982), 96. Also in RRK to DMF, March 26, 1977, DMFC, Box 4, "Rait-Kovaleva, Rita, 1968–1978." Translation Yana Skorobogatov. By karass, Rait was referring to one of the key principles of the religion that Vonnegut fabricated—Bokononism—especially for people who think religion is ridiculous. The karass is the organizing principle, or "team," cited in the Book of Bokonon, which ignores national, institutional, occupational, familial, and class boundaries. "If you find your life tangled up with somebody else's life for no very logical reason," wrote Vonnegut, "that person may be a member of your karass." (Kurt Vonnegut, *Cat's Cradle* (Dial Press Trade Paperbacks, 2010), 2.)
[31] RRK to DMF, rec'd February 1, 1974, DMFC, Box 4, Folder 3, "Rait-Kovaleva, Rita, 1963–1976."
[32] Rita Rait-Kovaleva, "Nit' Ariadny" ["Ariadna's Thread"], in *Redaktor i perevod* [Editor and translation], ed. E.B. Kuz'mina (Kniga, 1965); Rait-Kovaleva, "Just remembrances"; Rita Rait-Kovaleva, "Vse lushchie vospominaniia" ["All the best memories"], in *Trudy po russkoi i slavianskoi filologii IX: Literaturovedenie* [Works on Russian and Slavic Philology IX: Literary Studies], ed. B.F. Egorov, Iu.M. Lotman, and V.T. Adams (Tartu State University, 1966).
[33] RGALI 3401/1/630 (No date, 1970s). The draft remembrance was entitled "Upushchennaia Liubov" ["Missed Love"].

Library, University of Louisville). Donald Fiene prepared many of these "bio sketches" for university and state department administrators during several unsuccessful attempts to bring Rita Rait for a visit to the United States.

Raisa Iakovlevna ("Raisa, daughter of Iakov") Cheromordik was born in April 1898 in the village of Petrushovo in Kherson province. Then in the Russian Empire, Kherson city is now in present-day Ukraine.[34] Both her parents were Jewish, although apparently Rita usually only admitted to having a Jewish mother. There are several versions of the story of how Raisa Chernomordik came to take the name "Rita Rait." Rita sometimes said that one of her childhood governesses was a Scot called Miss Stewart who taught her English from childhood. Purportedly "it was this influence that later led her to take the [Scottish sounding] pseudonym of Wright."[35] Another version holds that the great futurist poet and artist Vladimir Mayakovsky, a close colleague of Rita's in Moscow in the 1920s, suggested to her the pseudonym "Rita Rait."

Rita's parents belonged to the intelligentsia, and her family was well off. Her father, Iakov Efimovich Chernomordik (1871–1931), was a politically conservative country doctor. Rita said he was a gentle, Chekhov-type doctor. Rita's mother, Emma Il'inichna Chernomordik (1876–1960), was a teacher and member of the Marxist Social-Democratic Party. Emma Chernomordik was the product of what Rita called a "German-French" upbringing. Emma introduced Rita and her four younger siblings to classic German and French authors, including Friedrich Schiller and Victor Hugo. Youthful Rita, however, preferred Oscar Wilde and Charles Baudelaire. (Meanwhile, Rita winked, she read Guy de Maupassant—in French—in secret.)[36] The Chernomordiks must have conversed freely in Russian, German, and French. With a Scottish governess around who no doubt tutored Rita and her siblings in English, English was likely spoken in the home as well. Donald Fiene said that Rita spoke English with a British accent.[37]

Despite this rich early literary and linguistic education, Rita described her "breezy, warm" provincial childhood as "wrapped in surgically sterile cotton."[38] Rita graduated from the Kursk gymnasium for women in 1917, and

---

[34] In early March 2022 Russian forces captured the city of Kherson and most of Kherson province. Ukrainian forces liberated Kherson city on November 11, 2022. As of writing, Russia still occupied a portion of Kherson province.
[35] DMF to KV, July 14, 1979, DMFC, Box 4, Folder 5, "Rait-Kovaleva, Rita, 1976–1982."
[36] RRK to Konstantin Markovich Azadovsky (hereafter KMA), December 5, 1971, Personal archives of Konstantin Markovich Azadovsky, Correspondence (hereafter, KMAC).
[37] Donald M. Fiene, "J.D. Salinger in the Soviet Union—A Brief Report." Unpublished manuscript. DMFC, Box 4, "Rait-Kovaleva, Rita, 1963–1976."
[38] Rait-Kovaleva, "Best memories," 264.

in 1917–20 she studied natural sciences and medicine at Kharkiv Medical Institute. This was during the years of the Bolshevik Revolution with its socio-political upheavals and aftermath. Kharkiv province and Rita's native Kherson province both went from being part of the Russian Empire to part of the Soviet Union (Ukrainian Soviet Socialist Republic), and Rita was confused by the situation around her. She wrote, "My first year at university passed by in a muddle of complete lack of understanding about what was happening . . . through the kaleidoscope of ever-changing governments in Kharkov and homesickness for my family still in Soviet Russia."[39] As for her choice to study medicine, Rita later explained that she had tried to follow in the footsteps of her father, but her heart was never in the sciences and medicine. Her true calling, she felt, was to study literature and languages, and as a medical student in Kharkiv she devoted all her free time to literary circles. She also taught advanced English in so-called "Dickens groups." According to Rait's memoirs, in Kharkiv her friends included the poets Anastasia Aleksandrova, Vladimir Bessmertnyi, Velimir Khlebnikov, and Grigorii Petnikov.[40]

Alexander Winogradow met young Rita in 1917 at the Kharkiv Medical Institute where he taught chemistry. He recounted his impressions of her in a letter to Donald Fiene in 1966. Winogradow was struck by Rita's "giftedness, lucidity, breadth of worldview, and the unconditionality of her humanistic ambitions." He was especially impressed by her deep knowledge of foreign languages, literature, and poetry. "It's difficult to fathom when, where, and how she developed this knowledge. In addition to an extraordinary ("cosmic") memory, she had to have had a deep interest and love not only of poetry and literature, but of people!"[41]

Although she suspected it was not her true calling, Rita persisted in her medical education. In 1920 she transferred to the medical faculty of Moscow State University, and later (in 1923–4) to Moscow Medical Institute. During a short trip to Moscow in 1920 to work out the details of her transfer, Rita boldly telephoned Vladimir Mayakovsky from a telephone booth. She called him at the offices of ROSTA, the Russian Telegraph Agency where he directed the production of propaganda posters, the so-called "satirical windows." Rita explained that she had translated some of Mayakovsky's poetry into German. Would he like to hear it?

---

[39] Rait-Kovaleva, "Just remembrances," 237. Kharkiv is rendered "Kharkov" in Russian.
[40] Rait-Kovaleva, "Best memories," 266.
[41] Alexander Winogradow to DMF, November 21, 1966, DMFC, Box 4, "Rait-Kovaleva, Rita, 1961–1989."

Mayakovsky immediately invited Rita to visit him at ROSTA. There she also met his colleague and lover, Lili Brik. Rita became a member of Mayakovsky's and Brik's inner circle, which included Lili's husband, Osip Brik, the poet Boris Pasternak (who Rita fell in love with), Nikolai Aseev, and other luminaries of the Moscow literary and artistic scenes. Mayakovsky was taken with Rita's German translations and invited her to translate his play "Mystery-Bouffe" into German for a performance at the June 1921 Congress of the Third Communist International. This was Rita's first major translation. Although her translation was one of "German for non-German speakers" and, as Rita put it, "never would have stood up for real German readers," Rita's ability to replicate in translation the rhythm, alliteration, and "word-fashioning" (made-up words) of Mayakovsky's writing put her on the map as a talented young translator.[42]

Rita led something of a triple life in Moscow in the early 1920s. She was a medical student but also a young woman swept up in the intellectual and creative ferment of the Russia of the 1920s, especially the futurists' movement. She lived in a kaleidoscope of social, artistic, and literary experimentation and debate at a time when the new regime was still taking shape. The sky seemed the limit. When Rita was not attending lectures and labs for her medical degree, she was running back and forth between two very distinct literary circles. In the early 1920s, and really, for the rest of her life, she lived at the literary border between the old and the new. During the afternoons Rita worked at ROSTA, where in her position as "permanent part-time staff member of the artistic section" Rita was charged with proofing the text of ROSTA's "satirical windows" and proposing themes for poster series.[43] Mayakovsky asked Rita to focus on what she jokingly called "girly" topics: "sanitation and hygiene, children, clothing drives, and literacy campaigns."[44] In Mayakovsky's circle Rita was marinated in ideas about the new society, and the nihilist and futurist movements. "With all our hearts, all our hearing and our sight, we absorbed the poetry, voice, and lines of Mayakovsky, and the flawless instinct of youth and revolutionary truth told us this was the

---

[42] Rait-Kovaleva, "Best memories," 267.
[43] Mayakovsky worked on the "satirical windows" of ROSTA from October 1919 to February 1922. He mentioned Rita Rait as one of the text writers. See Vasily Katanyan, *Khronika zhizni i deiatel'nosti Maiakovskogo 1919* [Chronicle of the life and works of Mayakovsky 1919], accessed June 3, 2020. http://mayakovskiy.lit-info.ru/mayakovskiy/bio/katyanyan-hronika/1919.htm
[44] Rait-Kovaleva, "Just remembrances," 245. ROSTA posters (originals and copies) for which Rait-Kovaleva provided the text are housed at RGALI.

epitome—this was the true high poetry of revolution and a revolution in poetry."[45]

At the same time, Rita does not seem to have been completely on board with the futurists. The futurists rejected the art of the past, eschewed any sentimentality, and privileged construction over style. Even while immersed in the futurists' movement, which she later called "its own form of iconoclasm in the arts," Rita was nevertheless drawn to the "classics," too, especially the symbolists.[46] So after working at ROSTA in the afternoons, she spent her evenings with a group of like-minded would-be poets and writers. They listened to lectures and seminars under the auspices of "LITO," the literary wing of the People's Commissariat for Enlightenment. At LITO Rita was part of a new literary "studio," under the tutelage of the writers and symbolist poets Valery Bryusov, Vyacheslav Ivanov, and Andrei Bely.[47] In contrast to the urgent, "boiling" work at ROSTA—to crank out texts for propaganda posters—the literary evenings at LITO were more casual and laid-back. The LITO studio was saturated with Russian symbolism, a movement centered on using art to evoke a feeling rather than to depict reality. Rita also loved learning about the history of poetry and lingering over the "old mammoths" of poetry and literature of the past. Rita later attributed her skill as a writer and translator to her training at LITO. "They taught us precision; the great poets and great literary masters sharpened our sight and our hearing."[48]

All of this—Rita's attraction to the symbolists and her reluctance to jettison wholesale the "old masters"—prompted Mayakovsky to teasingly call Rita an "aesthetic."[49] She rejected this label as a terrible insult, but did admit to having "indeterminate artistic worldviews."[50] Rita appreciated "art for art's sake," but also for its social-political significance and utility. She valued function AND construction, form AND style. Rita was a mediator, a go-between channeling multiple worlds and movements. She was, in a word, a medium. A translator.

As a young adult in Moscow, Rita soaked in the influence of scores of creative people and their competing ideas about remaking the world. These formative years instilled in her a deep "tolerance," a quality that was difficult to come by at the end of the 1920s.[51] Rita was heavily influenced by time

---

[45] Rait-Kovaleva, "Just remembrances," 248–9.
[46] Rait-Kovaleva, "Just remembrances," 248.
[47] Eventually the LITO studio intersected with courses from the Palace of Culture and became the first Literature Institute (also called the Bryusov Institute). Rait-Kovaleva, "Just remembrances," 252.
[48] Rait-Kovaleva, "Best memories," 281.
[49] Rait-Kovaleva, "Just remembrances," 248.
[50] Rait-Kovaleva, "Just remembrances," 252.
[51] RRK to DMF, August 12, 1978, DMFC, Box 4, Folder 5, "Rait-Kovaleva, Rita, 1976–1982."

spent with Mayakovsky, the Briks, Pasternak, and the Aseevs in Pushkino, a dacha community outside Moscow. When Mayakovsky died by suicide, Rita's name was penciled in on the highly restricted guest list of people allowed to attend his funeral.[52] Rita accompanied Lili Brik home from Mayakovsky's funeral and considered Brik her life-long best friend.

Rait graduated with her medical diploma from Moscow State University in 1923. She preferred medical research to practicing medicine and relocated to Leningrad in 1923 or 1924 to pursue a PhD (kandidat) degree in physiology. She worked in the laboratories of the famous Professor Ivan P. Pavlov. During these years (1924–30), Rita continued her work with languages and taught foreign languages at a military academy. While on vacation in Sevastopol in 1928, Rita fell in love with a navy submarine officer named Nikolai Petrovich Kovalev. He had grown up in Kursk, where Rita attended the women's gymnasium. The match was a curious one, as Kovalev had little if any interest in languages and literatures.[53] By 1931, the couple lived together in Leningrad. Rita continued her research in Pavlov's laboratories and simultaneously taught foreign languages at the Leningrad Military Academy. In 1933, Rita and Nikolai (Rita called him "Nikolka") relocated for Nikolai's work to Vladivostok, in the Russian Far East. Their daughter Margarita was born there in October, 1933. Letters Rita wrote to the writer, journalist and poet Maria Shkapskaia during 1933 and 1934 reveal that she was a devoted, but very scared and lonely new mother.[54]

The Kovalevs left Vladivostok in 1934 or 1935 because Nikolai had health problems. The couple was quite destitute.[55] Between 1935 and 1938 Rita worked as a researcher at Pavlov's Brain Institute in Leningrad. Like many Soviet citizens her life was strongly impacted by the purges of the late 1930s. Rita's sister Elena, a medical doctor, was arrested and sent to a labor camp in 1937. Elena's husband was shot, and Elena later died by suicide. The Kovalevs

---

[52] RGALI 336/5/124/24ob. ("ob" is the Russian abbreviation for *oborot* (*obratnaia storona*), or "back side of the page.")

[53] Author interview with Mikhail Levitin, October 18, 2019, Moscow.

[54] RGALI 2182/1/449/11–17. It is interesting that Rait chose Shkapskaia to confide in about how overwhelmed and lonely she felt as a new mother. Shkapskaia was known for her 1920s poetry about different forms of maternal joy, loss, grief, and struggle. Shkapskaia's poetry invoked a supportive community of women, especially mothers. Barbara Heldt argues that "Shkapskaia's poetry of the early 1920s comes closest of any writing in Russian to inscribing the female, the maternal, body into Russian culture" (Barbara Heldt, "Motherhood in a Cold Climate: The Poetry and Career of Mariia Shkapskaia," *The Russian Review* 51, no. 2 (April 1992): 160). Shkapskaia stopped writing poetry in 1926 and was nearly forgotten as a poet until a volume of her poetry was republished in London. (Maria Shkapskaia, *Stikhi* [Poems] (Overseas Publications Interchange Limited, 1979)).

[55] RRK to Maria M. Shkapskaia, March 30, 1934 or 1935. RGALI 2182/1/449/23.

subsequently adopted Elena's son, Sasha (Rita always called him "Shurik"). Sasha Kovalev later perished as a war hero while serving in the Soviet Navy during the Second World War. Tainted by her relationship with her sister and brother-in-law, and also possibly because one of her lab assistants was the daughter of an "undesirable," Rita was accused of "lack of loyalty." She lost her position at the Brain Institute in 1938 practically on the eve of her dissertation defense.[56] Politically stained by association, Nikolai was dismissed from the Navy but was "rehabilitated" a year or two later.

Things could have been much worse for Rita. Although she had been far away in the Russian Far East, and was a medical researcher, she maintained her keen interest in literature and translation. She considered the great, politically "problematic" poets, writers, and literati of the time to be her dear friends and allies. Yet, not a highly regarded writer in her own right, Rita was in a less precarious position than some of her colleagues. Throughout her life Rita managed to carve out a relatively safe space for herself to live and work in oppressive political conditions. She did so while maintaining friendships with politically "dangerous" individuals and even—eventually, when it was "safe"—writing about them. Rita's memoirs about Mayakovsky's and Nabokov's inner circle in the 1920s were published in 1962 and 1966, and her "Meetings with Anna Akhmatova" appeared in 1966.[57]

Rita joined the Union of Writers of the Soviet Union in 1939 and from that time made her living as a translator and writer. In 1941 Nikolai, Captain of the first rank, flag-officer, and mechanical engineer, was stationed with the White Sea Flotilla. The rest of the family—Rita, Margarita, and Sasha—joined Nikolai in Arkhangelsk after being evacuated from Leningrad.[58] In Arkhangelsk, Rait created materials for local radio broadcasts as a special

---

[56] RGALI 3401/1/630/3-4. In this unpublished memoir (undated, was in 1970s) dedicated to the memory of Kornei Chukovsky, "Missed Love," Rait recalled that she was offered back her position in the laboratory two months later. She refused it, however: the specially-operated-on dogs she studied for her dissertation had died of starvation in her absence, and she could not bear the thought of starting her experiments again from scratch.

[57] Rita Rait-Kovaleva, "Vstrechi s Akhmatovoi" ["Meetings with Akhmatova"], *Literaturnaia Armeniia* [Literary Armenia] 10 (1966): 54–62. The published versions of Rait's memoirs were self-censored. She produced more detailed memoirs that have not yet been published. Author interview with Lev Sobolev, October 24, 2019, Moscow.

[58] Rita and the children were evacuated to a LitFond (Literary Foundation) camp. At both national and republic levels the Writers' Union had LitFonds responsible for material and logistical support of union members. Through LitFond, union members could receive housing, work trips, vacations, deficit consumer goods, and so on. The LitFond camp where Rita and the children ended up was at Gavrilov Iam, as described in the memoirs of cyberneticist Viktor Il'ich Varshavskii, "Potok soznaniia" ["Stream of consciousness"], accessed May 21, 2020. http://is.ifmo.ru/important/_potok.pdf

correspondent for the Soviet Information Bureau. She wrote articles for *Moscow News*, and wrote as a theater critic for the *Pravda Severa* (Truth of the North) newspaper.[59] After the Nazis bombed American and British ships bringing supplies to the Soviet forces in the northern ports, Rita was called to work as an English-Russian translator in the hospital where the American and British wounded were treated. She also developed programming for the International Sailors Club ("Interclub"), where Soviet and Allied soldiers met for cultural exchange and entertainment. In a letter she wrote to the leadership of the Writers' Union of the USSR in August 1945, Rita described the difficulties of working as a translator "in the periphery." She had little time to work on translating books or plays, since she was busy doing "oral translations" and leading discussions, concerts, and readings for the Interclub. She also edited a monthly Interclub newsletter in English and Russian.[60] Working with Allied soldiers, including Brits and Americans, enriched Rita's vocabulary. She was known to "curse like a sailor" in English from then on.[61]

In May 1944, the Kovalevs' adopted son Sasha was killed in naval action, and Nikolai Kovalev died of hypertension in 1947 at the age of forty-eight. Rita struggled through very lean times as a housing-insecure single mother. She and young Margarita lived in a series of navy dormitories and run-down apartments, first in Leningrad, and finally in Moscow. As a Leningrader, Rita struggled to get translating assignments in Moscow, where she was an outsider. Rita credited Lili Brik with facilitating her gradual resurrection as a professional translator. Thanks to Brik's intervention Rita obtained some paid work at a movie studio dubbing films from German, French, and English.[62] Bit by bit Rait began to carve out a space for herself in the competitive world of literary translation in the Soviet Union. And this was not an easy world in which to make a living. On one hand, in the Soviet Union the translating profession attracted a disproportionate number of intellectuals with politically "problematic" backgrounds, including Jews and formerly imprisoned persons. Like Rita Rait, rarely were professional translators

---

[59] Archive Inquiry (Spravka No. 655/5-4;September 25, 2019) prepared for the author about Rita Rait-Kovaleva's personal fond at RGALI (631/39/4810).
[60] RGALI 631/15/645/3.
[61] DMF to LGL September 26, 1978, pp. 1-2, DMFC, Box 4, "Leighton, Lauren Gray, 1978-1979."
[62] RRK to DMF, August 12, 1978, p. 4, DMFC, Box 4, "Rait-Kovaleva, Rita, 1976-1982."

members of the Communist Party.[63] Yet, translators were highly respected, in part due to the long history of Russian poets (Alexander Pushkin among them) working as translators.[64]

Although it may be easy to think of translation as a non-political activity, in fact in the Soviet Union, as elsewhere, literary translation was carefully controlled. Providing Soviet readers with literature translated from foreign languages was an important component of the "literary foreign policy" of the USSR.[65] In this context, translation is a political act. Choices of who, what, and how to translate are decisions that easily reveal ideological commitments. In the Soviet Union, intellectuals with stains on their record, especially "problematic" writers, found refuge in working as translators of foreign literature. "From all indications, Soviet authorities approved of the existence of translation as a purgatory for authors in disfavor."[66] Translation was a fallback profession for frustrated or politically repressed writers. It offered talented authors unable to publish their own work an opportunity to sublimate their need to write while allowing them to make a decent living.[67] When in 1968 the great translator and scholar of poetry translation Efim Etkind pointed out in print that many great poets in the Soviet Union had become professional translators and were unable to publish their own writing, he was dismissed from the Union of Soviet Writers.[68] Prominent examples of writers-cum-translators in the Soviet Union ("translators by necessity")

---

[63] Maurice Friedberg, *Literary Translation in Russia: A Cultural History* (The Pennsylvania State University Press, 1997), 17. This is also borne out in a "Memorandum on the Work of the Foreign Translators" Section of the Soviet Writers' Union (SWU)" dated 1953: "The section of foreign translators is comprised of 100 members and candidates of the SWU, 94 of them are not party members and 10 translators are members of the CPSS [Communist Party of the Soviet Union], most of them with postwar experience. The party stratum (*partiinaia prosloika*) is very small in comparison with other sections." (RGALI 631/26/28).

[64] Carl R. Proffer, "Introduction: American Literature in the Soviet Union," in *Soviet Criticism of American Literature in the Sixties: An Anthology*, ed. Carl R. Proffer (Ardis, 1972), xv.

[65] Deming Brown, *Soviet Attitudes Toward American Writing* (Princeton University Press, 1962), 4.

[66] Friedberg, *Literary Translation*, 79.

[67] Friedberg, *Literary Translation*, 79.

[68] The offending sentence, which caused controversy, publication delays, and disarray of an important two-volume work, is in Efim Etkind, "Introduction," in *Mastera russkogo stikhotovornogo perevoda* [Masters of Russian Literary Translation], ed. Efim Etkind (Leningrad: Sovetskii pisatel', 1968), 71. For a transcript of the April 25, 1974 meeting in the secretariat of the Leningrad Writers' Organization excluding Etkind from the Writers' Union, see "Protokol No. 9 Zasedaniia Sekretariata Leningradskoi pisatel'skoi organizatsii 25 aprelia 1974 goda" ["Protocol No. 9 of the Meeting of the Board of the Leningrad writers' organization April 25, 1974"], *Revue des etudes slaves* 70, no. 3 (1998): 719–23.

included Boris Pasternak, Marina Tsvetaeva, and Anna Akhmatova, all three of whom Rita Rait admired.[69] Early in her career, Rait, too was a translator by necessity. After all, her career in scientific-medical research was destroyed by what she called the "fury and losses of 1937" (the Great Terror).[70] But as her talents and acclaim grew, Rait established herself as one of the Soviet Union's greatest translators. She longed to be a writer in her own right. She published a series of memoirs of the 1920s, as well as two major literary biographies of Scottish poet Robert Burns, and French Resistance writer and activist Boris Vilde. But translation was Rait's primary outlet to channel her passion and talent for prose writing.

Rita struggled mightily after the Second World War to secure housing, scratch out a living, and support her young daughter. The years 1946 to 1955—the very height of the Cold War—were extremely difficult for literati such as Rita. Cultural exchange was all but impossible, and any affinity for American literature and culture was not tolerated. As Deming Brown noted, "At the height of the cold war, Soviet isolation from the West had been so complete and Soviet doctrine so rigid that genuine cultural contacts with America were virtually impossible. Intellectual activity that led to any kind of overt admiration for American culture had been dangerous in the extreme."[71] Stalin's death in 1953, and Khrushchev's "secret speech" in 1955, which acknowledged the "excesses" of Stalin's reign of terror, paved the way for the Thaw. The Thaw was the period from the mid-1950s to the mid-1960s that some literary scholars call the "decade of euphoria."[72] It brought renewed opportunities for cultural diplomacy between the USSR and the West. Literature in translation was a major cultural dimension of the policy of *détente*.[73]

During the Thaw, the arts—including literature and translation—became staging grounds for cultural diplomacy between the USSR and Western countries. In the mid-1950s, the Soviet state cultural apparatus worked to facilitate increased translation and publication of foreign (including Western) literature for Soviet readers. The journal *Foreign Literature* and an associated publishing house was launched in 1955. This was a huge endeavor that introduced the massive Soviet readership to foreign classics and contemporary prose. Hitherto unavailable works by an increasing menu

---

[69] Friedberg, *Literary Translation*, 79.
[70] RRK to DMF, August 12, 1978, p. 1, DMFC, Box 4, "Rait-Kovaleva, Rita, 1976–1982."
[71] Brown, *Soviet Attitudes*, 174–5.
[72] Maurice Friedberg, *A Decade of Euphoria: Western Literature in Post-Stalin Russia, 1954–64* (Indiana University Press, 1977).
[73] Friedberg, *Decade of Euphoria*, 6.

of so-called "bourgeois writers" could be framed as exposing "the existential dilemmas of life under capitalism."[74]

Foreign Literature was not the first journal to introduce Soviet readers to foreign literature. From 1928 to 1943 a predecessor, *International Literature* (*Internatsional'naia literatura*) provided readers with information about cultural and literary life outside the Soviet Union.[75] *International Literature*, conceived as "the oracle of a global revolutionary movement," envisioned a worldwide readership and was published in several languages.[76] The journal's mission and reach ebbed and flowed with the changing tides of cultural collaboration with the West during the troubled 1930s. After the Great Terror of 1937 the journal began a decline resulting in its closure in 1943. With the journal's demise, Soviet readers lost an important source of information about global cultural and literary developments.[77]

By 1955 it was time to try again, and *International Literature*'s successor, *Foreign Literature*, was launched. Although reminiscent of *International Literature*, the new journal's goals and scope were distinct. *Foreign Literature* was a journal for a domestic, not an international, audience. Its main purpose was to acquaint the Soviet reading public with literary developments abroad. The journal's editorial policies "reflected a liberalized attitude toward the literature of the West, and specifically of America."[78] The journal's geographic scope was far-reaching. It included translations and criticism from the literatures of Western countries, socialist countries, and countries of the developing or so-called "third" world.[79]

During 1955–61, *Foreign Literature* published translations of the following American writers, among others: Erskine Caldwell, Howard Fast, William Faulkner, Lorraine Hansberry, Ernest Hemingway, Langston Hughes, Jack Kerouac, Arthur Miller, J. D. Salinger, Carl Sandburg, William Saroyan, John Steinbeck, Anna Louise Strong, Walt Whitman, and Tennessee Williams. *Foreign Literature* heralded a widespread sigh of relief—indeed, a Thaw—across the Soviet publishing world. Finally world literature was sanctioned for translation for a Russian language readership. At the same time, the perhaps unexpected popularity of translated foreign literature

---

[74] Gilburd, *To See Paris*, 106.
[75] The journal went through several name changes, reflecting the priorities of different editors-in-chief and shifts in the journal's mission. It was founded as *Herald of Foreign Literature* [*Vestnik inostrannoi literatury*] in 1928, renamed *Literature of the World Revolution* [*Literatura mirovoi revolutsii*] in 1930, and then *International Literature* in 1933. Safiullina and Platonov, "Literary Translation," 240.
[76] Brown, *Soviet Attitudes*, 176.
[77] Safiullina and Platonov, "Literary Translation," 262.
[78] Brown, *Soviet Attitudes*, 176.
[79] Proffer, "Introduction," xxii.

among voracious Soviet readers sparked inconsistencies in Soviet policies. In 1958 and 1959, strictures were added that threatened to slow down and decrease the number of Soviet translations of foreign works. Paradoxically, the expanded publication of Western books caused a tightening rather than a slackening of Soviet censorship.[80] Soviet publishing houses had to balance multiple priorities. They had to simultaneously publish works that were politically and morally acceptable according to official state doctrine, and books that would sell and keep the publishing houses financially viable. When it came to translations of foreign literature, publishers seemed to be constantly letting cats out of bags and trying to stuff them back in again. They practiced damage control when a foreign author suddenly became unacceptable, due to political statements they made, or political actions they took.[81]

During the 1950s and 1960s Rait was at the epicenter of the "international cultural traffic" of which translation of foreign literature was a key component.[82] An incomplete list of books Rita Rait translated for Soviet publishing houses in the 1950s and 1960s includes Dyson Carter, *The Future is With Us* (1952); Graham Greene, *The Quiet American* (1956); Sinclair Lewis, *Babbit* (1959); Sean O'Casey, *Five One-Act Plays* (1960); Mark Twain, *Life on the Mississippi* (1960); *The Diary of Anne Frank* (1960); Heinrich Böll, *The Clown* (1964); John Priestley, *Sir Michael and Sir George* (1965); J. D. Salinger, *Catcher in the Rye and other stories* (1965); Franz Kafka, *The Process* (1965); William Faulkner, *The Town* (1965) and *Soldier's Pay* (1966); and Nathalie Sarraute, *The Golden Fruits* (*Les Fruits d'or*) (1969). Rita's translations of myriad other stories and books by James Galsworthy, Bernard Malamud, Howard Fast, William Faulkner, Ernest Hemingway, and others were published in the "thick journals" of the official Soviet publishing apparatus.

It was during this time—the late 1950s and 1960s—that Rita Rait built her reputation. Rait's translations of Böll's *The Clown* and Kafka's *Process* were high impact cultural phenomena. In 1968 a play of *The Clown* ("Eyes of a Clown") based on Rait's translation premiered to great acclaim at the Mossovet Theater. The director was the great actor Gennadii Bortnikov, who also played the starring role of Hans Schnier.[83]

Rait's 1960 translation of *Catcher in the Rye* was another tremendously important literary and cultural event. It prompted widespread debates among

---

[80] Friedberg, *Decade of Euphoria*, 25.
[81] Natalia Kamovnikova, *Made Under Pressure: Literary Translation in the Soviet Union, 1960–1991* (University of Massachusetts Press, 2019), 159–60.
[82] Friedberg, *Literary Translation*, 13.
[83] See http://teatr.pro-sol.ru/pictures/index14.htm, accessed June 7, 2020.

Soviet readers and literary critics about translation practice, language taboos, and American society. Rait solidified her role as an unparalleled cultural conduit of American literature for Soviet readers. Rait proudly wrote in 1966 to her friend Sara Ginsburg in New York City that her friend Aleksandr Tvardovskii (editor of *New World* from 1950–4 and 1958–70) had called to congratulate her on her translation of Faulkner's *Soldier's Pay*, which had recently been serialized in the journal *Don*. Tvardovskii said Rita had helped "Russian readers to discover Faulkner."[84] That same year Rita Rait would read Kurt Vonnegut for the very first time. She would launch her quest to help Russian readers to discover Vonnegut, too.

Soviet schools of translation and Rita Rait

There were five main "pioneers" of the Soviet school of translation. Rita Rait was a disciple, and in the first two cases, a devoted friend, of four of them: Kornei Chukovsky, Samuil Marshak, Valery Bryusov, and Ivan Kashkin (the fifth "pioneer" was Mikhail Lozinsky).[85] Also important as founders of Soviet translation practice were Maxim Gorky and Boris Pasternak, the latter of whom Rita knew and fell in love with in the early 1920s. Her approach to translation was deeply influenced by all these mentors. In many respects Rait's translation practice exemplified the main tenets of the Soviet school of translation.

Scholars of translation practice in the USSR often cite V. M. Rossels on the four accepted postulates of the Soviet school of translation, the so-called "Gorky-Chukovsky-Kashkin doctrine."[86]

(1) Any literary text is translatable.
(2) A translator, like the original author, should study not only the text, but the everyday life conditions of the setting and characters.
(3) Translation as a literary process is prioritized over translation as a linguistic process.
(4) A literary translation should be neither "precise" (i.e., literal, with unwavering fidelity to the original text) nor "free." The translation's artistic impact on readers should equal that of the original text on its readers.

---

[84] RRK to SG, June 5, 1966, p. 4, BA-RRK.
[85] Leighton, *Two Worlds*, 9.
[86] Adapted from Friedberg, *Literary Translation*, 95.

The tension between literal (word-for-word) and literary ("artistic") translation is clear. A historic review of translation practice in the Russian Empire reveals that the same debates animated discussions of translation practice in the eighteenth century as during the Soviet period. To what extent should translators render "accurate," even "literal" translations of the original, versus translations that were more "artistic" and "free?" Arguments in favor of the practice of "free" translation usually carried the day, but there were continuous debates about exactly how freewheeling a translation should be. Overall, the Soviet school had a clear preference for translations that "flowed" and were "readable" in Russian. Peter the Great himself, the tsar who initiated the translation of secular books into Russian, including *belles-lettres*, blazed the trail for "free" or "literary" translations. His 1724 pronouncement required that translations be "clear and easy to understand, eschewing 'lofty Slavonic words.'" He rejected literal translation on principle. "It obfuscates the meaning of the original, familiarity with which then becomes a virtual necessity for the Russian reader."[87]

It is telling that only one of the "pioneers" of Soviet translation—Mikhail Lozinsky (1886–1955)—was a dyed-in-the-wool literalist. Literalism in translation was quite popular in the 1920s and very nearly dominated translation theory and practice in the Stalinist period. But literal translation eventually became taboo and was almost universally rejected by Soviet translators. Literal translations, so-called "technologically exact renditions" of original texts, were deemed too mechanical, devoid of creativity, and even damaging.[88] Kornei Chukovsky, a leading man of letters (poet, theoretician, writer, linguist, literary critic, literary historian, and foremost Walt Whitman expert), was considered a premier practitioner and trend-setter of the Soviet school of translation. An early proponent of literalism, Chukovsky wrote the Soviet school's "Bible," *A High Art*. There he insisted that "the translator must renounce his individual peculiarities. He must learn to mimic another person's gestures, inflections of voice, mannerisms, and forget his own ego . . . This is required by our epoch, which prizes above all scientific truth, documentary quality, precision, and authenticity."[89] Chukovsky altered this advice, however, when literalism fell out of favor and even became dangerous.[90]

---

[87] Quoted in Friedberg, *Decade of Euphoria*, 28.
[88] Friedberg, *Literary Translation*, 87.
[89] Kornei Chukovsky and Andrei Fedorov, *Iskusstvo perevoda* [The art of translation] (Akademia, 1930), 24, quoted in Friedberg, *Decade of Euphoria*, 110–11.
[90] Friedberg, *Literary Translation*, 111.

In a reversal of Chukovsky's path *away* from literalism, another of Rita Rait's mentors, Valery Bryusov, made a conversion *to* literalism. He suffered disenchantment with his earlier belief in the "universality of European civilization." Now believing each civilization to be unique, Bryusov figured that literalist translations were best, since only they could reflect this uniqueness.[91]

Albeit for different reasons, leading Soviet translation theoreticians, *and* leading Soviet translators rejected literalism. Ivan Kashkin was arguably the most influential Russian translator of the era of Socialist Realism, the Soviet artistic doctrine obligatory for all creative writers from the mid-1930s to the early 1980s. Kashkin, who was known as a great translator of Hemingway, insisted on the need for firm theoretical underpinnings for Soviet translation practice. For ideological reasons he rejected literalism in favor of "free" or "creative" translation, which he called "realist" translation. "Our Soviet literary translation is not at all 'a photographer's craft,' but creative assimilation."[92] Kashkin instructed translators to "perceive and reproduce the reality of the original in the light of our world view." Translators should "strive to convey to our readers everything that is progressive ... This should be accomplished without undue burdening of the text with unnecessary detail that is characteristic only of the alien linguistic structure and sometimes should not be translated at all."[93] Essentially, Kashkin instructed translators to make sure ideological (read: socialist realist) "truth" shine through their translations. That is, to make sure they were ideologically correct. He was also, perhaps, giving them license to engage in light censorship of foreign literary texts. This could have included omission of sexually suggestive scenes, deletion of remarks "disrespectful" or disparaging of the Soviet Union, and so on.[94] In our discussion of Soviet censorship of translated works below, we shall see examples of these tinkerings made possible by an "artistic" approach to translation.

"Artistic-realist" translation was the safer practice. It was the politically sanctioned approach, one which allowed translators and editors leeway to massage, rephrase, and reinterpret original texts, bringing them in line with "correct" ideology. Especially at the height of the Stalinist anti-Semitic

---

[91] Friedberg, *Literary Translation*, 146.
[92] Friedberg, *Literary Translation*, 103.
[93] Ivan Kashkin, *Dlia chitatelia-sovremennika: Stat'i i materialy* [For the Modern Reader: Articles and Materials] (Sovetskii pisatel', 1968), 443, 447, 490, 479, 451; quoted in Friedberg, *Literary Translation*, 104.
[94] Friedberg, *Literary Translation*, 105.

purges in the early 1950s, the charge of literalism was weaponized and used especially against Jewish translators.[95]

Many translators, Rita Rait included, preferred free translation because it offered them much more latitude to exercise their own writerly craft. The opportunity to consider oneself at least a minor "co-author" of the text was no doubt appealing. It was much more fulfilling to put one's own contemporary "spin" on a translated work for a Russian readership, than to mechanically duplicate it as primarily a linguistic, instead of literary, exercise. Realist translation practice allowed translators to "enliven" and enrich the texts they worked with. Rita Rait did this exceptionally well.[96]

The notion of "stylistic key" was a cornerstone of Soviet translation theory. This concept is summed up in the fourth tenet of Soviet translation: The translation's artistic impact on readers should equal that of the original text on its readers. Finding the stylistic key involved discovering the basic elements of the original author's signature style and working out how to successfully render those elements in the target language.[97] To successfully translate a work, the translator needed to identify and lock into the underlying elements of the author's craft. She must channel the features of style, intonation, and rhythm that coalesced to form the entire essence of the work. Rait took this maxim to heart, and her ability to tune into an author's "stylistic key" was one (open) secret of her success as a translator of "difficult" authors such as Salinger, Vonnegut, and Sarraute.

Rita Rait certainly was influenced by Kashkin, but there is no evidence that she was a Kashkin acolyte. She was not one of the so-called *kashkintsy*, the group of mostly female protégés of Kashkin who dominated the Soviet translation field in the 1960s.[98] Rait developed her own distinct translating craft under the influence of two other great giants of Soviet translation, Samuil Marshak and Kornei Chukovsky. Marshak was a children's poet and "gentleman translator," a "prosperous and politically conformist member of the literary establishment."[99] He was also a dramaturg, theorist, editor, and teacher. Rita first met Marshak in 1924 in Leningrad. A few years later Marshak took her under his wing to encourage her in what he hoped was her

---

[95] Friedberg, *Literary Translation*, 83.
[96] Burak, "The Other," 26–30.
[97] Leighton, *Two Worlds*, 101.
[98] Khmelnitsky, *Sex, Lies, and Red Tape*, 189.
[99] Friedberg, *Literary Translation*, 114.

emerging interest in writing books for children.[100] Rait was drawn to Marshak as a "master of the spoken word, a brilliant improvisator, with a colossal memory for poetry and prose."[101] But she had no intention of becoming a children's author.

It was not until nearly twenty-five years later, around 1948, that Rita officially became Marshak's mentee. At a writers' retreat near Riga she assisted Marshak in correcting final drafts of his monumental collection of translated Shakespearean sonnets. They worked together frequently for the next sixteen years. Rita's main roles, it seems, were fact checker (are you sure that type of bug has wings? Is that constellation visible in summer?) and sounding board for Marshak's translations. She would read his translations aloud and point out potential glitches or flaws. Rita supposedly never proposed improvements herself but left those to Marshak.[102] With Marshak Rita exercised a practice she carried through her life, one commented on frequently by those who knew her well—reading "out loud."[103] Rita and her colleagues, from Mayakovsky, to Marshak, were interested not only (and perhaps not primarily) in words on the page, but in how poetry and prose—in the original or in translation—sounded to the ear. This is one major distinction between literal and artistic translation. A literal translation may be correct, but sound "wooden." An artistic translation is a lyrical translation, pleasing and interesting when read aloud. Rait valued writing that delivered a true voice, with "live intonation," especially when read aloud.[104]

Rita acknowledged Marshak as her primary mentor. She dedicated her important 1965 article on translation practice, *"Nit' Ariadny"* (Ariadna's Thread) "in memory of my friend and teacher S. Ia. MARSHAK—the best translator and editor I have ever known."[105] Marshak, president of the international Federation of Robert Burns clubs, was the foremost expert in the Soviet Union on Robert Burns, whom he helped make widely popular. (Marshak also translated Blake, Keats, and Shakespeare, among others.) Rait shared his love of Burns in particular. With Marshak's encouragement she published a biography of Burns, which she dedicated to Marshak.[106] Rait also

---

[100] Marshak had seen an illustrated children's book Rait had written about a big factory in Leningrad, *Red Triangle*. Rita Rait-Kovaleva, "Nadpisi na knigakh" ("Book inscriptions"), in *Ia dumal, chuvstvoval, ia zhil: vospominaniia o S.Ia. Marshake* [I thought, I felt, I lived: remembrances of S. Ia. Marshak], ed. B.E. Galanov, I.S. Marshak, and Z.S. Papernyi (Sovetskii pisatel", 1971), 260.
[101] Rait-Kovaleva, "Book inscriptions," 261.
[102] Rait-Kovaleva, "Book inscriptions," 264.
[103] Rait-Kovaleva, "Book inscriptions," 264.
[104] Rait-Kovaleva, "Book inscriptions," 266.
[105] Rait-Kovaleva, "Ariadna's Thread," 5.
[106] Rita Rait, *Robert Burns* (Molodaia Gvardia, 1959).

translated Burns' prose, and she edited and provided the Introduction and Commentary for a collection of Marshak's translations of Burns' poems.[107]

It was Kornei Ivanovich Chukovsky, who Rait aptly called a "legend" of Soviet cultural life, whom Rita credited for one of her first big breaks. It is likely that Chukovsky read and was affected by an early (1960) excerpt from Rait's groundbreaking translation of J. D. Salinger's *Catcher in the Rye*.[108] Duly impressed, Chukovsky suggested Rait translate, under his editorship, Mark Twain's *Life on the Mississippi*. Rait blazed through the Twain translation, which was published later that same year (1960).[109]

Rait and Chukovsky became especially close one summer in the 1960s in Peredelkino, the famous writers' colony outside Moscow, where Chukovsky had a house (now a house-museum). He was finalizing his magnum opus, *A High Art: On the Principles of Artistic Translation*. It was the culmination of Chukovsky's long and esteemed career as the Soviet Union's leading visionary of the art of translation, and Rait enjoyed debating translation issues with him as he touched up the final draft. Chukovsky and Rait agreed on many points, including their distaste for translators who peppered translations with "*otsebiatina*." Literally "from the self," *otsebiatina* connotes "drivel from oneself—" unnecessary embellishments, explanations, or "improvements" to the text thrown in by over-eager, self-important translators. This was artistic translation taken too far, a translator pretending to know better than the text's original author, unable to stop themselves from whispering cues from offstage. Yet, Rait and Chukovsky had at least one major disagreement about translation practice: Rita could not abide when translators left in "witty" words and dialecticisms from the original text. She thought these stuck out like a sore thumb in foreign contexts where they no longer made sense. Chukovsky was indifferent to such transgressions, which Rait called "hyperanimation" (*ozhivliazho*).[110]

Rita acknowledged Chukovsky's mentorship. She was gratified that he singled out her and her translation of *Catcher* for praise in *A High Art*.[111] It was the first time Rita had been praised in print. She took Chukovsky's public praise to mean that "he affirmed the total legitimacy of the approach

---

[107] Robert Burns, *Robert Burns in the Translations of S. Marshak* (Pravda, 1979).
[108] Rait learned that Chukovsky's daughter Lidia ("Liusha") had read Rita's translation of *Catcher* aloud to him, and that he was especially impressed with it. Rait, "Missed love," 15 (RGALI 3401/1/630).
[109] Rait's translation of Twain's *Life on the Mississippi* was published as Volume Four of a twelve-volume Russian-language Twain series by the State Foreign Language Publishing House (Goslitizdat). Chukovsky was editor-in-chief.
[110] Rait, "Missed Love," 6.
[111] Kornei Chukovsky, *Vysokoe iskusstvo: o printsipakh khudozhestvennogo perevoda* [A high art: on principles of artistic translation] (Iskusstvo, 1964), 95–6.

to translation that I consider correct."¹¹² But Rait rejected the suggestion that she was "one of the many translators who were schooled" by Chukovsky.¹¹³ She explained in a letter to Donald Fiene that she met Chukovsky after he had read her translation of *Catcher*. That is, after she already had honed and proven her craft. Further, she insisted that her own translation method was "completely different."¹¹⁴ The "complete difference" of Rait's translation craft is important to understand. For this difference is what made her so perfectly suited to translate Kurt Vonnegut's unique prose for a "completely different" readership— Soviet readers in the 1970s.

Rait's translation practice: "I translated the word Bastard EIGHTEEN different ways"

Rita Rait articulated her golden rule of translation as follows. "The reader [of the translation] must understand, see, and feel everything that the reader of the original text understood, saw, and felt."¹¹⁵ To achieve this, Rait believed a translator must become fully immersed in the world of the author. The translator had to understand the author's intention in writing the text. She must strive to "know all there is to know about the book's author— his biography, his 'background,' including his upbringing and linguistic surroundings."¹¹⁶ Rait stressed the importance of intonation. A translator must hear and recreate the voice of the original author.¹¹⁷ For this to be possible, Rait encouraged young translators to "only translate authors that you love, or [authors] who you at the very least, feel and understand."¹¹⁸ Olia Bueva, who read Vonnegut in Rait's translation as a girl in Soviet Moldova, believes Rait's attention to the original author's voice was a big part of the books' success. "Rait has Vonnegut's self-effacing voice."

Rita Rait focused on translating the "essence" (*sushchnost'*) of a work. She worked not according to a "grammatical 'code,'" but by delving into the "essence" of a work by accessing what she called "emotional information." Rait believed that taking some translator's license was acceptable—perhaps

---

¹¹² Rait, "Missed love," 14–15.
¹¹³ Leighton, "Rita Rait-Kovaleva's Vonnegut," 413.
¹¹⁴ RRK to DMF, August 20, 1981, p. 1, DMFC, Box 4, Folder 5, "Rait-Kovaleva, Rita, 1976–1982."
¹¹⁵ Rait-Kovaleva, "Ariadna's Thread," 5.
¹¹⁶ Rait-Kovaleva, "Ariadna's Thread," 8.
¹¹⁷ Leighton, *Two Worlds*, 99.
¹¹⁸ RRK speech at Writers' Union of the USSR Seminar for Young Translators, December 22, 1956. RGALI 2854/1/129/7.

even necessary—to truly convey, in Russian, the true "essence" of a work. One example she liked to use was her approach to Holden Caulfield's voice in her translation of *Catcher in the Rye*. Some critics scolded Rait for translating the word "bastard" using eighteen different words in Russian. For Rait, her choice to translate "bastard" eighteen different ways was a perfect example of her credo. "I TRANSLATE—FEELING, REALITY, IMPLICATION..."[119] Translating "bastard" eighteen different ways crystallized Rait's commitment to privilege context and essence over form and "grammatical code."

When translating a work, Rait strived to fully inhabit the text and its setting. She felt she lived with the authors and their heroes. Rait compared her approach to the Stanislavski method of acting, where actors seek to fully recreate and inhabit the lifeworld of their character by studying the character's background, motivations, and emotions. Similarly, Rait believed, a translator must recreate the "back story" of a text's main characters. Rait believed that from the very first reading of the original text, the translator,

> must imagine as clearly and realistically as possible the heroes of the work. The translator must become intimately familiar with their physical appearance, manner of being, their habits, and life rhythm—not to mention their personality, spiritual inclinations, and fate. One must verify—do you see the character, do you hear his voice, even the timbre of his voice.[120]

Rait advised a young colleague in a letter in 1970, "Begin, with intention, slowly, "entering into" the protagonists' characters and the characteristics of their speech: try to see them CLEARLY, down to their gait and their voices, let them become your constant companions..."[121] If a translator managed to do all this—conjure up the character's back story and motivations, and fully see and hear the character (their mannerisms and gestures, their voice and personality)—then the character would "start speaking in Russian, while remaining an Englishman or a Frenchman, a medieval priest or a modern American beatnik."[122]

---

[119] RRK to DMF, August 20, 1981, DMFC, Box 4, Folder 5, "Rait-Kovaleva, Rita, 1976–1982."
[120] Rait-Kovaleva, "Ariadna's Thread," 8.
[121] RRK to KMA, October 25, 1970, p. 2, KMAC.
[122] Rait-Kovaleva, "Ariadna's Thread," 8–9. Rita's approach here resonates with that of Boris Pasternak, who translated Byron, Shelley, Shakespeare, and many others into contemporary Russian. Pasternak's goal was to revive the classics for modern Russian readers, in a language they could relate to. Etkind, "Introduction," 69.

Learning about the lives of Western authors and trying to imagine their characters' life worlds and "back stories" was, of course, a difficult task for Soviet translators, who rarely had the opportunity to travel abroad. An odd yet defining trait of Soviet translators was their forced immobility outside the bounds of the Soviet Union.[123] They also lacked access to foreign reference books.[124] Rait was rather an exception in that she did make extended trips to the UK and France, which helped her contextualize her work on Robert Burns, Nathalie Sarraute, and Boris Vilde. She also spent time in Prague, invaluable for her translations of Kafka. But despite several epic attempts to invite her to the United States, Rait was never able to visit the land of Billy Pilgrim.

Rita envied her Western colleagues who could travel widely, at will, and even on a whim. In letters she contrasted her own stuck in place-ness with others'—especially Vonnegut's—freedom to travel, to spend a few days here (Paris!), a few days there (Rome!). In a 1975 letter to Fiene she wrote, "How I long to see him . . . It is so painful when your friends are sown across the whole world—and you are cut off from them . . ."[125] Many of her letters included wistful thoughts about her own desires to travel to Europe and the United States. She noted the unrealistic nature of these desires, and the heaps of bureaucratic red tape and eons of planning time that realizing any of these trips would require.

Nevertheless, Rait did have considerable contextual knowledge of where Vonnegut fit into American literature. A life-long voracious reader of foreign literature, Rita kept as up to date as possible on the literary scene in the United States and other Western countries. Friends frequently sent her books from abroad. In early 1973 Fiene sent her *The Vonnegut Statement*, a collection of essays about Vonnegut's work compiled and edited by Vonnegut's primary bibliographer, Jerome Klinkowitz.[126] She was in touch, via post, telephone (rarely—international calls were expensive), and in person, with numerous American friends and colleagues, many of whom traveled to Soviet Russia on academic exchange programs such as IREX, ACLS, and Fulbright. There was one good friend in particular, an American translator living in Moscow named Margaret (Peggy) Wettlin, who Rita often asked about Americanisms, slang, etc.

---

[123] Gilburd, *To See Paris*, 155.
[124] Friedberg, *Literary Translation*, 117.
[125] RRK to DMF, August 2, 1975, p. 1, DMFC, Box 4, Folder 3, "Rait-Kovaleva, Rita, 1963–1976."
[126] RRK to DMF, February 24, 1973, p. 1, DMFC, Box 4, Folder 3, "Rait-Kovaleva, Rita, 1963–1976."

Sections of Rita Rait's typed drafts of her translations of Vonnegut's books are in her "fond" (archive) at RGALI.[127] The drafts include typed and handwritten edits and corrections presumably made by Rait herself. They illustrate that for Rita, translation was a constant process. In one illustrative case, over several pages handwritten in thick blue marker, Rita tries out some fifteen different ways to translate one sentence from Vonnegut's Preface to *Slapstick*.[128] Archival materials show that Rait was constantly editing, correcting, and adjusting, even after the translation had already been published. It was as if she never considered a translation "finished," or "perfect."

Several factors coalesced in Rita Rait's choice to translate Kurt Vonnegut's novels. By the mid to late 1960s, when she first read Vonnegut, she was a very specific kind of cultural figure in the Soviet Union. Rita was a self-described living "museum piece of the 1920s" with her finger on the contemporary literary pulse of the West. She was a "translator of their MOST FASHIONABLE AUTHORS," as Rita put it in a letter to Lili Brik.[129] Rait's life "connected the late Soviet years—the kitchen-table conversations about eternal things, the home jam-packed bookshelves, the domesticity of friendship—with the early Soviet avant-garde and internationalism."[130] Rait constantly surrounded herself with young representatives of the cultural intelligentsia—writers, artists, translators, theater folk. She kept herself relevant, fashionable, and contemporary. Indeed, Rait embodied the principle of "contemporariness" described by Giorgio Agamben. She possessed "a singular relationship with one's time, which adheres to it and, and the same time, keeps a distance from it."[131] In this she had much in common with Vonnegut, whose writing utilized strong elements of Agamben's contemporariness. "The contemporary is he who firmly holds his gaze on his own time so as to perceive not its light, but rather its darkness."[132] This critical gaze of contemporariness—seeing one's time through grey-colored glasses, if you will—animates all of Vonnegut's prose. As a "contemporary," one who is in one's time but not necessarily of it, Vonnegut frequently drew on his experiences during the Second World War (a formative period for all Soviet citizens) to reflect critically on the present. This is likely one major characteristic of Vonnegut's work that so attracted Rita Rait and Soviet readers to it.

[127] RGALI 3337/1/8.
[128] RGALI 3337/1/8/23-29ob
[129] RRK to Lili Brik, no date, RGALI 2577/1/417/15.
[130] Gilburd, *To See Paris*, 118.
[131] Giorgio Agamben, "What is the Contemporary?" in *What is an Apparatus? And other Essays* (Stanford University Press, 2009), 41.
[132] Agamben, "What is the Contemporary?" 44.

Rait also loved the challenge of translating Vonnegut's unique, sometimes fabricated, lexicon. She loved, and excelled at, translating slang and jargon, finding the absolute right and best way to render these words and phrases in Russian. She had honed this skill when translating Salinger with wild success, and it served her well with Vonnegut. Rait loved to play with language in everyday life. In her Russian-language letters to colleagues and friends she constantly threw in "Ukrainian, English, French and German words." She invented words using a mishmash of different languages and loved sharing her little daughter Margarita's funny baby talk phrases with friends. Rita sometimes took up these phrases and used them in her everyday speech. Therefore, Vonnegut's tendency to invent words and use unique, playful terms and phrases, fit perfectly with Rait's love of unusual, creative wordsmithing and speech. Rait wrote to Donald Fiene in late 1969, "I am quite delighted by this writer. He is awfully like me in the way he thinks and talks. I myself talk like that in Russian and, when I can, in English as well."[133]

Rita also must have connected with Vonnegut's unique style of writing, which has been described as "both lax and gnomic, 'telegraphic schizophrenic.'"[134] Vonnegut's style made him especially interesting—and difficult—to translate. Reflecting on Rait's Vonnegut translations, literary scholar Lauren G. Leighton explained:

> His sentences, following each other in a matter-of-fact tone, repeat in structure.... Vonnegut's style, his voice, is so casual as to seem banal—banality is both his style and the theme most often conveyed in his style—but his casualness actually heightens his irony.... The connection between banality and irony in his style (a connection that conveys his despair) is a delicate one, so that an incorrect choice of lexical equivalent or ordering of syntax could give Russian readers the wrong idea about Vonnegut.[135]

No doubt Rait enjoyed the challenge of working out how to replicate Vonnegut's style—his use of repetition, banal lexicon and trite phrases,

---

[133] RRK to DMF, November 17, 1969, DMFC, Box 4, "Rait-Kovaleva, Rita, 1968–1978." Translation Yana Skorobogatov, "Kurt Vonnegut in the U.S.S.R." (master's thesis, University of Texas at Austin, 2012), 5. https://repositories.lib.utexas.edu/handle/2152/19910

[134] Ihab Habib Hassan, *Contemporary American Literature, 1945–1972: An Introduction* (Ungar, 1973), 47. In a May 1980 letter to Leighton, Fiene quoted Hassan and said he had "carried that phrase around in my head for ten years, hoping to find an occasion to use it, but I never have." DMF to LGL, May 5, 1980, p. 2, DMFC, Box 4, Folder 2, "Leighton, Lauren Gray. 1980–1991." Thanks Don—this one's for you.

[135] Leighton, *Two Worlds*, 98–9.

laconic voice, and colloquialisms. As Rait translated Vonnegut, she sought to speak with Vonnegut's singular voice, to sustain Vonnegut's style, voice, and intonations.[136] Rita even likened her translations of Vonnegut to a kind of photograph. Inspired by the photography of Vonnegut's second wife Jill Krementz, whom Rait met in Moscow in 1974, Rita wrote to a friend in New York, "Tell Jill, that now, when there's discussion of my translations, especially the translations of Kurt: It's not a literal translation (*podlinnik*), of course. It is a Jill Krementz photograph; that is, a TRUE, <u>faithful portrait of the original</u>, rendered in a different language."[137]

Even Rait, a virtuosic translator, encountered some significant challenges when translating Vonnegut. She faced the daunting task of channeling Vonnegut's unique tone, register, and style. What is more, she faced the considerable challenge of identifying the provenance and meaning of certain culturally-specific references in his work. Then, she had to render those into something intelligible for a Russian reader unfamiliar with the American context. For guidance in this endeavor Rita frequently relied on Donald Fiene. Her letters to Fiene when she was working on *Cat's Cradle* were peppered with queries: Who or What is a Hoosier, and how do you pronounce it? What is Spencer County? A Prairie State/r (is it Texas)? The International Order of Odd Fellows? A Hobby Shop? Pall Malls are cigarettes, right?[138] After learning that a "Hoosier" was a "citizen of Indiana," Rait was reluctant to translate the term phonetically. "Huzher" sounds like the Russian word for "worse." She did not want to offend "the good people of Indiana."[139] (In the end, Rait did use "huzher.") And while Rait initially searched for an English equivalent for "Bokononisms" like karass, Wampeter, and Boko-maru, she finally decided to translate them phonetically. "They sound just fine in Russian," Rait decided.[140]

While translating *Slaughterhouse-Five*, Rait again asked Fiene to explain 7-Up, zap gun, crankcase drainings, and barbershop quartet.[141] Having signed a contract with *Foreign Literature* to translate *Breakfast of Champions*, Rita once more reached out to Fiene for guidance. How, she wondered, might one

---

[136] Leighton, *Two Worlds*, 99–100.
[137] RRK to LV, October 21, 1974, BA-RRK.
[138] Rait, "Reflections on Kurt Vonnegut," 94. Rita Rait was asked to contribute a piece for this festschrift, but it had not been received by the publishing deadline. Therefore, this remembrance attributed to Rait, was actually penned by Donald Fiene. It relied heavily on letters he had received from Rait about her friendship and work with Vonnegut.
[139] RRK to DMF, August 31, 1969, DMFC, Box 4, "Rait-Kovaleva, Rita, 1968–1978." Translation Yana Skorobogatov, "Kurt Vonnegut," 8.
[140] Skorobogatov, "Kurt Vonnegut," 8.
[141] Rait, "Reflections on Kurt Vonnegut," 94.

translate "doodley-squat?"[142] Rait worked on *Cat's Cradle* in 1969 before she had been in personal contact with Vonnegut. In line with her maxim to learn as much as possible about the authors she translated, Rait inquired of Fiene, "Who is Vonnegut-Senior (ours, after all, is Junior!)? What does our Vonnegut do—where did he study, what is he like? Do you have his portrait?"[143] Two-and-a-half years later, Rita would meet Kurt Vonnegut, Junior, in Paris, and have *her* portrait taken, with him, by the famous American photographer Jill Krementz.

Rait's translations of Vonnegut's novels are considered canonical in Russia today. Many assume that Rait took liberties with the texts, that she "improved" upon Vonnegut's prose in her process of translation. This raises the question, when people read Rait's Russian translations of Vonnegut, are they reading Vonnegut? Or are they reading Rita Rait? The notion that Rait's translations were superior to Vonnegut's originals is fueled by a well-known anecdote, possibly apocryphal, probably an urban legend, and no doubt embellished. The great satirical Russian writer Sergei Dovlatov included this apocryphal story in his *Solo on Underwood: Notebooks*.[144] Some version of this anecdote is often repeated when Rita Rait's name comes up in conversation. According to Dovlatov:

"At one point, I was Vera [Fedorovna] Panova's secretary.[145] Once Vera Fedorovna asked me:

"Who, in your opinion, has the best Russian language?"
I probably was supposed to say – You do. But I said:
"Rita Kovaleva"
"Kovaleva?"
"Rait."
"You mean Faulkner's translator?"
"Faulkner, Salinger, Vonnegut."
"You mean Vonnegut sounds better in Russian than Fedin?"

---

[142] Rait, "Reflections on Kurt Vonnegut," 95.
[143] RRK to DMF July 25, 1969, DMFC, Box 4, "Rait-Kovaleva, Rita, 1968–1978."
[144] Sergei Dovlatov, *Solo on Underwood: Notebooks* (Tret'ia volna, 1980). http://lib.ru/DOWLATOW/dowlatow.txt
[145] Vera Panova was a prominent journalist, novelist and playwright, who in the 1950s was elected as a member of the Presidium of the Union of Soviet Writers. She was a three-time recipient of the prestigious Stalin prize. Panova knew very well who Rita Rait-Kovaleva was, for Panova had written the afterword to Rait's translation of *Catcher in the Rye* published by Foreign Literature in 1960. See Raisa Orlova, "Istoriia odnogo poslesloviia" ["History of one afterword"], *SSSR: Vnutrennie protivorechiia* [USSR: Inner contradictions] 13, ed. Valery Chalidze (Chalidze Publications, 1985), 122. https://vtoraya-literatura.com/pdf/sssr_vnutrennie_protivorechiya_13_1985__ocr.pdf

"Absolutely, no doubt."
Panova thought and responded:
"How terrible!"

Further, unless I'm mistaken, something similar happened with Gore Vidal. He was in Moscow. Muscovites started asking him about Vonnegut. They were inspired by his novels. Gore Vidal remarked: 'Kurt's novels aren't nearly as good in the original...'"[146]

One of Rait's closest friends, the theater director Mikhail Levitin, often references a version of Dovlatov's story when speaking about Rita. When I interviewed Levitin in Moscow in 2019, his summary of the story was as follows: "Once Dovlatov... (he worked for the great Vera Panova) and she asked him once, 'Who writes better than anyone in Russian?' He said, 'Rita Rait writes the best in Russian.' She said, 'The translator? Better than Fedin? How terrible.'" However the story is told, there are two take-away messages. The best Russian writer is not a writer at all, but a translator, Rita Rait. And Rait's translations, including of Vonnegut, are improvements on the original works.

Levitin told the Dovlatov-Rait story in response to my question, "Why did people here love to read Vonnegut?" Levitin continued,

> Rita channeled Kurt (*proniklas' Kurtom*).[147] She got it right. When you are translating, you just have to get it right. You have to make the line your own. She translated KURT, not Kurt's books. She was able to translate PEOPLE—the authors of the books. She translated THEM. She was concerned with THEM first and foremost. Some people criticized her for that. "In this line there's not a single word the author wrote." She would answer, "And? Does it contradict what he wrote?" "No, it doesn't." "So why are you criticizing me? Is it worse than the English?" "No." "Then don't criticize me." Her whole life, she couldn't understand that. Because she was free. They were translators. And she was a writer, a poet, a co-author. Co-author, that's it—she was, more than anything, a co-author.

Conceptualizing translation as "co-authorship" could imply that the translator is bringing too much of themselves—their own proclivities, voice,

---

[146] Dovlatov, *Solo on Underwood*, no page.
[147] It is difficult to adequately translate the meaning of Levitin's phrase. The Russian-English dictionary definition of "proniknut'sia" is "be imbued with, imbue one's mind with, be filled with." In Levitin's usage it means "to be saturated with," or "to channel."

and stylistic devices—to the work. However, this transgression was one Rait could not abide and would have avoided at all costs. Indeed, in his thorough treatment of Rait's translations of four Vonnegut novels, scholar Lauren Leighton effectively absolved Rait of the charge of seeking to "improve upon" the texts. In Leighton's assessment, "Her modifications are not motivated by a desire to improve Vonnegut, and she does not succumb to the temptation to create for herself . . . Rayt has not reinterpreted Vonnegut; she has instead exercised tact and taste in her choices . . ."[148] He continued, "Rayt's rearrangements of syntax do not disrupt Vonnegut's steady narrative tone or vary his laconic voice. Rather . . . her substitutions and modifications almost always facilitate her intent to recreate an American writer in Russian."[149] And finally, "Rayt is both imaginative and inventive, but she does not attempt to create for herself; her work is not an opportunity to express her own literary 'I.' She reveals respect for the rights of the original author and, at the same time, for the integrity of the original text."[150]

In his analysis Leighton seems to imply what other scholars, including Alexander Burak, stated more explicitly. Soviet translators, including the "Kashkintsy" school, and later Rita Rait, actually developed a new literary style in Russian literature. Burak coined this the "Russian Amerikanskii literary substyle."[151]

> I submit that Rait-Kovaleva's translation follows the Kashkintsy's lead in creating a special field, or "zone" in Russian-language literary texts that became reserved specifically for Russian-style "Americanese"—the Russian "Amerikanskii" literary substyle. Although accepted by the Soviet literary establishment, this style of translating was shaping up as a distinctive mode of verbal expression that was not exactly "ours" (*nash*—Soviet). In contrast to the mainstream writing of the time, it was subtly alluring, attractive, and voguish, because, in an Aesopian sort of way, it half suggested the idea of freedom, the idea of democracy, the state of being able to say and do what you wanted to say and do in opposition to the totalitarian constraints of life and self-expression in the Soviet Union of the 1960s.[152]

---

[148] Leighton, *Two Worlds*, 102–3. In this work Leighton spelled Rait's last name "Rayt."
[149] Leighton, *Two Worlds*, 104.
[150] Leighton, *Two Worlds*, 107.
[151] Burak, "The Other," 20–6.
[152] Burak, "The Other," 78.

It is Rait's "systematic enlivenment" of translated texts via this distinctive Russian Amerikanskii substyle that caused some readers to credit her with "enriching" the Russian language with her translations of Vonnegut, Salinger, and other American authors. It is one reason Rait and other Soviet translators in the 1960s and 1970s have been called the "quiet heroes of revolution."[153] On the other hand, Rait knew there was a fine line between finding an author's stylistic key and tuning to it in the Russian translation, versus slipping into the kind of "hyperanimation" that she abhorred.

Rait recognized her translations as superior and she sought to improve on or repair *others'* translations of Vonnegut, "her" author. Rait took it upon herself to retranslate Vonnegut to save his work from sub-par if well-meaning translators. For instance, as Fiene relayed to Vonnegut in a 1978 letter:

> In her seminar for the American professors [visiting Moscow], Rita spoke in detail about how she translated *Rosewater*, how she corrected the errors of the two pathetic (though sweet) women translators whose botch was published in the journal Aurora. For the first thing, she changed the title. The title is derived from the spoken words of Diana Moon Glampers. The ladies had her saying (for their title): Da blagoslavit vas Bog, Mr. R. But that is what a priest would say in a church service. Rita's title is: Dai vam Bog zdorov'e, Mr. R., which is how a Russian woman of Diana's class would express it. The back translation is "God give you health . . ." It has a wonderful authentic sound in Russian. She saved your book for you.[154]

Still, Rait's translations of Vonnegut are not perfect, and she made choices that rub some translation studies specialists the wrong way. She also made some mistakes. A catalog of these is provided by Michael Khmelnitsky in his dissertation, "Sex, Lies, and Red Tape: Ideological and Political Barriers in Soviet Translation of Cold War American Satire, 1964–1988." Whereas Fiene and Leighton tend to emphasize the "brilliant equivalences" Rait conjured for difficult "Vonnegutisms" and elusive references to Americana in his work, Khmelnitsky reads her translations more critically. He takes issue with Rait's "modus operandi at the word level" (her tendency to "depart from normative semantic usage"); her "approach to conveying idiomatic concepts and realia" (culture-specific material objects); and her "approach to reader competency" (overuse of footnotes).[155] Although Rait's translations of Vonnegut have

---

[153] Burak, "The Other," 27, quoting translator and cultural commentator Vadim Mikhailin.
[154] DMF to KV, September 16, 1978, p. 11, FIEN, Folder 4, "1978."
[155] Khmelnitsky, "Sex, Lies, and Red Tape," 247–70.

become canonical and led a generation of readers to fall in love with Vonnegut, they are not problem-free, as we shall see.

Pushing through "a complicated author like Kurt"

When Rita Rait embarked on translating *Slaughterhouse-Five* and *Cat's Cradle* in 1968 and 1969, she had no guarantee, and possibly not much hope, that the translations would ever see the light of day. Rita reported to her friend Lili Brik in a December 1969 letter:

> During 1968–69 I translated Kafka's "Zamok" [The Castle] . . .and two small novels of my now-favorite—Kurt Vonnegat [*sic*]. His work is a <u>little</u> reminiscent of Osip [Brik]'s "*Nepoputchitsa*" ["the Misfit"] in its laconicism and absence of any embellishment and contrivance . . .His last novel is just wonderful: it's called "Slaughterhouse Five, or the children's crusade . . ." I'm sending the manuscript to *Novyi Mir* (*New World*) . . .Actually, you might not like it: it is sort of "black humor" with a little science fiction thrown in.[156]

It is not clear whether Rait had secured a publishing contract before she translated *Cat's Cradle*, or if she embarked on the translation "cold" (without a contract) in the hopes of interesting a publisher with translation in-hand.[157] It was actually very common—the norm, really—for Soviet translators in the late 1960s and early 1970s to initiate translations on their own in the hopes of later interesting a publisher. Sometimes this was done in consultation with an editor, but oftentimes not. Some translations never got published. They became manuscripts "for the drawer," that is, work completed solely for the translator's own satisfaction.[158]

---

[156] RGALI 2577/1/417/29, 29ob. I believe Rita was referring to an unpublished work by Lili Brik's husband, Osip Brik, entitled "*Nepoputchitsa*" ["The Misfit"].

[157] Rait wrote to Donald Fiene: "Long ago I submitted an 'offer' (*zaiavka*) to the Young Guard editorial office—where [my translations of] Salinger and Malamud were published. And now they've sent me an agreement!" (DMFC, Box 4, Folder 2, "Rait-Kovaleva, Rita, 1968–78.") The "offer" was in essence a translator's application for translating a work of foreign literature. In this "pitch" the translator would argue for the value of the work they wished to translate, for a Soviet readership. Historical *zaiavka* documents are thus valuable for understanding the ideological framings—honing to official discourse—necessary to get a work approved for translation.

[158] Proffer, "Introduction," xvi.

Unfortunately, I have not found records in the archives of the Foreign Commission and the Translators' Section of the Writers' Union of the Soviet Union of discussions about Kurt Vonnegut and the suitability of his writing for translation for Soviet readers. Nor could I track the exact mechanisms through with Rita Rait pursued and secured contracts from journal and book publishers to publish her translations of Vonnegut. From reading her letters on the subject to correspondents such as Ariadna Efron (Maria Tsvetaeva's daughter), Lidia Chukovskaia (Kornei Chukovsky's daughter), and Lili Brik, however, I can make certain inferences. During this period—the late 1960s—Rita frequently undertook translations of at least a sample chapter or two on her own initiative. She then sought publishing contracts. This is the likely scenario with Vonnegut since, as her friend Mikhail Levitin explained, "She didn't get many [official] offers [to do translations]. Even from *Foreign Literature*. It all depends on the head editor, and I remember there was a head editor that didn't suit her. I'm sure that was the case. She didn't get any work, and she had to find literature [to translate] herself."

Another reason Rait was hard up for work in the late 1960s was political. She had traveled abroad, for months at a time, to the UK and France. She had taken a big gulp of Western-capitalist hospitality, literature, and daily life. This was enough to make her a suspicious Soviet citizen. Rait followed international politics with interest, even if she continued to reject politics as a "dirty business." During a trip to Paris to visit Nathalie Sarraute, Rita wrote to Donald Fiene in late February 1968:

> Do not overwork yourself and do not (most emphatically so!) get into politics—a game which is getting worse and worse for every decent person to take part in. . .I shall come to the USA if and when that war [in Vietnam] is over. . .I do not want to talk about it or about all the dirty things both sides are doing. . .(Read Mary McCarthy's "Vietnam").[159]

It is very doubtful that Rita would have written so openly about the Vietnam war and both sides' atrocities if she had been posting letters from the Soviet Union instead of France. She both acknowledged and concealed this fact in a subsequent letter to Fiene, also written from Paris. "If you have any questions for me to answer from here—fire away. (I don't want to say that I cannot write too many things from home, but it is so much quicker to write from

---

[159] RRK to DMF, February 27, 1968, pp. 5–6, DMFC, Box 4, Folder 3, "Rait-Kovaleva, Rita, 1963–1976."

here...)."[160] On the very next page of this letter, Rita revealed that she indeed was following American politics, especially the debate over the Vietnam war, quite closely. She had read Hans Magnus Enzensberger's recently published diatribe in *The New York Review of Books* excoriating the US government and outlining his reasons for leaving the United States for residence in Cuba.[161] (Rita called Enzensberger's piece "a most offensive letter.")

Rait presented an outwardly "apolitical" stance, never joined the Communist Party, and never considered emigrating or getting deeply involved in political dissent. Fiene characterized Rait as having been "more or less a Marxist" in the 1920s, and a life-long supporter of "Communist social programs."[162] He insisted that she judged people for their human qualities. He said she refrained from labeling people "along political lines."[163] Rait wrote to Fiene in 1966:

> No matter how critical we (my sort of people) are to many things that happen in our country, we never want to go and do anything that could do even the slightest harm... And, as I told you, we want to clean up all the dark and cobwebby corners of our house ourselves, because we know better how to do it properly.[164]

This was also the impression Vonnegut had formed of Rait. Consider his letter to William Styron in June 1974. "We are going to Moscow in October, to see my translator, and perhaps yours, too—Rita Rait (*Puma Paum*). She is one of those who wants to stay there, and, with a little help from her friends, to make the Soviet Union more amusing and humane. Fat chance, I suppose."[165] Overall Rait preferred not to rock the political boat. She was cautious about crossing the line into political dissidence. At the same time, she offered support—material, and moral, at least—to Soviet dissident writers. Rait's friendship with and moral support for dissidents, coupled with

---

[160] RRK to DMF, March 2, 1968, p. 4, DMFC, Box 4, Folder 3, "Rait-Kovaleva, Rita, 1963–1976."
[161] RRK to DMF, March 2, 1968, p. 5, DMFC, Box 4, Folder 3, "Rait-Kovaleva, Rita, 1963–1976." See Hans Magnus Enzensberger, "On Leaving America," *The New York Review of Books*, February 29, 1968. https://www.nybooks.com/articles/1968/02/29/on-leaving-america/
[162] Donald M. Fiene, "J.D. Salinger in the Soviet Union—A Brief Report." DMFC, Box 4, "Rait-Kovaleva, Rita, 1963–1976."
[163] DMF to William H. Luers, October 16, 1966, DMFC, Box 4, Folder 1, "Rait-Kovaleva, Rita, 1961–1989."
[164] RRK to DMF, November 9, 1966, DMFC, Box 4, Folder 3, "Rait-Kovaleva, Rita, 1963–1976."
[165] Wakefield, *Kurt Vonnegut—Letters*, 216–17. In the letter Vonnegut wrote Rita's name twice—once in English, and a second time in parentheses in Cyrillic.

her own reluctance to challenge the system, left her in an ambiguous position. Although one close friend remembers her as a "minor dissident," others characterize her as a "scared citizen." Rait's fellow translator Shimon Markish called Rait "a very experienced translator and very Soviet in that sense that she never made any false steps capable of bringing on the displeasure of the authorities."[166]

As noted in Chapter One, Rita had "stains" on her own political biography, due to her sister and brother-in-law's arrest during the purges, as well as the former's death by suicide and the latter's political execution. Rait was subject to suspicion on several grounds. There was the matter of her "cosmopolitan" background (read: Jewish intellectual roots) and her deep interest and knowledge of foreign literature. She had friendships with writers and scholars in problematic countries, especially the United States. She had traveled abroad, though infrequently and no doubt under close monitoring. At home, she maintained close relationships with cultural figures targeted for political repression.

Rait was personally acquainted with a host of literati, intellectuals, and other cultural figures who ran afoul of the Soviet government. She was close friends with some who suffered prison sentences, labor camps, and exile. Among these were Yuli Daniel and Andrei Sinyavsky. Rita's friend Lynn Visson remembers that when she knew Rait during the early 1970s, Rait was "buying carton after carton of cigarettes for [Yuli] Daniel, who was back in Moscow after his release from prison."[167] Rait deeply admired and frequently corresponded with Lidia Chukovskaya, a great supporter of Soviet dissidents who was monitored closely by the KGB. She supported the controversial young theater director Mikhail Levitin, who in the early 1970s was not given work for political reasons. In a 1972 letter to her friend and protégé Konstantin Azadovsky (who would in 1980 be sentenced to a labor camp on false drug possession charges and fully rehabilitated in the 1990s), Rait wrote that she thanked her lucky stars each morning that "UP THERE they seem to have forgotten about me."[168]

In this context, what arguments might Rait have presented to the editorial boards of literary journals and publishing houses, to convince them to publish Kurt Vonnegut? If she had undertaken this task two decades earlier, right after the Second World War and before Khrushchev's secret speech

---

[166] Shimon Markish, "*O perevode*" [On translation], *Ierusalimskii zhurnal* [Jerusalem journal] 18 (2004). Antho.net. Translation Michael Khmelnitsky, "Sex, Lies, and Red Tape," 297.
[167] Lynn Visson, email message to author, August 20, 2019.
[168] RRK to KMA, April 1972, KMAC.

acknowledging the excesses of Stalinism, her ideological argumentation would have been strong. In the early 1950s Rita Rait led the "English Group" of the Foreign Commission of the Translators' Section of the Soviet Writers' Union. During those years she also struggled to get translation work. She may have felt the need to prove her loyalty through active participation in "politically correct" debates. In the RGALI archives I found a 1952 letter from Rita Rait to the editors of the literary journal *New World*. The letter offers clues about how translators in the early 1950s would have been compelled to argue for translating foreign authors. In her letter, Rita, who at the time was dabbling in translation from Bulgarian, requested a contract to translate a story, "Song of a Person" ("Pesnia o Cheloveke"). It was a work by Khristo Ganev about the life and work of Bulgarian poet Nikola Vaptsarov. In her pitch Rait stressed the ideological correctness of Ganev's story. She explained that Vaptsarov was "shot by the fascists" a decade earlier.[169] Records of Rait's speeches at meetings of the Foreign Commission also index ideological concerns at the center of the translation enterprise. At a 1954 meeting, Rita delivered strong remarks about the important "counterpropaganda" work that journals such as *Literary Gazette* were doing.[170]

By the late 1960s and early 1970s, getting permission to translate and publish foreign—even American—authors was not as hard. Still, Rait would have had to argue for the "usefulness" of Vonnegut's prose for a Soviet readership. Officially, the Soviet book publishing industry was primarily an ideological endeavor. Publishing was guided by the policies of the Communist Party. The main evaluation criterion for publishing any book was whether it would be "useful" to the cause of building Communism. Economic factors were secondary.[171] In reality, this evaluation of "usefulness" was surely aspirational, and publishing houses' operations were more pragmatic and flexible. Further, publishing books by Soviet sympathizers, or at least those foreign authors who could be "framed" as such, had propaganda value.[172]

While no one would call Vonnegut a Soviet sympathizer, he was a relatively "convenient" author for the Soviet government. He offered strong critiques of the United States, especially the excesses of American capitalism and the wrong-headedness of the Vietnam war. It did not hurt that in some corners of the United States his books had been banned, and his freedom of speech trampled. Vonnegut's status as a veteran of the Second World War was another boon to his acceptability. That he was a war veteran who spoke

---

[169] RGALI 1702/4/336/119.
[170] RGALI 631/26/34/74–5.
[171] Friedberg, *Decade of Euphoria*, 17.
[172] Friedberg, *Literary Translation*, 210.

out virulently against the American war in Vietnam was almost too good to be true.

Nevertheless, Rait likely kept her political and ideological argumentation to a minimum when she pitched Vonnegut in translation to Soviet publishing houses. By the late 1960s and early 1970s, Rait was less active in the Foreign Commission of the Writers' Union. She certainly leveraged her pull there and enjoyed her status as a senior translator. Rait frequently led seminars for beginning translators. But she refrained from political discussions in the open and urged others to do the same. Rait, like Vonnegut, positioned herself as a "citizen of the world." She was more interested in world peace and mutual understanding than in Cold War rivalries between nations and political-economic systems. As Fiene noted in his letters to U.S. State Department officials, Rait believed that change in the Soviet system had to come from within, from Soviet citizens, not from external influences. For Rait, introducing Soviet readers to great Western literature was a means to that end. Vonnegut's novels endeared Soviet readers to ridiculous but loveable characters (many of them Americans), raised moral questions of universal importance (scientific ethics, social inequality, the existence of free will), and included healthy doses of anti-capitalist harangue (from an American writer!). His books, especially in Rait's lively translations, would have had an automatic appeal.

Still, the process to get permission for a foreign work to be translated and published was daunting. As Rita described in a letter to Fiene (July 25, 1969), translating a work was just the first, and perhaps not even the most difficult, step in the publication process of foreign literature in the Soviet Union. "Hip hip, hurray! I'm finally translating Cat's Cradle!!!!! I just signed the contract with Young Guard [publishing house]. The book will be out early in 1970; I will finish it toward November—but after that will follow still many stages, as in a flight to the moon."[173] This "spaceflight" was choreographed by Soviet publishing practices, with its own rules and internal dynamics, and at least five levels of approval. As Gregory Walker observed in 1978:

> A publishing-house considering translation of a foreign work must. . .obtain at least two recommendations for the translation from scholarly institutions or specialists, and secure the agreement of the appropriate chief editorial office in the State Committee for Publishing before submitting details of the work for "coordination" to the State Committee . . . The choice of translators, and of authors to write any

---

[173] RRK to DMF, July 24, 1969, DMFC, Box 4, "Rait-Kovaleva, Rita, 1968–1978." Translation Yana Skorobogatov, "Kurt Vonnegut," 6.

notes or introduction to the work, must be approved by a senior editor or the head of an editorial office.[174]

For Rait, an established translator but not a favorite of publishers, all of this would have involved a lot of string-pulling and negotiation.

It should be noted that Kurt Vonnegut himself played no role at all in these negotiations about *Cat's Cradle* and *Slaughterhouse-Five* in 1969–72. The Soviet Union did not sign onto the Universal Copyright Convention (UCC) until 1973. The UCC required publishers to pay royalties to foreign authors whose works they translated and published. Before the Soviet sign-on, translations of foreign works were published in the USSR without permission from foreign authors. Vonnegut confirmed in 1974 that he had not known in the late 1960s that his books were being translated into Russian. "To the best of my knowledge, the books of mine which have been published in the Soviet Union are *Utopia-14* (*Player Piano*), *Cat's Cradle*, and *Slaughterhouse 5*. I was not consulted at all about their translation. I was not even informed that they were being published."[175]

When the Soviet Union did adopt the UCC, there were no "grandfather" clauses. That is, foreign authors of works that had been translated and published in the Soviet Union prior to May 27, 1973, could not expect to receive retroactive royalties for those books. The new requirement to get permission from foreign authors to translate and publish their works in the USSR, to have authors sign contracts, and to pay them royalties, added layers of red tape to the process. By 1976, the new office of the All-Union Agency for Authors' Rights (VAAP) had 400 employees in its Moscow office alone. UCC strictures slowed down the already glacial process of publishing translated works in the USSR.[176]

In this context, Rait became very nervous when publication of her translations of *Cat's Cradle* and *Slaughterhouse-Five* was stalled. Rait complained in a letter to Ariadna Efron in February 1970.

> Everything is somehow hung up (*v "podveshennom" sostoianii*). I have submitted THREE books—with little result: it is not clear whether the editorial board will accept Vonnegut for *New World*, what will happen with [Kafka's] *Castle*, what will happen with Vonnegut's other little novel

---

[174] Gregory Walker, *Soviet Book Publishing Policy* (Cambridge University Press, 1978), 119.
[175] Letter from Kurt Vonnegut to Maurice Friedberg, September 12, 1974. In Friedberg, *Decade of Euphoria*, 21.
[176] Friedberg, *Literary Translation*, 16.

(*romanchikom*) [*Cat's Cradle*] with "Young guard" . . . I rushed and rushed—[and] for what!?!?!¹⁷⁷

In a follow-up letter Rait repeated, "All three submitted books—two of Vonnegut's and one of Kafka's—are going nowhere . . ."¹⁷⁸ Three months later, in May, Rita had finally heard good news from the editor of *New World*, who said she'd translated *Slaughterhouse-Five* "jauntily."¹⁷⁹

The UCC made Rita's practice of pre-translating foreign literature to pitch to publishers all but obsolete. Until an author contract with the publisher was agreed on, it made no sense to embark on a time-consuming translation project. Rait received a copy of *Slapstick* from Donald Fiene in early 1976 and hoped to translate it.¹⁸⁰ But at the end of that year she wrote Fiene that she was not yet translating *Slapstick*, because "there is no agreement (yet!)."¹⁸¹ In a follow-up letter to Fiene she further explained, "Don't forget that to translate without an agreement is NONSENSICAL . . ."¹⁸²

The controversy over *Slapstick* is a good example of how the Soviet Union's foreign relations affected decisions about translation and publication of foreign literature in the late 1970s. The problem with *Slapstick*, from the Soviet point of view, was not Vonnegut's portrayal of the USSR, or communism. Concerns about vulgarity and sexual content were not germane, either. Rather, the problem was Vonnegut's portrayal of China and the Chinese people in the book. Ironically, permission for Rita to translate *Slapstick* was stymied not by tensions between the United States and the Soviet Union. The major concern was how the Chinese might react to certain Sino-relevant details in the book. Rita explained to Lynn Visson in a January 1977 letter.

> We are holding off on translating "Slapstick" for now, since it has funny bits about the Chinese, along the lines of how they learned to make tiny little people, and they get SWALLOWED by mistake, and this causes "Green Death"(!). So they are asking me to WAIT—until it is clear whether our relations [with China] will improve or not . . . Lenochka, of course you understand that this is irrelevant to both literature and "common sense," but that's 'la vie' as the French say.¹⁸³

---

¹⁷⁷ RRK to Ariadna Efron, February 11, 1970, RGALI 1190/3/438/62, 62ob.
¹⁷⁸ RRK to Ariadna Efron, February 18, 1970, RGALI 1190/3/438/63.
¹⁷⁹ Rait, "Reflections on Kurt Vonnegut," 95.
¹⁸⁰ RRK to DMF, March 4, 1976, p. 2, DMFC, Box 4, "Rait-Kovaleva, Rita, 1976–1982."
¹⁸¹ RRK to DMF, December 3, 1976, p. 2, DMFC, Box 4, "Rait-Kovaleva, Rita, 1976–1982."
¹⁸² RRK to DMF, January 5, 1977, p. 1, DMFC, Box 4, "Rait-Kovaleva, Rita, 1976–1982."
¹⁸³ Copy of letter from RRK to LV, January 13, 1977, pp. 1–2, DMFC, Box 4, Folder 5, "Rait-Kovaleva, Rita, 1976–1982."

Rita followed up with Fiene in late 1980. "Tell [Kurt] that no one wants to translate "Slapstick" because of the Chinese [characters] !!!!! Recently the journal *Neva*—where they <u>Love</u> both me and Kurt—turned it down!!!!"[184]

One book that Rita Rait never sought permission to translate was *Mother Night*.[185] It would have been pointless to seek such permission, due to the book's ideological nature and its portrayals of the Soviet Union, Soviet socialism, and totalitarianism. Rita chided Donald Fiene for continuing to inquire about her plans to translate *Mother Night*.

> There's a lot you don't understand—you have a different 'program' in your brain! For instance, you ask when I'm going to translate "Children of the Night" [Mother Night].[186] All of us—Misha [Mikhail Levitin] the [theater] director and my mathematician friends and everyone who has read this miraculous book—laughed: don't you understand that it is impossible to translate it—due to the THEMES—all those people, sitting in different corners of the world, they can't be depicted as Kurt depicts them.[187]

What Rait meant, but could not write in a letter to Fiene (which most certainly would have been read by Soviet authorities), was that no Soviet publisher would agree to a book that was so explicitly anti-Soviet. The characters George Kraft-Potapov and Resi Noth were nefarious Soviet agents. Vonnegut used silly names and place names to make fun of Russia and Russians. His critique of utopian thinking and the "totalitarian mind" was a clear attack on Soviet socialist thought.

Slapstick and *Mother Night*, then, were not translated in the 1970s Soviet Union due to geopolitical and ideological concerns. *Slapstick* was translated into Russian only in 1988, and the translator was not Rita Rait, but her

---

[184] RRK to DMF, October 10, 1980, p. 2, DMFC, Box 4, "Rait-Kovaleva, Rita, 1976–1982." However, archival materials show Rita could not help herself from playing around with some early translation ideas for *Slapstick*—as early as 1976 she tried out various Russian translations for "Hi ho" and phrases from the book's Preface (RGALI 3337/1/8). Rait's translation of just the first chapter of *Slapstick* did appear, in 1976, in *Literary Gazette*. It is unclear whether Vonnegut granted permission.

[185] *Mother Night* was translated into Russian by Russian-Jewish emigres living in Israel in 1976 and 1977. Donald Fiene noted that even that text was "cut by 1/3." Fiene believed the text was "probably set for pub. in USSR, then rejected." Donald M. Fiene, "Kurt Vonnegut in the USSR: A Bibliography," *Bulletin of Bibliography* 45, no. 4 (1988): 226.

[186] Rita wrote in a side bar: "'Mother night'—it's impossible—'*Mat' noch*' sounds stupid [in Russian]!" RRK to DMF, March 26, 1977, p. 2, DMFC, Box 4, "Rait-Kovaleva, Rita, 1976–1982."

[187] RRK to DMF, March 26, 1977, p. 2, DMFC, Box 4, "Rait-Kovaleva, Rita, 1976–1982."

daughter, Margarita Kovaleva. *Mother Night* first appeared in Russian in 1990.

In 1977, Rita Rait lamented in a letter to Fiene how "difficult it is to 'push through' (*probit*) a complicated author, like Kurt."[188] But she and other translators HAD managed to get four of Vonnegut's novels published in translation, along with a healthy list of his stories and essays. They translated Vonnegut into Russian, Ukrainian, Lithuanian, Estonian, etc. How did they do it?

One obvious answer is: censorship. In Soviet publications, the most politically and morally "inappropriate" aspects of Vonnegut's writing were edited, sometimes lightly, sometimes heavily. They might be left out altogether. One lexical-statistical analysis of Rait's translations of *Cat's Cradle* and *Slaughterhouse-Five* found that the Russian translations were shorter—by about 20 percent—than Vonnegut's original texts.[189] It is true that the Russian language is generally more "economical" than English. Ideas often can be expressed in Russian with fewer words. There are single-word equivalents in Russian that require entire phrases to express in English. However, omissions and censorship explain at least partially the abbreviated nature of the Russian-language translations.

Censorship—no ogres allowed

American literary scholars and critics interested in writing, translation, and publishing in the Russian Empire and the Soviet Union have always been interested in censorship. Censorship of the written word, particularly translations from "the West," has a long history in Russia. This history stretches back to tsarist times. The Imperial censorship blotted out passages of text deemed "blasphemous," that is, showing lack of respect for Church or state. Any translated text might be censored, whether prose, poetry, general nonfiction, imported reference works, and so on.[190] Censorship of Western texts and ideas only escalated in the Soviet Union.

---

[188] RRK to DMF, March 26, 1977, p. 2, DMFC, Box 4, "Rait-Kovaleva, Rita, 1976–1982."
[189] Andrey Kutuzov, "Change of Word Types to Word Tokens Ratio in the Course of Translation (Based on Russian Translation of K. Vonnegut's Novels)," 2010, p. 5, accessed April 2, 2020. https://arxiv.org/ftp/arxiv/papers/1003/1003.0337.pdf
[190] Friedberg, *Literary Translation*, 142. See also Marianna Tax Choldin, *A Fence Around an Empire: Russian Censorship of Western Ideas under the Tsars* (Duke University Press, 1985).

It is tempting to think of censorship as a monolithic process adhering to uniform and strict rules. We imagine the agents of censorship as soulless bureaucrats in shabby grey suits. However, a close "reading" of censorship practices in a specific and in a broad sense, reveals a different picture. Censorship, at least during the Stagnation period when Vonnegut's novels first appeared in Russian translation, was a non-linear, somewhat nested phenomenon.

Tracking how Vonnegut was translated for publication in the Soviet Union confirms Annette Kuhn's insight that when considered through a focus on specific "events" and "instances," censorship is the product of a "heterogenous ensemble" of practices and relations.[191] This was certainly true for literary translations of foreign works in the late 1960s and 1970s in the Soviet Union. Multiple agents—translators, editors, censors—played a role in the process.[192] Translators and editors of foreign translations were by definition cultural and political mediators. They could use this position to adhere to and enforce the state censorial instructions and institutions, but also to undermine them. They could use their position to allow as much or as little information as possible to get through the filter of censorship.[193] Literary scholar Samantha Sherry argues that censorship is best conceptualized as "a set of variable practices that reflect the struggle of agents in the cultural field, even in a seemingly 'closed' system" such as the Soviet Union in the 1960s and 1970s.[194] Clues I have gleaned about Rita Rait's struggles to have her translations of Vonnegut's novels published in the USSR support Sherry's thesis.

Most scholars of Soviet censorship agree that it was a multi-stage process. Brown noted in the early 1960s that the practice of censorship operated most severely in the choice of works to be translated, rather than in the translation process itself.[195] Leighton put it like this:

> The process of censorship in Soviet literature is more elaborate than the writer's conditioned reflexes. There are committees at the Union of Soviet Writers; there are sessions of criticism and self-criticism; there are editors and whole editorial boards; there are methods of selection, revision, and approval of texts. Writers work closely with editors and

---

[191] Annette Kuhn, *Cinema, Censorship and Sexuality, 1909–1925* (Routledge, 1988), 8.
[192] Samantha Sherry, "Better Something than Nothing: The Editors and Translators of Inostrannaia literatura as Censorial Agents," *Slavonic and East European Review* 91, no. 4 (2013): 732.
[193] Sherry, "Better Something," 733.
[194] Sherry, "Better Something," 758.
[195] Brown, *Soviet Attitudes*, 7.

publishers to negotiate what each interested party thinks can and should, or cannot and should not, be put into print.[196]

Soviet publishing houses were closely linked to the government. They were attached to a variety of institutions, including educational establishments, journals, branches of the Communist Party, affiliates of the Writers' Union, and industrial enterprises. Publishing houses were controlled by the State Committee for Printing and Publishing of the USSR Council of Ministers, which coordinated the technical and commercial aspects of publishing. Political considerations were the purview of the Main Administration of Literature and Publishing Affairs, also known as the State Committee on Censorship, or Glavlit.[197] Tensions arose for publishers needing to navigate between sometimes competing considerations of publication. There was the commercial imperative to offer books that readers would buy, and the political imperative to publish books that were ideologically acceptable. When it came to translations of foreign works, a balance had to be struck. The ideal foreign book was one that Soviet readers would clamor for. It also had to be a book that, with minimal shaving and tweaking, was politically acceptable. That is, it could not criticize the Soviet Union and state socialism, and it could not praise the U.S. and Western capitalism. A lot of Vonnegut's writing fit all these criteria.

Editors—not translators or Glavlit censors—exercised the bulk of censorship of foreign translations. Often, therefore, censorship occurred at a middle stage of production. As Carl Proffer wrote in 1972, "The normal American view of an ogre from Glavlit (the censorship board whose number appears in every Soviet book) with a small head and red pencil oversimplifies matters. The editors are the ones who do the majority of crossing out, and they tend to be so cautious that Glavlit has little left to do."[198] Multiple scholars have confirmed this. Soviet translators were "barely aware of Glavlit or censors during their work."[199] The Soviet publishing system was structured so that only adjacent levels of the multilevel process had direct contact. Translators worked most closely—almost exclusively—with their direct editors. Editors exercised a "multiple habitus."[200] They were charged with simultaneously

[196] Leighton, *Two Worlds*, 36.
[197] Leighton, *Two Worlds*, 37; Vladimirov, "Soviet Censorship," 17. The name of the censorship organ was changed several times after its founding in 1922. In 1953 it was renamed to the Main Administration for the Protection of Military and State Secrets in Print attached to the Council of Ministers of the USSR.
[198] Proffer, "Introduction," xxiv.
[199] Kamovnikova, *Made Under Pressure*, 153.
[200] Sherry, "Better Something," 741.

maintaining ideological standards set by state institutions while also preserving the literary integrity and quality of the published works. A translated text had to go through numerous layers of editorial action before being published in the journal *Foreign Literature*, for instance.

> At the first stage, the translated typescript was checked... editors made both stylistic and "political" changes at this point. Once the required amendments were made—the process could take two drafts—the typescript was printed and checked again, eventually being signed off by the editor responsible for that section. Five copies of the printed proofs were produced; the first was the printing copy; the second was signed by the chief editor and his deputy; the third was sent to the "checking section," which verified and signed off facts, dates and names. The fourth and fifth copies were distributed to members of the editorial board. Once it had passed through the tight net of editorial control, the text was approved for printing. Subsequently, as was the case with all literary publications, the galley proofs were checked by a Glavlit agent. The final printed versions were submitted to Glavlit once again before the issue was approved for distribution. At each stage in the sometimes long and drawn-out process of publication, the editor acted as a gatekeeper, approving both style and content.[201]

The editorial and production process would have been similar at all major literary journals and state publishing houses throughout the country. For translations of foreign literature there was an additional layer of oversight. This was the Translators' Section of the Soviet Writers' Union. It regulated admission, certification, and training of translators, as well as codification and internalization of censorship norms.[202]

Translators like Rait acted as "artistic mediators who channeled the words of others," but they also were tasked with adhering to and enforcing political norms imposed by the Soviet ideological discourse.[203] Sometimes translators themselves engaged in a certain level of censorship. This occurred even in initial drafts, in anticipation of editors' and Glavlit censors' responses. Donald Fiene and Rita Rait frequently discussed her approach to translation. She admitted to preemptive censorship. Fiene wrote to Vonnegut, "She automatically reduces all obscenities to expressions that can be published, but that still convey to sophisticated readers the tone and flavor of the

---

[201] Sherry, "Better Something," 741.
[202] Sherry, "Better Something," 745.
[203] Sherry, "Better Something, 748.

original. She has constant battles with editors over allowable political stuff and the like. She herself curses like a sailor, has no personal objections to obscenities."[204]

Here Fiene homed in on the two main categories of Soviet censorship. These were "political stuff" (politics) and "obscenities" (morality). Any dialogue, character, description, or scene that could be interpreted as critical of the Soviet Union and its peoples, Marxist-Leninist ideals, or the system of state socialism, was subject to censorship.[205] This included critical remarks made by the author or voiced by literary characters.[206] Translators publishing in *Foreign Literature* tended to leave potentially politically sensitive material in their initial drafts. They left the decision to editors whether to retain or jettison problematic "political stuff."[207]

Censorship pertaining to "morals" focused most directly on anything of a sexual nature, but also included violence, obscenities, and other forms of "vulgarity" or "indecency." In the Soviet Union, official attitudes toward sexuality and the body were governed by the notion of "naturalism." Naturalism encompassed physiological functions and distortions, "the bodily effects of illness or poverty, psychic derangement, ugliness in nature and in people."[208] In Soviet literary criticism, reference to "naturalistic scenes" was code for anything sexual.[209] "Descriptions of sex, violence, bodily functions and so on were excised or heavily modified before translated works appeared in print." Whereas translators often left "political stuff" in their texts for editors to decide about later, they tended to preemptively modify or omit sexually explicit and "vulgar" content. Thus it was translators who took the lead in so-called "puritanical" censorship.[210] It is an open question whether translators tended to make such modifications on auto-pilot. Maybe they could gauge how sanitized a translation would need to be to see the light of day. Or perhaps this moral scrubbing reflected translators' own sense of propriety and internalization of accepted norms. When it came to translating

---

[204] DMF to LGL September 26, 1978, pp. 1–2, DMFC, Box 4, "Leighton, Lauren Gray, 1978–1979."
[205] Marianna Tax Choldin noted an additional category for censorship: "portrayals of Soviets as non-European barbarians." Mariana Tax Choldin, *Garden of Broken Statues: Exploring Censorship in Russia* (Academic Studies Press, 2016), 90.
[206] Friedberg, *Literary Translation*, 139.
[207] Sherry, "Better Something," 752–3.
[208] Gilburd, *To See Paris*, 110.
[209] Khmelnitsky, "Sex, Lies, and Red Tape," 26.
[210] Herman Ermolaev, *Censorship in Soviet Literature, 1917–1991* (Rowman and Littlefield, 1997), 46–7, 93–4, 175–6.

Vonnegut, this Soviet "Victorian chastity," as Rita Rait called it, had its greatest impact on *Breakfast of Champions*.[211]

The typewriter and the green marker: Censorship of *Breakfast of Champions* and *Slaughterhouse-Five*

Michael Khmelnitsky conducted a detailed analysis of Rait's translations of four of Vonnegut's novels, including *Breakfast of Champions*. His findings reveal an unexpectedly high level of modification of the texts, serious censorship that Khmelnitsky attributes almost entirely to Rait, not editors or Glavlit censors. Khmelnitsky claims that Rait took exaggerated liberties with Vonnegut's texts. She made them more anti-American, more politically correct, and much more prudish than was necessary, even in the confining environment of Soviet publishing in the era of Stagnation. Khmelnitsky believes Rait moved between various translation techniques—realist, improving, and free—to make Vonnegut uber-acceptable politically, to augment the text and make it her own, and to liberally "soften" allusions to anything sexual or violent. He tracks how Rait "domesticated" the text by substituting culturally familiar objects and situations for references Soviet citizens would find unfamiliar. Khmelnitsky argues that the resulting Soviet Russian-language versions of Vonnegut's books were fundamentally different from the original texts. He says Vonnegut's intended messages were lost. Khmelnitsky characterizes Rait as a scared and overly compliant agent of the Soviet ideological machine, who had fully internalized the self-censorship process.[212]

Khmelnitsky's analysis of the Russian translations of Vonnegut, contextualized within his deep knowledge of translation studies, is based on his comparative reading of Vonnegut's original texts and Rait's finalized (published) translations. Another important part of the story, however, is Rait's own views and deliberations about censorship. Access to these views is limited, but in various archives I have found letters written by Rait to colleagues in which she discussed some aspects of the censorship process. At RGALI I also found several drafts of Rait's translations of Vonnegut, with editor's markings. Using these materials, it is possible to track the editing and censorship process at least partially from the perspective of the translator.

---

[211] RRK to DMF, March 14, 1981, p. 1, DMFC, Box 4, Folder 5, "Rait-Kovaleva, Rita, 1976–1982."
[212] Khmelnitsky, "Sex, Lies, and Red Tape," 257.

This adds an important dimension to Khmelnitsky's critiques and allows Rait herself to speak into the conversation.

RGALI has a 123-page document, a draft of Rait's translation of *Breakfast of Champions* (Chapters 15–24 and Epilogue). It is described as a "typescript with translator's corrections and notes."[213] However, upon examination, it is unclear whether all the suggested "corrections" are Rait's. The use of different pens to insert and change words, make notes in the margins, and excise entire sentences and paragraphs (with big "X's"), indicates the work of multiple readers. Although it is impossible to know for sure, I believe Rait's editor was probably wielding the green felt-tip marker to excise entire sentences and sections of her translation. This is especially likely given that the sections crossed out with the green pen contain other, smaller edits in Rita Rait's handwriting. These are words crossed out with black and blue ink, with alternative word choices inserted. This suggests that the "light" editing was done by Rait in pen first, and then someone, most likely her editor, came behind with a green marker and crossed out the offending sections. Examining these documents confirms other scholars' observations that translators tended to exercise a certain degree of censorship themselves during the first drafts of their translations, particularly when it came to descriptions of sex and violence. But editors also played a big role in "puritanical" censorship.

What were the sections of Rait's translation of *Breakfast* that were excised by the green felt pen-wielding editor? Not surprisingly, the editor marked out most of Vonnegut's discussions in Chapter 15 of comparative penis lengths and comparative measurements of women's busts, waists and hips.[214] The sentence introducing Vonnegut's famous inventory of penis sizes and women's measurements was left in, but Rait had preemptively softened it. "Dwayne Hoover, incidentally, had an unusually large penis" became "Dwayne Hoover, incidentally, had unusual masculine qualities."[215] The editor also crossed out Vonnegut's discussion of monthly orgasm rates.[216] Other examples show omissions or softening of explicit references to sex organs and the sex act. Rait had pretty accurately, though not fully, translated Vonnegut's passage about the sexual revolution and women's pleasure. Vonnegut wrote, "The key to their pleasure, they said, and scientists backed them up, was the clitoris, a tiny meat cylinder which was right above the hole in women where men were supposed to stick their much larger cylinders."[217] Rait had directly translated

---

[213] RGALI 3337/1/5.
[214] Kurt Vonnegut, *Breakfast of Champions* (Dial Press Trade Paperbacks, 2006), 148–9.
[215] RGALI 3337/1/5/9.
[216] RGALI 3337/1/5/21.
[217] Vonnegut, *Breakfast*, 155.

Vonnegut's description of the clitoris, and even specified "vagina" for "the hole in women." But she left out "where men were supposed to stick their much larger cylinders." The editor came behind and crossed out this entire section. A thrice-underlined fat green checkmark graces the margin beside the crossed-out section. The section was most emphatically excised![218]

The Soviet translation of *Breakfast* suffered other forms of censorship. In his close comparative reading of Vonnegut's source text with Rait's translation, Khmelnitsky counted thirteen omitted passages.[219] He is especially critical of Rait's "domestication" of Vonnegut's text. Khmelnitsky rejects Rait's substitution of idiomatic concepts and America-specific material objects with ones more familiar for Soviet readers. This was an aspect of Rait's translation practice fully in line with the realist school.[220] Khmelnitsky also objects to the inclusion of thirteen footnotes and numerous parenthetical notes, athough he acknowledges these were probably imposed by Rait's editor.[221]

How did Rait justify the extensive modifications made to *Breakfast of Champions*? In a letter to her friends Lynn Visson and "Vova" in New York in late 1973, Rait explained the editing that would need to be done on *Breakfast*.[222] Rait did not use the word "censorship" but instead said the novel would need to be "bowdlerized." The Oxford English Dictionary defines bowdlerize as "to expurgate (a book or writing), by omitting or modifying words or passages considered indelicate or offensive; to castrate."[223] For emphasis, Rait hand-wrote "bowdlerise," in English, in an otherwise typed Russian-language letter. (Two other words Rait hand-wrote in English were "prude" and "four-l. words.") The letter sums up tactfully and with humor the lengths to which Rita Rait went to ensure Soviet readers the pleasure of reading Vonnegut's latest novel. It details the artistic sacrifices she make to do so, and her concern about explaining these concessions to the author.

> Lenochka, I have a diplomatic request: I need you to explain to my favorite author, that the publishing of his latest book has been delayed. It's all still being decided, but he needs to know AHEAD OF TIME that a few things will need to be "bowdlerised" somehow, because in

---

[218] RGALI 3337/1/5/13. Khmelnitsky included a list of "Sexual Passages Omitted from the Russian Text of Breakfast of Champions" (1978 edition); see Khmelnitsky, "Sex, Lies, and Red Tape," 487–8.
[219] Khmelnitsky, "Sex, Lies, and Red Tape," 270.
[220] Khmelnitsky, "Sex, Lies, and Red Tape," 254–8.
[221] Khmelnitsky, "Sex, Lies, and Red Tape," 258–62.
[222] RRK to LV and Vova, November 18, 1973, BA-RRK.
[223] Etymology of "bowdlerize," according to the Oxford English Dictionary: "the name of Dr. T. *Bowdler*, who in 1818 published an edition of Shakespeare, 'in which those words and expressions are omitted which cannot with propriety be read aloud in a family,'" accessed May 28, 2020. https://www.oed.com/viewdictionaryentry/Entry/22199

the Russian tradition such "not-for-print" (*nepechatnye*) words and expressions are UNACCEPTABLE [*NEPROKHODIMY*, "will not get through"]. I wrote him about this earlier, and asked him to confirm in writing that he trusts ME—HIS TRANSLATOR, to shall we say, soften a few things—after all I did this beautifully in "Slaughterhouse [Five]" and in "Cat['s Cradle]" and it didn't prevent those works from being hugely successful. Tell him to trust me and to also make peace with the fact that two or three drawings—WHILE PRESERVING ALL THE OTHER ONES—will also be excluded [*vykinuty*, "thrown out"].

Tell him that it's very important and interesting for this book to be published, and I'm confident that I'll be able to preserve EVERYTHING IMPORTANT—all that childish naivete, humor and sadness. And it's no big deal to give up the long descriptions of measurements of various "anatomical parts." I know it's a parody of those magazines (I've seen enough of them!) where sex maniacs brag about their "merits" in inches . . . I know that this "trend" has trickled down to everyone, and I'm not so much of a "prude" (given my medical background!) that I would give this a second thought or worry about it at all. But Russian literature has always taken a DIFFERENT approach to such things, and what's more, all the corresponding terms to English Anglo-Saxon four-l[etter]. words in Russian sound so vulgar and awkward, that not even the most lenient censor—AND ESPECIALLY NOT A SINGLE READER WITH GOOD TASTE, would ever interpret them as they were meant by the author of the English text. There's nothing to be done: it's a function of LANGUAGE, and not MORALS. . .

In the end, what's the tragedy here? THIS work will be published in ONE LANGUAGE WITHOUT all those references to customs in big closed scientific institutions—or it will be related in OTHER WORDS relating the same idea. BUT THE INTERNAL IDEA, THE ENTIRE HUMANISTIC SIDE, which for me, is most IMPORTANT in Vonnegut, which is what I love him for, will be read once more by a HUGE READERSHIP. And lots of people read and continue to read the book in English, so the majority of linguists, English specialists, and so on can still enjoy the boyishly mischievous escapades . . . This is what I am begging you to tell Kurt Vonnegut.

Rait's attempts to rationalize "puritanical" censorship ("bowdlerising" of the novel's sexual content and sexual illustrations) show how Soviet translators sometimes justified their own censorship choices as an artistic act.[224] "It's a function of LANGUAGE, and not MORALS . . ."

---

[224] Sherry, "Better Something," 751.

Rait indicated in a follow-up letter to Lynn Visson in early 1974 that she was still negotiating the publishing agreement for *Breakfast* with the editors of *Foreign Literature*. With the caveat that she did not "love the *For. Lit.* people very much," Rita explained why she wanted *Breakfast* published in that journal in particular. *Foreign Literature* was a familiar entity, having previously published many of her translations. There were two additional advantages to publishing *Breakfast* with *Foreign Literature*. "They are able to print the book WITH KURT'S OWN ILLUSTRATIONS," and, Rita noted, it was a journal which, geared toward a more "experienced" (*iskushennaia*) readership, could "allow itself many more liberties." Rita vowed not to make any unnecessary abridgements. She would simply "substitute more precise— and decorous—medical terms—LIKE KURT DOES, ANYWAY!"[225]

Obviously, Rait was not able to follow through on this latter promise. Entire sentences and sections referring to sex and reproductive anatomy were excised from the Russian version, most likely by Rita's editor. Rait appears to have reconciled herself to censorship norms as an unavoidable, if unfortunate and even amusing, aspect of Soviet translation and publishing. In a 1981 letter she poked fun at an American critic's review of her translations of Vonnegut's novels. The review had called Rait out for censorship:

> Everything he writes is correct, save several precious accusations [against] ME!!!! In place of uncensored words—[I used] censored [words]! [And I substituted] several DIRECT references to certain countries [with] neutral words . . . O, SANCTA SIMPLICITAS!!! Doesn't the wise professor understand our "Victorian" chastity? You tell him that I went through the 'school of four-letter words' during the war . . . I've heard a lot of curse words in my time and if here I'm unable to get them across in Russian EXACTLY, well, what can you do?[226]

It should be noted, however, that Rait herself was annoyed by American authors' insistence on describing the human body in sexual terms. She found that superfluous. In a January 1973 letter to Donald Fiene, Rita described her recent meeting in Paris with the writer James Jones. "He gave me a stack of his books, and like always, I'm stunned by the physiological-anatomical complex, which is COMPLETELY MECHANICALLY inserted into the most serious of themes . . . It is annoying, like when you unexpectedly bite into a

---

[225] RRK to LV, January 28, 1974, BA-RRK.
[226] RRK to DMF, March 14, 1981, p. 1, DMFC, Box 4, Folder 5, "Rait-Kovaleva, Rita, 1976–1982."

peppercorn in your soup—completely unnecessary . . ."[227] In this and other letters to her American friends, Rait made it clear that she was not at all squeamish when it came to the human body and bodily functions. She was trained as a doctor, after all. But why, she wondered, did American authors insist on wallowing in all this?

Several year later, Rait contemplated translating Vonnegut's 1979 novel *Jailbird*. He had sent her the page proofs before it was even published in the United States. Besides the fact that there was "too much politics in the new book," Rait also admitted that she was also turned off by the "filth" that she found in *Jailbird*.[228] "I'm a bit tired of sex-bombs, bedroom scenes etc.—even my dear Kurt . . . smeared the wonderful novel [*Jailbird*] with all kinds of 'filth' . . ."[229] I am not convinced by Khmelnitsky's claim that "Rait pathologizes sexuality in her translation[s]" of Vonnegut's books.[230] But her complaints about American authors' obsession with "filth" do evince a certain level of exasperation and potential internalization of the very norms of Soviet- "Victorian chastity" she poked fun at in letters to friends.[231]

When challenged by Western scholars for her translation choices, including censorship, Rait got prickly. In an overall highly laudatory article evaluating Rait's translations of *Slaughterhouse-Five*, *Cat's Cradle*, *Breakfast of Champions*, and *God Bless You, Mr. Rosewater*, Lauren G. Leighton pointed out several clear instances of censorship of the texts.[232] Rait called his article "very sweet, and funny," and concluded that "there are a lot of things here he doesn't understand."[233] Rait felt attacked for making amendments that were in fact dictated by her editor, perhaps the one wielding the green felt-tipped pen. In a letter to Fiene, which she invited him to share with Professor Leighton, Rait insisted that many edits were not her fault, but rather were required by

---

[227] RRK to DMF, January 28, 1973, p. 2, DMFC, Box 4, Folder 3, part 3, "Rait-Kovaleva, Rita, 1963–1976."
[228] RRK to DMF, June 15, 1979, p. 2, DMFC, Box 4, Folder 5, "Rait-Kovaleva, Rita, 1976–1982."
[229] RRK to DMF, September 28, 1981, p. 2, DMFC, Box 4, Folder 5, "Rait-Kovaleva, Rita, 1976–1982." In July 1979, Fiene wrote to Vonnegut and expressed his concerns that Rait would get "cold feet"—because of "all the Watergate stuff, the politics" in *Jailbird*, and decide not to translate it. His fears were justified. Rait did not translate *Jailbird* and it appeared in Russian translation only in 1992. DMF to KV, July 6, 1979, p. 1. FIEN, Folder 5, "1979–1980."
[230] Khmelnitsky, "Sex, Lies, and Red Tape," 286, 288–9.
[231] RRK to DMF, March 14, 1981, p. 1, DMFC, Box 4, Folder 5, "Rait-Kovaleva, Rita, 1976–1982."
[232] Leighton, "Rita Rajt-Kovaleva's Vonnegut," 416–17.
[233] RRK to LV, September 2, 1981, BA-RRK.

her editor. "My favorite editor changed especially much in 'Breakfast—' [he] even changed the words 'abort,' 'uterus' and 'body...'"[234]

Rait was ecstatic that all but two of "KURT'S OWN ILLUSTRATIONS" (there were more than 130 of them) appeared in the Soviet translation of *Breakfast*. Rait undoubtedly worked with the editor on captions. First, the drawings had to make sense in the Soviet cultural context. Second, they had to make sense for readers of Rait's translation, given the amendments made to the text.

With the discussion of relative penis lengths and measurements of women's busts and hips taken out of the book, Vonnegut's drawing of "an inch" no longer made sense, and was omitted. Also missing from the Soviet version was Vonnegut's illustration of the "hairy vulva" explaining the "wide open beaver" joke in Chapter 2. Rita and her colleagues substituted a rather ingenious, only slightly muted, version of the "wide open beaver" schtick. "Wide open beavers" became "unbuttoned minks" (*norki—naraspashku*), complete with an illustration of a mink Vonnegut drew himself at Rait's request. Many Vonnegut lovers and Rait fans applaud this substitution as exceptionally clever. The word for "mink" in Russian—*norka*—contains a double-entendre. It is also the diminutive form of the word *nora*, or "burrow/hole." (Minks may be slightly more culturally familiar for Russian speakers than beavers, though neither holds any inherent cultural sexual connotation in Russian.) Thus, Soviet readers encountered "unbuttoned mink caves," which successfully related a sexual innuendo replicating Vonnegut's intention in spirit, if not exactly in form.[235] What is more, "*norki—naraspashku*" has an irresistible lilt and alliteration in Russian. It is a phrase that sticks in one's brain and became part of Vonnegut enthusiasts' unique lexicon. And although the "hairy vulva" illustration did not appear in the Soviet publication to explain the "unbuttoned minks" joke for those who didn't get it, Rait's translation did that work. "The thing which excited news photographers so much, was simply the place from which babies are born."[236] Explicit illustrations that remained in the Soviet version of *Breakfast* include the famous image of "an asshole" and the drawing of rather industrial-looking "female underpants."

Vonnegut knew that Soviet publishers were swapping out the beaver for a different animal. He even drew the mink for Rait during his brief Moscow trip in October 1974. However, he misremembered what the substitute

---

[234] RRK to DMF, March 14, 1981, DMFC, Box 4, Folder 5, "Rait-Kovaleva, Rita, 1976–1982."
[235] Khmelnitsky, "Sex, Lies, and Red Tape," 263.
[236] Kurt Vonnegut, *Zavtrak dlia chempionov* [Breakfast for champions], trans. Rita Rait-Kovaleva (AST, 2018), 28.

mustelid was. Vonnegut thought Rait had used a weasel, instead of a mink. Vonnegut wrote Donald Fiene in July 1975, "I knew a little about the beaver's being changed to a weasel. I didn't know the linking of the animal with the mons veneris was to be eliminated. I drew her [Rita] a weasel during our visit to Moscow. In fact, she made me draw about ten of them."[237] (It is hard to tell whether Vonnegut drew a mink or a weasel for the Soviet edition of *Breakfast*—it looks like a cross between the two!)

Rait's Russian translation of *Slaughterhouse-Five* was also censored. In 1972 Ann C. Vinograde picked through Rait's 1970 translation of *Slaughterhouse-Five*. "As a whole the translation is faithful to the original ... in many small instances, however, the translated text contains apparently deliberate changes which are not justified by translator's license."[238] Vinograde sorted these changes into three categories—politics; obscenities and sex; and miscellaneous. She noted that the translator tinkered with any derogatory references to Russian soldiers, softened all references to sex, and changed and omitted some words and phrases. Vinograde did not mention Rita Rait's name at all in the review. She referred to the translator only (and erroneously) as "he."

Rait herself acknowledged that some "replacements" had been necessary in her translation of *Slaughterhouse-Five*. "Of course, I had to take out all the four-letter words ... but I replaced them with such euphemisms that everyone will understand what the soldiers are really saying."[239] For instance, whereas Vonnegut had Roland Weary calling Billy Pilgrim a "dumb motherfucker," in Rait's translation Weary said, "Get out of the road, blankety-blank [*tramtararam*] your mother." Though less explicit, the meaning ("blank your mother") is hardly lost. Instead of "fairies" (meaning, homosexuals), the Russian version used "vagrants." Rait might have substituted "vagrants" here because Vonnegut used the word "fairies" in context with (though not in reference to) "Communists."[240]

Khmelnitsky wondered how Rait had dealt with the dozen or so phrases and passages in *Slaughterhouse-Five* that caused a New York school board to ban the book in the mid-1970s.[241] He found that the "offending excerpts" survived, but they were considerably softened. "Why don't you go fuck yourself?" becomes "Go you-know-where!" "Pecker" becomes "groin." "Balls ... bouncing gently on the floor" becomes "hurt, hurt my various places."

---

[237] Wakefield, *Kurt Vonnegut—Letters*, 222.
[238] Vinograde, "A Soviet Translation," 14.
[239] Rait, "Reflections on Kurt Vonnegut," 95.
[240] Leighton, "Rita Rajt-Kovaleva's Vonnegut," 417.
[241] Board of Education v. Pico, 457 U.S. 853.

"Semierect" becomes "excited," as does "jerk off."[242] Rait translated "silly cocksucker" as "fool."[243] Leighton noted how Rait cleverly relayed sexual references into non-offensive Russian. "'... [Well, brother ... it was clear what you'd been dreaming about]' is [Rait's] telling substitute for 'man, you sure had a hard-on.' ['He was the right kind of man'] might reduce the obviousness of 'he had a tremendous wang', but it gets the idea across."[244]

Other modifications were of a more political nature. True, not much in *Slaughterhouse-Five* is explicitly anti-Soviet to begin with. Still, in the Soviet translation anything even remotely critical of the Soviet Union was modified.[245] Vonnegut's Billy Pilgrim remembered "two Russian soldiers who had looted a clock factory." The Russian version dropped the "looting" phrase. However, the two Russian soldiers still had "a horse-drawn wagon full of clocks" in the desolation of Dresden after the firestorm. Any perspicacious reader would surmise the soldiers had stolen the clocks. Derogatory references to Russians were modified or omitted. "The Russians ... killing and robbing and raping and burning" was changed to "rumors of the coming of the Russians." "The Russians, who occupied Dresden after the war, who are in Dresden still [in 1969]," became simply "the Russians who had occupied Dresden after the war."[246] In another side-stepping of international politics, Rait's translation also dropped Vonnegut's mention of a "promiscuous Polack." Vonnegut's references to "East Berlin and West Berlin" appear in Russian as just "Berlin." In the Russian translation the phrase "by secret ballot in a free election" was trimmed to "in a free election." Khmelnitsky believes the translated text thus "mocks the idea of holding a vote in a camp for war prisoners."[247]

The real story here, however, is that *Slaughterhouse Five* got published in the Soviet Union at all. Rait's text barely squeaked through to publication across two issues of the journal *New World* in early 1970. *Slaughterhouse-Five* appeared just before the hounded editor-in-chief Aleksandr Tvardovskii was finally forced to resign, and his editorial board was disbanded. Years prior, Tvardovskii had published Solzhenitsyn's controversial *One Day in the Life of Ivan Denisovich*, some of Solzhenitsyn's other stories, Il'ia Ehrenburg's memoirs, and other "defiant" works.[248] By 1968, after a string of scandals and hardships for Tvardovskii and his editors, *New World* was in grave trouble. The

---

[242] Khmelnitsky, "Sex, Lies, and Red Tape," 285.
[243] Khmelnitsky, "Sex, Lies, and Red Tape," 285.
[244] Leighton, "Rita Rajt-Kovaleva's Vonnegut," 416.
[245] Leighton, "Rita Rajt-Kovaleva's Vonnegut," 416.
[246] Khmelnitsky, "Sex, Lies, and Red Tape," 277.
[247] Khmelnitsky, "Sex, Lies, and Red Tape," 271.
[248] Dina Spechler, *Permitted Dissent in the USSR: Novy Mir and the Soviet Regime* (Praeger, 1982), 219–27.

literary-political establishment found the journal increasingly undesirable. State censors ramped up pressure. Glavlit cracked down on proposed manuscripts.[249] In fall 1968 ideological interference in literary publishing escalated in the wake of the Warsaw Pact invasion of Czechoslovakia. As Khmelnitsky observed, *Slaughterhouse-Five*, which appeared in the March and April 1970 issues of *New World*, was "one of Tvardovskii's last gifts to his readers" just before he was forced to leave the journal.[250]

All over the USSR

Rita Rait was not the only Russian translator of Vonnegut's novels and stories. As already mentioned, the first of Vonnegut's works to be published in the USSR was Marat Brukhner's translation of *Player Piano* (titled *Utopia 14*). Donald Fiene informed Vonnegut about it on May 12, 1972. "I'm aware, incidentally, that a guy named Brukkhner [*sic.*] translated *Player Piano* into Russian in 1967 (as *Utopia 14*)." Fiene continued, ". . . but it seems to be Rita Rait that has made you so much loved and admired in Russia these days. She must be your soul sister or something . . ." Indeed, Rait had something of a monopoly on translations of Vonnegut. She fiercely guarded access to the author and his work. She prized her reputation as "Vonnegut's translator." Rait did "share" Vonnegut with her daughter Margarita, and she may even have delegated some portions of Vonnegut's novels to Margarita to translate. Some of the edited page proofs of *Breakfast* in the RGALI archive are hand-labeled "Margarita's." Margarita mostly translated Vonnegut's short stories, while Rita took on the novels. Between them, they had a near lock on Vonnegut translations. A 1981 compiled volume of Vonnegut translations published in Kishinev, the capital of the Moldovan Soviet Socialist Republic, contains Rait's translations of three novels (*Slaughterhouse-Five*; *Cat's Cradle*; and *God Bless You, Mr. Rosewater*). Of the book's fourteen translated stories, eight translations are attributed to Margarita Kovaleva, and four to Rita Rait. Margarita's translations of *Slapstick*, *Sirens of Titan* and *Dead-Eye Dick* all appeared in 1988, a year before her mother's death.

As a rule, Soviet publishing trends were established in Moscow and Leningrad. Publishers in the non-Russian republics then followed suit. According to this pattern, translations of Vonnegut in the USSR first appeared in Russian in the main centers of Soviet Russia (Moscow and Leningrad).

---

[249] Kozlov, *Readers of Novyi Mir*, 296–7.
[250] Khmelnitsky, "Sex, Lies, and Red Tape," 117.

Then translations cropped up in other Soviet republics, often in the republics' official languages (e.g., Ukrainian, Estonian). *Cat's Cradle* was published in Moscow in 1970, but a Latvian translation appeared only in 1973. Not until 2016 was a Ukrainian translation published.[251] *Slaughterhouse-Five* was published in Moscow in 1970. The first Ukrainian translation was issued in Kyiv in 1976. This lag indicates stronger ideological control over translation and publication of foreign literature in the various republics compared to the center of Soviet Russia, especially Moscow and Leningrad.

In Soviet Ukraine, the power center enacted policies of russification and suppression of the Ukrainian language and Ukrainian literary translation to varying degrees throughout the country's Soviet period (1919/39–91). Stalinist repressions targeted literati and literary translators, who were either killed or exiled to camps. The murdered Ukrainian artists and writers of the 1920s were Ukraine's "executed renaissance." Those who survived, many of them former political prisoners, led the 1960s Ukrainian dissident movement. In this context, the authorities scrutinized translation activity in Ukraine during the Thaw and Stagnation periods. Nevertheless, the Kyiv-based monthly Ukrainian-language journal of literature, *Vsesvit* (*Universe*), founded in 1958, "developed a sophisticated policy of encouraging Ukraine's urban population, increasingly russified in the 1960s–1970s, to read in Ukrainian by publishing texts by Western authors unavailable in Russian translations."[252] It was precisely in this journal—*Universe*—that some of the first Ukrainian Vonnegut translations were published, including "Tomorrow, Tomorrow and Tomorrow" (1979), "Fortitude" (1983), and *Slapstick* (1984).

The extreme censorship of the 1973 Latvian translation of *Cat's Cradle* is further evidence that the non-Russian Soviet republics experienced greater ideological control than the center. The book was "so extensively purged and altered politically, ideologically and linguistically that it was retranslated by the same translator in 2002 and published with a statement on the cover that the new version did not contain any censorial restrictions and is in fact a totally different rendering of the source text."[253] The American Slavicist Donald Fiene deserves credit for the popularization of Vonnegut in

---

[251] Kurt Vonnegut, *Kolybel' dlia koshkyi, roman* [Cat's cradle, a novel], transl. A. Nemirova (Book Club "Klub Simeinoho Dozvillia," 2016).

[252] Vitaly Chernetsky, "Nation and Translation: Literary Translation and the Shaping of Modern Ukraine," in *Contexts, Subtexts and Pretexts: Literary Translation in Eastern Europe and Russia*, ed. Brian James Baer (John Benjamins Publishing Company, 2011), 49.

[253] Gunta Locmele and Andrejs Veisbergs, "The Other Polysystem: The Impact of Translation on Language Norms and Conventions in Latvia," in Baer, ed., *Contexts, Subtexts and Pretexts*, 297.

the Baltic Republics of the USSR. In one of Fiene's first letters to Vonnegut, in September 1972, Fiene informed Vonnegut that Valda V. Raud had translated *Slaughterhouse-Five* into Estonian. She wished to send Vonnegut her translation.

> Mrs. Raud is about sixty, I guess. I've also been writing to her off and on for ten years or so. I sent her copies of your books, too . . . The standard pattern seems to have established itself. Since you've proved popular in Russian, you'll be available in the top ten USSR languages in a couple of years—after Estonian: Latvian and Lithuanian; and then Georgian, Armenian, Azerbaizhanian [*sic*.] and God knows what else. Have a good time spending all that money, if you get over there again.[254]

Two years later, in October 1974, Vonnegut did get "over there" to the Soviet Union again. And some 2000 rubles (worth about $2,700 at the time)[255] in royalty payments was waiting for him. According to Rita, the Soviets had "generously" deposited the funds in a savings account.[256] (They were not required to pay authors any royalties prior to 1973, when the USSR joined the UCC.) But contrary to Fiene's lighthearted wish, Vonnegut did not "have a good time spending all that money." He was not allowed to withdraw any rubles. He signed the entire account over to Rita Rait.

---

[254] DMF to KV, September 19, 1972, FIEN, Folder 1, "1972–1974."
[255] On January 1, 1975 the official exchange rate of the Soviet ruble to the U.S. dollar was .7300 rub. to $1 USD, accessed May 28, 2020. https://en.wikipedia.org/wiki/Soviet_ruble
[256] KV to DMF, October 25, 1974, FIEN, Folder 1, "1972–1974."

4

Interlude

Rendezvous in Paris, 1972

It was May, 1972. Rita Rait was disappointed that Kurt Vonnegut would not visit Moscow as part of Nixon's entourage. But she was delighted to learn of Vonnegut's warm attitude toward her. His cable to Donald Fiene had ended, "YOUR EXCELLENT LETTER MADE ME FALL IN LOVE WITH RITA."[1] In a May 30, 1972 letter to a colleague, Rait quipped that she hoped Fiene had "told [Vonnegut] that 'Rita' is no longer 20 years old . . . But I'm sure he described my translations and my indefatigable character."[2]

Rait persisted in her quest to meet Vonnegut in person. She once more enlisted Fiene's assistance in late August 1972. Fiene again wrote to Vonnegut. Would he please visit Moscow? It should be possible for Vonnegut to secure an invitation to the USSR from the Foreign Commission of the Writers' Union. "If you are going to be in Europe in October, Rita will also be there that month, mostly visiting Nathalie Sarraute in Paris. (She's been working on arrangements for this trip for a couple of years.) She would like to see you then if not eventually in Moscow."[3]

On her end, Rita wondered if her long hoped-for trip to Paris would materialize. Each step in the process was nerve-wracking. Rait had two goals for her extended stay in Paris. First, to work closely with Sarraute, whose novel *The Golden Fruits* she was translating. Second, to do research for her biography of Boris Vilde, a Russian émigré active in the French Resistance during the Second World War. Rait wrote to a colleague on August 4, 1972:

> Now, some secret news: my papers have returned from one important office and went to MID [Ministry of Foreign Affairs], for the new foreign passport and French visa. I don't know what will happen, but everyone

---

[1] KV to DMF, May 17, 1972, FIEN, Folder 1, "1972–1974."
[2] Liubov' Kachan, "Ee velichestvo perevodchik! Rita Rait" [Her majesty the translator! Rita Rait], accessed November 22, 2023. https://www.proza.ru/2012/02/29/434.
[3] DMF to KV, August 30, 1972, FIEN, Folder 1, "1972–1974."

is "giving me hope." I don't believe in such happiness but nevertheless I wrote my friends in Paris, that if everything comes through, I will try to arrive in September . . . They responded with wonderful letters, they are waiting, they've prepared a room for me . . . Now all that is left is THE FLIGHT![4]

Around the same time, Fiene again wrote Vonnegut.

> Rita Rait is pleading with me to get in touch with you, hoping you will write, phone, telegraph or visit her in Paris. . .This would make her very happy. She's a nice intelligent lady. She wants to give you a couple of your books in Russian that she brought to Paris with her. She wants to talk with you, etc.

He included the address where Rait would be staying in Paris.[5] For her part, Rait thought she might build on the exposure she had given Vonnegut in the Soviet Union. Perhaps she could introduce him to the French reading public, who, she contended, were unfamiliar with Vonnegut's books. "I would like him to write me here—OR TO VISIT PARIS, if he's so rich! . . . He is little known here (don't tell him this) and I will 'propagandize' him—but has he been translated into French????"[6]

Happily, Donald Fiene, Kurt Vonnegut, and Rita Rait were all to be on the European continent in fall 1972. They just had to figure out—in a world before the internet, email, cellular phones, and instant messaging—how, when, and where to meet one another. On October 12, Vonnegut telegrammed Fiene (who was already in Paris) from New York City. IN ENGLAND BROWNS HOTEL LONDON OCTOBER 21 TO 31 STOP HAVE NOTIFIED RAIT STOP HAVE REQUESTE (*SIC.*) RENDEVOUS ANYWHERE STOP YOU COME TO [*SIC.*] STOP KURT VONNEGUT.[7]

As it happened, Rait, Fiene, and Vonnegut never did manage to meet all together as a trio. Fiene and Vonnegut, and their respective partners Judy Fiene and Jill Krementz, had a long lunch at Brown's Hotel in London on October 27. They discussed many issues, but mostly Rita Rait, Russian literature, Vonnegut's life and work, and Fiene's collection of glass telephone-

---

[4] Kachan, "Her majesty."
[5] DMF to KV, October 5, 1972, FIEN, Folder 1, "1972–1974."
[6] RRK to DMF, October 1, 1972, p. 2, DMFC, Box 4, Folder 3, "Rait-Kovaleva, Rita, 1963–1976."
[7] KV to DMF, October 12, 1972, FIEN, Folder 1, "1972–1974."

pole insulators.[8] Meanwhile, Rita had finally made it to Paris. Vonnegut phoned her to arrange a meeting for October 28. "You'll recognize me easily—I'm tall, very tall, with big hair, and a big mustache..."[9] Vonnegut and Krementz flew to Paris to spend two days with Rita. Rait got her first glimpse of Vonnegut in the lobby of the small Paris hotel where Vonnegut and Krementz were staying. "An extremely tall man rose from a deep chair to greet me; he was very elegant with a curly cap of hair and completely childlike, wide-open eyes."[10] The trio covered a lot of ground during the whirlwind two-day rendezvous. There was a photo session or two courtesy of Krementz, a trip to Versailles, and meetings with the American writers James Jones and Mary McCarthy.

Rait later recalled the lovely evening spent at Versailles with Vonnegut and her young friend Nathalie Goutbrod. A Russian émigré and teacher of English, Goutbrod was likely invited because she had a car. She could provide both transportation and affable company. The friends arrived at Versailles toward evening. Other tourists had left, so they enjoyed the quiet beauty of the gardens in peace. Rait joked that this was her early fiftieth birthday present for Vonnegut—"Versailles in the fall" (he would turn fifty on November 11).[11] She had brought other "presents" for Vonnegut—difficult-to-acquire copies of her published Russian translations of *Slaughterhouse-Five* and *Cat's Cradle*.[12] Rait found the evening magical. "In an English restaurant, just near the park, we were the only guests, and they treated us like millionaires passing through: all the props of the 'sweet life:' roses in crystal vases, candles in antique copper candlesticks, luxurious service, exquisite food. Until late in the evening we talked, asked one another about many things, laughed, debated..."[13]

Young Nathalie Goutbrod recalled the evening at Versailles with Rait and Vonnegut a bit differently. She described her impressions in a charming

---

[8] Donald M. Fiene, "First Meeting," in Krementz, ed., *Happy Birthday*, 92. Fiene also described his meeting with Vonnegut in a letter to Jerome Klinkowitz (hereafter JK): DMF to JK, March 5, 1973, DMFC, Box 4, Folder 2, "Klinkowitz, Jerome "Jerry," 1971–1977."

[9] Rita Rait-Kovaleva, "Kanareika v shakhte, ili moi drug Kurt Vonnegut" ["Canary in a coal mine, or my friend Kurt Vonnegut"], in *Slaughterhouse Five, Cat's Cradle, God Bless You, Mr. Rosewater, or Pearls before Swine; Stories*, by Kurt Vonnegut, trans. Rita Rait-Kovaleva (Literatura artistike, 1981), 6.

[10] Rait-Kovaleva, "Canary," 6.

[11] Rait-Kovaleva, "Canary," 13–14.

[12] RRK to DMF, October 1, 1972, p. 2, DMFC, Box 4, Folder 3, "Rait-Kovaleva, Rita, 1963–1976."

[13] Rait-Kovaleva, "Canary," 14.

letter to Donald and Judy Fiene. Goutbrod's observations shed light on some important dynamics of the Rait-Vonnegut relationship.

> You'll probably be very jealous when I tell you that whereas you spent two and a half hours in London with Kurt Vonnegut, I spent nearly seven hours with him in Paris and Versailles! He did come to see Rita Rajt and she asked me whether I would like to join them—I couldn't make it both days because I was to go to Germany for a few days but in order to meet the great man I postponed my departure by a day. I then hastened to buy two of his books: "Slaughter-house five" and "Welcome to the Monkey House" but had to read only a few chapters from either, among [them] his self-portrait in "Welcome to the monkey house"—I found his self-portrait irritatingly self-confident and consequently was surprised and relieved to see that in real life he seemed to be much more likeable: gentle and almost shy and with a touch of sadness in his eyes which I didn't expect to find at all. It is true that his private life was no longer what it was in his self-portrait: I suppose one should never proclaim how lucky and happy one is!
>
> Rita was extraordinarily nervous at the thought of meeting him and partly to try and overcome her nervousness and partly because she can't help herself, she kept talking about herself all the time, hardly ever asking him anything or letting him say anything! And though what she had to say was interesting, I had much rather on that particular day have heard him speak! And I was surprised that as his translator she shouldn't try and know him as a person: alas she sounded terribly self-centered and it was extremely difficult to deviate the conversation from her own self. I made a few attempts and then gave up![14]

Goudbrod again remembered the evening she spent with Vonnegut and Rait in Versailles in a letter to Donald Fiene two years later. She mentioned an "article that dear Rita Rait wrote in a Soviet magazine in January of last year," about the lovely Paris-and-Versailles meeting with Kurt Vonnegut.[15]

---

[14] Nathalie Goutbroud to Donald and Judy Fiene, May 29, 1973, DMFC, Box 3, "Goutbroud, Nathalie "Natasha," 1972–1996." Goutbrod's chosen spelling for Rita's surname in the 1972 letter was "Rajt."

[15] Goutbroud was referring to Rita Rait-Kovaleva, "Kanareika v shakhte" ["Canary in a coal mine"], *Rovesnik* 1 (1974): 16–19. A version of the piece later appeared as the Introduction to a 1981 collection of Vonnegut's translated books and stories. The "canary" piece was also translated and published in journals in Estonian (1974) and Lithuanian (1981).

I was shown a copy of it by a friend who saw Rita in Moscow several times in the summer. No doubt sooner or later you'll see the article yourself so I'll make no comments except that there is one sentence in it which really stands out and must explain Rita's passion for K. V. In it she says of him that she "had never met anyone who was so good at being silent and listening" . . . to her I guess!! And that was certainly true of our visit to Versailles! But I must stop being beastly![16]

Krementz, a renowned photographer, did not venture to Versailles with the others, so there is no photographic evidence of the excursion. Krementz did, however, document other aspects of the 1972 Rait-Vonnegut Paris rendezvous. She took several striking portraits of Rait, possibly in Vonnegut and Krementz's hotel room, or perhaps at the Paris residence where Rait was lodging. Rait later used one of these portraits as her "press photo" in one edition of her book about Vilde.[17] Krementz also took a charming photo of Vonnegut and Rait sitting on a couch. Vonnegut's lanky arm is draped behind Rait's back and over her shoulder. She has taken hold of just the tip of his index finger. Vonnegut signed a copy of the photograph for Donald Fiene, in all caps: "For Donald Fiene, who created this meeting between Rita Rait, my translator in the Soviet Union, and myself in Paris on October 28, 1972."[18]

Later, after Vonnegut and Krementz had left Paris, Rait was invited to lunch with the writers James Jones and Mary McCarthy. The lunch seemed similarly luxurious as the dinner at Versailles, again with "all the props of the 'sweet life.'" But Rait evaluated it with a more critical eye. In a letter to Fiene, she described the wonderful but "paradoxical" luncheon.

> He [James Jones] invited me and Mary McCarthy—whom I've known for a long time through my Nathalie Sarraute, and we lunched in fine style—silver, porcelain, a maître-d—at the Hotel Spaniard, the five of us: James and his wife, Mary and her husband, and me!!!! And the maître-d, or butler, it turns out, CAME TO PARIS TO DO HIS DOCTORAL STUDIES AT THE SORBONNE—and makes money on the side serving rich Americans!!!!!!!!!! I was floored by this paradox!!![19]

---

[16] Nathalie Goutbroud to DMF, November 9, 1975, DMFC, Box 3, "Goutbroud, Nathalie 'Natasha,'" 1972–1996."
[17] Rita Rait-Kovaleva, *Chelovek iz muzeia cheloveka: povest' o Boris Vil'de* [Man from the museum of man: the story of Boris Vilde] (Sovetskii pisatel', 1982).
[18] FIEN, Folder 9, "1972, Oct. 28. Photograph of Kurt Vonnegut."
[19] RRK to DMF, January 28, 1973, DMFC, Box 4, Folder 3, "Rait-Kovaleva, Rita, 1963–1976."

Figure 4.1 Kurt Vonnegut photographed with Rita Rait by Jill Krementz in Paris on October 28, 1972. All rights reserved. Photograph by Jill Krementz. Used with permission. Courtesy Lilly Library, Indiana University, Bloomington, Indiana.

Invite Rita Rait to America!

Rait's Paris rendezvous with Vonnegut, her subsequent luncheon with American literati, and her reflections on the circumstances of these interactions crystallize several important tensions of the Rait-Vonnegut relationship. They also telescope the circumstances of Soviet-American friendships and cultural diplomacy more generally during the 1970s. These tensions were at once born of practicalities and symbolic of deeper Cold War tensions, both personal and political. One obvious difference between Rait's circumstances and those of her American colleagues was Rait's extremely limited freedom to travel outside the Soviet bloc. Her extended visit to Paris, to do archival research for her book on Vilde, and to consult with Nathalie Sarraute on *The Golden Fruits*, was a great exception. The trip was the "last hurrah" for an already elderly woman with a full career behind her. Rait had not believed until the last moment that her Paris trip would materialize. It took months to arrange and involved miles of red tape, and she reckoned it would be her last European adventure.

The Americans' circumstances could not have been more different. They did not have to get permission from their government, and from their trade union, to travel to Europe. They did not have to travel with a group of fellow citizens, among them obligatory "informants" (*stukachy*) who kept a watchful eye on others' comings and goings. They had the freedom of movement, and the financial means, to travel on a whim. Rait envied Vonnegut these possibilities to travel freely. She contrasted his frequent international travels with her own relative stuck-in-placedness.

Differential access to "the props of 'the sweet life,'" also separated Rait and her American colleagues. She was wowed by fine dining in the "English" and "Spanish" restaurants in Versailles and Paris and was unused to "luxurious service." Rait had never had the means to enjoy this bourgeois lifestyle, and she never would.[20] All her life, Rait struggled to keep herself and her daughter financially afloat. Vonnegut never seemed to fully understand this. His concern about receiving royalties for the Russian translations of his works was a constant stressor for Rita. In this context, one might note Rita's surprise at meeting a doctoral student from the Sorbonne working as a maître-d for "rich Americans." That Rait saw this as a great "paradox" sheds light on some of the grim realities of life for the intellectual and literati class in the 1970s Soviet Union.

American authors—members of the intellectual class—could enjoy international European travel and fine dining, and EVEN be "served" by a Sorbonne-educated maître-d. Such things were not possible for most Soviet intellectuals. Perhaps in the Sorbonne doctoral student, Rait saw glimpses of her own colleagues back in the USSR. They were highly educated, accomplished scholars, writers, and artists kept closely in check. They were not permitted "the sweet life," professionally, financially, or otherwise. They couldn't even fully express themselves creatively. Perhaps Rita believed that success and fortune had come too easily to the "rich Americans," without sacrifice or obstacle. Perhaps she believed the situation demeaning to the "real intellectual" in the dining room at the Hotel Spaniard—the Sorbonne student. Rait and her Soviet colleagues could well identify with the doctoral student's "paradoxical" situation. They, too, balanced the pursuit of a vocation,

---

[20] In her published memoirs about Mayakovsky and his circle in the 1920s, Rait recalled how Mayakovsky and Lili Brik once invited her to a "private cafeteria," which turned out to be a lavish restaurant in a luxurious old apartment. Not used to such finery, Rait declined to eat a "mysterious fish and vegetable concoction, which smelled tantalizingly of cream butter, only because I didn't know whether one should eat it with a fork or a spoon!" Rait-Kovaleva, "Best memories," 273.

of a higher calling, with an obligation to serve. But the scholar-maître-d's burden was temporary and relatively manageable. He served rich Americans. Rait and her colleagues served a harsher master—the Soviet state.

This fact Vonnegut *did* seem to recognize. He wrote to Loree Rackstraw as he was preparing to visit Rait in Moscow in October 1974. "She [Rita] is one of those who want to stay there, but who is heartbroken over the regime's cruelty to its artists and intellectuals. I am supposed to bring a lot of razor blades, so her friends can be clean-shaven in jail. Some lark..."[21] Around the same time, Vonnegut wrote to his cousin Mary Glossbrenner.

> I'm going over... [to Moscow] to see my seventy-six-year-old translator, a magnificent woman who took a doctor's degree in physiology under Pavlov. She has been allowed out of the worker's paradise only four times in her entire life. We got to know her during one of those times—in Paris. Now she will probably never be allowed out again. She has made friends with too many of the wrong people.[22]

Rait, who would not have known he wrote such things about her and her colleagues, thought Vonnegut never fully understood her circumstances. Rait found Vonnegut naïve about the Soviet system and how people like her lived. She did not think he fully appreciated how precarious was her work, and indeed her very existence. Without a doubt, the historic Rait-Vonnegut rendezvous in Paris laid a foundation for a life-long correspondence, collaboration, and friendship. But the two did not always see eye to eye. They could not avoid the push and pull of Cold War politics.

The pair's correspondence picked up in the wake of Paris. Rita informed Donald Fiene in December 1972 that "Vonnegut wrote a couple of wonderful letters to me!" and "Yesterday I had an 8-minute phone conversation with Jill and Kurt (the Lit. gazette paying!) and he promised to 'start working on an invitation' for me. If it really works out I might come [to the USA] in spring!"[23] Rita told Fiene at the end of January 1973 that Kurt had sent her some record albums, but she had not received them yet.[24] Rait took an interest in Vonnegut's family, in particular in his son Mark Vonnegut, whom

---

[21] Loree Rackstraw, *Love as Always, Kurt: Vonnegut as I Knew Him* (De Capo Press, 2009), 53.
[22] Wakefield, *Kurt Vonnegut—Letters*, 219.
[23] RRK to DMF, December 1972 (undated postcard), DMFC, Box 4, Folder 3, "Rait-Kovaleva, Rita, 1963-1976."
[24] RRK to DMF, January 28, 1973, DMFC, Box 4, Folder 3, "Rait-Kovaleva, Rita, 1963-1976."

she called "little Vonnegutik." Rita also liked the fact that one of Vonnegut's daughters was an artist and children's book author.[25]

Rait did not let herself get too excited by Vonnegut's and Fiene's repeated campaigns to bring her for a lecture tour to the United States. She did not think she would be given permission to go, and she was right. An early centerpiece of Vonnegut's advocacy of Rait was his editorial in *The New York Times Book Review* on January 28, 1973, entitled "Invite Rita Rait to America." The piece aptly and in characteristic Vonnegut style described Rait, her remarkable life, and her literary achievements. Vonnegut emphasized Rait's apolitical nature. ". . . If she gets here, it will be discovered that she is comparably unenthusiastic about, in fact strikingly ignorant of, economic and political affairs." Fatally, however, Vonnegut used several paragraphs to decry the "piracy of books as practiced so smarmily in the U.S.S.R." He averred that "other socialist countries make more honorable and open deals." Several of Rait's friends were appalled at the piece. Some did not appreciate the playful tone with which Vonnegut described Rait, his elder by several decades. The letter's general "lighthearted tone" put off others.[26] One colleague found the piece "too facetious."[27] Had Rait's friends known Vonnegut had been paid $150 for the editorial, they would have been incensed.[28]

Rait herself did not seem upset. No doubt she was delighted by Vonnegut's praise of her, her work, and her professional stature in the Soviet Union. She did chafe that he'd gotten her age wrong. Rita had just turned seventy-five and he gave her age as "nearly 80!"[29] But Vonnegut's open critique of "piracy" in the USSR surely confirmed his naiveté when it came to life in the Soviet Union and Soviet-American politics. Vonnegut's editorial was framed as a plea to American bureaucrats at universities and the State Department to invite Rait to America. Did he not realize the Soviet bureaucrats were the ones who needed convincing? Demeaning the Soviet publishing industry would not help the cause. Rait wrote to friends in New York. "Read all those funny things—I'm afraid he really spoiled it by mentioning all those authors, and so on . . . Well, we shall see."[30]

---

[25] RRK to KMA, April 1, 1974, p. 3, KMAC.
[26] RRK to DMF, April 12, 1973, p. 1, DMFC, Box 4, Folder 3, "Rait-Kovaleva, Rita, 1963–1976."
[27] RRK to DMF, April 5, 1973, p. 2, DMFC, Box 4, Folder 3, "Rait-Kovaleva, Rita, 1963–1976."
[28] Earnings Statement for $150 to Kurt Vonnegut, Jr. from *The New York Times* for "Guest Word: Invite Rita Rait to America," payroll date February 3, 1973. Kurt Vonnegut Manuscripts (hereafter KVM), Publishing Records. Box 20, "Royalty Statements."
[29] RRK to SG and Esia, February 6, 1973, BA-RRK.
[30] RRK to SG and Esia, February 6, 1973, BA-RRK.

In a letter to Fiene dated February 24, 1973, Rait expressed gratitude for Vonnegut's intervention but critiqued his simplicity. The *Times* op-ed revealed "he has no idea of all the complications connected with such an invitation. Despite the fact that he considers my English to be 'excellent,' I have a hard time explaining many things to him."[31]

Throughout the spring and summer of 1973 Rait wrote letters to friends and colleagues to express her joy with Vonnegut while lamenting his naiveté. On April 23, 1973, Rait wrote to Lili Brik.

> Vonnegut sent me a funny telegram from New York . . . Silly (*glupyi*) Vonnegut is CONVINCED that in October I will come to the University of Iowa, and he wrote me a long letter about how quiet it is there, how nice, what a sweet little town it is, in the cornfields—and how he will be my "happy host" in New York . . . He doesn't understand anything . . . But somehow, ALL SORTS OF MIRACLES are happening for me all the time, like Paris . . . There's always one chance in a million [that it will happen] . . . But I don't even dare to think about it.[32]

In June, Rait informed Fiene about the nice telegram Vonnegut had sent for her birthday. "Happy birthday, Sweetheart you are heroine of world literature also beautiful see you in October." Rita reflected, "Dear dear Kurt! But absolutely unable to understand what is what here."[33] In a July 1973 letter to Brik she reiterated, "And Vonnegut keeps writing and writing me—wonderful letters, but he doesn't understand anything . . ."[34]

Vonnegut probably understood more than Rait gave him credit for. The *Times* op-ed was just the first of several open critiques Vonnegut made of Soviet authorities and the USSR's treatment of intellectuals. In 1975, Vonnegut sent a cable to the Union of Soviet Writers urging them to defend Andrei Amalrik, a writer recently sentenced to hard labor.[35] In 1974, he supported the case of Efim Slavinsky with colleagues from PEN, an advocacy organization created to protect freedom of creative expression and to defend the human rights of all writers. (PEN America formed in 1922 with a mandate to protect freedom of creative expression and to defend the human rights of all writing professionals. It is the largest of more than 100 PEN Centers worldwide that

---

[31] RRK to DMF, February 24, 1973, p. 1, DMFC, Box 4, Folder 3, "Rait-Kovaleva, Rita, 1963–1976."
[32] RRK to Lili Brik, April 23, 1973, RGALI 2577/1/417/49, 49ob.
[33] RRK to DMF, June 5, 1973, p. 1, DMFC, Box 4, Folder 3, "Rait-Kovaleva, Rita, 1963–1976."
[34] RRK to Lili Brik, July 22, 1973, RGALI 2577/1/417/51ob.
[35] Wakefield, *Kurt Vonnegut—Letters*, 225.

constitute the PEN International network.)³⁶ Vonnegut defended Alexander Ginzburg in the late 1970s, among other campaigns. He carefully weighed decisions about participating in these rights defense campaigns. Vonnegut was aware that the wrong kind of intervention could make things worse for dissidents and their friends and families.

Rait did not like Vonnegut's outspoken activism on behalf of Soviet dissidents and those out of political favor. She believed that Western writers could do more to help improve the situation in the Soviet Union through their writing than by publicly critiquing the system. Foreign writers should leave it to those living in the Soviet Union to work on improvements from the inside. Rait summed up her views on the subject in a letter to Fiene in May 1974. Vonnegut had informed Rait that he had been elected Vice President of PEN. In this role he would be compelled to "defend the writers of Iran from the Shah." Rita was concerned that if Kurt engaged in similar "defense" of writers of the USSR, the translation of his work would be disallowed. This had happened to Bellow, Malamud, Graham Greene, and Böll. She preferred that Vonnegut "not get involved . . . [but rather] offer his smart, good and useful books to millions of readers—that is the best means to influence this crazy, crazy world." He should, she believed, "not defend someone with LETTERS, but defend truth and honesty WITH HIS BOOKS."³⁷

Of course, Rita was not about to advertise these thoughts widely. Such ruminations were for private letters and conversations. In public she preferred to look on the bright side. She emphasized Vonnegut's role—and the role of writers in general—in uniting like-minded people from all walks of life. To this end, she quoted Vonnegut in her "Preface" to the 1981 Russian-language anthology of Vonnegut's novels and stories.

> People often suffer from loneliness, from a feeling of disconnection with others, and with life. We no longer have large families, kind neighbors, and childhood friends. A writer has to become the "link," he can unite those around him who think as he does, who believe in the same things he does . . . Don't try to take away from me my faith in the happiness of humankind.³⁸

---

[36] PEN America, "About Us," accessed August 30, 2025. https://pen.org/about-us/.
[37] RRK to DMF, May 25, 1974, p. 3, DMFC, Box 4, Folder 3, "Rait-Kovaleva, Rita, 1963–1976."
[38] Rait-Kovaleva, "Canary," 6.

5

Vonnegut and Soviet Readers

In Donald Fiene's astute and chatty analysis of Vonnegut's "popularity in the Soviet Union and his affinities with Russian literature," he described how beguiled were educated Soviet citizens of the early and mid-1970s with Vonnegut's writing and ideas. "On a trip to the Soviet Union in December of 1975, I found that almost every educated Russian I met was a Vonnegut fan . . ."[1] Fiene's interlocutors in Moscow incorporated "Vonnegutisms" into their daily speech. Some believed themselves (or at least aspired to be) part of Vonnegut's karass. Rita Rait was pleased to hear from a friend who had seen a young man on the Moscow subway wearing a large homemade button pin on his jacket—a portrait of Kurt Vonnegut.[2]

But *why* did Soviet readers of a certain ilk embrace Vonnegut's prose so readily and so fervently? As explored in Chapter 8, the official Soviet narrative on Vonnegut emphasized his political utility. Literary critics assigned Vonnegut the role of humoristic satirist of American wrong-headedness and cultural degradation, a committed fighter in the worldwide (communist) "struggle for peace." But the Soviet readers who devoured Vonnegut's books were not reading him for enlightenment in politics. This chapter tracks how Soviet readers heard Vonnegut speaking directly to their own lives and experiences. How did Vonnegut speak into the specific challenges of the era of Stagnation in the USSR, as well as into the global crisis of US-Soviet animosities during the Cold War?

There was not one "Kurt Vonnegut in the USSR." There were multiple Kurt Vonneguts in the USSR. Soviet citizens read Vonnegut's novels and stories for a host of reasons. They liked his sardonic style, humor, and sarcasm. Science fiction fans were drawn to Vonnegut. Reading Vonnegut helped Soviet readers engage with philosophical and moral ideas and debates. This, in turn, helped readers imagine for themselves alternate futures. Young people especially read Vonnegut to find membership in a community of readers. They read Vonnegut to be cool and "Western." Like other foreign authors translated for the Soviet market, Vonnegut offered readers a window to the West and

---

[1] Fiene, "American Dissident," 259.
[2] RRK to SG, April 6, 1975, BA-RRK.

to Western culture. Vonnegut's prose offered readers an escape. Escape from the sometimes-stultifying daily existence in the period of Stagnation. Escape from the wooden, predictable language of official discourse. Escape from the overdetermined official ideology which left little room for creativity or debate.

As described in Chapter 3, Rita Rait played a key role in popularizing Vonnegut's writing for the Soviet readership. Rait was often asked "why they love Kurt." She characteristically depoliticized the reasons for Vonnegut's popularity among Soviet readers. Rita downplayed the political and critical aspects of Vonnegut's prose. Instead, she emphasized Vonnegut's unique, clear writing style and his humanity and truthfulness as a writer. Rait stressed that Vonnegut was popular with Soviet readers NOT for political reasons, but for "human" reasons.

> The young people here love Kurt not for the transitory things in his writings, but for the permanent ones, unchanging in value, that the author understands and that he tells about so beautifully, so engagingly, so masterfully. They love him for the same reason I do: for "that unwavering band of light" that he sees in every living creature. . . . They love Kurt because he invented "karass" and "duprass" and explained the utter emptiness of "granfalloons" everywhere in the world. . . . They adore him for that gift of "eternal childhood" that he preserved within himself; for the fact that he feels pity for all human beings; that he has almost no "villains" in his works; that he knows how to laugh—and is also laconic; that he is a great master of <u>style</u>, one of the best representatives of "naked prose" free of cute ornamentation; that despite certain "risqué expressions," he is a man deeply chaste, <u>very pure</u>. I am proud that to me fell the great honor of being his translator, of bringing to my friends—and they are now also Kurt's friends—all the charms of his works and—if I may express it so—the beauty of his soul.[3]

Certainly, Rait was correct to emphasize readers' love of Vonnegut's refreshing, direct style and his dry, cynical tone. Soviet citizens were marinated in—and very weary of—the artificial, predictable, official ideological language that saturated daily life in the USSR. Vonnegut poked fun at banalities of thought

---

[3] RRK to DMF, March 26, 1977, DMFC, Box 4, "Rait-Kovaleva, Rita. 1968–1978." Emphasis in original. Translation Yana Skorobogatov, "Kurt Vonnegut," 9–10. In Vonnegut's fabricated religion of Bokononism, "duprass" is a karass composed of only two people. A "granfalloon" is a false karass, a proud and meaningless association of human beings. Marc Leeds, *The Vonnegut Encyclopedia: An Authorized Compendium* (Greenwood Press, 1995), 213, 269.

and speech. This gesture surely resonated with Soviet readers so relentlessly exposed to the wooden vocabulary of official discourse. Vonnegut was a playful, irreverent author. Reading Vonnegut, particularly in Rita Rait's literary translations, was pleasurable. No doubt, readers could understand—and enjoy—Vonnegut without mining his prose for underlying meanings or symbolic references to politics, religion, and ethics.

Yet, Soviet readers' affinity for Vonnegut was based on more than escapism and reverence for this charming American author. Raisa, one of my interviewees, was fifteen or sixteen years old when she first read Vonnegut. Raisa recalled that Vonnegut's unique "artistic form" of writing helped readers to "overcome" or "conquer" the difficult subject matter in his books. In her experience, reading Vonnegut was a kind of soft launch for budding young readers to start considering hard philosophical questions and ethical dilemmas. Nataliya Shulga, who read Vonnegut as a young teenager in the 1970s in Kyiv, the capital of the Ukrainian SSR, expressed a similar idea. "First, I came [to Vonnegut] as a science fiction lover, but very quickly I realized, no, it's not just science fiction. It is philosophy. It is fundamental questions about human beings, their presence on the planet..." Another interviewee, Leonid, grew up in Leningrad. He said Vonnegut and other foreign authors supplied an escape route for young people beginning to question the Soviet system who were hungry for new perspectives and critiques. Reading fiction—including world literature—with embedded sociological and philosophical critiques was a way for these people to sublimate their eclectic interests "without going to jail."

Rita Rait knew very well that Soviet readers found important philosophical, social, and political messages in Vonnegut's work, in *her* translation. In the stifling political climate of the 1970s, however, she did not want Vonnegut's political relevance—and his appeal to the increasingly restless Soviet youth—advertised. She admonished Donald Fiene, who in 1977 was exploring the question of Vonnegut's popularity in the USSR, not to politicize the question of Kurt's popularity in his scholarly publications.

> I am very worried about your article on Kurt's popularity here: you SHOULD NOT use political fictions (*vydumki*) to explain WHY our young readers love him . . . if you start to invent something about "oppositions" and so on, they may get angry at him—and then you can kiss the play—our play, which is eliciting ENCORES—goodbye.[4]

---

[4] RRK to DMF, March 26, 1977, p. 2, DMFC, Box 4, Folder 5, "Rait-Kovaleva, Rita. 1976–1982."

(Rait was referring to the Soviet Army Theater's staging of "The Wanderings of Billy Pilgrim," described in Chapter 7.) Rait constantly implored Fiene not to entangle his analysis of Vonnegut's popularity in the Soviet Union with politics. She called politics "a temporary phenomenon." Constant phenomena, she wrote, included "good literature, and all primordial noble human feelings:" "I translate Vonnegut," Rita explained, "because he wrote that instilled within living creatures is 'an unwavering band of light' (*Breakfast of Champions*)."[5] If Fiene insisted on emphasizing Vonnegut's political appeal to Soviet readers, Rait warned, "you can really harm Kurt and his friends here."[6]

Rita had waged this particular battle for years. She'd weathered waves of repression and had fought mightily to translate key "problematic" American and British authors for a Soviet readership. She feared that to emphasize "political symbolism" in foreign writing would deprive people in the USSR of the opportunity to read Western literature. By the time she implored Fiene in 1977 to leave off enumerating the underlying political reasons for Vonnegut's popularity in the Soviet Union, Rita had been trying to break him of his "searching for symbolism" habit for nearly ten years.

In this respect, it is informative to look back on a charming letter Rait wrote Fiene in March 1968. Her reflections were not about Vonnegut, whom she had not yet begun to translate. They were about the Russian writer Isaac Babel, in whom Fiene had a nascent interest. Fiene had asked Rita for feedback on his preliminary thoughts about the "political symbolism" in Babel's writing. Rait teased Fiene for trying too hard to find hidden meanings in the work of a writer like Babel who was "so clear and precise." This is exactly how Rait evaluated Vonnegut's writing—as clear and precise. And she tried to translate him for the Soviet readership clearly, and precisely. Her humorous rejection of Fiene's "discovery" of political symbolism in Babel presages her refusal ten years later to accept his thoughts about Vonnegut's "political appeal."

> Why should one try to find a hidden meaning in what is absolutely clear and above board? <u>Nothing</u> was disguised in Babel's works: it is an absolutely brilliant, if a bit surrealistic picture of people and times. <u>No character</u> stands for any other but what he is or was: Babel wrote at a period when one could show absolutely everything. Why should he

---

[5] RRK to DMF, October 25, 1977, p. 2, DMFC, Box 4, Folder 5, "Rait-Kovaleva, Rita. 1976–1982."

[6] RRK to DMF, March 26, 1977, p. 3, DMFC, Box 4, Folder 5, "Rait-Kovaleva, Rita. 1976–1982."

depict some Red Army soldier, who is an embodiment of all that was good—and bad!—then, and think of, say, Lenin or Bukharin etc.? It sounds quite artificial to me to try to plant some hidden thoughts into things so clear and precise.

But of course if you start deciphering literature from the Freudian point of view you certainly can find anything you want: it might as well be an Oedipus complex or any other syndrome, but why the dickens do you want to do it?!? On the other hand if you take the author at his word you may find exciting things about the beginning of many changes that have come about later on.

Of course I might be quite quite wrong in my "realist" or rather "surrealist" approach, but it sounds absolutely irrelevant to the real meaning of Babel's works, this identification of the figure of Savitsky with King David or Lenin. Why not Archangel Gabriel or Thomas Moore, or any fighting spirit at all?!?!...

There is an acute danger in making these "discoveries..." I knew Babel quite well. He was never religiously minded, nor politically much involved. All he wanted to do is to give a many-sided and multicolored picture of his time, with a precision and an insight that were more like a picture, say, of Bosch than an Esopian thingumbob [sic.] ...The details, the dialogues, the coining of new images—everything he did was unexpected, fresh, very precise, very laconic and condensed... all this 'political symbolism' you try to inject artificially into Babel, seems quite quite immaterial, when one sees that magic power of evoking things in a few sentences admirably constructed, and devoid of any artificiality at the same time.[7]

Rait insisted that writers be "taken at their word," not probed for "hidden meanings" that would reveal more about the prober, than the probed. Taking writers and their writing at "face value" was a safer—and depoliticized—approach. It was also the only approach Rita could take if she wanted to stay in business as a translator of potentially controversial Western authors. Rait did believe that books like *Cat's Cradle* and *Slaughterhouse-Five* had something to "teach" Soviet readers. She just downplayed any political relevance of Vonnegut's writing and emphasized instead his "humanity" and kindness.

Late 1973 and early 1974 was a particularly tense period in US-Soviet relations. Détente between the two superpowers was severely threatened by

---

[7] RRK to DMF, March 9, 1968, pp. 2-6, DMFC, Box 4, Folder 3, "Rait-Kovaleva, Rita. 1963-1976."

tensions in the Middle East.⁸ Rait hoped that more American writers would produce books like Vonnegut's. She wanted books that could be translated into Russian to "teach people something, to instill something in them," instead of books that were too political and anti-Soviet, which would not get translated.⁹ When a version of her article, "Canary in a coalmine, or my friend, Kurt Vonnegut" was selected as the Foreword of a collection of four Vonnegut novels and fourteen stories published in Kishinev in 1981, Rait practiced what she preached. Her piece was politics-free. Rait sketched Vonnegut's biography and described their long-time friendship. She acknowledged that forewords usually include an analysis of the author's work "from the point of view of style, artistic elements," and so on.¹⁰ But instead of venturing her own analysis of Vonnegut's work, Rait quoted an entire page from literary critic Alexei Zverev's analytical foreword from a Vonnegut compilation published by Artistic Literature (*Khudozhestvennaia literatura*) in 1978.¹¹ It was a safe move. Zverev's assessment had gone over well, and adding her own spin would have been superfluous and possibly risky. Rait ended her article with a friendship-of-the-peoples type imbrication to Soviet readers. "Try to love Kurt Vonnegut, like thousands of people from all the countries of the world, including ours, already do."¹² This was an easy ask.

The fan base

Who was reading Vonnegut in the USSR? Vonnegut's fans were educated Soviet citizens who connected with his science-fiction-like scenarios and dystopian worlds. They eagerly grappled with the provocative questions he raised about human morals, soulless bureaucracies, and empty ideologies. Vonnegut fans were primarily young people, including secondary school and university students, and members of the "technical intelligentsia." My interviewees identified the "technical intelligentsia" as those Soviet citizens who were drawn to both science and the humanities, who also had a strong interest in sociology and politics. Many Vonnegut fans were influenced by

---

[8] Jonathan Haslam, *Russia's Cold War: From the October Revolution to the Fall of the Wall* (Yale University Press, 2011), 271–6.
[9] RRK to DMF, rec'd February 1, 1974, p. 1, DMFC, Box 4, Folder 3, "Rait-Kovaleva, Rita. 1963–1976."
[10] Rait-Kovaleva, "Canary," 15.
[11] Alexei Zverev, "Signal prodesterezheniia" ["Warning signal"]. In *Boinia nomer piat', ili Krestovyi pokhod detei, i drugie romany* [Slaughterhouse-Five, or the Children's crusade, and other novels], by Kurt Vonnegut (Khudozhestvennaia literatura, 1978), 3–19.
[12] Rait-Kovaleva, "Canary," 16.

Charles Snow's *The Two Cultures*, which was translated into Russian in 1973. Snow complained that the sciences and the humanities, which represented "the intellectual life of the whole of western society" had become split into "two cultures." He warned that this division was a major impediment to solving the world's pressing problems.[13] Snow's framing resonated with Vonnegut's well-known observation that the literary establishment had wrong-headedly divorced itself completely from science and technology. Any writer who "knew how a refrigerator worked" was dismissed as an author of (mere) science fiction.

Vonnegut often dealt with questions of scientific and technological innovation (usually, innovation gone wrong, or technology taken to its disastrous extremes). This was familiar subject matter that appealed to readers in the Soviet Union accustomed to reading Soviet literature about science, technology, and engineering. As explored by Rosalind Marsh, the "scientific and technological revolution" was a pervasive theme in Soviet life beginning in the mid-1950s. Scientific progress—its nature and its consequences—featured prominently in Soviet literature.[14] The Soviet technical intelligentsia fit Snow's criteria for the ideal cultural person as one who "has great knowledge of literature but also knows how the world works," as one interviewee, the sociologist Elena Gapova, put it. Vonnegut appealed to those with an interest in science and the ethics of science, who also wanted to explore the humanities and social sciences. Several of my Vonnegut-fan interviewees who had been educated in the hard sciences said that in another country they would have pursued the social sciences, probably sociology. But in the USSR, they'd been compelled to go into hard science (chemistry, biology) because it was "safe." The opportunity to read a novel with "both sides of the brain," so to speak, was one reason for Vonnegut's appeal to the Soviet technical intelligentsia.

Rita Rait described Vonnegut's style early on as "sort of 'black humor' with a little science fiction thrown in."[15] This style had particular appeal for young readers in the USSR. Vonnegut fans I interviewed often lined him up alongside Bulgakov, whose *Master and Margarita* became available to Soviet readers around the same time as Vonnegut's books. Readers paired Vonnegut with the Strugatsky brothers, beloved Soviet science fiction authors of the 1960s. Soviets read Vonnegut alongside foreign sci-fi writers in translation,

[13] Charles P. Snow, *The Two Cultures and the Scientific Revolution: The Rede Lecture, 1959* (Cambridge University Press, 1961).
[14] Rosalind J. Marsh, *Soviet Science Fiction Since Stalin: Science, Politics and Literature* (Barnes and Noble Books, 1986), 31–64.
[15] RRK to Lili Brik, December 26, 1969, RGALI 2577/1/417/29, 29ob.

including Ray Bradbury, Robert Sheckley, and Isaac Asimov, who Vonnegut later succeeded as president of the American Humanist Society. Publication of original and translated science fiction fell precipitously in the 1970s, as the political atmosphere tightened and the space for critique narrowed.[16] Demand for sci-fi was high, but supply was low. This is precisely when Vonnegut appeared in translation in the USSR. Some regarded Vonnegut as one among several of the "contemporary non-realist authors" from the West to whom they had access, at a time when such access was very limited.[17] Vonnegut's fellow foreign non-realist writers in translation who Soviets read widely included Isaac Asimov, Ray Bradbury, Arthur Clark, Gabriel Garcia-Marques, Iris Murdoch, and later, William Golding and Tom Wolfe (*Bonfire of the Vanities*). (See more on Vonnegut and science fiction fandom below.)

University students and youth were prime consumers of Vonnegut in the Soviet Union. Viktoria was a student in the Department of Foreign Languages at Kyiv State University (now Shevchenko National University) in the late 1970s and early 1980s. She remembered that Vonnegut was just "in the air" among university students. He was not required reading on the syllabus of her "American Literature of the 20th Century" course. Obligatory authors were Hemingway, Faulkner, Dreiser, Steinbeck, Sinclair, and Twain, many of which the students read in the original English when it was available. "But definitely not Vonnegut. He was just in the air among the student community." For Viktoria, after slogging through Faulkner or Dreiser, with their "long passages of explanation and complex sentences, reading Vonnegut was like reading a newspaper." What Jess Ritter wrote about American students and Vonnegut in the early 1970s was true for Soviet students, too. "They [students] react to him as a myth-maker and fabulist rather than as a dramatic and narrative novelist. Vonnegut hangs ideas on his fables, making them easily accessible to young readers."[18]

Vonnegut's straightforward, pared-down writing style appealed to young readers. And his novel lexicon gave young people a new, hip vocabulary to use among themselves. Soviet youth made Vonnegut part of a larger package of "cool." Listening to jazz, rock, and the Soviet bards (Vysotskyy, Okudzhava), wearing blue jeans, and reading the Strugatsky brothers and Vonnegut—these were all ingredients of the "contemporary" lifestyle Soviet young people wanted to cultivate. Reading Vonnegut was one "checkbox"

---

[16] Rafail Nudelman, "Soviet Science Fiction and the Ideology of Soviet Society," *Science-Fiction Studies* 16, no. 1 (1989): 53.

[17] Author's interview with "Raisa," June 8, 2020, electronic correspondence.

[18] Jess Ritter, "Teaching Vonnegut on the Firing Line," in *The Vonnegut Statement*, ed. Jerome Klinkowitz and John Somer (Delacorte Press/Seymour Lawrence, 1973), 38.

in a list of ways Soviet youth pursued "American" culture to be cool and contemporary. Consider Nadia's story.

> I studied in a regular Moscow school—no specialization, no subjects taught in English—but in my circle of friends (some from our school, some from others) it was customary to debate elements from the world of American culture. It [American culture] was magnetic and irresistible. We knew music (not only the Beatles and the Rolling Stones, but also Led Zeppelin, Queen, etc.), we knew American classic [literature] (adults, our parents from intelligentsia families, tried to push Harper Lee's *To Kill a Mockingbird* on us, but we preferred *Catcher in the Rye*; they pointed us towards Mark Twain, but we read *The Great Gatsby* and *Tender is the Night* by Fitzgerald; we were carried away by Hemingway) . . . And on this wave of love for everything American; of desire to wear "fades," (that is, blue jeans that faded the more you wore them); to have access to Wrigley's chewing gum, and [our] adoration of "Yellow Submarine," somebody in our circle of friends mentioned K. Vonnegut.

In Nadia's clique, imitating an American lifestyle, including reading Kurt Vonnegut and other "cool" American authors, was part of living a "contemporary" lifestyle as a Soviet teenager. Reading translated prose in the *Foreign Literature* journal already signaled one's "contemporariness." As Andrei Bitov observed, readers subconsciously thought of the journal *Foreign Literature* as being titled *Contemporary Literature*. "Foreign" equaled "contemporary." *Foreign Literature* contained the "alternative canon of the intelligentsia" of the 1970s and 1980s.[19] Other signals that one was "contemporary" included traveling to festivals or on camping trips or "expeditions" (most likely inside the USSR because of travel restrictions). "Contemporary" people listened to the VOA or the BBC (which was often jammed).

Elena Gapova is a sociologist now living in the United States who read Vonnegut as a Soviet teenager. She noted that familiarity with American culture, including through books, was considered prestigious. Applying her sociologist's lens to the phenomenon forty years later, Gapova said she now realizes that Soviet teens gobbled up foreign, especially American, literature, to accumulate social and cultural capital. "Somehow, we knew what to read." Gapova reflected on how *Foreign Literature* was structured, and how it was consumed. Each issue was divided into three sections: Western literature,

---

[19] Bitov as cited by Iuliia Vishnevetskaia et al., "Genom russkoi dushi" [Genome of the Russian soul], *Russkii reporter* [Russian reporter] 5, no. 283 (February 7, 2013).

socialist literature (especially from East-Central Europe) and "Third World" (postcolonial) literature. "Everyone read the Western literature. A few people read the socialist. And no one read the postcolonial."
Teen readers of Vonnegut in the Soviet Union sought a "dialogue" with the West. Raisa went on to become a historian of Russian journalism and literature.

> Vonnegut, Böll, Salinger—these authors, like foreign literature in general, were very important for Soviet society in the 1960s, which was striving for a dialogue (and first, an understanding) with the western world. People were thirsty for the air of freedom and greedily caught it wherever they could. The separation (*raz"edinenie*) seemed unnatural, and the iron curtain oppressed and suffocated us.

Some who read Vonnegut—a sanctioned writer, not banned in the Soviet Union—were also readers of samizdat and forbidden material. Examples were Solzhenitsyn's books and the *Chronicle of Current Events*, the unofficial newsletter about human rights abuses that circulated between 1968 and 1983. Vonnegut was not "dissident literature," but some Vonnegut fans read him alongside dissident literature. Interlocutors often mentioned the book *In Search of Melancholy Baby*, by Soviet émigré writer Vassily Aksyonov. In that book Aksyonov relates his adventures moving to America, after a lifetime of imagining what life in America must be like. He also describes his former life in the USSR "loving the States." Among a certain subset of Soviet society, anything American was considered valuable and cool. "There was a period when we spoke to our friends almost entirely in quotes from American movies."[20] Aksyonov's book resonated with Vonnegut fans, who sought glimpses of the "real America" in Vonnegut's books.

Yana Skorobogatov observes that "the typical Soviet Vonnegut reader fit somewhere in between 'conformist' and 'reformist,'" a broad demographic produced by the atmosphere of Stagnation.[21] Vonnegut was one of the relatively few Western authors available to Soviet readers. They read him together with the other "must reads" of Western literature—Salinger, Hemingway, Maugham, Nathaniel Hawthorne, Flannery O'Conner, Heinrich Böll, Remarque. Vonnegut fans often read him alongside (and confused him with) Joseph Heller, the author of *Catch-22*. Like Vonnegut, Heller wrote about war, employed a similar cynicism, and wrote in timelines that jumped

---

[20] Vassily Aksyonov, *In Search of Melancholy Baby* (Vintage Books, 1989), 18.
[21] Skorobogatov, "Kurt Vonnegut," 11.

back and forth. (One Muscovite interviewee, Sergei, a Vonnegut fan as a teenager, said that during his life he had only read a couple of books more than one time—Vonnegut's *Slaughterhouse-Five*, and Heller's *Catch-22*.) Several interviewees read Vonnegut around the same time they read Richard Bach's *Jonathan Livingstone Seagull*. One mentioned Herman Hesse's *Steppenwolf* as coterminous with Vonnegut in his own readerly memory. This indicates that some Soviet readers may have taken a personal spiritual journey as they explored Vonnegut alongside Hesse, Bach, and others.

There is some debate over whether "highbrow" readers of the Soviet literati intelligentsia read Vonnegut, or not. It was in Rita Rait's interest to argue that literati indeed read Vonnegut. "Here Vonnegut is a favorite of the intelligentsia; the [political] 'elite' and 'the people,' (*narod*) don't read him, or Faulkner, or Kafka. But if students are considered 'the people'—then they read him and love him."[22] Others made a distinction between what kind of "intelligentsia" Vonnegut appealed to in the Soviet Union. The technical intelligentsia: Yes. The cultural intelligentsia (elite literati): No.[23] In general, a broad demographic of educated Soviet readers seems to have read Vonnegut, "the kind of people who subscribed to *Foreign Literature*" as many of my interviewees put it. This included scientists, professors, engineers, teachers, university students, and often, precocious Soviet "tween-agers."

Reading Vonnegut: The pleasures of recognition

Vonnegut's Soviet readers saw themselves in his characters, in the moral and social conundrums he explored, and perhaps even in Vonnegut himself. Reading Vonnegut in the Soviet 1970s was to engage in what Eleonory Gilburd has called "the pleasures of recognition." Gilburd wrote about the "Soviet lives" of Western imports—novels, films, paintings, etc.—during the Thaw period of the 1950s and 1960s.

To understand how the Soviets made sense of what they read and saw, I rely on the notion of translation—as a mechanism of transfer, a process of domestication, and a metaphor for ways cultures interact. Meanings emerged at the confluence of a translated text and Soviet context. To

---

[22] RRK to DMF, May 25, 1974, p 4, DMFC, Box 4, Folder 3, "Rait-Kovaleva, Rita. 1963–1976."
[23] Author interview with Konstantin Azadovsky, October 31, 2019, St. Petersburg, Russia.

a large degree, then, the Soviet pleasures in things Western were "the pleasures of recognition."[24]

I am persuaded by this notion that Soviet readers "recognized" themselves and their reality, their own life experiences and aspirations, in Vonnegut's writing. Readers' interpretations of Vonnegut—their understandings of his works and incorporation of his ideas into their world views—depended to a great extent on their own positioning in a particular (Soviet) cultural and political context.

Vonnegut's characters were accessible to the Soviet reader because his writing featured "simple people," people of "simple origins." This was a commonality that Vonnegut believed American and Russian literature shared. In an interview with Vonnegut, journalist A. Mirchev pointed out that American writers had been very influenced by the Russian writers of the nineteenth century, and that American writers—Hemingway, Steinbeck, Faulkner—had made a big impact on Russians. Vonnegut responded:

> I think both our societies are peasant societies, of the people. In our [American] literature, as in Russian [literature], we wrote about common people, not the nobility, [or] the elites. If you look carefully at French, English, and Spanish literature—they worship and highly value elite people, the bluebloods and so on. Which we don't do at all. I think this is why we [Americans and Russians] have so much in common. We all write about "simple people." Who, in the end, are not so simple. But they have humble roots.[25]

Having recognized themselves in Vonnegut's characters, Soviet readers could then have a good laugh at themselves. Vonnegut superfan Nataliya Shulga felt this deeply. "[Vonnegut's] black humor is just a medicine to cure stupidity and ignorance people express in their social life. We found that laughing at ourselves helps us to stay healthy."[26]

Vonnegut's unique narrative style and viewpoint also helped readers feel "close" to him. Raisa explained, "I was most charmed by his manner of narration—[telling] a story from the point of view of a hero, who sits in an uncomfortable relationship with the author himself. It was difficult to take in the whole picture through his point of view, but that's precisely what was so

---

[24] Gilburd, *To See Paris*, 1–2.
[25] "A. Mirchev" was Aleksandr Minchin, writing under a pseudonym. Mirchev, "Interview," 445.
[26] Nataliya Shulga to KV, November 10, 1995, KVM, Box 3, Folder 12, "1995–1997."

interesting about [Vonnegut's narrative] style." This narrative style, this form of "voice," was new to Soviet readers. It was not something they "recognized," but something they warmed to. Vonnegut's narrator—who seemed to be Vonnegut himself—was warm and inviting, a wise friend you'd want to spend time with. My interviewees frequently did not remember the plots of Vonnegut's books. Rather, they referenced certain flashpoints in his writing that had stuck with them—particular characters, a discrete scene, a snatch of dialogue, or some concrete "take away" idea. Several remembered how as teenagers, they had copied down key sayings and phrases from Vonnegut's writing and displayed them—maybe just for themselves, maybe for others—in their most private spaces. "My impressions from Vonnegut were so strong back then that I copied down some of his phrases and arranged them under the glass top of my writing desk."[27] When she was a young bride, another interviewee made a banner with a quote from *Jailbird* and hung it on her bedroom wall, as a reminder to her husband. "Love may fail, but courtesy will prevail." (Some forty years later she remembered the line as something like, "Love me less, but treat me better.")[28]

After recognizing themselves and their daily struggles in Vonnegut's books, Soviet readers took the next steps: pondering, debating, and problem-solving. Vonnegut helped readers grapple with contemporary social, political, economic, moral, and existential debates that were relevant to their lives. As Skorobogatov noted:

> Despite Vonnegut's fictional flourishes, pessimism, and sometimes naïve idealism, Vonnegut fans [in the Soviet Union] read his books not as absurd, dark, and entertaining fiction, but as serious, cautionary tales of mankind's capacity for destruction: warnings for people living in the present day to heed as they contemplated the future . . . In his stories . . . [they] . . . found warnings of man's inherent culpability, his capacity to act unreasonably and against all logic. They believed that simply reading Vonnegut's novels made them that much better equipped to cope with the problems, both present and future, around them.[29]

Muscovite Evangelina was reading Vonnegut as a young teenager during the early to mid-1980s, when three General Secretaries of the Communist Party of the USSR died in quick succession. Brezhnev in November 1982, Andropov in February 1984, and Chernenko in March 1985. Ideas she'd

---

[27] Author interview with "Nadia," May 11, 2020, electronic correspondence.
[28] Author interview with Nataliya Shulga, March 16, 2020, virtual.
[29] Skorobogatov, "Kurt Vonnegut," 16–17.

taken from *Cat's Cradle* helped Evangelina process this strange occurrence. "We live in a mosaic of happenstance, there is no free will, we cannot predict the future, and we have no control over what happens to us." Evangelina saw the "demise of the Gen Secs one right after the other" through this lens of "happenstance." What if one or the other of them hadn't died? She recalled reading or hearing some possible scenarios. "If X hadn't died, he would have tightened the screws, perestroika wouldn't have happened. . ."

Another reader, Nataliya Shulga, fell in love with Vonnegut's books as a teenager in Soviet Ukraine. She believed that Vonnegut used his characters (e.g., Kilgore Trout), "to deliver the questions people [are] afraid to ask themselves and each other."[30] For Nataliya—and other interviewees echoed this as well—the "red thread" running through all of Vonnegut's prose was the question, "How should a decent person live in an indecent society?" This was a question of immediate importance to Soviet teens in the 1970s. They felt trapped in a corrupt, boring social and political system. In this environment, Soviet subjects had to compete for resources. "You had to fight, you had to grab, you had to get. You had to use your paws and teeth." Here Nataliya named the true "villains" in Vonnegut's novels—inhumane systems that catch people up, grind them down, and pit them against one another. Nataliya aligned herself with the misfits, those "decent people" who stood out in a totalitarian society.

> It's a decent person who holds values, appreciation of their own life and the life of others, who would never do any brutal things against their family members or their society and stuff like that. These people look stupid in this society. They look stupid . . . and that's what we were discussing when we were teenagers . . . by [the] definition of society I am exactly Kurt Vonnegut's character: a decent person in an indecent society.

In identifying with Vonnegut's "stupid" heroes, young Nataliya found license to re-orient her own moral compass to pursue a "decent" life in Soviet Ukraine.

Vonnegut helped Soviet readers think through important existential issues. These included the appropriate role of science and technology in society, and the relevance of ethics to scientific advancements. By what moral codes should people live their lives, as individuals and as members of collective society? Vonnegut's writing enabled readers to reflect on the nature

---

[30] Nataliya Shulga to KV, November 10, 1995, KVM, Box 3, Folder 12, "1995–1997."

of ideology, free will, human agency, and emerging discourses on human rights. Many readers were particularly taken with Vonnegut's ruminations on what Leonid from Leningrad/St. Petersburg, called "scientific inventions without borders." The ethical side of scientific-technological advancement was important to these readers, several of whom went on to careers in the hard sciences.

Again, the example of Nataliya Shulga is pertinent. "First I came [to Vonnegut] as a science fiction lover, but very quickly I realized—no, it's not just science fiction. It is philosophy. It is fundamental questions about human beings, their presence on the planet, the society." Nataliya also commented on Vonnegut's unique style. She found it at once simple yet provocative. She was stimulated by his "black humor, his way of saying trivial things, but in a way that gets to your mind. It forces you to think and ask the question, Why?" Nataliya says that *Cat's Cradle* and its exploration of ethics in science influenced her choice to pursue a scientific career. Reading the book raised important questions for her about "how responsible science should work." It underscored the danger of blindly following ideologies of any kind, including a blind reverence for scientific advancement, or even "strange religions" such as Vonnegut's Bokonism. Nataliya, now an administrator in the educational-scientific sphere, says that to this day, "*Cat's Cradle* has been the guidebook for my life." In her days of teaching science students in Ukraine, she assigned *Cat's Cradle* as required reading, to help students think about and debate scientific ethics.

Raisa had a different reaction when she read *Cat's Cradle* at age fifteen or sixteen around 1970.

> After reading it I gladly gave it to my friend. He loved this book and was glad to have it for himself. I felt much better, too. That book weighed especially heavily on my soul, as no other book had before or since. . . . Maybe the genre of anti-utopia just isn't for me. That book made a really hard, suffocating impression on me.

The scenarios *Cat's Cradle* proposed, including the prospect of a scientific invention gone horribly wrong (Ice-9), was just too much for Raisa's young teenage self to contemplate.

Ivan, who grew up in Novosibirsk, reported being similarly stunned—traumatized, really—by Vonnegut's novel *Deadeye Dick*. He read it as a young teen in 1986 when the translation by Margarita Kovaleva and Rita Rait was serialized in *Foreign Literature*. "I liked it, even though it is a terrible (*strashnyi*) book. It is the source of certain phobias for me to this day." Ivan was moved by the "impossibility of undoing a mistake—even one committed by a young boy—for him, for strangers, and for the entire family." The scenario—young Rudy Waltz unleashing a string of tragedies when he mistakenly shoots a woman across town from the cupola of his family home—resonated with stories Ivan heard from medical students who worked for the emergency services. Stories his mother's friend told him about Novosibirsk's psychiatry wards also reminded Ivan of Rudy Waltz. *Deadeye Dick* instilled a sensitivity in Ivan to the fact that "catastrophe can happen in an instant, but it lasts forever; you cannot atone for inflicting such damage." These thoughts revisited him when his own son reached adolescence. "This fear returns, a neurosis comes out [of me] as if voiced by Vonnegut's characters." Ivan recalled that even though his friends and family also read *Deadeye Dick*, he never discussed the book with anyone. "It's like there were too many taboo themes in that text, and we feared a kind of sympathetic magic. If one were to talk about all those horrible things that might happen to a person or to a family, then you might 'catch' [and experience] those horrible things yourself."

Raisa was compelled to shed *Cat's Cradle*, which was too heavy. Ivan experienced psychic discomfort thanks to *Deadeye Dick*, but he liked the book nevertheless. These stories reveal how Soviet readers' engagements with Vonnegut were not uniformly pleasant. But they were often productive, whether positively, negatively, or both. Vonnegut prepared young Soviet readers to engage with work by other challenging authors. Nadia said that reading Vonnegut as a high school student "prepared" her to read the difficult prose of the French polymath and novelist, Boris Vian.

"Humanity"/humanism

Soviet readers of Vonnegut frequently appeal to his "humanism," "humanity," or even "humaneness" (*gumannost'*). Vonnegut, his Soviet readers insist, did not take sides. He approached his characters first and foremost as humans, not as products of a particular socio-political environment. He did not embrace the Soviet Union; nor did he reject it. He was extremely critical of America, but saw the good in that country, too. For Soviet readers, Vonnegut's view of the world was not a binary one—it was not "black and white." "[Vonnegut's] unique brand of humanism appealed to a generation of readers who had been taught to view the world as a contest between good and evil: Bolshevism versus Menshevism, socialism versus fascism, communism versus capitalism. Vonnegut's world was far less binary."[31] Skorobogatov further argued that for

---

[31] Skorobogatov, "Kurt Vonnegut," 36.

Soviet readers, Vonnegut's moral relativism "challenged the legitimacy of the Cold War's bipolar framework, one that hinged on a divisive rhetoric that cultural and person-to-person exchange between east and west would eventually erode."[32]

When Soviet readers of Vonnegut talk about his "humanity" or "humaneness," they mean many things. They believe Vonnegut himself was a "humane" person, that "the values he expresses in his novels are deeply felt by him."[33] Tamara, a Vonnegut fan originally from Arkhangelsk who is highly spiritual and practices Zen Buddhism, describes Vonnegut as a "heart opener." "He combines philosophy, mystery, and fairy tales, when raising important humanistic issues."

I asked theater director Mikhail Levitin, who staged a play based on *Slaughterhouse-Five* at the Soviet Army Theater in 1976 (see Chapter 7), why Vonnegut was so popular with Soviet readers.

> Humor. Humor, and Rita's sixth sense about form. Rita's composition ... or his composition in Rita's translation. I don't know. But most of all, of course, his warmth and humor about humanity. People really needed someone writing like that in those days. You can't say that Faulkner wrote with warmth and humor. No way. But he [Vonnegut] did—with warmth and humor. And for the most part we understood him. It was like a sort of dance, an awkward dance by a person who doesn't dance very well. A really strange dance. A dance of life or something.

Fiene, too, believed it was Vonnegut's "humanity" that Soviet readers most appreciated. Fiene was deeply interested in Vonnegut's affinities with the great Russian writers, especially Fyodor Dostoevsky. He noted that both Vonnegut and Dostoevsky had great "compassion for the insulted and injured, for people 'who have no use.'"[34] "I think that both Dostoevsky and Vonnegut are concerned with the problem of how to love the unlovable—and that is why modern Russians like Vonnegut so much. He is concerned with all of humanity in a broad and sweeping way, much as were the great 19th -c.

---

[32] Skorobogatov, "Kurt Vonnegut," 39.
[33] Fiene, "American Dissident," 268.
[34] DMF to RRK, April 5, 1977, p. 1, DMFC, Box 4, Folder 5, "Rait-Kovaleva, Rita. 1976–1982."

Russian writers."[35] (See more about Vonnegut's affinities with Russian writers below.)

Vonnegut frequently explored a flip side of "humanity" in his books—people's encounters with inhumane bureaucratic obstacles. His readers in the USSR could identify with these scenarios. Bureaucracy was a frustrating feature of everyday life for people in the Soviet Union, where "the bureaucracy managed to turn a routine procedure into a complicated one."[36] As Fiene observed, "One reason for Vonnegut's popularity in the Soviet Union is that the average reader there is able to identify with Vonnegut's fictional victims of manipulative rulers and heartless, ubiquitous bureaucracies—and to feel that Vonnegut is his spokesman."[37] Vonnegut's critiques of soulless bureaucracies resonated just as deeply with Soviet readers as did his "humanism," that antidote to bureaucratic inertia.

Critique of war

The Red Army's victory in the Second World War, and the glorification of sacrifice and near deification of Soviet war heroes, was an immutable foundation of Soviet ideology. According to historian Donald Raleigh,

> a mythologized cult of the Great Patriotic War grew up with the [Soviet] Baby Boomers, replacing the Revolution of 1917 as the foundation story for the Soviet state that people could identify with, because they lived through the conflict. The cult of World War II evolved after 1945 to serve changing state needs, reaching its apogee under Brezhnev.[38]

Soviet citizens, including children, were inundated with stories of heroic figures to be emulated, a veritable "pantheon of historical and contemporaneous examples of self-fashioned Soviet heroes."[39] At the front

---

[35] DMF to RRK, April 5, 1977, p. 1, DMFC, Box 4, Folder 5, "Rait-Kovaleva, Rita. 1976–1982." Fiene likewise emphasized Vonnegut's "humanity" at length in an article he wrote that year for the *New York Times Book Review*, but most of that discussion was edited out of the published version. Donald M. Fiene, "Vonnegut—Big in Russia," *New York Times Book Review*, April 3, 1977. https://www.nytimes.com/1977/04/03/archives/vonnegut-big-in-russia-vonnegut-in-russia.html

[36] Donald Raleigh, *Soviet Baby Boomers: An Oral History of Russia's Cold War Generation* (Oxford University Press, 2011), 239.

[37] Fiene, "American Dissident," 270.

[38] Raleigh, *Soviet Baby Boomers*, 252.

[39] Raleigh, *Soviet Baby Boomers*, 251.

of this hero parade were the Soviet leaders, especially Lenin. Next in line were the war heroes. Then came all kinds of other heroes and heroines—labor heroes (Stakhonovites, the "shock workers"), mother heroes, and even child heroes like Pavlik Morozov, the boy who denounced his father to the authorities.

When she decided to translate *Slaughterhouse-Five* for a Soviet readership, Rita Rait consciously stepped into heated debates about "deheroicizing" the Second World War.[40] A generation of Soviet citizens was drenched in the glorification of the Soviet victory over the fascists. The irreverence of *Slaughterhouse-Five* was quite a shock. Billy Pilgrim was not the kind of hero Soviet readers were used to. So strange was Billy Pilgrim, with his nervous collapse and space-and-time travel to distant planets. So relatable, so human, was Billy Pilgrim, with his little battlefront organ and his ridiculous boot with no heel.

Slaughterhouse-Five in translation landed just as the Soviet myth economy of the Second World War was beginning to crack. Why, some Soviet citizens began to ponder, had it been necessary to sacrifice some 27 million Soviet people in the war effort? Could different measures toward victory have been taken? And was it really the Nazis who starved Leningrad's residents during the long siege? Maybe Stalin was at fault for not giving up the city. These rumblings of doubt were fertile soil for *Slaughterhouse-Five*'s revelations about the brutality and utter senselessness of war. Reading *Slaughterhouse-Five* exposed Soviet teenagers like Evangelina to new details about the war. "My fellow students and I had been exposed to a totally different story of the war. As schoolkids we were taken to lots of war films and such. But we knew nothing about the 'second front,' about convoys . . . We didn't know about the bombing of Dresden, either."

Nataliya Shulga's father was a highly decorated hero of the Second World War, a former artillery commander. She explained why Vonnegut's portrayal of war in *Slaughterhouse-Five* was such a "bomb" for Soviet readers. First, Vonnegut described the war from the point of view of American and British soldiers. He dispelled the Soviet myth that the allied forces played little or no role in fighting the Nazis.

> It's like nobody else was fighting Nazis, only Soviets. . . . We won the war against Nazis—there was no information about contributions by British, French, Americans. . . . We heard it was a coalition, but. . .that they didn't want to fight the Nazis—[that] they pretended, but they didn't. . . . Only

---

[40] Friedberg, *Decade of Euphoria*, 312–15.

Soviet people defeated the Nazis and Hitler . . . that's what we heard at school.

Further, Vonnegut's critique of war as a dirty business fought by "simple people . . . [who] were not well trained," was a welcome intervention for Soviet citizens tired of the glorification of war.

> I have my father here, who also did not like this glorification of the war . . . he was a hero . . . and he hated the war. And here, Vonnegut, who explains that war is nothing good. It's really a terrible experience, especially for young people, especially for those who cannot find the reason why it's going on. Why it's terrible destruction, you know? . . . I think to me, I realized it when I was very young. Because of my father's story, it was like a story of our family.

Vonnegut's description of war as "the children's crusade: a duty-dance with death" was a gut punch to the established Soviet narrative. Skorobogatov summed it up well.

> Kurt Vonnegut's incisive critique of past and present wars made a lasting impression on his Russian [and other Soviet] readers. Indeed, out of all of his political and social musings, it was his portrayal of the horrors, emptiness, and downright absurdity of war that became his greatest moral and intellectual legacy behind the Iron Curtain.[41]

Evangelina drew on Billy Pilgrim's post-war difficulties in *Slaughterhouse-Five* to try to understand the so-called "afgantsi," young Soviet men returning from fighting in Afghanistan, many of whom seemed to have PTSD (post-traumatic stress disorder). Vonnegut offered her an "important lens" that evoked her sympathy for returning soldiers.

One Vonnegut reader in the USSR observed in 1982, ". . . nobody here is ever going to write about war like Vonnegut did—that would be considered a mockery."[42] Indeed, most Soviet war literature struck a very different tone. Nikolai Sholohov's famous story "Fate of a Man" dwelt on the horrible loses imposed by the Nazis on one man, Andrei Sokolov. Sokolov could only start postwar life anew by adopting an orphan boy who was as alone and forlorn as he was. Konstantin Simonov's *The Living and the Dead* trilogy (later a favorite book of Vladimir Putin) portrayed the experiences of Red Army soldiers

---

[41] Skorobogatov, "Kurt Vonnegut," 19.
[42] Nikolai Rabotnov, diary entry for June 11, 1982. https://corpus.prozhito.org/note/19055.

during "Operation Barbarossa," Germany's invasion of the Soviet Union.[43] Although Simonov's characters are relatable individuals with many flaws and misgivings, ultimately the book is a tribute to the heroism and tenacity of the Red Army soldiers, for whom victory was everything.

Those authors who did write critically about the Second World War—so-called "lieutenants' prose"—were not considered part of the official Soviet literary canon. This included Nekrasov with his *Front-Line Stalingrad*. The novel depicted the horrible violence of the war on the Eastern Front and some of the Red Army's worst failings such as cowardice, losses, and retreat. Okudzhava's irreverent play, "Bud zdorov, shkoliar" (To your health, schoolboy) was a farce about a tank that invaded a high school dance. The tank senselessly dragged young men to war, as they morphed into faceless marching uniforms.

Just when the immutable Soviet narrative of the Great Victory began to fray around the edges, Vonnegut and Billy Pilgrim barged in. For a generation brought up on stories of Red Army heroism and a devastating yet "just" war, thinking of Dresden as containing "tons of human bone meal in the ground," and the war as a "children's crusade," a youngsters' "duty dance with death," was a revelation. This is precisely how Valentina described her engagements with Vonnegut and *Slaughterhouse-Five*. Born in Soviet Ukraine, Valentina eventually moved to Saratov (in the Russian SSR), and then to Moscow. Vonnegut's portrayal of the Second World War as a war fought by teenagers made a strong impression on her. She had only been exposed to official portrayals of war "through the prism of heroism." Vonnegut's approach was much different. The young people in his book had "no idea what they were doing, no idea what was happening to them." Valentina realized how "the times can put you in a meat grinder. The dreams of a young person can be destroyed in one minute."

This notion of being "swept up with the times" resonated strongly with stories that circulated in her family. Valentina's parents and grandparents had survived German occupation in Soviet Ukraine. They spoke of war and its horrors as a facet of "everyday life." "Terror became normal.'" The tales her parents and grandparents spun out about the war were unlike official Soviet narratives of war heroes. Their stories were closer to Vonnegut's narrative of war as the "children's crusade." Reading Vonnegut confirmed for Valentina what she already suspected: war is not heroism.

---

[43] Zita Ballinger Fletcher, "Our Review of Putin's Recommended Book: The Living and the Dead," *HistoryNet*, April 15, 2020. https://www.historynet.com/our-review-of-putins-recommended-book-the-living-and-the-dead/.

Vonnegut as quasi-science fiction, socialist escape, and vehicle for human rights discourse

Vonnegut also appealed to members of the technical intelligentsia and students in the Soviet Union because these constituents had at least one thing in common: an affinity for science fiction. As in the United States, many Soviet fans of Vonnegut were initially drawn to his writing thanks to their already-existing interest in reading science fiction. Of course, Vonnegut's use of genre is wide-ranging and difficult to classify. His first six novels have been "alternatively labeled science fiction, black humor, satire, schizophrenic fiction, fabulation, fantasy" and more besides.[44] It is undeniable that many of his works contain strong elements of science fiction. No surprise, then, that early in his career some readers and critics considered him a science fiction writer.

Science fiction, or what many scholars call "speculative fiction," was an important literary genre from the early days of the Soviet Union. Sci-fi was an appealing vehicle for socialist ideology and revolutionary dreaming. Early Soviet science fiction was no fringe genre. Until the end of the 1920s, mainstream writers were key producers of Soviet science fiction, or at least writing with sci-fi elements. These included Valery Bryusov, Vladimir Mayakovsky, Aleksei Tolstoy (*Aelita*, 1923), Evgeny Zamiatin (*We*, 1920–21), Alexander Beliaev (often called Russia's Jules Verne, author of *The Air Seller*, 1929), and Mikhail Bulgakov (*The Fatal Eggs*, 1923; *Heart of a Dog*, 1924).[45] Many of these established authors used elements of science fiction to explore alternate ideologies and their potential future consequences, sometimes by describing anti-utopias. Such approaches (usually they were critiques) quickly fell out of political favor. From the late 1920s to the 1950s, Soviet science fiction was mainly a "convenient service genre" to confirm and disseminate the official ideology, a "means of affirming and legitimizing the official myth" of state socialism.[46]

However, with Stalin's death and destalinization's opening of a temporary space to question established ideology and imagine alternate futures, the 1960s saw a boom in Soviet science fiction. Science fiction grew in popularity among readers and received serious attention from literary critics. The literary "thick journals" printed science fiction. Publishing houses formed divisions devoted to publishing science fiction in the original and in translation.

---

[44] Donald E. Morse, *The Novels of Kurt Vonnegut: Imagining Being an American* (Praeger, 2003), 24.
[45] Nudelman, *Soviet Science Fiction*, 39.
[46] Nudelman, *Soviet Science Fiction*, 44–7.

Leading newspapers and journals published serious discussions of the genre. Nudelman notes about the 1960s, "In theoretical articles of the period, SF [science fiction] is perceived as a specific artistic 'laboratory' where various societal and historical models are placed under scrutiny." One example is the novel by Boris and Arkady Strugatsky ("the Strugatsky brothers"), *Hard to be a God* (1964), in which scholars at the Institute of Experimental History undertake a comparative study and "rectification" of various societies.[47]

Soviet science fiction fans of the period read works of homegrown authors such as the Strugatsky brothers, Ivan Efremov, and Kir Bulychev. Bulychev wrote an extremely popular science fiction book series for children and young adults called *Alisa Selezneva*, which featured an eponymous teenage heroine. They also read foreign sci-fi writers in translation, including Isaac Asimov, Ray Bradbury, Arthur Clark, Stanislaw Lem, Robert Sheckley, and others. Three of Vonnegut's works appeared in the extremely highly regarded twenty-five-volume series published by Young Guard publishing house between 1965 and 1976, *Biblioteka Sovremennoi Fantastiki* (BSF, Library of Contemporary Science Fiction). BSF published *Player Piano* in 1962 under the title *Utopia 14*, and an anthology in BSF in 1973 featured two Vonnegut stories (translated by Margarita Kovaleva), "The Barnhouse Effect," and "EPICAC." The anthology also featured foreign and Soviet science fiction writers such as Azimov, Bradbury, Arthur Clark, Efremov, Stanislaw Lem, Vladimir Savchenko, Sheckley, Clifford Simak, and the Strugatsky brothers, among others.

Starting in the 1970s, with the period of Stagnation, the political atmosphere tightened once more and the space for critique of the Soviet system narrowed. The most popular Soviet science fiction writers (the Strugatskys, Efremov) found it progressively difficult to publish. Other established sci-fi writers increasingly considered part of the political "opposition," found it impossible. Publication of original and translated science fiction fell precipitously, in serialized and book form.[48] This is the environment in which Vonnegut's books first appeared in the Soviet Union.

---

[47] Nudelman, *Soviet Science Fiction*, 49. *Hard to be a God* was part of the Strugatskys' Noon Universe series, in which highly developed human agents control the development of less advanced peoples. Life is characterized by high levels of social, technological, and scientific advancement (much higher than in contemporary society). The books thus served as a critique of contemporary life.

[48] Nudelman, *Soviet Science Fiction*, 53.

Demand for sci-fi was high, but supply was getting low.[49] Lovers of science fiction snatched up Vonnegut. Readers who identified Vonnegut primarily as a science fiction writer often lined him up beside the Polish author Stanislaw Lem, author of *Solaris*, *The Star Diaries*, *The Cyberiad*, and others.

As mentioned above, science and technology were common and respected topics in Soviet fiction in general. Soviet fiction often included scientists, engineers, and other techie-types as protagonists. The genre featured topics such as scientific progress and complicated techno-scientific inventions. By the 1970s and 1980s the limitations of the "scientific-technical revolution," which had been a major preoccupation in the Soviet Union since the early 1960s, were increasingly explored in Soviet fiction. It acted as "a counterweight to the increasing emphasis on science in Soviet society, stressing the value of morality and the life of the individual."[50] Vonnegut's cautionary tales about science and technology run amok were right in line with this homegrown genre of critical fiction, and Soviet readers did not need to be sci-fi fans to connect with Vonnegut's subject matter or major themes.

Some interviewees mentioned Vonnegut's interesting experiments with time as a feature that drew them to his writing. Evangelina, who was not a science fiction fan, said she considered "Tralfalmadore and all that" as mere "inserts" in the books, "interludes" that allowed Vonnegut to experiment with time. In this she likened him to Carlos Castaneda and Richard Bach, who she was reading around the same time. For readers who were not science fiction fans, Vonnegut's surrealist style—mixing realism with fantasy—exposed them for the first time to non-linear plot lines and timelines. Viktoria from Kyiv noted the novelty for Soviet readers who had only been exposed to the "classics" (Dostoevsky, Tolstoy), and had not yet read Bulgakov's *Master and Margarita* or Andrei Platonov's fiction. "Reading Vonnegut, we understood that different styles are possible."

Vonnegut's use of satire to poke fun at society and politics also charmed Soviet readers. Fans of Soviet satirists liked Vonnegut, too. They read him alongside authors such as Fazil Iskander, whose book *The Goatibex Constellation* (*Sozvezdie kozlotura*) (1966) was a "remarkable satire of

---

[49] Finding Vonnegut's *Slaughterhouse-Five* translated in the pages of *New World* must have been a real treat for readers. In Issue 4 in 1970, where the second half of Rait's translation of the book appeared, besides Vonnegut and a poem by Evtushenko ("Kazan University") there was very little of interest. Unless, of course, readers wanted to read the article "N.K. Krupskaia about the figure of V.I. Lenin in Literature and Art," or a piece entitled, "Science is developing according to Lenin."

[50] Marsh, *Soviet Science Fiction*, 10.

Lysenko's genetics and Krushchev's agricultural campaigns."⁵¹ (Iskander, who was born in Abkhazia, was sometimes called "the Abkhazian Mark Twain".)

In a collection of essays, *Socialist Escapes: Breaking Away from Ideology and Everyday Routine in Eastern Europe, 1945—1989*, scholars examine how beaches, concert halls, stadiums, and other sites offered citizens in Soviet bloc countries "escape venues." In these spaces they could "acquire their own agency in the field of culture, leisure, and entertainment," to "escape" socialism "without leaving it."⁵² Fürst and McLellan further explore socialist escapes, including hippie communes, underground rock music scenes, and yoga collectives, in their volume *Dropping out of Socialism: The Creation of Alternative Spheres in the Soviet Bloc*.⁵³ We should add *reading* to this list of "socialist escape" routes. Many Soviet citizens, especially young people, immersed themselves in books to break the stultifying boredom they experienced during Stagnation. One needed hobbies and distractions to flavor the "blandness" of life, and reading was one such pastime. Educated families amassed impressive home libraries. Many of my interviewees who were young people in the 1970s remembered spending hours and hours of down time poking through their parents' many shelves of books.⁵⁴

Some Vonnegut fans surely experienced reading works by him and other foreign authors in translation as a form of living *"vnye"* ("not inside") socialism. As described by anthropologist Alexei Yurchak, living *"vnye"* was the practice of living mentally, emotionally and intellectually outside the system, while physically stuck in place in the Soviet Union.⁵⁵ But the readers I talked to framed reading as a temporary escape. Reading was a pastime to, well, pass the time, and experience something different to their daily lives, which were typically "conformist."

Take the example of Snezhana, a native Muscovite who started reading Vonnegut in 1981 at the age of nineteen. (Today she is an educator and sociologist.) Shezhana described herself as living a sort of double life as a

---

⁵¹ Karen L. Ryan-Hayes, *Contemporary Russian Satire: A Genre Study* (Cambridge University Press, 2006), 15.
⁵² Alexander Vari, "Introduction: Escaping the Monotony of Everyday Life under Socialism," in *Socialist Escapes: Breaking Away from Ideology and Everyday Routine in Eastern Europe, 1945-1989*, ed. Cathleen M. Giustino, Catherine J. Plum, and Alexander Vari (Berghahn Books, 2013), 4.
⁵³ Fürst and McLellan, *Dropping Out of Socialism*.
⁵⁴ Some interviewees mentioned it was easier to find good books for purchase in rural areas than in cities. Viktoria, born in Soviet Ukraine, remembered that for his work her father frequently traveled to Ukrainian villages. There he would purchase "good books" that could not be found in cities. In this way the family accumulated a very respectable and large family library.
⁵⁵ Yurchak, *Everything Was Forever*, 126-57.

young adult during the early 1980s. She was a Komsomol (All-Union Leninist Young Communist League) organizer who worked at the regional Komsomol office (RaiKom) during the day. She took courses at a local institute in the evenings. She evaluated this "official" part of her existence as typical of a Soviet citizen during Stagnation. "Everything was very black and white—this is good and necessary and you have to do it." At the same time, however, Snezhana said her most poignant memories of that time include "other stuff that was interesting and fun." The "other stuff" included her love affair with a slightly older architecture student and hanging around with him and his friends. Snezhana described them as "borderline *neformaly*" (hippies) who "listened to jazz and read samizdat."

These young architects "practically forced her" to read Vonnegut. They discovered Mikhail Bulgakov's *Master and Margarita*, which they insisted on reading aloud to her, at the same time Vonnegut's writing entered their lives. Thus, Snezhana will forever associate Vonnegut and Bulgakov in her mind. Other Western writers she read at the time were Theodore Dreiser, John Galsworthy, and Jack London. Snezhana also recalled reading some samizdat Solzhenitsyn. A certain kind of science fiction appealed to her as well, "not the spaceship kind," but rather "social science fiction" like that of the Strugatsky brothers, the kind that explored "what might happen to people of the future."

Snezhana used the trope "living a double life" to describe her teenage years as a Komsomol organizer and student who hung out with "borderline hippies" and read Solzhenitsyn, Bulgakov, and Western literature in translation. But Snezhana did not perceive deep contradictions in these pastimes. She certainly did not narrate herself as having "checked out" of socialist society. Many of the Vonnegut fans I interviewed, unlike some members of the "last Soviet generation" described by Yurchak, did not really articulate themselves as having lived in an ideological space of "*vnye—*" simultaneously inside and outside of the system of late socialism. Yurchak described the "*vnye*" phenomenon as "deterritorialization of late Soviet culture, which was not a form of opposition to the system."[56] Instead, my interviewees took lessons and inspirations they found in Vonnegut's writing and applied them in ways relevant to their own experiences as young people living through the period of Stagnation.

At the same time, some interviewees expressed their fondness for Vonnegut's writing in terms of the questions it prompted about human nature, moral choices and free will. Vonnegut prompted reflections

---

[56] Yurchak, *Everything Was Forever*, 28.

about their own existence as young people feeling ground down by the dehumanizing machinations of an authoritarian state. Skorobogatov reminds us that Vonnegut's work came to the Soviet Union at just the time that "some of the country's leading scientists, including Andrei Sakharov and Andrei Tverdokhlebov, enlisted themselves as leaders of Russia's democratic movement."[57] On the heels of the Prague Spring in 1968, Sakharov had published his famous article "Thoughts on Progress, Peaceful Coexistence and Intellectual Freedom." He synthesized his arguments about the "dangers linked with the scientific-technical revolution" and what he called the "trinity of freedoms:" the freedom to obtain and distribute information; freedom for open-minded and fearless debate; and freedom from pressure by officialdom and prejudices.[58] The links that dissidents such as Sakharov drew between scientific and intellectual life and universal human rights, resonated with Vonnegut's writing. Skorobogatov argues:

> Around the same time that Sakharov wrote his article, other scientists were beginning to shed the widely held view that science and technology represented a panacea for society's many illnesses. Instead, they began to look for answers to questions about Russia's future in the technological age: how to reach that harmonious balance between man-made and machine-made production; how to maintain a centralized state without stifling innovation; how to maximize collective output without compromising an individual's physical and emotional wellbeing. Critical interest in Vonnegut's dystopian science fiction reflected this reversal in attitudes towards science and technology and the birth of a new concern with the welfare of the individual. On the dawn of the 1970s, technological and scientific utopias were giving way to the utopia of human rights.[59]

Several interviewees took up reading and other "escapist" but "questioning" habits in the wake of the Prague Spring, which disappointingly failed to produce any new freedoms or room for debate in the Soviet Union. Vonnegut readers were tuning into his humanism and sympathy for wayward souls and outcasts with one ear, and his critique of corrupt human morals and dehumanizing, abusive institutions with the other. Sakharov and other dissidents spoke into this conversation with eloquence and bravery, and Soviet readers took notice. As we will explore in Chapter 10, Vonnegut

---

[57] Skorobogatov, "Kurt Vonnegut," 48.
[58] Skorobogatov, "Kurt Vonnegut," 49–50.
[59] Skorobogatov, "Kurt Vonnegut," 50.

was already speaking out in defense of Soviet dissident writers, including Solzhenitsyn, Amalrik, Ginzburg, and others.

Kurt Vonnegut and the deficit effect

Just because Soviet citizens were in love with Vonnegut's books and read them widely, does not mean that Vonnegut's books in translation were easy to come by. In fact, the opposite was true. Soviet readers of Vonnegut experienced an ironic juxtaposition. They thoroughly enjoyed Vonnegut's critique of capitalism, with its overabundance of useless goods resulting in crass over-consumption, while themselves experiencing shortages of all manner of goods, including Vonnegut's books.

In her seminal book, *What Was Socialism, and What Comes Next?*, anthropologist Katherine Verdery builds on the groundbreaking work of economist János Kornai and his analysis of "actually existing socialism" as an economy of shortage. Verdery pinpoints the system of centralized planning as the weak spot that made socialism fall. Since everyone at every level of the bureaucracy hoarded materials and padded budgets in anticipation of not being able to fulfill "the plan" (quota) for production, in socialist economies there were widespread shortages.[60] People experienced shortages of all kinds of consumer goods, from shoes to trousers to typewriter ribbons to nail polish. Most central for our discussion, they experienced a deep shortage of books. One huge problem was a lack of paper. The ideological priority of the Soviet publishing industry was to push out millions of copies of Party publications and miscellaneous literature. There simply was no paper left with which to publish literary translations. In this situation, at one point Goskomizdat (The State Commission for Publishing) instated a requirement that citizens could only purchase belletristic literature if they brought in a certain amount of waste paper (*makulatura*, "literature fit for pulp") for recycling.[61] As Maurice Friedberg explained,

> In September 1974, government agencies announced that nine book titles would be printed in half a million copies each . . . . To obtain a copy of one of these, one would have to deliver to a storehouse twenty kilograms of scrap paper . . . . The list of books. . .[was] to lure Soviet

---

[60] Katherine Verdery, *What Was Socialism, and What Comes Next?* (Princeton University Press, 1996), 19–38.
[61] Walker, *Soviet Book Publishing*, 363.

citizens into collecting and hauling the heavy bundles of old newspapers, magazines, and unwanted volumes."[62]

According to literary scholar Konstantin Azadovsky, "Anything that was published and had the least bit of significance was 'in deficit.' It was simply unimaginable that you could ever buy a book in a bookstore. This was a characteristic trait of socialism, just like abundance was and is a trait of capitalism."[63] Indeed, in the 1960s and 1970s Soviet Union, popular titles, which were published in relatively small print runs, sold out at bookstores in a matter of hours. As Klaus Mehnert famously put it, there were "too many Russians [sic.] chasing too few books."[64] In 1978, Rita Rait wrote to Donald Fiene, "Our book-lovers have gone completely mad: as soon as a book is published, it's impossible to find it anywhere!!!! We really love to read, especially translations! And classics, of course!"[65]

In her letters to Fiene, Rait complained constantly that newspapers, journals, and books "flew off the shelves in five minutes." She had terrible trouble tracking down copies of the "thick journals" with her translations of Vonnegut. Rait became frustrated by Fiene's requests for newspaper clippings about Vonnegut, her translations, and so on. She tried to explain the "deficit" of printed materials to him.

> Thankfully I'm not giving up hope on seeing the collected Vonnegut [come out] in my lifetime; remember one thing: only "Cat's Cradle" came out as a separate book, and "Breakfast" and "Slaughterhouse" were printed in journals—and it's been rather impossible to publish them [in book form]—not because [readers] don't love Kurt, quite the contrary: yesterday at the theater the young actors [in the Soviet Army Theater adaptation of *Slaughterhouse-Five*] brought CLIPPINGS OF HIS NOVELS FROM THE JOURNALS and asked me to autograph [them]! All the issues where "Slaughterhouse" was printed have disappeared from all the libraries: at the TsTSA [Central Soviet Army Theater] youth are still teeming to the play, asking for encores, but somehow the publishing house still can't manage to publish the book.[66]

---

[62] Friedberg, *Decade of Euphoria*, 76.
[63] Email from Konstantin Azadovsky to author, April 14, 2020.
[64] Klaus Mehnert, *The Russians and Their Favorite Books* (Hoover Institution and Stanford University Press, 1983), 13–30.
[65] RRK to DMF, October 30, 1978, p. 1, DMFC, Box 4, Folder, 5, "Rait-Kovaleva, Rita. 1976–1982."
[66] RRK to DMF rec'd January 5, 1977, p. 2, DMFC, Box 4, Folder, 5, "Rait-Kovaleva, Rita. 1976–1982."

A year later, in 1978, Rait's translations of several of Vonnegut's novels were published as a collection by Artistic Literature. The 727-page volume included *Slaughterhouse-Five*, *Cat's Cradle*, *Breakfast of Champions*, and *God Bless You, Mr. Rosewater*. "50,000 copies—sold out the same day they hit the store."[67] Rita didn't even have published copies of everything of Vonnegut's she had translated. She wrote to Fiene, "It's a lot harder for me to get ahold of articles than for you: everything here disappears (*raskhoditsia*) so quickly that you don't have a chance to grab a book—even the one with your [own] translations. . ."[68] It was not until the next year, in 1979, that Rait could obtain copies of the 1978 collected volume she had translated. A friend of Rait's from Akademgorodok, a Siberian city nearly 2,000 miles from Moscow, was able to track down five copies of the book for Rita.[69]

In the socialist economy of shortage, there were certain shortage items—like books—that were used over and over. Books, even those printed on low-quality paper (which many were) could weather sustained use as people worked out creative systems for accessing, distributing, and redistributing them. At times, Soviet citizens could leverage their access to hard-to-get books to procure favors or goods and services. This was part of the Soviet "*blat*" economy, the "economy of favors," described so thoroughly and eloquently by sociologist Alena Ledeneva in *Russia's Economy of Favours: Blat, Networking and Informal Exchange*.[70] One such story is the following, as told by Rita Rait to Donald Fiene, who in turn relayed the story to Kurt Vonnegut:

> Rita told me a story reported by a librarian friend in Riga. A bathroom in the library developed serious plumbing problems. It was rotten to the core. The plumber came and just shook his head. While poking around behind panels and closets he came upon some tattered, discarded books. One of these was Cat's Cradle. The plumber showed the librarian the book, said he had been searching for it for five years. If she would give him the book, said the plumber, he would guarantee a repair job on the bathroom (with all new fixtures) that would last until the millennium. Of course he was given the book.[71]

---

[67] DMF to JK, April 12, 1979, DMFC, Box 4, Folder 1, "Klinkowitz, Jerome. 1976–1984."
[68] RRK to DMF, May 24, 1974, p. 1, DMFC, Box 4, Folder 3, "Rait-Kovaleva, Rita. 1963–1976."
[69] Kachan, "Her majesty."
[70] Alena Ledeneva, *Russia's Economy of Favours: Blat, Networking and Informal Exchange* (Cambridge University Press, 1998), 11–38.
[71] DMF to KV, September 16, 1978, p. 11, FIEN, Folder 4, "1978."

Michael Khmelnitsky reported another "*blat*"-like arrangement for obtaining Vonnegut in translation. "In the 1970s, when Vonnegut was selling like hot cakes, my father had to do electrical work as a favour in order to be able to buy the 1978 collection of translated novels; the book (once again, one in 50,000) was simply unobtainable."[72] There are surely more examples of barter and trading goods and services for access to hard-to-get books. During my research I heard about many ingenious strategies individuals and families devised to obtain, preserve, and share translations of foreign literature, Vonnegut included.

Several interviewees remembered how difficult it was to secure a subscription to *Foreign Literature*, even though the journal's print run was an impressive 700,000 copies in the early 1970s.[73] They recalled their parents "sharing" a subscription to the journal with other families or friends. These young peoples' personal experience of reading Vonnegut in *Foreign Literature* was one of "having to quickly read it and give it back."[74] Another technique for sharing "hot" translations published in journals like *Foreign Literature* was to disassemble each issue, pull out the most interesting sections or stories, and reassemble them by "sewing" the pages back together. Some relied on their own sewing skills, while others took the little volume to a "book binding shop." The result was a small homemade magazine that could be saved and/or passed around. These ersatz volumes might be a "greatest hits" compilation of favorite items from *Foreign Literature*, *Literary Gazette*, or *New World*. Or they might be a "one-stop" collection of one author's prose that had been published over several issues of the "thick journal." Nadia offered a vivid example.

> In the 1970s and 1980s my family was proud to have a subscription to the thick journals, including "Inostranka" [*Foreign Literature*]. At the end of the year, all the best stuff published that year would be ripped out of the journal, put into a separate collection, and sent off to a book binders. I still have two of these "homemade" volumes with two novels of Vonnegut at my dacha. A remembrance of those times.

Some "self-publishers" of these homemade collected volumes would create covers for the compilations, illustrating the contents. They might also include a makeshift Table of Contents, thus adding their own creative touches to the "re-publishing" process.

---

[72] Khmelnitsky, "Sex, Lies, and Red Tape," 134–5.
[73] Vishnevetskaia et al., "Genome of the Russian Soul."
[74] Author interview with "Ivan," May 11, 2020, electronic correspondence.

The fact that journals and books of translated foreign literature were hard to access may have been part of their charm. If something was in deficit, it must be worth reading. (As Leonid put it, "Forbidden fruit is sweet.") Most readers obtained such coveted books on the black market, signed up at local libraries in a long queue to reserve the journal, or borrowed the books from friends. Sometimes journals like *Foreign Literature* were accessible through one's workplace. Evangelina from Moscow recalled that her mother's workplace had a library, and employees could put their name in the very long queue to check out *Foreign Literature*. That is how young Evangelina got access to foreign literature, by picking up *Foreign Literature* when it was "lying around the house." Evangelina, who spent a lot of time in libraries as a girl, credited "really great librarians" with giving her excellent reading recommendations, including Vonnegut.

Some eager readers would travel long distances to purchase impossible-to-access books, which were sometimes easier to acquire in smaller cities and towns. Nataliya Shulga from the Ukrainian SSR recalled how in 1981 her husband traveled by train from Kyiv to Kishinev, the capital of the Moldovan SSR, to purchase a collected volume of Vonnegut novels and stories that had just been published there. It was impossible to find in Kyiv and he guessed correctly that if he acted quickly, he could score a copy of the book in Kishinev, the "source" city, which had a much smaller population that Kyiv. Once the coveted collected volume was acquired and hungrily read by Nataliya and her husband, they began to loan it out to friends under strict conditions. Nataliya insisted that friends who wanted to borrow the anthology leave their passport in her possession as insurance the book would be returned. "Otherwise people would steal it! It was a very rare book!" She estimates she loaned the book to at least thirty people.

A very few lucky readers, however, didn't even have to wait until translations of Vonnegut hit the presses to acquire and read them. One interviewee whose parents were a few degrees of separation "acquaintances" with Rita Rait, obtained page proofs of Rait's translations from friends—who had obtained them from Rita—before they were even published. Ironically, far from tearing people apart, the deficit of quality printed material brought people together around shared goals and interests. The deficits helped build a community of readers. By sharing books, by working so hard to find, read, and redistribute them, Soviet readers were also sharing a culture, and a lifestyle. By necessity, because the books were hard to get, reading Vonnegut in the 1970s and early 1980s in the USSR was a thoroughly social and interactive experience.

Vonnegut and other Western writers engendered communities of readers in the Soviet Union in other ways, too. Vonnegut's sui generis vocabulary, his "cultist language," was ready-made for binding his readers together. Vonnegut is full of literary memes that Soviet readers could extract and use in daily speech. Expressing "Vonnegutisms" provided "cool" social glue for readers.[75] One interviewee recalled how using "Vonnegutisms" was a signal that "you are one of us," along the lines of the communities of "*svoi*" ("our own") that developed within Soviet culture. As one interviewee explained, a person could utter a term or phrase from the Vonnegut oeuvre ("*takie dela*" (so it goes); "karass," "*Led*-9" (Ice-9)) and an appropriate response or understanding would signal the interlocutor's cultural progressiveness. Lack of understanding marked them as culturally backward. As one Leningrader recalled, the word "karass" was a kind of signal among people of his (university student) generation in the early 1970s. "If you said 'karass' and a person's eyes lit up, you knew he had read *Cat's Cradle*, and that's all you needed to know." Evangelina remembered how "Ice 9" became a central meme of an arctic expedition she took with friends in the early 1980s. Someone had left the pot of porridge outside the mess tent, and it took four hours to heat it up. From then on, for this group of friends, "porridge" was always "Ice 9."

Reading Vonnegut accomplished other forms of "social work" in the context of late socialism. Vonnegut fans the world over frequently imagine themselves as a member of Vonnegut's karass, and his readers in the Soviet Union were no different. But some applied their affinity for Vonnegut's books and his ideas in novel forms of outreach. They used Vonnegut to extend or enhance their own relationships with other important people in their lives. Snezhana, for example, fell in love with Vonnegut's writing in the early 1980s as a young adult. She connected intensely with some of the "real life advice" that Vonnegut offered in *Cat's Cradle*. These ideas became almost like her personal credo or even calling card. Snezhana recalled some of this powerful "real life advice." "It is PEOPLE who decide if an act is sacred, or profane, or taboo, or miraculous" (here she used the example of Boko-maru in *Cat's Cradle*). "Any religion or ideology can be invented, layered with rules and rituals, and become considered as 'sacred.'" That is, all religions and ideologies are socially constructed. After she read *Cat's Cradle* and *Sirens of Titan*, Snezhana could not fathom how she had managed to live her life to that point without those books. In an effort to enlighten others, specifically key romantic partners that came through her life, over the years she gave copies of *Cat's Cradle* to three different men. "I wanted them to experience the book as I had, and I thought it might help them understand me better, too." Snezhana identified so deeply with the tenets of *Cat's Cradle* (as she interpreted them),

[75] Hassan, *Contemporary American Literature*, 46.

that she imagined the book as a manifestation of her own fundamental moral and social convictions. By sharing the book with important people in her life, she felt she was sharing a part of her inner self. Snezhana insisted that *Cat's Cradle* was the only book she had gifted so "intentionally." One could also interpret Snezhana's practice as a sort of litmus test. If the intended partner did not appreciate Vonnegut, perhaps Snezhana's tentative investment in the new relationship was not really worth it.

Some Vonnegut devotees invested their own talents and imagination to become his co-creators. These super fans were seeking—and perhaps finding—a relationship with Vonnegut himself. Importantly, these creative endeavors of co-production were often collaborative projects that further solidified Vonnegut's community of readers. These are poignant examples of how socialist subjects carved out small communities of "*svoi*" (our own).

To illustrate, we can continue with the example of Nataliya Shulga from the Ukrainian SSR. When she was sixteen years old, Nataliya engaged deeply with Vonnegut's characters and scenarios from his books. She embarked on a kind of fan fiction project to imagine what these American characters might have looked like. Nataliya explored and condensed episodes and key tropes from across Vonnegut's oeuvre into a series of six original illustrations. She undertook this project with her friend Oleksandr Kotlyarevskyy. Nataliya's fellow art school and music school student, Oleksandr was just twelve years old. As Nataliya explained the project,

> [Vonnegut] inspired us as artists, right? His language, his heroes, all these fantasies. So as artists, we worked with the text and we discussed the text. . . . he was a multi-faceted author. . . . he stimulated your personal creativity . . . [That's] why each illustration . . . It's not just an illustration. It has a lot of text involved in that. It's not just one moment, it's a whole set of pages, or dream of Billy Pilgrim or Kilgore Trout, you know, so it's like a portrait of the hero, the way we try to imagine it for ourselves . . . So [Vonnegut] gave people some material to work with or think about and discuss.

Her and Oleksandr's families were close, Nataliya explained, because they were "part of the same pool of intelligentsia." Her and Oleksandr's parents and grandparents were steeped in mathematics and the hard sciences but were also distinguished musicians. Nataliya's parents, like many members of the Soviet intelligentsia, were able to amass an impressive home library, some 2,300 books, Nataliya estimated. Still, a lack of information about the United States made it difficult for the two Soviet teenagers to render accurate representations of characters and scenes in Vonnegut's books. One of the first drawings Nataliya and Oleksandr worked on included an American policeman. As we looked at the illustration together in 2020, Nataliya laughed that the "American" policeman she and Oleksandr had drawn looked something like a British bobby crossed with a German officer.

> This guy, a policeman, it was among the first [of our drawings]. Imagine, we don't have a single piece of information [about] how American policemen look like. We went through the libraries. We were searching through newspapers, through magazines, the magazine *Amerika*. We could not find a single photo about how American policemen look... And here we are... discussing, trying to come up with how American policemen should look like. So, it's a pure fantasy. And [now] you can compare how a real [American] policeman looked in 1977. He didn't look like that... we could find how British policemen looked, how German policemen looked, but because America was the number one enemy—there was nothing. The only thing we learned at school about Americans was that they hate us, and they kill Black people. That's it. Nothing else.

Here, Nataliya indexed one of the tropes through which Soviet citizens were conditioned through Soviet reporting and pervasive propaganda to view the United States through a lens of racial injustice.

Nataliya went on to explain that to consult the magazine *Amerika* she turned to her high school biology teacher, whose husband was an academician and member of the National Academy of Sciences. His books had been translated and published abroad, giving him access to hard currency. This allowed the couple to subscribe to the journals *Science*, *Nature*, and *Scientific American*, as well as the journal *Amerika*. Still, Nataliya found no pictures of American policemen in the *Amerika* journal. "There were photographs of some protesters but there was no policeman on the photograph. It was an anti-Vietnam War protest, but there were no policemen there... So, this one [our drawing of an American policeman] is pure fantasy, produced by the minds of kids sixteen and twelve years old."

Nataliya marveled that she and her friend Oleksandr were able, as artists, to collaboratively complete the illustration project, which included six detailed drawings. They used colored pencils of thirty-six different shades. "We really drew it together. It's also unusual, you know. Imagine, artists who do it together! They are all very egotistical and protective and stuff like that." Here Nataliya implied that there was something unusual or unique about Vonnegut's work that drew fellow creatives together in smooth collaboration. Oleksandr eventually completed the drawings, including the "pure fantasy"

English-German-"American" police officer, for his "diploma" project as a student at the art institute in Kyiv.[76]

On the one hand, the illustrations, and the stories behind them, reveal the limits of the collective construct Yurchak described as "the Imaginary West" in late socialism. "The Imaginary West" was the "diverse array of discourses, statements, products, objects, visual images, musical expressions, and linguistic constructions that were linked to the West by theme or by virtue of their origin of reference, and that circulated widely in late socialism."[77] The two teens went on a literal quest around the city of Kyiv for information about one particular aspect of American culture—what does an American policeman look like?—but came up empty-handed. Despite being children of the intelligentsia with access to musical, artistic, and literary educations, the two teenagers were unable to find a single picture or firsthand description of that most basic feature of American life: a cop.

On the other hand, the illustration project reveals the deep reach of global literature into Soviet life in the 1970s and 1980s. It highlights Vonnegut's impact on young readers in particular. Nataliya found Vonnegut's writing of deep and lasting relevance to her existence as a moral being, a "decent person in an indecent society." Nataliya and Oleksandr spent countless hours poring over Vonnegut's books and rendering key scenes, characters, and events based on their "fantasies" about life in the West and their own artistic sensibilities. Nataliya underscored the distance between the United States and the USSR, and the teens' inability to access certain kinds of information for the project. But she also emphasized the close bond she and Oleksandr formed as they created the drawings together. The two creators inspired one another and complemented each other's talents. The story of Nataliya and Oleksandr's drawings crystallizes how Vonnegut inspired young Soviet readers to activate, gauge, and exercise their own moral compasses as individuals in late socialist society. This resulted in personal soul-searching about "how one should live." It also led some fans to undertake co-creations with Vonnegut and other readers as they explored his ideas and shared them with others.

---

[76] Nataliya, who spent many years in the United States as a postdoctoral researcher, mailed high-quality color copies of the drawings to Vonnegut in 1995. The drawings, and correspondence between Nataliya and Vonnegut, are housed in the Kurt Vonnegut Papers at Indiana University's Lilly Library. This is just as Vonnegut had predicted, in a generous letter he sent to "Natalia Shulga, former Ukrainian, now World Citizen," dated Nov. 22, 1995: "What will become of Alexander's illustrations? They have already become particular treasures in my archives, and will one day repose in the library of some university." KV to Natalia Shulga, November 22, 1995, KVM, Box 1, Folder 12, "1995–1997." (Alexander is the Russian rendering of Oleksandr.)

[77] Yurchak, *Everything Was Forever*, 161.

Leonid and his flatmates were university students in Leningrad in the 1970s. They creatively engaged with Vonnegut's fabulations, including his "false religion," Bokononism. Their story provides another example of the vital forms of sociality that Vonnegut fans enacted during the period of Stagnation. The friends compiled all the tenets of the "false religion" of Bokononism from Vonnegut's various novels and typed them up into a "Primer." (See Figure 5.7) In their own samizdat operation, the students distributed copies of the Primer among friends. They thereby introduced other young people to Vonnegut's writing. In this way, translations of Vonnegut provided models for the creation of new cultural forms in the Soviet Russian context. A specific youth culture, however small, centered around a lexicon of Vonnegutisms, the ludicrous tenets of Bokonon, the "sociological" notions of karass and duprass, and so on.

Leonid explained further (and with an ironic tone) that reading Vonnegut as a university student was part of his "commune" experience. Leonid and his friends had graduated high school in 1968. They had watched the Prague Spring with hope that a similar opening might occur in the USSR. When the protests in Czechoslovakia were repressed, they were disappointed, and their mood turned sour. By 1972, Leonid and a friend were renting one room in a two-room apartment in Leningrad. University students gathered around the clock to hang out and discuss politics and literature. They began to call their quarters a "commune." While the young people did, in some ways lead a communal existence (e.g., sharing meals), they approached the idea of the "commune" ironically. They invoked the ideas of the anarchist communist Pyotr Kropotkin and poked fun at socialist slogans. A homemade banner on one wall of their room sarcastically lauded the "Definitive Third Year of the Five-Year Plan" (the young men were in their third year at university). After the failed Prague Spring, Leonid and his peers coped with disappointment and disillusionment by telling jokes and exercising irony. He recalled some pithy phrases from the Polish satirical writer Stanislaw Jerzy Lec that he and his friends repeated endlessly. "When smashing monuments, save the pedestals—they always come in handy." "Sometimes they close the windows to the world with newspapers." "Okay, so you broke through the wall with your head. What will you do in the neighboring cell?" Leonid explained that "Vonnegut was on that same side: irony and humor in all things, but at the same time the serious sayings of Bokonon. The first and second books of Bokonon, when you put them all together, you get a kind of truth, actually." The "publisher" of the students' 1973 samizdat "Book of Bokonon" was listed as "Kommunizdat," or "Commune Publ."

The "commune's" samizdat Bokonon Primer illustrates well how Vonnegut variously inspired the complex ethos of these university students in Leningrad. Leonid explained that his parents had bought him a typewriter so he could type his university thesis. Instead of completing his thesis, he and his friends (sitting in their rented room with the "Five Year Plan" banner on the wall) used the typewriter to type out the Books of Bokonon. This act of teen rebellion manifested the young people's profoundly ironic world view and their resistance to conform to expectations of "proper students." At the same time, Leonid insisted that he and his peers found meaning, "a kind of truth," in the teachings of Bokonon as fabricated by Vonnegut. He recalled some of these "truths" during our interview. "Unusual travel suggestions are dancing lessons from god." "All of the true things that I am about to tell you are shameless lies." When Leonid told me about the samizdat Books of Bokonon, I asked him if he still had it. He said he doubted it, but he went to search his bookshelves. Leonid returned with a folder containing the samizdat Book and exclaimed, "I did not expect to find it. You see, Bulgakov was right, manuscripts don't burn."

Making the familiar, strange, and Vonnegut's other affinities with Russian and Soviet literature

In some way Vonnegut's writing was ideal for foreign readerships, due to his tendency to explain the obvious. As Fiene noted, quoting Vishnevsky, a Soviet reviewer of *Breakfast of Champions*, Vonnegut uses a technique "of 'making strange,' the common objects he draws and describes. That is, he describes a revolver, for instance, as though it were unfamiliar to the reader, calling it 'a tool whose only purpose was to make holes in human beings.'"[78] For an American readership already familiar with the objects Vonnegut over-explains, this technique does the anthropological work of "making the familiar, strange." It helps readers to critically distance themselves from the obvious—from the standard, or "normal"—to question the "natural" order of things. For a foreign readership, explaining the obvious worked to acquaint readers with unfamiliar contexts, phenomena, and consumer objects. Lauren Leighton mused in a letter to Donald Fiene.

> KV always explains things—it is his way to explain the obvious—what a cereal is, what is the name of a drink and why—things that everyone knows. Poor Rita R-K—her Russian readers must think she inserts them

---

[78] Fiene, "American Dissident," 271.

for their benefit. Or on the other hand, it is almost as if KV wrote this way because he has a foreign readership in mind.[79]

Rita Rait, however, did not want the Soviet readership to feel like total strangers to Vonnegut's world. She frequently "domesticated" his text for readers of Russian. She sometimes substituted culturally familiar equivalents for specific "Americanalia" in Vonnegut's texts. In *Cat's Cradle* Rait substituted the more familiar "soccer" for American football, though the English and Russian words are both *"futbol."* In *Breakfast of Champions* "professional golfers" became "play on a team," and "a hamburger" became "chopped beefsteak" (*kotletka*).[80] Rait's translated texts often included footnotes to explain to Soviet readers the personages, places, and historical events with which Soviet readers may not have been familiar (e.g., Jonah and the whale, Betsy Ross, Houdini, *The Wonderful Wizard of Oz, A Tale of Two Cities,* the city of Springfield, Illinois).[81] In her quest to explain things for Soviet readers, Rait at times actively worked *against* Vonnegut's technique of making the familiar, strange for his readers. Her translator's task, to the contrary, was to make the strange, familiar for the Soviet reader.

In a general sense, though, Vonnegut's overall tendency for "strange making" of familiar situations and objects was a technique with which readers of Russian literature would have been familiar. Russian writers, especially Leo Tolstoy, used the technique of *"ostranenie"* (estrangement or defamiliarization), which served to "make strange" common objects and situations. *Ostranenie* was a term coined by the great Russian formalist Viktor Shklovskii (who was a friend of Rita Rait's—they spent time together at Soviet writers' retreats. See Figure 5.8). Shklovskii first used the term *ostranenie* in his 1929 essay *"Iskusstvo kak priem"* (Art as device). He described the technique as putting "common objects and situations under a new light to produce an ontological estrangement, thus provoking, on the part of the reader, a vision *(videnie)* of the object and not its recognition (*uznavanie*)."[82]

One famous example of Tolstoy's use of *ostranenie* is his description of an opera in *War and Peace.* "Pieces of painted cardboard and oddly dressed men and women who moved, spoke and sang strangely in a patch of blazing light." The purpose of *ostranenie*, in both Tolstoy's and Vonnegut's hands,

---

[79] LGL to DMF, November 6, 1979, p. 1, DMFC, Box 4, Folder 1, "Leighton, Lauren Gray. 1978-1979."
[80] Khmelnitsky, "Sex, Lies, and Red Tape," 257–8.
[81] Khmelnitsky, "Sex, Lies, and Red Tape," 259–60.
[82] Ilaria Sicari, "Paratext as Weapon: The Role of Soviet Criticism in the Cultural Cold War," *Translation and Interpreting Studies* 15, no. 3 (2020): 368, ftn. 20. https://doi.org/10.1075/tis.20081.sic

was to offer a social critique. For Vonnegut, the fondness for *ostranenie* may have developed from his years of studying anthropology at the University of Chicago. "Making the familiar, strange" is a fundamental tenet in cultural anthropology that helps scholars develop critical distance from the so-called "natural" order of things. Soviet readers, having read Tolstoy and other giants of Russian literature, would have recognized this familiar technique in Vonnegut's writing. However, Soviet literary critics could not openly identify Vonnegut as practicing *ostranenie*. References to the "dangerous" and taboo Russian Formalism were disallowed. Instead, critics performed a "terminological inversion." They framed Vonnegut's technique as one of "alienation" (*otchuzhdenie*), an eminently politically correct theoretical term from the very core of Marxist-Leninist theory.[83] (This is why Vishnevsky, the critic Fiene cited for the insight about "strange making" in Vonnegut's work, did not use the term "*ostranenie*" to make his observation.)[84]

Vonnegut shared other similarities with the great Russian, Ukrainian, Kyrgyz, Abkhazian, and other writers with whom Soviet readers were familiar. Donald Fiene outlines Vonnegut's "affinities" with such writers in the scholarly article he wrote about Vonnegut in the USSR, "Kurt Vonnegut as an American Dissident: His Popularity in the Soviet Union and His Affinities with Russian Literature." Vonnegut's most obvious indebtedness to Soviet literature was one he himself acknowledged. For the plot of *Player Piano*, Vonnegut admitted, he "cheerfully ripped off the plot of *Brave New World* [by Aldous Huxley], whose plot had been cheerfully ripped off from Eugene Zamiatin's *We*."[85] In his treatment, Fiene points out some possible comparisons between Vonnegut and Leo Tolstoy. Both used the technique of *ostranenie* as a vehicle for social criticism. Vonnegut also shared a few thematic touchpoints with Maxim Gorky. Painting in broad strokes, Fiene describes Vonnegut as "a man possessed by the messianic, the apocalyptic, the eschatological, and the chiliastic—preoccupations so obviously 'Russian' in character. . .that there is really no need here to cite parallels."[86]

In the end, though, Fiene is most convinced by Vonnegut's similarities to Dostoevsky. He finds numerous parallels between the two writers, including their sentimentality, their shared preoccupation with psychosis, and the "tendency of both to dramatize in a single work of fiction one major idea, often exaggerating it to an extreme limit." Because both writers attended

---

[83] Sicari, "Paratext as weapon," 369.
[84] S. Vishnevsky, "Kogda real'nost' absurdna. . ." [When reality is absurd], *Inostrannaia literatura* 2 (1975): 209–13.
[85] Kurt Vonnegut, "Playboy Interview," in *Wampeters, Foma & Granfalloons (Opinions)* (Delta Publishing Co., 1974), 261.
[86] Fiene, "American Dissident," 272.

continuously to basic moral questions in human relationships, Fiene additionally suggests they could be called "philosophical novelists." Fiene pulls examples from various Vonnegut plotlines and characters to suggest parallels with Dostoevsky's works, most notably *The Brothers Karamazov*. He also, however, notes many things that separated Dostoevsky from Vonnegut, especially their different takes on the existence of God. Dostoevsky was a firm and reverent believer in a traditional God, and Vonnegut was an atheistic humanist.[87]

For his part, though, Vonnegut himself rarely named Dostoevsky—or any other Russian or Soviet author—as a major influence. He did mention Dostoevsky in *Slaughterhouse-Five* and *Breakfast of Champions*. When Fiene and Vonnegut first met in London in October 1972, Vonnegut named Dostoevsky as his favorite Russian writer.[88] He promptly stopped doing so, however, when Fiene warned him that Rita Rait (who Vonnegut was due to meet for the first time in Paris the next day) abhorred Dostoevsky. Rita called Dostoevsky a veritable sadist and much preferred Chekhov.[89] From then on, Vonnegut tended to name two authors as his favorite "Russian" writers—Chekhov, and Gogol (who was actually Ukrainian-born).[90] He told a Russian émigré interviewer in 1987, "For me, the most humane writer, the one I would most like to resemble—is Chekhov. And the writer, who was as funny as possible—Gogol." After expressing his admiration for Solzhenitsyn and a few other contemporary Russian writers, Vonnegut concluded, "I can tell you that my favorite book from an earlier period of literature is *Master and Margarita*."[91]

None of the Vonnegut devotees from the former Soviet Union I spoke with drew parallels between Vonnegut and Dostoevsky, Gogol, or Chekhov. They did, however, talk a lot about Vonnegut's similarity to Bulgakov (on the example of *Master and Margarita* in particular). Parallels include both authors' time-and-space-jumping techniques, reference to coincidences or chance occurrences that shaped the course of history (but which may not

---

[87] Fiene, "American Dissident," 274–7. Some would argue that although Dostoevsky very much wanted to believe in God, he never really managed to do so.
[88] DMF to LGL, December 21, 1978, p. 4, DMFC, Box 4, Folder 1, "Leighton, Lauren Gray. 1978–1979."
[89] Rait found Dostoevsky "cruel and unjust . . . when he writes with RELISH about all sorts of 'nasty' things . . . Dostoevsky has NO compassion, only in "The IDIOT" does he portray a real person . . . and he made him an IDIOT . . ." RRK to DMF, March 26, 1977, p. 3, DMFC, Box 4, Folder 5, "Rait-Kovaleva, Rita. 1976–1982."
[90] See Oleh S. Ilnytzkyj, *Nikolai Gogol: Ukrainian Writer in the Empire: A Study in Identity* (De Gruyter, 2024), which argues for Gogol's identity as a Ukrainian Russian-language imperial writer.
[91] Mirchev, "Interview with Kurt Vonnegut," 274–7.

have been coincidences at all), and their overall quasi-magical realist style. In this regard, Soviet readers also frequently lined Vonnegut up alongside another foreign favorite—Gabriel García-Márquez.

Readers in the Soviet Union read Vonnegut for many of the same reasons people in the United States or any other country read Vonnegut. To connect with his characters. To try and see themselves in those characters. To ponder existential questions. To have a good laugh, including at themselves. To temporarily escape reality. But Soviet readers had their own, local and unique, reasons for gobbling up Vonnegut's books in quick succession. Reading foreign literature, including Vonnegut, was a window to the West. It was a peek into a strange and only sometimes wonderful world of capitalism and the "imagined West." With her masterful and sometimes "domesticating" translations of Vonnegut, Rita Rait made this experience one of pure joy and adventure. In their particular socio-political milieu, Soviet readers could pretty much find what they wanted to find in Vonnegut's prose. They found philosophical debate, sci-fi fantasies, cultural and political commentary, and linguistic backflips. In spite of the censor with his green pen, they found a little bit of raciness, pseudo-vulgarity, and almost even, sex. As Nadia remembered, "I can still recall (I was a young girl then, a star student, raised on the stories of Turgenev. . .) the drawing of an anus and a written description of that orifice [in *Breakfast of Champions*]. Until that point in my life I had never encountered such a 'discovery!'"

Tracking down hard-to-acquire foreign literature in translation, including Kurt Vonnegut, was a quest for Soviet citizens during Stagnation. The quest's reward was an intense period of feverish reading, since most books were lent for a maximum of forty-eight or seventy-two hours. The quest's reward was access to a social network of like-minded readers, all hungry for new imaginings, a new language, and maybe a new way of life. Reading Vonnegut and other foreign authors gave people in a society with restrictions on freedom of speech a fresh shared vocabulary to discuss morality and the meaning of life. As Raisa explained, "In my family we talked in citations— citations from Russian and Soviet literature." Vonnegut fans could take this one step further and communicate in the strange and secret language of Bokonon, or Tralfalmadore, or Dwayne Hoover or Eliot Rosewater.

Herein lies the important work of cultural diplomacy that Vonnegut's books accomplished in the hands of Soviet readers. They could recognize themselves in Vonnegut's characters. If this was true, if Soviet readers could understand these Americans in Vonnegut's books (these strange humans, deeply flawed but loveable), and even see themselves in these characters, perhaps Cold War animosities—the rifts between the Soviet and American peoples—were not unbridgeable, after all.

Plate 5.1 A scene from *Breakfast of Champions*. "[The driver told Kilgore Trout], 'I was arrested for speeding down there [in Libertyville, Georgia] ... I had some words with the policeman, and he put me in jail.'" By Nataliya Shulga and Oleksandr Kotlyarevskyy. Courtesy Lilly Library, Indiana University, Bloomington, Indiana.

Plate 5.2 A scene from *Slaughterhouse-Five*. "Billy was working on this letter in the basement rumpus room of his empty house . . ." By Nataliya Shulga and Oleksandr Kotlyarevskyy. Courtesy Lilly Library, Indiana University, Bloomington, Indiana.

Plate 5.3 A scene from *Slaughterhouse-Five*. "One time on maneuvers Billy was playing 'A Mighty Fortress Is Our God,' with music by Johann Sebastian Bach and words by Martin Luther . . ." By Nataliya Shulga and Oleksandr Kotlyarevskyy. Courtesy Lilly Library, Indiana University, Bloomington, Indiana.

Plate 5.4 A scene from *Breakfast of Champions*. "The words in the book, incidentally, were about life on a dying planet named Lingo-Three, whose inhabitants resembled American automobiles . . ." By Nataliya Shulga and Oleksandr Kotlyarevskyy. Courtesy Lilly Library, Indiana University, Bloomington, Indiana.

Plate 5.5 A scene from *Breakfast of Champions*. " . . . Kilgore Trout found himself standing on the shoulder of the Interstate . . . There were no bridges across the creek. He would have to wade." By Nataliya Shulga and Oleksandr Kotlyarevskyy. Courtesy Lilly Library, Indiana University, Bloomington, Indiana.

Plate 5.6 A scene from *God Bless You, Mr. Rosewater*. "Trout, the author of eighty-seven paperback books, was a very poor man and unknown outside the science fiction field." By Nataliya Shulga and Oleksandr Kotlyarevskyy. Courtesy Lilly Library, Indiana University, Bloomington, Indiana.

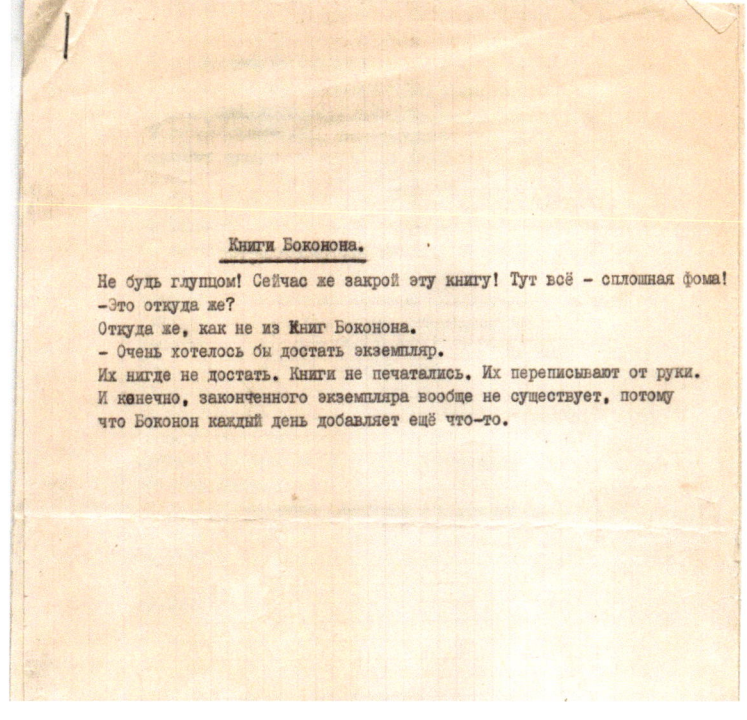

Plate 5.7 A samizdat Russian-language "Book of Bokonon" that synthesizes all references to Bokononism across Vonnegut's novels. Leningrad, 1973. Used with permission.

Plate 5.8 Viktor Shklovskii and Rita Rait, Yalta, 1963. Courtesy Russian State Archive of Literature and Art, Fond 3112, opus 1, item 270, document 3.

6

Interlude

Five Days in Moscow, 1974

In late October 1974, a functionary named T. Kudriavtseva submitted a report to the Foreign Commission of the Writers' Union of the USSR. She called it "A Report on Kurt Vonnegut's trip to the USSR October 14–19, 1974."[1] Kudriavtseva was Vonnegut's official interpreter during his trip to Moscow. That she submitted this report signals that the Writers' Union probably issued Vonnegut his invitation to visit the Soviet Union. But "interpreter" Kudriavtseva undoubtedly had another role, one that was hidden from Vonnegut. Her job was to watch and report on his every move. In fact, Kudriavtseva was instructed to cultivate Vonnegut as a Soviet ally. Rita Rait thoroughly thwarted this venture with her characteristic flair.

Kudriavtseva's report is almost the only *official* evidence available in Russia about Vonnegut's 1974 trip to Moscow. He left few other traces, save a few photographs taken by his partner (in life and in travel) Jill Krementz. These photos ended up in some archives and personal collections of people he met. Vonnegut left no traces at the Ukraina hotel where he and Krementz stayed, at least no traces anyone was willing to share with an American anthropologist. As far as official records go, we must rely on his interpreter-handler's official (if witty) report.

> In accordance with the telegram received from our embassy in Washington, the editors of the journal *Inostrannaia literatura* [*Foreign Literature*] invited K. Vonnegut to remain [in the USSR] for a[nother] week as a guest of the journal after the end of his tourist trip. An itinerary for his 10-day stay in the USSR was drawn up, including a three-day trip to Tbilisi [in the Soviet Republic of Georgia], meetings with readers of the Library of *Foreign Literature*, with MGU [Moscow State University] students, with publishers and journals "*Vokrug sveta*," [Around the world] "*Nauka i zhizn*," [Science and life] "*Foreign Literature*," the

[1] RGALI 631/27/1692.

publisher "Progress," with the All-Union agency for authors' rights [*po avtorskim pravam*], and with the writers' and poets' unions. I delivered the editor-in-chief's invitation to Vonnegut during dinner at the hotel "Ukraina," where he was staying. Vonnegut thanked me, and citing Jill's affairs, said that he likely would not be able to stay. The next day at the journal *Foreign Literature* he announced that he could not accept the invitation, since work obligations awaited Jill in Rome.

Kudriavtseva went on to describe Vonnegut's activities during the five-day visit.

In spite of the brevity of Vonnegut's stay in Moscow, we nevertheless were able to show him some things and organize several meetings. In addition to driving around the city, seeing the Kremlin, the house-museum of A.P. Chekhov, and Novodevichy cemetery, and also the Arkhangel'skoe estate museum, Kurt Vonnegut met with American Studies specialists at the Library of *Foreign Literature*, with a collective from the journal "*Rovesnik*" [Fellow] and was the guest of A. Voznesensky, and also saw the ballet Anna Karenina at the Bol'shoi Theatre. The leadership of the journal "*Foreign Literature*" organized a lunch for him, which was attended by K.M. Simonov and first secretary Flem of the U.S. Embassy in Moscow with his wife.

Kudriavtseva recounted some encouraging aspects of Vonnegut's visit. She underscored the positive things he said about the Soviet Union during the trip.

In his conversations with me Vonnegut heartily underlined how glad he is that he is being published in the Soviet Union, and in such good translation. He liked Moscow very much, and he liked the hotel where he stayed. He found the meeting with A. Voznesensky especially interesting, where the discussion was on artistic method, on the selection of themes, and the citizenship responsibilities [*grazhdanstvennosti*] of the writer.

At the meeting at the Library of I.L. [Foreign Literature] Vonnegut expressed his deep gratitude to the Soviet army for ridding the world of fascism (at the end of the war Vonnegut was in Dresden and was a witness to the firebombing that befell the city).

Kudriavtseva complained that Rita Rait-Kovaleva thwarted her attempts to cultivate Vonnegut. She also noted the caution and skepticism of his "co-traveler," Jill Krementz.

At the same time, influenced by his co-traveler, who approached everything with much prejudice and skepticism, which became especially obvious after she and Vonnegut spent the evening with his translator R. Rait-Kovaleva, Vonnegut was very nervous about his honorarium. The evening before his departure he received the honorarium and deposited it on his bank-book, which he left in the custody of R. Rait-Kovaleva. This is explained by the fact that she successfully convinced Vonnegut, how poor translators are here and how little they earn. ~~When Vonnegut handed her his last 20 rubles before his departure at the airport, she took them gratefully, saying "it would cover taxis for her until the end of the month."~~[2]

Overall R. Rait conducted herself ~~very~~ strangely. She talked Vonnegut out of all the meetings that were proposed to him, such that the few things we managed to organize were done, so to speak, "in spite of" [her]. No one from the journal [Foreign Literature] was invited to a single meeting at her home—and Vonnegut was at her home on the 15th, 16th, and 17th, after the meeting with Voznesensky. During the visits at the journal "I.L." [Foreign Literature] and during the lunch in honor of Vonnegut, R. Rait—in the presence of representatives of the U.S. Embassy—complained that even though she had been invited by several American universities, she had not yet been in the USA, and she asked, what kind of invitation was required, for her to travel [there]? No doubt, in the near future such an invitation from Vonnegut will arrive for her.

Curiously, during the first evening of his visit in Moscow Vonnegut asked me a lot of questions: how does one become a member of the writers' Union; according to what principle does Litfond work; why don't Soviet writers join Pen-club; how are authors paid; and is it still possible to see the exhibition of abstractionists at Izmailova [museum]?[3]

In response to the latter question, I said that it [the exhibition] had already closed due to a lack of interest in such "works." R. Rait immediately interjected and said, that nothing of the sort: the exhibition had been so popular that visitors couldn't get close to the paintings.

---

[2] Strikethroughs in the original.
[3] Reference is to "the biggest officially sanctioned show of modern and unorthodox art by Soviet painters since the avant-garde movement . . . in the nineteen-twenties," which drew an estimated 10,000 viewers. Hedrick Smith, "A Soviet Artist Displaying his Work at the 'Second Fall Outdoor Art Show' Near Izmailovo Park in Moscow," *The New York Times*, September 30, 1974, p. 73, accessed November 22, 2023. https://www.nytimes.com/1974/09/30/archives/excited-russians-crowd-modern-art-show-russians-some-excited-others.html.

> I will not offer many other such analogic utterances, I will just say that during the last days [of his visit] Vonnegut did not ask me any questions at all.

After outlining these difficulties, Kudriavtseva ended her report on a rather unconvincing positive note.

> He [Vonnegut] left thoroughly satisfied with his visit to Moscow, but still with a cloud in his head, which due to the brevity of his visit and the energetic interference of R. Rait, who thwarted attempts to make contact with him,—it was not possible to completely dispel. Nevertheless, I am convinced, that much can be accomplished here—we just have to show him more of our life and our people.

Kudriavtseva's account of Kurt Vonnegut and Jill Krementz's five days in Moscow is a remarkable document. Contrary to expectations of such an official report, the style was not dry and obtuse. Kudriavtseva was a witty observer of the complex dynamics at play in Vonnegut's unofficial visit to the USSR. We see the Americans Vonnegut and Krementz pulled this way and that, roped into several formal events and meetings. With Rita's help, they struck a balance and spent plenty of quality time with Rita and her friends, at her home, away from the watchful eye of the interpreter-handler. For Vonnegut, and for Rait, finances were a core concern of the visit. Vonnegut wanted to collect the money he'd earned from the publication of his books in the USSR. Rait wanted to help him spend it. Soviet officials were not indifferent to the question of money, but the ideological stakes were of more pressing concern. Kudriavtseva and other functionaries Vonnegut encountered were to show him the very best of the Soviet system. They had to frame the Writers' Union, publishing, and everyday life in the rosiest of terms. Rita Rait's purpose, conversely, was to tell it to Kurt straight. She pointed out flaws in the design and showed him a good time hanging out with true artists.

A major tension in the visit's planning and execution was a tug of war between two modes of travel: official and unofficial, curated and casual. Vonnegut and Krementz journeyed to the USSR on tourist visas. Their express intention was to spend their time informally, "to avoid endless and pooping official receptions," as Kurt wrote to a friend in New York.[4] The trip was arranged through Intourist, whose helpful staff insisted Vonnegut

---

[4] KV to LV, June 7, 1974, BA-RRK.

add Leningrad and Kyiv to his itinerary.[5] But he stood firm. His only destination in the USSR was Moscow, specifically to visit Rita. Then he and Jill would continue to Rome.[6] Leaning on Krementz's work obligations in Rome, Vonnegut turned down a proposed ten-day extension to their USSR excursion. It would have taken the couple to Tbilisi for three days. And it would have added a slew of literary-focused meetings in Moscow to their itinerary.

On one hand, Rita considered her quest to protect Kurt and Jill from the bureaucrats most successful. "It was a feverish four-and-a-half days, and all the time they were trying to 'wrench' them from me and subject them to all sorts of boring people, but they [Kurt and Jill] held firm, and we spent nearly the entire time together."[7] But upon reflection, Rita worried that Kurt had not enjoyed his visit to Moscow as much as he might have, despite her best efforts. Because "here he is SO WELL KNOWN and SO BELOVED," he was subjected to various "boring meetings," including a really "boring breakfast." Even though Rita had vigorously tried to protect him, she was not able to completely sequester him from "his devotees." Rita believed that "all the official editorial mess [*sueta*]" had sabotaged Kurt's trip.[8]

Vonnegut was glad to have met Voznesensky and Simonov. He later described them as "the only distinguished writers I shook hands with" during the trip.[9] Vonnegut characterized everyone else he met at the formal events as "cultural hacks mostly."[10] He was likely unimpressed by the big reception at the Hotel Ukraina that drew staff from the U.S. and Soviet Embassies to meet him. An uneven highlight of the official itinerary was an outing Rita Rait was allowed to join—the ballet *Anna Karenina* at the Bol'shoi Theatre. Rita described the performance later to a friend in New York. She expressed sympathy for "poor 50-year-old Maya Plisetskaya," who had "no business dancing in that ballet." "Only a couple of times she was Maya, Miracle of Nature, and the rest of the time she lay on the floor and wept."[11]

Of course, Kudriavtseva's report could not capture certain important details of Vonnegut's trip. For instance, how his friends—especially Rita

---

[5] RRK to DMF, July 24, 1974, pp. 2–3, DMFC, Box 4, Folder 2, "Rait-Kovaleva, Rita. 1968–1978."
[6] KV to Don Farber, October 3, 1974. KVM, Box 1, Folder 26, "1974, Oct.-Dec."
[7] RRK to SG, December 23, 1974, p. 1, BA- RRK.
[8] RRK to DMF, June 6, 1975, DMFC, Box 4, Folder 2, "Rait-Kovaleva, Rita. 1968–1978."
[9] Wakefield, *Kurt Vonnegut—Letters*, 221. In 1977, Vonnegut wrote of Voznesensky, who as a sanctioned and favored writer of the Soviet establishment was frequently in New York: "He has beautiful Italian clothes—and gets to fuck just about anybody he likes, I expect." KV to DF, November 11, 1977, FIEN, Folder 3, "1977."
[10] Wakefield, *Kurt Vonnegut—Letters*, 221.
[11] RRK to LV, October 21, 1974, BA-RRK.

Rait—carefully prepared for his trip. Or how Vonnegut spent his "down time" in Moscow when released from the "endless and pooping official receptions." Rita Rait was excited, but extremely nervous, in the days, months, and even years leading up to the visit. As usual, she took matters into her own capable hands. She enlisted the assistance of an impressive roster of friends and colleagues across the globe, all in the interest of bringing "our dear Kurt" to the Soviet capital.

Rita prepares

Even before she met Vonnegut in Paris in October 1972, Rait was already encouraging him to visit Moscow. She coached him to request an invitation from the Foreign Commission of the Writers' Union. Rita helpfully advised Kurt to ask if he could pay for his stay in Moscow from royalties from the Soviet translations of his writing. If he asked politely, Rita assured him, the Writers' Union would help.[12] Unluckily for Kurt, Soviet officials declined this sensible scheme. Instead of paying for travel, hotel, and other expenses in rubles they had lying around in Soviet bank accounts, foreign visitors like Vonnegut were compelled to contribute to the Soviet economy. This was accomplished by injecting valuable U.S. dollars into the system.[13]

Rita was more worried about Vonnegut coloring within the lines during his visit. She didn't want him making a poor impression by saying the wrong things. His books (in her translation!) could be rejected for publication. Vonnegut could become *persona non grata* for the literary establishment. Rita shared these fears in several letters she wrote in summer and fall 1974 as Vonnegut's trip drew closer. By July, Rita had nearly finished her translation of *Breakfast of Champions*. She dreaded any ideological mishaps during Vonnegut's trip. "Just one slip of the tongue while he's here, and all would be kaput!"[14] She did not want Vonnegut's reputation sullied. And she did not want her hard work translating *Breakfast* to be for naught.

Rait articulated slightly different concerns about Vonnegut's impending visit in a letter to her friend Sara Ginsburg in New York.

> Of course now I'm all worked up: I'm waiting for dear Kurt Vonnegut.... Tell Lenochka [Lynn Visson] that the telegram made a

---

[12] DMF to KV, August 30, 1972, FEIN, Folder 1, "1972–1974."
[13] Wakefield, *Kurt Vonnegut—Letters*, 218.
[14] RRK to DMF, July 22, 1974, p. 2, DMFC, Box 4, Folder 2, "Rait-Kovaleva, Rita. 1968–1978."

WONDERFUL IMPRESSION and everybody here is trying to do ALL THEY CAN for Kurt's visit—extend it, get him an honorarium, and so on. I DON'T KNOW what will come of this: but I don't think he'll be disappointed and [I'm hopeful] his trip will be pleasant and even USEFUL for him.

Yesterday I got a letter from him in which he promised to bring some record albums—good ones, I hope!—and he also asks: "What else would delight you?" How could I possibly explain to him that if it were possible to get warm shoes for me and for Margaritka—we could warm our paws all winter long...you have to spend so much time and energy here to acquire anything, and I CANNOT GO ANYWHERE... I'm writing to Lenochka about this too, and about other little things, such as typewriter ribbon (OLIVETTI and OLIMPIIA—13 mm.)

Underneath this, Rita handwrote, using two different pens: "my size—37 Margaritka's—38." Just in case, she clarified, "(feet)."[15]

Rita had multiple concerns. Would Kurt enjoy the visit, and would it be "useful" for him? How might she tactfully ask him to bring some much needed and hard-to-get consumer goods for her and her daughter, especially shoes and typewriter ribbon? This tension—Rait as Vonnegut's protector, but also his supplicant, in the Soviet shortage economy—is a "red thread" throughout their long and lively relationship.

Although Vonnegut was no doubt looking forward to seeing Rita Rait again, he had an additional preoccupation. He wanted copyright acknowledgment, and royalties, for the translation and publication of his works in the USSR, especially *Breakfast of Champions*. It was his first book published after the Soviet Union entered the UCC, which mandated the payment of standard royalty fees to foreign authors. Kurt's impending travel to Moscow was announced to the American community of writers in the October 1974 issue of the *PENewsletter*.

> Kurt Vonnegut will be visiting the USSR Oct. 13-19 to see his translator, Rita Rait.... While in the USSR, Vonnegut will check into his royalties account there. Just before his departure, his publishers, Seymour Lawrence (Delacorte), learned that the Soviet journal, Literarnaya [*sic*.] Gazeta had published two chapters from Breakfast of Champions without permission, acknowledgment of copyright, or payment of fees to Vonnegut. In response to a query by the publishers to the Soviet journal,

---

[15] RRK to SG, no date, BA-RRK.

Editor O. Prudkov replied that under the provisions of Soviet civil legislation, "reproduction in newspapers of the works of literature, the sciences and the arts in the original and in the translation, is permitted without the author's consent and without the payment of royalties. . . . Our newspaper is not going to pay the requested royalty." Vonnegut, his publishers, and American P.E.N. are challenging the Soviet ruling.[16]

Three nights in Moscow

Vonnegut's interpreter-handler T. Kudriavtseva reported that Vonnegut was at Rita Rait's home on the evenings of October 15th, 16th, and 17th. No one from the journal *Foreign Literature* was invited to join the informal soirees. Who *had* Kurt Vonnegut and Jill Krementz spent their evenings with at Rita Rait's apartment? An undisputed highlight of the trip was time spent with the collective of young theater directors and composers who were in the process of staging a theater adaptation of *Slaughterhouse-Five*. (For details see Chapter 7.) As Fiene explained to Professor Lauren Leighton, "Vonnegut was in the USSR during the writing of the play and met all the authors, composers, the director and many of the actors . . ."[17] Rita herself reflected,

> I think he enjoyed his visit and our young friends—the director, actors, scholars, etc. They are the wonderful leading, smart young ENLIGHTENERS (as Diderot and D'Alambert said in the 18th century), and very honest, good people. It's the group that is staging here in Moscow the dramatization (*instsenirovka*) based on Slaughterhouse-Five—I keep asking Kurt if he'll come for the premier in September.[18]

Another evening, Kurt came to Rita's place without Jill (who was resting at the hotel), and the trio sat quietly—Rita, Kurt, and Margarita.[19]

Rait was convinced that Kurt's most memorable meeting was with Mikhail Levitin. He was the young theater director whose career she'd helped resurrect by suggesting he stage a theater adaptation of *Slaughterhouse-Five*, "The Wanderings of Billy Pilgrim." Levitin—as well as composer Vladimir Dashkevich and poet and dramatist Yulii Kim—met Kurt Vonnegut and Jill

---

[16] "Vonnegut to Russia," *American PENewsletter*, October 16, 1974.
[17] DMF to LGL, September 26, 1978, DMFC, Box 4, Folder 1, "Leighton, Lauren Gray. 1978–1979."
[18] RRK to SG, April 6, 1975, p. 1, BA-RRK.
[19] RRK to LV, October 21, 1974, p. 2, BA-RRK.

Krementz at Rita Rait's apartment on October 15th, Margarita Kovaleva's birthday. Rita recalled, "Kurt and Jill arrived like Santa Claus with a suitcase full of books, records, jeans, and ball point pens.... It was really funny when Margaritka dressed up like a cowboy and Kurt got down on his knees to roll up her britches..."[20]

Jill Krementz documented the evening in several spirited photos. One shows Vonnegut sitting in front of a small table, surrounded by Rait, Kim, Levitin and Dashkevich. They are smiling and rapt with attention. Vonnegut is holding forth. He balances a cigarette between the index and middle fingers of his right hand, and gesticulates with his left fist held in the air. Vonnegut is smiling, too. Rita shared copies of the photo with her young friends, and it circulated quite widely in literary and artistic circles in the Soviet Union. Vonnegut brought home a storied memento as well. Rita gave him an ornate silver candlestick, an heirloom passed to her by a friend during the Second World War. Vonnegut's granddaughter Nellie treasures the candlestick to this day.

Rita reflects

Rita Rait wrote to friends and colleagues to debrief about Vonnegut's Moscow visit. The letters fill in details about the "endless and pooping" receptions and other official events to which Vonnegut was subjected. Konstantin Simonov was the secretary of the Soviet Writers' Union. Like Vonnegut, he was a veteran of the Second World War who wrote on war themes. Vonnegut's meeting with Simonov took place at the "Dom Literatov," the House of Littérateurs. Jill Krementz photographed Vonnegut and Simonov during an informal smoke break. Simonov is holding a pipe, and Vonnegut a cigarette. Simonov, in profile, is speaking and grinning at Vonnegut. Vonnegut looks straight into the camera, chin slightly lifted, with a smile on his face. His pinstriped pants are hitched halfway up his shins to reveal long dark socks and soft, slightly scuffed suede shoes.[21]

---

[20] RRK to LV, October 21, 1974, p. 1, BA-RRK.
[21] In an article about his interview with Vonnegut in 1982, Sergei Dovlatov noted: "In front of us sits a curly-haired, lanky man in a shapeless sweater and soft suede shoes. This is how all American students used to dress twenty years ago." Sergei Dovlatov, "... Poetomu budet voina: Beseda s Kurtom Vonnegutom" [Therefore there will be war: Conversation with Kurt Vonnegut], *Novyi Amerikanets* [New American] 101 (15–January 21, 1982): 24–5. Article is reproduced at https://dzen.ru/media/azibuli/dovlatov-beseduet-s-vonnegutom-5d81a730027a1500ad140c3b.

Figure 6.1 Candlestick presented to Kurt Vonnegut in Moscow in 1974 by Rita Rait-Kovaleva. Photograph by Nanette Vonnegut. Used with permission.

Rita's letters provided heartwarming insights about Vonnegut's visit to the Library of *Foreign Literature* for a chat with readers. Vonnegut began by saying, "First thing, please give my regards to the Red Army, which liberated me from the German camp." He laughed, then added, "And thereby made an invaluable contribution to literature!"[22] After that,

[22] RRK to SG, April 6, 1975, BA-RRK.

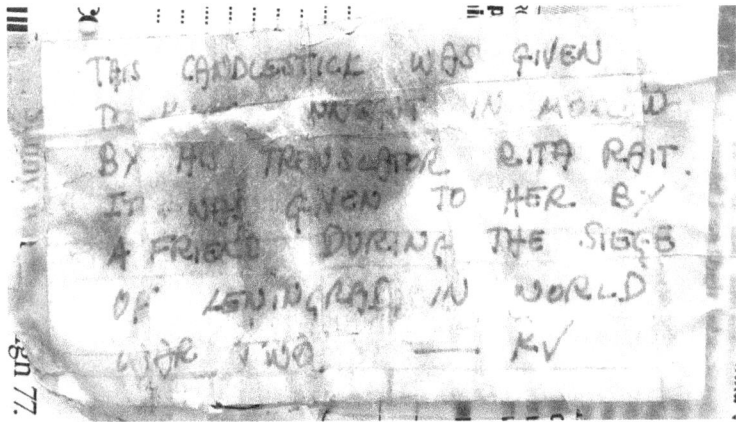

Figure 6.2 Kurt Vonnegut's inscription on a candlestick presented to him in Moscow in 1974 by Rita Rait-Kovaleva. Photograph by Nanette Vonnegut. Used with permission.

"Everybody laughed, and applauded, and the boring grey ice was broken . . ."[23] Rita seemed alternately worried and elated by Vonnegut's visit to Moscow. The opportunity to spend time with Vonnegut in person (her second of three such meetings during her lifetime) undoubtedly confirmed for her his greatness as a writer and human being. She found him generous, patient, and kind. A year later, Rita wrote to an American friend, "I think of Kurt fondly, always, I really love him and Jill. Their photo is on my desk."[24]

Kurt reflects

Vonnegut's own preoccupations with the visit were twofold. First, he tried to "behave himself." He didn't want to compromise Rita or damage his own reputation as an acceptable foreign writer in the USSR. Second, he was frustrated and slightly amused. The Soviets had paid him some royalties for publishing translations of his books (and this before the USSR signed onto the ICC). However, there was no real way for Vonnegut to withdraw and spend the funds.

> I was able, incidentally, to open a savings account over there. Crazy
> I have about two-thousand rubles on deposit, earning two per cent a

---

[23] RRK to LV, October 21, 1974, BA-RRK.
[24] RRK to LV, October 1975, no date, BA-RRK.

year. I gather that several favored writers have been allowed to do this. As far as I know, I am the first American. Also: they were petrified by the international copyright agreement, because they thought foreign literature would cost them so much. They are now elated, because writers are charging them on the average less than half of what they expected to pay. Please don't publish this fact anywhere. I am advising my brother writers only in conversations.[25] It wasn't Rita who told me this news, but people might assume that it was and want to hurt her in some way.[26]

As we learned from Vonnegut's interpreter-handler Kudriavtseva, he had transferred the 2,000 rubles to a "bank book" (bank account). He left it "in the custody" of Rita Rait.

Vonnegut's papers contain few personal reflections about the writers, theater folk, and other culturally minded comrades he met in Moscow. He did, however, enjoy telling the story of how one Soviet citizen had correctly interpreted his "vibe" as a writer. ". . . I spoke once at the Lenin Library in Moscow, and there were scholars in American Literature there in an amphitheatre, and a professor stood up at the end of my speech and said—'I think I can characterise you,' and I said—'Fine, what is that?' And he said—'you are a writer in favour of democracy', and I said 'yes, that's about right.'"[27]

Vonnegut did not want his trip to result in any negative repercussions for Rita.

> Rita is generally fine, and I was glad to learn from the guys at the Moscow bureau of the NYTimes that they all know how important she is culturally. They were eager to meet this legendary person, and I was delighted to perform the introductions.... I behaved politely. The theory is that my good behavior would do a lot to loosen up travel restrictions on Rita.... That country sure is full of envy, by the way. Simonov drank a toast to this effect: "We all argue as to who our finest novelist is, who our finest poet is, who our finest playwright is—but nobody argues about who our finest translator is. It is indisputably Rita Rait." The faces of other translators at the table shriveled as though drenched with lemon juice.[28]

---

[25] This was not actually the case; Vonnegut published this information in "Writers, Vonnegut, and the USSR," *American PENewsletter*, November 17, 1974, pp. 1–2.
[26] Wakefield, *Kurt Vonnegut—Letters*, 220.
[27] Transcript of "Christopher Bigsby in conversation with Kurt Vonnegut," Kaleidoscope broadcast, September 20, 1984, interviewer Christopher Bigsby, program producer Carroll Moore, KVM, Box 2, Folder 19, "1984, Mar.-Dec." The event may have been at the *Foreign Literature* Library. Nowhere else is the Lenin Library documented as part of Vonnegut's itinerary.
[28] Wakefield, *Kurt Vonnegut—Letters*, 220–1.

Figure 6.3 Kurt Vonnegut photographed with Konstantin Simonov by Jill Krementz in Moscow, October 1974. All rights reserved. Photograph by Jill Krementz, used with permission. Courtesy Russian State Archive of Literature and Art, Fond 2871, opus 3, item 354, document 17.

"The usual state of affairs—SNAFU—continues"

In 1966, Donald Fiene began a multi-years-long campaign to bring Rita Rait to the United States. He envisioned a university lecture tour on literature and translation in the Soviet Union. Fiene enlisted support from faculty and administrative colleagues at Indiana University, the University of Michigan, and the University of Tennessee. He also tapped a prominent former official in the State Department. On the U.S. side, it was smooth sailing. Fiene obtained official invitations and secured the necessary funds for Rita's travel. The challenge, however, was convincing the Soviet government, specifically the gatekeepers at the Writers' Union, to approve her exit visa.

After Vonnegut met Rita in Paris in 1972, Fiene and Vonnegut started working together in earnest to get her to the United States. They spent countless hours and reams of paper on the endeavor, this time soliciting additional invitations from the University of Iowa and Harvard. It was all for naught, and the Soviets prohibited *any* writers or translators from visiting the United States on official business. Vonnegut sent a laconic letter to Fiene.

> Dear Don—What can we do? We raised the money. We mobilized the academic community to welcome Rita. An invitation was sent to her more than six weeks ago. It was either lost or intercepted, most likely intercepted. . . . [Paul] Engle told me on the phone that the cultural attaché in Washington had told him that there weren't going to be ANY exchanges of writers and translators during the coming year. So there we are, and fuck all.[29]

The great hope was that Kurt's successful visit to Moscow in 1974 would shake loose some goodwill and enable Rita to make the U.S. tour. Unfortunately for everyone involved, including university students in the great states of Tennessee, Michigan, Iowa, and Indiana who would have benefited from the wisdom of Rita Rait, this was not to be.

In 1975 and 1976, renewed efforts by Fiene, Vonnegut, and various university administrators to bring Rita to the United States all ended in disappointment. By March 1976, Rita realized she would probably never travel to America. She declared that "they" [the Writers' Union bureaucrats] were not "holding" her or preventing her from going to the United States. They simply were not *helping* her. "They say, 'First we'll send who WE want to, and later on . . .' But 'later' is a very broad concept, and I have no time

---

[29] Wakefield, *Kurt Vonnegut—Letters*, 200–1.

to wait . . ." Perhaps, Rita hoped, she could instead travel to Dresden, in the GDR, and meet Kurt there. "I could write a wonderful article about it in *Novyi Mir*," she mused.³⁰

Rita's scheme to meet Vonnegut in Poland also hit a dead end.³¹ It was not just that the Soviet state deemed Rita "unfit" for travel to the capitalist West. She couldn't even travel to friendly socialist states in East-Central Europe. In her letters of late 1976 and early 1977 Rita avoided criticizing her colleagues at the Writers' Union. She insisted that no one was "preventing" her from traveling to the United States. She was wrong.

In March 1977, Writers' Union official Georgii Markov sent a telegram to the University of Tennessee's Chancellor Jack E. Reese. "In response to your telegram the Union of Writers of the USSR informs [you] that a trip by Rita Rait to the USA is not foreseen in our plan for the current year STOP At the end of last year we sent a representative delegation of translators of American literature to the USA STOP At present our efforts are directed toward preparing a mutual Soviet-American meeting of writers STOP."³² In a letter to Vonnegut, Rita reported that the head of the Writers' Union, Professor Nikolai Fedorenko, had disallowed her travel. "Everything was held up on the W. [Writers'] Union level . . . alas . . . the usual state of affairs— SNAFU—continues."³³

These official protestations, Rita averred, and all that business about her travel not being part of the "plan," were just a ruse. They were flimflam, cover up for the real reason the authorities denied her the gift of international travel: Jealousy. She wrote to Fiene, "By the way, don't publish about me—you have no idea how much ridiculous jealousy any superfluous 'promotion' of my humble work evokes! That's why the trip plans were stymied."³⁴ Mikhail Levitin said much the same when I interviewed him in 2019. "Once I accompanied Rita to a Writers' Union meeting. It was awful. The air crackled with tension. To be honest, Rita was rude, she was haughty. They didn't like her. Everyone was jealous of Rita, her monumental talent."

A smashing success in other ways, Vonnegut's five well-behaved days in Moscow failed to earn Rita even the shortest break from what Kurt sarcastically called "the workers' paradise." In fact, the very successful visit—

---

[30] RRK to DMF, rec'd March 4, 1976, p. 1, DMFC, Box 4, Folder 5, "Rait-Kovaleva, Rita. 1976–1982."
[31] RRK to SG, December 23, 1974, p. 1, BA-RRK.
[32] Telegram from Georgii Markov to Jack E. Reese, March 17, 1977, DMFC, Box 4, Folder 5, "Rait-Kovaleva, Rita. 1976–1982."
[33] RRK to KV, March 13, 1977, DMFC, Box 4, Folder 5, "Rait-Kovaleva, Rita. 1976–1982."
[34] RRK to DMF, March 26, 1977, p. 4, DMFC, Box 4, Folder 5, "Rait-Kovaleva, Rita. 1976–1982."

orchestrated, choreographed, and monitored so assiduously by Rita—may have increased the ire with which many colleagues and higher-ups regarded her. That she'd taught Kurt and Jill how to avoid boring official engagements made her an even bigger thorn in the Writers' Union's side. It didn't help matters that "she ha[d] made friends with too many of the wrong people," as Vonnegut put it.[35]

The Writers' Union's excuses for why Rita could not travel got more ridiculous with time. Much later, in 1984, Vonnegut was thrilled when Rita won Columbia University's Thornton Wilder Prize for a distinguished foreign translator of American literature. He had nominated her, with support from Arthur Miller and John Updike, and she was expected to travel to New York to receive the prize in person.[36] When she didn't show, Writers' Union officials, clearly desperate for an excuse, circulated a false rumor. They said Rita had broken her arm and was unable to travel. Rita did accept the Thornton Wilder Prize, not in New York at Columbia University, but at a sparsely attended ceremony at the Union of Writers headquarters in Moscow. Vonnegut relayed in a letter to Don Fiene what he'd heard from a colleague. "'The story about her [Rita] having broken her arm, and having been, hence, unable to come here for the prize, was repeated, although it is obviously untrue. There were blunter messages, such as, 'Her traveling days are over.'"[37] Rita Rait was never let out of the USSR again.

One can imagine the scene at the Soviet Writers' Union's muted ceremony. Tiny Rita, eighty-five years old and supposedly too infirm to travel, muscles her way to the front of the room to claim her prize. Far from being a broken old woman, "she is all business, as usual, and as indestructible as a self-sealing gastank," to quote Vonnegut's description of Rita in 1982.[38] She drops some names, mentions what a pity it is that she couldn't travel to New York to accept her prize, and see her friends Kurt Vonnegut and John Updike. Rita brags about several exciting translation projects she is working on, new works of foreign literature she can't wait to share with the Soviet reading public. Maybe a play or two in the works, as well. She picks up the Thornton Wilder prize, a fancy framed certificate nearly as tall as Rita. She stuffs the envelope with prize money into her catch-all handbag. I imagine her spinning around, glancing at the few Writers' Union "colleagues" gathered there, their faces once again shriveled in envy.[39] Rita then sails out of the room, head held high.

---

[35] Wakefield, *Kurt Vonnegut—Letters*, 219.
[36] KV to DMF, January 9, 1984, FIEN, Folder 6, "1981–1984."
[37] KV to DMF, August 22, 1984, FIEN, Folder 6, "1981–1984."
[38] KV to DMF, October 16, 1982, FIEN, Folder 6, "1981–1984."
[39] Wakefield, *Kurt Vonnegut—Letters*, 220–1.

7

The Wanderings of Billy Pilgrim, or Cinderella in the Concentration Camp

In 1975–6, a theater adaptation of Rita Rait's translation of *Slaughterhouse-Five* was staged under the title *The Wanderings of Billy Pilgrim*. This was another fascinating episode of Kurt Vonnegut's love affair with the Soviet Union.[1] Or rather, the Soviet Union's love affair with *him*. The musical was remarkable not only for its content and form but also for the unusual and unexpected venue where it was performed—The Soviet Army Theater in Moscow. Intriguing, too, was the offstage drama surrounding the production, which was held up numerous times for personal and ideological reasons.

The story of the *Wanderings of Billy Pilgrim* is a raucous one. It involves entanglements of personality, artistry, and ideology. *The Wanderings of Billy Pilgrim* offers several vantage points and unique insights into how the Soviet cultural establishment engaged with Vonnegut's work. We can explore what he meant for artistic communities, how Soviet audiences interpreted him, and the congruities and tensions between these different experiences of Vonnegut in the Soviet 1970s.

Act One: preparation

We do not know all the details of the decision to adapt *Slaughterhouse-Five* for the stage in Moscow in 1975. Given what we know about Rita Rait, it is not too outlandish to propose that taking *Slaughterhouse-Five* to the Soviet stage may have been Rita's idea. She loved and promoted Vonnegut's work, she had stature as a *grande dame* of the Soviet cultural and literary scene, and she frequently mentored young artists. She had translated several musical comedies and plays. She even wrote a few herself.

In the late 1930s, Rait translated J. B. Priestley's *Cornelius*, and in 1940 she translated Clifford Odets' *Golden Boy*. Rita later co-wrote a musical comedy,

---

[1] Mikhail Levitin's director's notes indicate the original title was to be *The Adventures of Billy Pilgrim*, later changed to *The Wanderings of Billy Pilgrim*. RGALI 3092/1/7/20ob.

THE WANDERINGS OF BILLY PILGRIM (AKA CINDERELLA)

MAIN (OFFSTAGE) PLAYERS:

Kurt Vonnegut, b. 1922, author of Slaughterhouse-Five
Mikhail Levitin, b. 1945, director
Mart Kitaev, b. 1925, scenographer
Mark Rozovskii, b. 1937, writer
"Iu. Mikhailov," (AKA Iulii Kim), b. 1936, writer
Vladimir Dashkevich, b. 1934, composer
Rita Rait, b. 1898, translator, unofficial PR manager for Kurt Vonnegut, wheel-greaser, international liaison, critic
Donald Fiene, b. 1930, scholar, critic, matchmaker, unofficial agent for Kurt Vonnegut

Figure 7.1 Imaginary playbill for *The Wanderings of Billy Pilgrim*, Moscow, 1975–6. By Jenny El-Shamy. Used with permission.

Familiar Stranger, with Abram Argo, who she endearingly called "Argosha."[2] In 1945, she wrote a libretto for a play with R. Kreitner entitled *O Suzannah, or an Extremely Complex Case*.[3] In 1971, Rait's translation of Heinrich Böll's

---

[2] RRK to Abram Markovich Argo, May 12, 1967, RGALI 1784/1/354.
[3] RGALI 3337/1/9.

Green Bird was staged to great acclaim at the Pushkin Theater in Leningrad. In a letter to Lev Kopelev, Rita called her translation "simply hooliganish!!!"[4]

Rait frequently took young artists under her wing. Mikhail Levitin, aged thirty when he directed the stage adaptation of *Slaughterhouse-Five*, was one of her favorites. Years later, Levitin reflected on Rita's masterful translation of *Slaughterhouse-Five*, a book he said was "impossible to stage."[5] Levitin recalled Rita's incomparable translation of Cinderella's lament after the clock struck midnight. Rait rendered "Goodness me, the clock has struck—Alackday, and fuck my luck" as *"B'iut chasy, iadrena mat', Nado s bala mne bezhat'!"* (In English, this is roughly, "The clock has struck, holy shit! Away from the ball I must git!") Levitin mused, "That's how Rita, the great Rita Rait, translated it. Or maybe she made it up herself, hoping that I, her little 'rootlet' (*koreshek*) (that's what she called me), would decide to stage it."[6]

Rita's "rootlet" did agree to stage an adaptation, and Rita played a major role in all stages of the production. As usual, she saw herself as a defender of Vonnegut and his artistic intentions. Rait was very concerned that the play should go forward in *her* translation, under *her* guidance. Letters to colleagues stressed her efforts to ensure that everything be rendered "like he [Kurt] wrote it." Under her supervision, Rita pledged, *The Wanderings of Billy Pilgrim* would be a "VONNEGUTIAN" production. She "HERSELF HAD SELECTED very good people—young, and talented" to produce the play.[7] These included writer Vladimir Dashkevich and the poet, bard, and dissident Iulii Kim. Kim could not publish under his own name, so he was masked as "Iu. Mikhailov" on the playbill.[8]

In memoirs and interviews, Levitin often refers to *The Wanderings of Billy Pilgrim* simply as "*Zolushka*" (Cinderella), after the operetta at the center of the play (see below). Dear "Cinderella" may have saved Levitin's theater career. Levitin had a promising start in the Moscow theater world at the tender age of twenty-three when he directed *How Mr. Mockinpott was Cured of his Sufferings* at the renowned Taganka Theater in 1969. But then

---

[4] RRK to Lev Kopelev, January 9, 1971, RGALI 2549/1/351/85-6.
[5] Mikhail Levitin, *Posle liubvi: Roman o professii* [After Love: A book about a profession] (AST, 2019), 53.
[6] Levitin, *After Love*, 53.
[7] RRK to DMF, June 6, 1975, DMFC, Box 4, "Rait-Kovaleva, Rita. 1968–1978."
[8] Because of his participation in the dissident movement, Kim was forced to quit his job as a schoolteacher and stop performing his songs on stage (Iulii Kim, "Kak ia stal dramaturgom" [How I Became a Dramatist], in *Mozaika zhizni* [Mosaic of Life] (Eksmo-Press, 1999), 117). He was allowed to continue writing for the stage and screen but had to adopt a pseudonym since his name was "poisoned." Kim believes everyone knew Iu. Mikhailov was actually Iulii Kim, but by writing under a pseudonym "the form was maintained." Author interview with Iulii Kim, September 30, 2023, telephone.

he alternately fell in, and mostly out, of favor with those who made decisions about Soviet theater.[9] When the opportunity to work on *Billy Pilgrim* came to him in 1974, he was out of work and getting desperate. Levitin had not staged a single play during 1972–3.

Levitin was motivated to stage a theatrical adaptation of *Slaughterhouse-Five* for several reasons. First, he was drawn to Vonnegut's writing. "People could understand him. He wrote simply and directly. His writing was like a dance on the page, a strange dance by someone who can't dance very well." Further, Levitin sensed a magical chemistry between Vonnegut's composition and Rait's translation, or, as he put it, Rita's "co-composition. "She was a co-author, that's exactly what she was, not a translator, but a co-author."

Levitin recalled walking into the Soviet Army Theater before work on *Billy Pilgrim* began and being completely overwhelmed by the gargantuan space. He called it a "Colosseum in the shape of a star," referring to the five-pointed red star emblematic of the Soviet Army. Levitin struck a deal with the performance hall where *Billy Pilgrim* would be staged.

> I walked into the hall when it was empty, and looked around. I said quietly: "Dear, dear stage. Gift me some work. They are banning me everywhere; please do this for me. What would it cost you? You defended the homeland, what would it cost you to defend one more person?" And the stage answered. Only the supplicant could hear it, but she answered. It was hard for her, too, to live with all those drums and trumpets. She needed humanity (*chelovechnosti*).[10]

It was this thread of "humanity" that bound together Rait, Vonnegut, and the young Levitin. Rita Rait called Levitin a "young Meyerhold." This signaled her high regard for Levitin, since Vsevolod Meyerhold was her favorite theater director. Rait frequently discussed Meyerhold in her letters to friends. He was a bold, innovative director famous for his "biomechanics" method of training performers, his radically stylized productions, and his hot temper. Accused of "formalism" for his supposed focus on form over political message, Meyerhold was arrested, tortured, and executed in 1939. Rita probably knew Meyerhold from her days working with Mayakovsky. She had translated Mayakovsky's play *Mystery Bouffe* into German, and Meyerhold had staged the play in Russian.

One can imagine parallels between Meyerhold's productions and Levitin's *Billy Pilgrim*, particularly the "Cinderella" "one-act song opera" which by all accounts was a carnivalesque affair. The entire operetta was crystallized in

---

[9] The staging of *Mr. Mackinpott* was based on the play by German writer Peter Weiss.
[10] Levitin, *After Love*, 55.

Figure 7.2 Entrance to the Soviet Army Theater, Moscow, with the billboard of the stage play *The Wanderings of Billy Pilgrim* after Kurt Vonnegut, directed by Mikhail Levitin, March 19, 1976. Courtesy of Sputnik.

Figure 7.3 Soviet Army Theater, Moscow, October 2019. Photograph by Sarah D. Phillips.

Rita's terrific rendering of that couplet, back-translated as "The clock has struck, holy shit! Away from the ball I must git!" Levitin believed he had assembled a uniquely talented and dedicated cast. "It's hard to act with your heart in that [Soviet Army] theater. But all my actors did so.... We allowed them to see us defenseless and wonderful in the Army theater. We weren't afraid they would close us [down]. Truth doesn't care what fools think of her..."[11] In Donald Fiene's papers there is a long, handwritten list of "all the actors and people associated with the play."[12] There are fifty-two names on the list, including the "incomparable" Liubov' Ivanovna Dobrzhanskaia, who Levitin said had never heard of him before rehearsals began. Dobrzhanskaia sat out five rehearsals until she was sure she trusted Levitin and wanted to take part in the play. Finally convinced, she rose from her seat and tersely dismissed the understudy. "Sit down, Olia. I'll take it from here."[13]

Mark Rozovsky and Iulii Kim (the latter writing under the pseudonym Iu. Mikhailov) received equal credit as the play's writers. But Kim claims to have done the bulk of the writing, and very quickly, too. According to Kim, soon after Rozovsky started writing the play (working from Rita Rait's book translation) he was called away to a project in the Russian Far East.

---

[11] Levitin, *After Love*, 57.
[12] DFM to RRK, January 6, 1976, DMFC, Box 4, "Rait-Kovaleva, Rita. 1968–1978." It is unclear where Donald Fiene acquired this cast list. Perhaps he copied it from a draft playbill in December 1975 when he attended two dress rehearsals of the play.
[13] Levitin, *After Love*, 56.

Kim's initial assignment had been to work on the "Cinderella" scene, the "play within a play" that constituted the musical heart of the production. He quickly completed this task. With time getting short, and Rozovsky still away, it fell to Kim to complete the play's script. Kim says he churned out the script in just two short weeks. Thus, said Kim when I interviewed him in 2023, "I went from being a little bit of a co-author, to being a *bona fide* co-author."

Intermission: it's falling apart

As discussed in the previous Interlude, there was real danger that the Soviet Army Theater staging of *The Wanderings of Billy Pilgrim* would never see the light of day. Production was stalled several times during 1975, for a host of political-ideological reasons. The premiere of *Billy Pilgrim* was planned for October 1974 to coincide with Kurt Vonnegut's visit to Moscow. As it happened, the play did not even go into dress rehearsals until November 20, 1975.[14]

All the offstage actors in the drama to launch *Billy Pilgrim* performed balancing acts to ensure the production was not squashed by the "ideology police" of the Soviet theater world. According to Iulii Kim, for rehearsals to begin, the play's script required approval from the first level of censors—the "military censors" of the Soviet Army. (This was because the play would be produced at the Soviet Army Theater.) These military censors gave the thumbs up. Next, the play went to the second level of censors—the Moscow city committee of the Communist Party, namely the official who answered for theaters and their repertoires. This official rejected the play because of what Kim called its "not very Soviet ideology." "The idea that the fate of the world depends on the *entire* world—the Soviet Union *and* the United States—that's what is called 'pacifism.' And that [Moscow] city committee of the [Communist] Party really couldn't stand this pacifism, especially that guy who was in charge of the theaters."[15]

The minute the word "pacifism" was audibly associated with the *Billy Pilgrim* play, action ground to a halt. (We might imagine Levitin, Kim, Rait, and all the others frozen on stage, mid-sentence, their mouths dropped open.) To publish Kurt Vonnegut's writing in the USSR, to keep him acceptable, and now, to stage a play based on his book, Vonnegut's allies had to pretend that Kurt was *not* what he very much was: a pacifist.

[14] Letter from RRK to Konstantin Simonov, November 20, 1975, RGALI 1814/9/2100/2, 4.
[15] Author interview with Iulii Kim, September 30, 2023, telephone.

Pacifism is the "principled opposition to war and violence as a means of settling disputes." Pacifism "may entail the belief that the waging of war by a state and the participation in war by an individual are absolutely wrong, under any circumstances."[16] Pacifism (which we will explore in relation to Soviet reception of Vonnegut's oeuvre in more detail in Chapter 9), was incompatible with official Soviet foreign policy after the Second World War. The cornerstone of that policy was the so-called "struggle for peace" (*borba za mir*). The roots of this discourse developed into Khrushchev's policy of "peaceful coexistence," which had profound impact on cultural policy in the USSR.[17] As Maria Cristina Galmarini summarizes, the "struggle for peace" was part of the Soviet bloc's propaganda efforts. As such, it "worked as a discursive weapon in the arsenal of Cold War politics."[18] Juliane Fürst details how the Soviet peace campaign was a solidarity-making exercise at home shot through with "anti-Westernism and Soviet/Russian glorification."[19] It was directed most forcefully to harness the collective energies of Soviet youth. Called the "Peace movement" at home, the policy was cynically dubbed the Soviet "Peace offensive" in the West.

The *borba za mir* narrative cloaked Soviet intentions under the banner of "Peace." But the narrative had *borba* (struggle, both ideological and armed) baked into it. There were "just" struggles and wars and "unjust" struggles and wars. Only struggles and wars on behalf of the proletariat, to overthrow capitalism, counted as "just." Such struggles were inevitable and necessary. Thus, Soviet foreign policy was fundamentally incompatible with pacifism, and any "outed" pacifist was fundamentally incompatible with the Soviet Union and its people. Writers, artists, and other cultural figures from foreign countries could only be sanctioned cultural ambassadors to the USSR if they were engaged in—or at least not obviously opposed to—the struggle for peace.

Billy Pilgrim's reputation was besmirched by the label of "pacifism." The production's future was in peril. Rita Rait was desperate to convince the authorities that Vonnegut was *not* a pacifist, but an "anti-fascist," engaged in the "struggle for peace." To carry off this ruse, she enlisted the help of powerful cultural figures to dress Vonnegut up as a "fighter in the struggle for peace." This adventure is a good example of how icons of Western literature

---

[16] Britannica.com: https://www.britannica.com/topic/pacifism
[17] Gilburd, *To See Paris*, 33.
[18] Maria Cristina Galmarini, *Ambassadors of Social Progress: A History of International Blind Activism in the Cold War* (Northern Illinois University Press, 2024), 138.
[19] Juliane Fürst, *Stalin's Last Generation: Soviet Post-War Youth and the Emergence of Mature Socialism* (Oxford University Press, 2010), 88.

and culture were smuggled into the Soviet Union by cultural mediators like Rita Rait who knew the ideological ropes and how to swing on them.

On February 4, 1975, Rita Rait wrote a desperate letter to the respected writer Konstantin Simonov, who had met Vonnegut in Moscow in October 1974. Simonov was a distinguished poet, playwright, novelist and correspondent famous for his service in the Second World War and war-themed writing. He held impressive posts in the Soviet literary world as on and off editor-in-chief of *New World* and *Literary Gazette*. Simonov was currently secretary of the Union of Writers of the USSR. Rita's letter noted how much Kurt had enjoyed his meeting with the director, scenarist, and composer for the *Billy Pilgrim* play when he'd visited Moscow. Rait then explained her dilemma.

> Even though the play was approved by PUR [the Political Directorate of the Soviet Army] and they liked it at the Ministry of Culture—Mark Rozovsky did the stage adaptation, Mikhail Levitin is the producer/director, and Vl. Dashkevich the composer—every now and then a doleful little editorial voice of some "doubter" sounds off: "Doesn't the play contain—it's terrible to say—PACIFISM?" So we decided to ask you—just because a play conveys the author's own experience of the senseless bombing of a peaceful city, does that necessarily mean it's "Pacifist?"

> Vonnegut is a terrific writer, and the play is outstanding. I'm glad he has taken a liking to us, and I don't want to disappoint him. YOU KNOW YOURSELF HOW DIFFICULT IT IS RIGHT NOW TO MAINTAIN FRIENDSHIPS WITH the major WESTERN writers. The staging of a play from one of Vonnegut's best novels will definitely be good for our foreign connections. *The struggle for peace is not pacifism at all* [emphasis added] and this has to be said.

> Dear Konstantin Mikhailovich, if you could write a few words to ME, saying that the novel is good and the play should also be interesting—we will all be very grateful. Right now, your words can simply "clear the air" from the doleful cloud of doubt. Even though the Theater's administration FULLY approved the play, and PUR, too, and even though the Ministry isn't worried, that the play is excellent, nevertheless somebody there is muttering about pacifism.[20]

[20] RGALI 1814/9/2100.

Borba za mir (struggle for peace) and rejection of "pacifism" were the organizing themes of Rita's letter to Simonov. Vonnegut was being called a "pacifist" writer. Rait knew the discourse must be shifted to present Vonnegut as an anti-fascist veteran who fought in a "just war," who was still engaging in the "struggle for peace."

Four days later, Simonov dutifully sent Rita Rait a letter as she had requested. Curiously, Simonov chose *not* to employ the *borba za mir* discourse directly. Instead, he stated his confidence that any play based on Vonnegut's excellent book would be "deeply humanistic and uncompromisingly anti-fascist."

> Dear Rita Iakovlevna,
>
> I am very grateful to You for the photographs you sent me.
>
> The meeting with Kurt Vonnegut was an enjoyable and important event for me; I admire and respect him very much—I admire him as an artist and as a person who stands up for what he believes in [literally: "occupies worthy positions as a citizen"]. His novel "Slaughterhouse Five," in my opinion, is one of the best books about the Second World War. I read it with huge interest and trepidation, since I saw firsthand (a few days after the city was freed) the destruction of Dresden, awful Dresden, mutilated by the barbarian American bombing, which had no military justification. It was a horrible sight, and it came back to me vividly as I read Vonnegut's book.
>
> For me, this is a book by a person who hates war—its cruelty, its barbarity—but who also believes it would have been wrong to give into the Fascists, that one had to—was compelled to—fight them, and fight to the end, until they were destroyed. Actually, this position is so close to my own, that it is one I share.
>
> You write that the Soviet Army theater is preparing a stage adaptation of Vonnegut's book. This is of great interest to me and I will be very grateful to receive an invitation to the performance or to a general rehearsal—in short, it will be interesting for me to see it as soon as possible.
>
> I am confident that the stage adaptation of Vonnegut's novel, in the spirit of the book, will be a deeply humanistic and uncompromisingly anti-fascist production. And it will be very interesting to see it.
>
> Thank You for Your letter.
> I shake your hand.
> With deep and longtime respect
> [Konstantin Simonov]

In his letter Simonov highlighted several crucial points. First, Vonnegut was a Second World War veteran with "civic values." He hated war but hated fascism even more, and thus had fought in a "just war." Second, Simonov endorsed *Slaughterhouse-Five* the book and insisted that he was eager to see the stage adaptation come to fruition. Konstantin Simonov was a giant literary figure whose life story and literary oeuvre mirrored Vonnegut's. His endorsement was, for the moment, enough to get *The Wanderings of Billy Pilgrim* unstuck from pacifist purgatory and back on track for production during fall 1975.

End Round One to save *Billy Pilgrim*. Rait/Levitin/Fiene/Simonov/Vonnegut, et al.: 1. Censorship: 0.

Six months later, however, Rita Rait was anticipating another struggle. It was a struggle not for peace, but for the play's resuscitation. In anticipation of some theater "VIPs" finding fault with the production, Rait sent Vonnegut a letter on August 11, 1975. She begged him to preemptively intervene with an endorsement. She asked Kurt to send an encouraging telegram to Levitin. Such a telegram could be shared with the authorities, to grease the wheels of the play's production.[21] In February Rita had asked Simonov to send a note directly to her. This time she pleaded with Vonnegut to address the letter to the play's director, Mikhail Levitin, but to send it care of Rita.[22]

Dearest Kurt

I was ever so happy to hear from Lynn [Visson] that you love me and that Chaghiz Khan [Aitmatov] our Kirghiz author gave you a whip, of all things—hope you won't use it on darling Jill.

Lynn met Peg [Margaret Wettlin] and Mike [Mikhail Levitin] at my place and we drank to you and Jill, to Mike's new daughter Olga (a month old) and of course to THE PLAY. The theatre is on tour now and Mike shall start rehearsing when they come back in September. I have seen three rehearsals, in a small rehearsal-hall. You would LOVE IT: it is so like you, quite unexpectedly NEW and at the same time TRUE to the novel, THE SPIRIT OF IT.

Now we'll have to fight very, very hard for it when the Repertory V. I. P.'s start humming and hawing. . . . Somebody asked already "and what does the Author think about it? Does he trust you to do it well enough?" ETC. ETC. ETC. Ad infinitum

---

[21] The letter may have been mailed by post. It is more likely that Rait asked her American friend Lynn Visson, who had been in Moscow, to courier the letter to the United States and deliver it directly to Vonnegut.

[22] RRK to KV, August 11, 1975, RGALI 3337/1/15.

That is why I want you to write a short letter to Michael Levitin (my friend Mike) and just wish him luck. Say something about Rita Rait having told you she liked what she saw, and how good it is THEY KEEP THE ORIGINAL TEXT INTACT. SEND THIS NOTE TO ME. Everybody WILL BE IN HEAVEN, me too...

Kurt dear, there is always and everywhere a bitter fight to fight. Sometimes I get desperate but try hard not to give up. Now I am fighting for Kafka, for my own book on French Resistance that is being fubar by the mag which accepted it, fighting hard to get a one room flat in our house for Margarita, (who loves you as much as I do),—ETC. ETC. ETC.[23]

But hope The good shall win—GOD WILLING...

Much love to you and Jill. DO WRITE ABOUT ALL YOU have been doing and about your little garden.

Vonnegut dutifully sent a note, in the form of a telegram. It was a masterpiece of the genre. Vonnegut congratulated Levitin and his colleagues and the cast and gushed his delight that the play was a go. He apologized for his absence at the premiere, and he gave the Red Army (in whose theater the show would premier) props for saving his life:[24]

The autographed poster [signed by all members of the play's cast] arrived today along with word your production is superb, faithful to my humble intentions and delightful to your audience. Nothing has made me so happy and proud. Place a chair in the wings for my soul on opening night—my body must remain here. The Soviet Army saved my life in 1945, now they give me a theater. If I could enlist I would. Much love to you, my brothers and sisters in the arts. [Signed] Private Vonnegut, formerly U. S. Infantry, serial number 12102964.[25]

Reflecting back in 2019, Levitin declared, "Kurt's telegram saved my play."[26]

---

[23] "Fubar:" fucked up beyond all recognition (U.S. military slang).
[24] Vonnegut's telegram to Levitin is an important cultural touchstone for those who read and loved Vonnegut in the Soviet Union. In October 2019 I was invited to Levitin's well-appointed office at the Hermitage Theater in Moscow to interview him about *The Wanderings of Billy Pilgrim* and his impressions of Rita Rait and Kurt Vonnegut. Levitin immediately asked his assistant to retrieve the telegram so he could show it to me.
[25] David K. Shipler, "Vonnegut's 'Slaughterhouse-Five' Staged in Moscow," *The New York Times*, January 13, 1976. See Chapter 9 for more details on Vonnegut's relationship with the Red Army.
[26] Levitin also mentioned that Rita Rait's close friend Lili Brik helped with navigating political minefields to get the play approved, but he did not say how, exactly.

Iulii Kim has a different recollection of why *Billy Pilgrim* finally got the green light. He credits the Thaw in US-Soviet relations engendered by the Soyuz Apollo Test Program. (The Soviet Soyuz and the U.S. Apollo spaceships were docked for joint scientific experiments and other exchanges during forty-four hours beginning on July 17, 1975.) When I interviewed him in 2023, Kim said that this "step towards peace" inspired the Party functionary holding up production to give the play the go-ahead.

End Round Two to save *Billy Pilgrim*. Rait/Levitin/Fiene/Simonov/Vonnegut, et al.: 2. Censorship: 0.

Donald Fiene and Kurt Vonnegut engaged in a lot of nail-biting and exchanged panicked letters about the status of *the Billy Pilgrim* production. Vonnegut wrote to Fiene on November 3, 1975, "I'm surprised that you expect to see a production of Slaughterhouse-Five in Moscow. The most recent information I had on that was that it had been cancelled—probably because I, as an officer of P.E.N., sent a cable to the Writer's Union, asking them to do all they could to protect the rights of [persecuted writer Andrei] Amalrik."[27] Fiene replied two days later.

> Dear Kurt, Bad news about the show being cancelled. I haven't had a letter from Rita since the summer though people who've seen her since then and brought me messages said nothing about the play being in trouble. Of course you did the right thing by trying to help Amalrik. I'll discuss it with Rita. . . . I hope I can meet some of the people involved in your play in Russia and talk to them. Maybe there's still a chance it will be put on.[28]

Fiene followed up with a triumphant November 24 letter. "Dear Kurt, According to the letter I got from Rita today, written Nov. 10, your play is still in rehearsal and scheduled for premiere probably in December. With luck I'll get to see one of the rehearsals. Where did you hear that the play had been cancelled?"[29]

End Round Three to save *Billy Pilgrim*. Rait/Levitin/Fiene/Simonov/Vonnegut, et al.: 3. Censorship: 0.

While Vonnegut was "gloomily convinced that his action [letter in support of Amalrik] had caused the production to be canceled," a conviction that

---

[27] Andrei Amalrik was a leading Soviet dissident and author of the controversial 1970 book *Will the Soviet Union survive until 1984?* (Harper and Row, 1981). He was arrested several times and sentenced to a labor camp before being expelled from the Soviet Union in 1975.
[28] DMF to KV, November 5, 1975, FIEN, Folder 2, "1975–1976."
[29] DMF to KV, November 24, 1975, FIEN, Folder 2, "1975–1976."

happily turned out to be wrong, he was probably unaware of another SNAFU (one of Rait's favorite expressions) that did nearly shut down the production. It had to do with the sudden publication in Paris of a French translation of Vonnegut's novel *Mother Night*.[30] Rita relayed the story to Fiene only after the fact, in a March 1977 letter.

> The play about Billy [Pilgrim] nearly flew out the window thanks to one old idiot, a writer, who heard from someone that IN PARIS A NEW (!!!!!) book of Kurt's was PUBLISHED, in French, in which, apparently, they are making fun of us!!!—and he ran to the theater to report this, and thereby nearly killed our wonderful play. Thank goodness I interfered, practically cussed out that old idiot and calmed down the entire administration of the theater (even the higher-ups); I explained that in this OLD novel [Mother Night], Kurt makes fun of . . . any and all "classified secrets" AROUND THE ENTIRE WORLD, which are popped, because they are usually nonsense."[31]

End Round Four to save *Billy Pilgrim*. Rait/Levitin/Fiene/Simonov/Vonnegut, et al.: 4. Censorship: 0.

Act Two: the show must go on

Whether it was Kurt Vonnegut's telegram, Konstantin Simonov's letter, the cosmonauts' joint maneuvers, or Rita Rait's salty protestations that did the trick, the happy outcome was the same. Showtime.

IN ATTENDANCE:

RITA RAIT: Attended the very first dress rehearsal of the play. In a letter to her American friend Lynn Visson, Rita bragged that she ALONE would get to watch this run-through. Towards the end of November there would be run-throughs for "VIPs." "The play is very unusual, bold, and VERY TALENTED, totally in the spirit of Meyerhold and all the most PROGRESSIVE tendencies in theater [these days] . . ."[32]

KONSTANTIN SIMONOV: According to his request, Rita Rait sent Simonov a card inviting him to the first general rehearsal.

---

[30] Fiene, "American Dissident," 266. Rita Rait never sought permission to translate *Mother Night*. It was not translated into Russian until 1991.
[31] RRK to DMF, March 26, 1977, pp. 2–3, DMFC, Box 4, Folder 5, "Rait-Kovaleva, Rita. 1976–1982."
[32] RRK to LV, October 1975 (no date), p. 1, BA-RRK.

If you only knew how we are looking forward to hearing your thoughts and impressions. The presentation to the artistic board of the Theater went very well, but we still want you, someone we believe in, to see it; we need your help. Kurt Vonnegut writes me wonderful letters. Recently he sent a wonderful note to the play's director, Mikhail Levitin, and said that he's "happy and flattered that the Soviet Army theater is staging a play from my novel . . ." He will be so glad when I tell him that you, too, took part in this endeavor.[33]

DAVID SHIPLER: Published a review of *The Wanderings of Billy Pilgrim* in *The New York Times*, January 13, 1976.

DONALD FIENE: Visited Moscow in December 1975. He attended two dress rehearsals of *The Wanderings of Billy Pilgrim*. On his return to the United States, Fiene stopped in New York to visit Kurt, and told him all about the play.

[Kurt] "immediately made up his mind to go to Moscow for the premiere. The next morning he placed phone calls to Washington, trying to make the necessary arrangements through the U.S. State Department. However, it was not possible to make arrangements in any easy manner. When the thing became too complicated, Kurt just gave up on it."[34]

Fiene submitted a laudatory review of the play to *The New York Times*, but it was rejected.

~~KURT VONNEGUT~~: In a letter to Sara Ginsburg dated April 6, 1975, Rita asked her to tell Kurt that as soon as he agreed, the THEATER (caps in original) where the premiere would take place could issue him an invitation.[35] If he had acted then, maybe there would have been time to make travel arrangements. Perhaps quick action from Vonnegut could also have shielded the play from Party functionaries' threats. Ever Kurt's cheerleader, after the play's opening Rait wrote to her American friend Lynn Visson.

Kurt's play (in our interpretation!) is performed to standing ovations. I am begging you, please call him, and tell him that I heard ALL HIS INTERVIEWS, where he spoke so wonderfully about us—and about me!—and so skillfully parried all the questions from the lady from

---

[33] RGALI 1814/9/2100/2, 4.
[34] DMF to RRK, January 6, 1976, p. 1, DMFC, Box 4, Folder 3, "Rait-Kovaleva, Rita. 1963–1976."
[35] RRK to SG, April 6, 1975, BA-RRK.

"Voice" [of America]. My friends in Riga, Leningrad, and Crimea all heard the interview, too—and they are all in awe!"[36]

Rait evaluated Kurt's VOA interview in rather different terms in a separate letter to Donald Fiene. The problem was not with Kurt, but with the interpreter, who, Rita averred, was "an idiot" who tried to "polish up" Kurt's words. She "made them somehow COLORLESS and flat."[37]

V. TUROVSKY: Published a review of *The Wanderings of Billy Pilgrim* in *Komsomol'skaia Pravda* [Komsomol Truth], February 6, 1976.

V. SIMUKHOV: Published a review of *The Wanderings of Billy Pilgrim* in *Trud* [Work], March 10, 1976.

THOUSANDS OF THEATER-GOERS, AT EIGHTY-FIVE PACKED PERFORMANCES. The Soviet Army Theater extended the play's run twice to meet popular demand.[38]

Reflections from within: director, writers, and cast members speak

How did director Mikhail Levitin describe the play written by Rozovsky and Kim, the privilege and challenge of staging of which fell to him? Recalling *Billy Pilgrim* in his memoirs, Levitin emphasized Billy's confused state of mind caused by the emotional and psychological trauma of his wartime experiences. He described Billy as "having gone half mad" from his experiences "under the bombing of his compatriots [the Americans and Brits]" in Dresden. "Everything in the world began to seem made up [to Billy] . . ." Far from describing Billy as a strong anti-war hero and a wise veteran, Levitin's Billy was confused, weak, and "defenseless."[39]

Levitin's reflections on *Billy Pilgrim* center the immorality and absurdity of the situation Billy was caught in. First, he was firebombed by "his own people," the Americans and the British. Second, he and his comrades were bombed in Dresden, a city that "according to international convention was protected from attack." Billy had found himself on the wrong side of the war, "on the side being bombed, instead of doing the bombing, and

---

[36] RRK to LV, no date, BA-RRK.
[37] RRK to DMF, rec'd February 19, 1976, p. 2, DMFC, Box 4, Folder 5, "Rait-Kovaleva, Rita. 1976–1982."
[38] Fiene, "American Dissident," 259.
[39] Levitin, *After Love*, 55–7.

you are getting bombed by your own [people]!"[40] This narrative castigated the Allied forces for the tragedy of Dresden. It conveniently ignored the possibility that the Soviet Union had urged Great Britain and the United States to bomb the city in retribution for Germany's destruction of the USSR's Eastern Front.[41]

The centerpiece of the *Billy Pilgrim* performance was a "one-act song opera" called "Cinderella." The memorable Cinderella "pantomime" the POWs performed in Dresden on Christmas Eve occupies only a few sentences in the novel *Slaughterhouse-Five*. *The Wanderings of Billy Pilgrim* featured a much-expanded Cinderella scene. It lasted thirty minutes and constituted its own "short opera." Levitin said it was the brief Cinderella scenario in *Slaughterhouse-Five* that made him want to stage it as a play. He was intrigued by the idea of men playing Cinderella using a clumsy boot instead of a magical glass shoe. Levitin's artistic team built the entire play around the Cinderella scene. Dashkevich reportedly called the *Billy Pilgrim* play "dull," but he conceded that viewers flocked to the theater to see the "Cinderella" mini opera.[42]

Really, why wouldn't audiences love the operetta? After all, it featured cross-dressing male soldiers. Hilariously, Cinderella was the largest soldier—a sergeant—who shaved her face before going to the ball. The mini opera had bawdy songs about "living for today," and a weak emcee who the ragtag Chorus constantly contradicted. A farcical and grotesque affair, the operetta thoroughly skewered organized religion. A happenstance Christmas "mass" devolved into the Cinderella "play," and the Chorus sang liturgical-sounding songs with raucous, blasphemous lyrics. The play likewise poked fun at everyday corruption in the Soviet Union. The "Good Fairy" was a black marketeer who traded favors for goods and unabashedly served "power, not truth."

The "Cinderella" operetta included several musings on how the allied forces had violated the pact to spare Dresden, a cultural landmark where masses of German refugees sought refuge. The POWs were overjoyed when they learned their destiny was Dresden, where "all the windows are intact," and "nighttime entertainment continues to this day" (e.g., romps with "ladies of the night"). The entire cast vowed to drive to Dresden together "in a white Mercedes." This grotesque scenario—the POWs and other hangers-on

---

[40] Levitin, *After Love*, 54.
[41] Skorobogatov, "Kurt Vonnegut," 30–1.
[42] Julia Vaingurt, *Soft Matter: The Poetics of Weakness in Late Soviet Socialism* (Northwestern University Press, 2025), 46.

happily driving to their deaths in Dresden, piled into a German car—perfectly captured the spirit of the zany "Cinderella" operetta.

The "Epilogue" of Cinderella encapsulated another tension screaming throughout the operetta. This was the conflict between good and evil, and the impossibility of distinguishing one from the other. The emcee excitedly informed the Chorus, "I've just made a discovery: I've just opened a dictionary. It turns out that conscience is a moral category. It's a moral category, 'Which allows one to unmistakably distinguish the bad from the good.'" Incredulous Chorus members lobbed protestations and counterevidence at the emcee. "But sometimes one must lie, in order to serve a higher purpose, what then? A just fight, to improve the world, may result in some collateral damage, what then? Man is just a creature of his environment; what can a weak man do when the inevitable is rushing at him, what then?" The emcee had no response, except to repeat his stale dictionary definition of "conscience" over and over, in a stammering voice. "A moral category, which allows one to unmistakably distinguish the bad from the good!"

And how did cast members evaluate the play? In one interview the renowned actress Liubov' Ivanovna Dobrzhanskaia described her role as Billy Pilgrim's mother.

> In this spectacle I play the mother of Billy Pilgrim, a man who lived through the barbaric bombing of Dresden in 1945. The war separated mother and son, and his illness is a source of pain and suffering for his mother. During the entire play my heroine tries to reach him, to return her son. I love this role; it is close to the roles I've played in recent years— roles devoted to high emotions, humanity, and sympathy. Since the play we are preparing is not exactly usual in form and content, of course it presents me with new acting challenges. Maybe this role will be more eccentric than my previous work. War still poses a threat to the world. So it is very important for art to promote humanism, and faith in social progress. Kurt Vonnegut's book is filled with passion for good, sympathy for people, and hatred for fascism; he is an author who, like his [book's] hero, survived the bombing of Dresden and loves to repeat: "If the Red Army had not liberated me from captivity, I wouldn't be alive today."[43]

Dobrzhanskaia dutifully hit the necessary ideological notes: the struggle for peace, belief in social progress, and disdain for fascism. And of course, Vonnegut's liberation by the Red Army.

---

[43] Liubov' Dobrzhanskaia, interview by A. Smolianskii and L. Levikova, *Sovetskaia kul'tura* [Soviet culture] 82, no. 4882 (October 10, 1975): 3.

By the end of the play's run at the Soviet Army Theater, seventy-eight-year-old Rita Rait was exhausted. According to the director Levitin, Rita attended many of the approximately eighty-five performances. She explained in a letter to a friend, "I had to go to the play frequently—I became something like a *public relations officer*—I accompanied reporters, and 'worked' (exactly 'worked') the guests during intermissions..."[44]

Act Three: critical response

Fifty years after its premiere, the play's full script is so far unavailable to researchers. This is one reason that scholars interested in the play's staging in Moscow have focused almost entirely on the "Cinderella" operetta in their scholarship, the script of which is available online.[45] It is impossible to provide a full overview and hindsight evaluation of *The Wanderings of Billy Pilgrim* at the Soviet Army Theater. We *can*, however, track the critical response to the play by Soviet and American critics. This sheds light on the ways Cold War politics played out in the arts. It also provides glimpses into the personal relationships that animated cultural diplomacy between the United States and the USSR.

Shortly after the play opened in Moscow, Donald Fiene, who had attended two dress rehearsals, wrote to Rita Rait. "On the morning of the 28th [of December] I wrote an article for the *New York Times* about the play. Kurt [Vonnegut] hand-carried the article to the newspaper himself. I don't know if my article will be published separately or not, since the newspaper was sending its reporter to cover the premiere."[46]

The *Times* reporter was David K. Shipler, a correspondent at the paper's Moscow bureau who would go on to lead the bureau in 1977–9. The *Times* published Shipler's review instead of Fiene's. According to Fiene, "Shipler had a copy of my article when he wrote his but didn't make much use of it."[47] Shipler thought the play "diminished" the book. It took as its "backbone the book's anti-war theme" and stopped there. Shipler found the play only "slightly zany," in contrast to Vonnegut's "bizarre, dreamlike, hilarious tragedy." Shipler

---

[44] RRK to LV, no date, BA-RRK. In an otherwise Russian-language letter, Rait wrote "public relations officer" in English.
[45] "Zolushka v lagere dlia voiennoplennykh. Chast' 1, 2" [Cinderella in the concentration camp. Part 1, 2], script of the "Cinderella" libretto from *The Wanderings of Billy Pilgrim*, available at www.bards.ru/archives/part.php?id=47773.
[46] DMF to RRK, January 6, 1976, p. 1, DMFC, Box 4, Folder 3, "Rait-Kovaleva, Rita. 1963–1976."
[47] DMF to JK, January 16, 1976, DMFC, Box 4, Folder 2, "Klinkowitz, Jerome. 1976–1984."

criticized the play's writers for leaving out many of Billy Pilgrim's character flaws, including his early fascination with violence, and his "vaguely rightwing sympathies." Whereas in the book Billy had expressed mild pride for his son's service as a Green Beret in Vietnam, the play had Billy mocking his son and ridiculing his service medals. Shipler concluded that "Slaughterhouse-Five probably needs *theater of the absurd* [emphasis added], a genre alien to the contemporary Soviet stage." The review was remarkable in not even mentioning the thirty-minute "Cinderella" operetta that anchored the play. Shipler noted blandly, "The production has music."[48] What *was* the operetta, with its bawdy banter, transvestism, and barbed jabs at religion, the Soviet economy, and human nature, if not "theater of the absurd?"

Shipler did quote in full the congratulatory telegram Vonnegut had sent to director Levitin. He included two paragraphs quoting Vonnegut about his confidence in Rita Rait, her translation, and her judgment.

> Mr. Vonnegut, reached here yesterday, said that he never saw the Russian script. "One of my closest friends, Rita Rait, who is in her 70's, translated my novel. She then worked closely with the authors and director. I have trust in her judgment in this matter and continue to do so. She is one of my favorite translators."[49]

This section delighted Fiene, who was otherwise disappointed. He was miffed that the *Times* declined to publish his own review of the play. He regretted that Shipler had not culled insights from Fiene's own report, which Vonnegut had shared with the paper.

Fiene sent copies of his own review to several colleagues, including Jerome Klinkowitz, Rita Rait, and Mikhail Levitin. Fiene enclosed a note to Levitin. "The author of the article in the Times poorly understands Vonnegut, and is still a little bit waging a Cold War. He's an idiot and a bad critic, but it's really good that he cited Kurt's telegram for the world."[50] Fiene sent a similar note to Klinkowitz. He enclosed both reviews—Shipler's published one, and his own unpublished one. "Here's an article about Vonnegut's play . . . The guy who wrote it is an obvious jerk, but he did a good job quoting Vonnegut's telegram for history. My own review of the play is also enclosed—a more humane and charitable response to a first-rate production."[51]

---

[48] Shipler, "Vonnegut's 'Slaughterhouse-Five.'"
[49] Shipler, "Vonnegut's 'Slaughterhouse-Five.'"
[50] DMF to Mikhail Levitin, January 19, 1976, DMRC, Box 4, Folder 3, "Rait-Kovaleva, Rita. 1963–1976."
[51] DMF to JK, January 16, 1976, DMFC, Box 4, Folder 2, "Klinkowitz, Jerome. 1976–1984."

In his review Fiene called the Russian interpretation of Vonnegut's *Billy Pilgrim* "deeply soulful—even religious." He praised the composers and the cast. Fiene described the audience's emotional response to several poignant scenes and highlighted the "Cinderella" operetta as especially entertaining. Fiene noted the play's unusual invitation of "sympathy for the <u>German</u> victims of World War II" (emphasis in original). Fiene made another curious point. He essentially thanked the Soviet Army Theater's board of directors for allowing the play to be staged there and opined that "the board members deserve special commendation for this."[52]

Fiene summarized his unpublished review's main conclusions two years later in a letter to Professor Laurie Leighton.

> The stage adaptation of Slaughterhouse Five was a completely free adaptation of the novel in the style of Meyerhold.[53] It was excellent. I saw it twice. The question of addition or deletion of material is irrelevant to such a dramatic interpretation. In fact the play was true to the spirit of the original and Shipler was absolutely wrong in his remarks. As a correspondent for the New York Times he was quite as guilty of subtle, propagandistic distinctions as are the more sophisticated Soviet reporters on American art and lit.[54]

For her part, Rita Rait was relieved that *The New York Times* declined to publish Fiene's "nice article."

> Thank Goodness your nice article was NOT published: all the last words [about] boards etc. are absolutely irresponsible: when will you grow up and stop telling things you are not supposed to shout about? All our difficulties in producing the play ARE NOT UNDERSTOOD BY YOU and the compliments you shower on the Board are poison to them. . . . Please DO NOT try to explain your point of view to me—I understand all your good intentions too well. . . . I can hardly read the awful xerox

---

[52] Donald M. Fiene, "Vonnegut Staged in Moscow," unpublished review enclosed in letter from DMF to RRK, December 29, 1975, DMFC, Box 4, Folder 2, "Rait-Kovaleva, Rita. 1968–1978."

[53] In his unpublished review Fiene wrote, "Levitin's production is a lively and lavish spectacle in the tradition of Vakhtangov & Meyerhold with most of the actors appearing continuously on stage as Billy Pilgrim, their creator, travels in time between the magical planet of Tralfamadore and the earthly city of Dresden, destroyed by firebombs on February 13, 1945." Fiene, "Vonnegut Staged in Moscow."

[54] DMF to LGL, September 26, 1978, p. 2, DMFC, Box 4, Folder 1, "Leighton, Lauren Gray. 1978–1979."

to translate it and I will spare poor Mike [Mikhail Levitin] from hearing how you interpret the Board's decisions.[55]

In the same missive Rita admonished Fiene to "Grow up, dear boy, do not get too enthused about things like 'generals deserving commendations' etc."[56] This screed from Rita indexed her growing frustration with Fiene and signaled the beginning of a chill in their relationship.

In his review, by praising the board and its positive decision, Fiene implied that Levitin, Rait, and the production team had faced challenges getting the play approved. Rita feared this kind of public criticism of the Soviet bureaucracy. She believed it produced only resentment among the authorities. Rita did not appreciate it when foreign writers, scholars, and public figures, including Kurt Vonnegut, aired critiques of Soviet restrictions on freedoms. Nor did she approve of praise when such restrictions were "overcome." Such efforts could backfire and make things worse. Rita's jibe about "generals deserving commendations" reflected her distaste for Fiene's praises of the "board of directors consisting chiefly of officers of the rank of general" who had approved the play's production. Rita considered such kowtowing toxic and counterproductive.

To make matters worse, back in the United States both Vonnegut and Donald Fiene kept flubbing their parts. They unwittingly continued to cast the specter of pacifism over *Billy Pilgrim* and his wanderings. Vonnegut perpetually played up the "pacifist" nature of *Slaughterhouse-Five*. This came out in Vonnegut's response to Shipler's review of the *Billy Pilgrim* play which called it excessively critical of the Vietnam War. When asked about this, Vonnegut offered a retort. "I would say that what's remarkable about this production is that its theme deals with pacifism. The Soviet [Union] has been reluctant to put on such plays, which makes the occasion most noteworthy."[57] On one hand, as Skorobogatov argues, "Vonnegut praised the play's anti-war message as a sign of progress in US-Soviet relations."[58] On the other hand, by conjuring up "pacifism" he threatened to undo Rita's careful work to disassociate the play from that ideologically unacceptable term.

Fiene, too, ruffled Rait's feathers when he described Vonnegut and his work as "pacifist" in print. Fiene called Vonnegut's telegram to Levitin "an astonishing telegram in light of the pacifist, antimilitarist theme of *Slaughter-

---

[55] RRK to DMF, rec'd February 19, 1976, DMFC, Box 4, Folder 2, "Rait-Kovaleva, Rita. 1968–1978."
[56] RRK to DMF, rec'd February 19, 1976, DMFC, Box 4, Folder 2, "Rait-Kovaleva, Rita. 1968–1978."
[57] Fiene, "American Dissident," 261.
[58] Skorobogatov, "Kurt Vonnegut," 26.

house Five—yet altogether understandable and delightful."[59] Further, in his unpublished review, Fiene described *The Wanderings of Billy Pilgrim* as "simply and profoundly pacifistic." Rait found this association naïve and dangerous, and she said as much in a scathing letter to Fiene.

> The word "pacifistic" ('simply and profoundly' as you so very explicitly stated) has an entirely DIFFERENT connotation in our language meaning NOT peace-loving (*miroliubivy*) but something Tolstoyan, 'not standing up to evil' (*neprotivlenie zlu*)—and that is NOT what the play is about: it is HUMANE, kind, very sad and even a bit fatalistic—like the novel. . . . That is why Billy is so helpless and why <u>he pities everybody</u>. . . . I have a record of Kurt reading 'Slaught. 5' and HE picked out THE VERY SAME aspect of the book."[60]

In his insistence that *Billy Pilgrim* was a "pacifist" play, Fiene threatened to wreck Rita's careful choreography to prove that the play was most emphatically *not* "pacifist" (and thus *not* a play about "not standing up to evil"), but rather a "humane" play rooted in the international "struggle for peace." If Rita Rait had ever found out that in his very first letter to Vonnegut in 1972, Donald Fiene had assured Vonnegut that his Russian translator Rita Rait was "not a Marxist, but an international humanist and pacifist," she may have tried to skin him alive.[61]

End Round Five to save *Billy Pilgrim*: Infighting between the players. Round inconclusive. Pause for "blood time."

For their part, Soviet critics evaluated *The Wanderings of Billy Pilgrim* very positively. In the newspaper *Labor*, V. Simukhov emphasized "the author's humanistic and anti-militaristic pathos." The critic underscored the twisted tragedy of Dresden. He approved of the Cinderella operetta's knowing description of Dresden as "an open city, by international arrangement . . . It has no troops or military installations. Half of the German refugees are already there, and more are expected. No bombs have fallen on it and will not fall—according to the agreement." Of course that was not true, since the allies broke the Dresden pact and firebombed the city to ashes. Simukhov wondered at the POWs' ability to find laughter and hope in the darkest of circumstances.[62] As Skorobogatov notes, Soviet audience members must

---

[59] Fiene, "American Dissident," 267.
[60] RRK to DMF rec'd February 19, 1976, p. 2, DMFC, Box 4, Folder 5, "Rait-Kovaleva, Rita. 1976–1982."
[61] DMF to KV, May 12, 1972, FIEN, Folder 1, "1972–1974."
[62] V. Simukhov, "Stranstviia Billi Pilgrima" [The Wanderings of Billy Pilgrim], *Trud* [Work] 58, March 10, 1976.

have seen in the play "proof that beauty and tragedy could coexist, that people could find ways to cope in even the most hopeless scenarios."[63]

Another Soviet critic writing for the youth-oriented newspaper *Komsomol Truth* dwelt on the play's anti-war message and "the hope it evoked for a future without war."[64] V. Turovsky emphasized Vonnegut's use of the word "slaughter" (as in *Slaughterhouse-Five*) to describe the war. The critic found this an evocative play on words to describe the horrors of Dresden. Watching the play and reading Vonnegut's book, Turovsky predicted, "would ensure that generations of readers do not forget the names Dresden, Hiroshima, and Nagasaki ... As long as this memory exists, as long as it hurts—as long as the flame smolders inside all of us—there will not be another war."[65]

In sum, the Soviet Army theater adaptation of *Slaughterhouse-Five* was a riotous affair in every sense. I haven't even mentioned the staging by Mart Kitaev, who covered the entire stage in white bandages. As Levitin later remembered,

> I had to thank the stage right away [for helping me], and I asked the wonderful artist Mart Kitaev to protect it from the war with bandages. To bandage the air—wounded by war—with [white] linen. . . At the end of the show the Germans wrapped every member of the cast in those very same white bandages. . . . This might seem symbolic, but there was no symbolism at all. I just wanted them to stay there forever.[66]

The Wanderings of Billy Pilgrim was a bricolage, a strange improvisational production open to multiple interpretations. Adapting Vonnegut's war novel for the Soviet stage was an adventure unto itself. It involved international intrigue, dissident writers working under pseudonyms, ideological acrobatics, and a theater shaped like a star. For American critic David Shipler, the play was a thoroughly Soviet affair, a straightforward anti-American, anti-war production. And "it had some music." For Soviet critics, the play channeled the humanism and hope of its author, Kurt Vonnegut. It offered "large doses of optimism for a new epoch void of the conflict and destruction of the past half-century."[67] For audience members, the play was a hilarious operetta, a "Cinderella" skit performed by hairy POW guys in drag, with semi-lewd

---

[63] Skorobogatov, "Kurt Vonnegut," 25.
[64] V. Turovsky, "Liudi i teni" [People and shadows], *Komsomol'skaia Pravda* [Komsomol Truth], February 6, 1976.
[65] Turovsky, "People and shadows." Translation by Yana Skorobogatov, "Kurt Vonnegut," 26.
[66] Levitin, *After Love*, 56.
[67] Skorobogatov, "Kurt Vonnegut," 26.

Figure 7.4 Scene from *The Wanderings of Billy Pilgrim*, staged at the Soviet Army Theater, Moscow, May 1976. Courtesy of the Russian State Documentary Film and Photo Archive, Private Collection of N.N. Bobrov (0-356381).

lyrics and lots of slapstick. That half hour of joy was bookended by the rest of the pretty forgettable play. For some theatergoers the play was their first encounter with Vonnegut, and it sparked a life-long interest in his work. For Rita Rait, the play was an "event," a triumph, another victory in her life-long quest to introduce America's best writers to the Soviet public. She continued to play her own best role. She was a conduit through which Soviet readers (and now, theatergoers) could explore American culture in all its confusing, fascinating, glory.

Post-production cast party: reflections

The Wanderings of Billy Pilgrim, including the offstage drama, was a cornerstone of director Mikhail Levitin's career. When I visited him in his office at the Hermitage Theater in Moscow in October 2019, I found several framed black and white portraits prominently displayed on his wall-to-wall bookshelves. There is an approximately five by seven inch portrait of a mature Rita Rait. Vonnegut's wife Jill Krementz probably took the photo

Figure 7.5 Scene from *The Wanderings of Billy Pilgrim*, staged at the Soviet Army Theater, Moscow, May 1976. Courtesy of the Russian State Documentary Film and Photo Archive, Private Collection of N.N. Bobrov (0-356382).

in Paris in 1972. Rait's photograph rests on the same shelf as a photo of the famous satirists Ilf and Petrov. In charming fashion, the two photos are arranged as if Rita and Ilf + Petrov are having a stare down. Somewhat less prominently, and situated several shelves lower than those two photos, is a head shot of Kurt Vonnegut. These mementos were not a hasty exhibition curated specially for my brief visit with Levitin. They are permanent and integral features of his daily work environment.

Levitin and Rita Rait became friends when he was a young director. They shared common interests and sensibilities in the arts. But *Billy Pilgrim*, he said, "really solidified our relationship." Levitin got to meet a lot of luminaries thanks to his association with Rita Rait. These included foreign scholars, writers, and artists. He met Donald Fiene, and he met Kurt Vonnegut. In letters to Vonnegut, Rita referred to Mikhail Levitin as "Mike," anglicizing his name for her American friend. (In his letters, Fiene called him "Misha.")

In Levitin, Rita saw a young, innovative director who "should have been born 100 years earlier."[68] In Levitin she saw Meyerhold, her favorite. In Rita, Levitin saw an embodied representative of his favorite period of Russian-

---

[68] Author's interview with Mikhail Levitin, October 18, 2019, Moscow.

Figure 7.6 Theater director Mikhail Levitin in his office at the Hermitage Theater, Moscow, October 18, 2019. Photograph by Sarah D. Phillips.

Soviet theater, the 1920s and 1930s. (Rita sometimes jokingly called herself a "living museum piece of the 1920s.") "I loved everything about her. She became like the air around me. She would come over to our apartment and watch our three children. Can you imagine! A figure of world literature, and she was happy to babysit!"[69]

Billy Pilgrim was an important play for Levitin and the play's cast for other, devastating reasons. Liubov' Ivanovna Dobrzhanskaia, the famous diva who played Billy's mother, began showing the first signs of dementia during rehearsals. Andrei Mayorov, who played Billy, suffered a major heart attack soon after the play's run. Levitin later recalled, "He [Mayorov] didn't sacrifice his life, but he sacrificed his heart, for the role of Billy Pilgrim."[70]

For his part, Donald Fiene was disappointed that *The New York Times* passed over his review of *The Wanderings of Billy Pilgrim*. And his relationship with Rita Rait was starting to show stress fractures. Fiene consoled himself

---

[69] Author's interview with Mikhail Levitin, October 18, 2019, Moscow.
[70] Levitin, After Love, 57, 60.

with a huge play poster he brought back from Moscow, signed by the entire cast. He delivered a signed poster to Kurt Vonnegut in New York, too. In a letter Fiene assured Rita, "Kurt was very pleased with the signed poster advertising the play. He went out the very next day to have it framed in glass. (I am going to have my poster framed also.)"[71]

CURTAIN

---

[71] DMF to RRK, January 6, 1976, p. 1, DMFC, Box 4, Folder 3, "Rait-Kovaleva, Rita. 1963–1976."

8

Finding Comrade Vonnegut

Vonnegut and His Soviet Critics

On May 15, 1974, Donald Fiene sent a letter to Rita Rait in Moscow to let her know he was starting seriously on a new project. He envisioned it as a short book about "the influence of Russian literature on Vonnegut . . . the Russian response to Vonnegut, and Vonnegut's current interest in Russia."[1] Fiene had been poking around the Indiana University library. He'd tracked down several of Rita and her daughter Margarita's Vonnegut translations. He'd found critical reviews of Vonnegut by a few prominent Soviet literary critics.

> It would be especially helpful to me if you would send me information about other articles on Vonnegut, aside from those I listed above. I know that there must be a lot more. . . . Please cut out and send me any articles that you see on Vonnegut from now in; perhaps you know some editors who save all these articles and could send me copies.[2]

Fiene's letter reached Rita in less than ten days. She answered immediately to enlighten Fiene about the ridiculousness of his request. Ironically, it would be more realistic for Fiene to send *her* copies of critical responses to Vonnegut's work published in the Soviet Union than for her to obtain these articles herself. "As for the reviews [you mentioned], I'd like to get the Zverev and El'sberg articles FROM YOU: I haven't seen them or read them. And for us, getting photocopies is harder than a trip to the South Pole."[3]

---

[1] Fiene was always interested in exploring parallels and shared sensibilities between Vonnegut and great writers such as Dostoevsky, Gogol, and Zamiatin. He felt Soviet critics had overlooked these topics (Fiene, "American Dissident," 270). Rita Rait was not interested in having this conversation with Fiene, who believed Vonnegut had most in common with Dostoevsky. Rait detested Dostoevsky and, anyway, preferred to consider Vonnegut on his own merits.
[2] DMF to RRK, May 15, 1974, DMFC, Box 4, Folder 3, "Rait-Kovaleva, Rita. 1963–1976."
[3] RRK to DMF, May 24, 1974, p. 2, DMFC, Box 4, Folder 3, "Rait-Kovaleva, Rita. 1963–1976."

On a trip to Moscow several years later, in 1978, Fiene learned for himself the truth of Rita's words. In a letter he sent after that trip to Jerome Klinkowitz, Fiene listed twelve translations and critical articles on Vonnegut published in the Soviet Union between 1974 and 1978, including articles in Russian, Lithuanian, and Ukrainian. Beside entries about two important articles by the critic A. Zverev, Fiene typed, "Have not seen this."

> It took me all summer to dig out this information from the Lenin Library in Moscow. No one hindered me in any way. I was treated royally in fact. But the Lenin Library is about as easy to find your way around in as the New York Public after an air raid by angry Arabs. I ordered copies of the same Ukrainian and Lithuanian newspapers every single week from June through the end of August. Nobody was ever able to find the fucking things. The week before I left I laid some roubles on them and said if they ever found them, please to send me photocopies. Three months later I got a big roll of real photocopies, shiny glossy prints as big as the original periodicals. I've had a stack of books sitting on them for an additional three months, and they aren't flat yet.[4]

Fiene eventually was able to round out his collection of Soviet critical commentary on Vonnegut's work, and he compiled a terrifically comprehensive resource, "Kurt Vonnegut in the USSR: A Bibliography."[5] It included translations of Vonnegut published in the USSR and in the émigré press abroad, and an impressive list of 184 published critical commentaries. Upon reading these reviews, Fiene determined, and I agree, that Soviet reviewers' and literary critics' assessments of Vonnegut's work were almost uniformly positive.[6] Fiene wrote to Vonnegut that so far, he had not run across *any* negative criticism of Vonnegut in the Soviet Union. "I really think you're their great symbol of peach between the nations."[7] Fiene made a similar claim in print.

> Certainly throughout the 1970s he [Vonnegut] was the most widely read contemporary American author in that country [the Soviet Union], while enjoying, in the bargain, total critical success. I say "total" because I have read virtually everything published on Vonnegut in the U.S.S.R.

---

[4] DMF to JK, January 28, 1979, p. 2, DMFC, Box 4, Folder 1, "Klinkowitz, Jerome. 1976–1984."
[5] Fiene, "Kurt Vonnegut in the USSR," 223–32.
[6] Fiene, "American Dissident," 263.
[7] DMF to KV, October 12, 1982, FIEN, Folder 6, "1981–1984."

between 1967 and 1982 and have yet to find even one word written against him!⁸

It is hard to overstate just how positively many Soviet critics evaluated Vonnegut the author, and Vonnegut the man. In his Afterword to the 1970 translation of *Cat's Cradle*, V. Skorodenko practically gushed.

> Kurt Vonnegut has shown us the world in which he lives and which he knows well. He has done this with the courage of a genuine patriot of a great country, with the dignity of a human being—an inhabitant of our rather small planet, and with the straightforwardness of a true artist.⁹

Having explored Soviet readers' reception of Vonnegut's prose in Chapter 5, the present chapter explores the Soviet literary establishment's critical response to Vonnegut's work. Since any published criticism had to conform to sanctioned ideology, critical response is a window onto how Vonnegut the writer was safe and perhaps even useful for the Soviet state. What messages did Soviet critics "find" in Vonnegut? How were these nuggets of wisdom delivered to the reading public? What inconvenient or politically incorrect aspects of Vonnegut's writing did Soviet critics conveniently overlook or ignore? This chapter explores these questions. It also tracks how Soviet critics made Vonnegut legible as an ally of the Soviet Union and a "fighter for peace."

Published reviews of Vonnegut in Soviet literary journals are the primary sources for this exploration. Of interest, too, are references made to Vonnegut and his work in Soviet literary newspapers like *Literary Gazette*. Literary critics in the Soviet Union often produced contextual reviews of literature in translation, so-called "paratexts" or "paratextual information." These pieces appeared alongside translations as prefatory or supplemental essays and reflections. They guided readers' interpretations of what they were about to read or what they had just read. These introductions or afterwords to translated articles and books did not constitute censorship, but they served a specific political purpose, as pithily described by Michael Khmelnitsky.

> The reason for the involvement of pre-eminent men of letters first needs to be clarified . . . the inclusion of a critical apparatus by a professional

---

⁸ Fiene, "First Meeting," 90.
⁹ V. Skorodenko, "O bezumnom mire i pozitsii khudozhnika (Roman K. Vonnegata [*sic*.] Kolybel' dlia Koshki)" [On the Absurd World and the Position of the Artist (K. Vonnegat's [*sic*.] novel Cat's Cradle)], Afterword to *Kolybel' dlia Koshki* [Cat's Cradle], transl. Raisa Rait-Kovaleva (Molodaia Gvardiia, 1970), 224. Translation Fiene, "American Dissident," 269.

authority (informally nicknamed the parovoz55 [steam locomotive] in the Soviet translation and publishing industries, for its ability to "pull" the text through various censorial and editorial apparatuses) ensured an additional safeguard for the work's publication.... [This was] because of the expectation of alignment of the foreign author with the communist project in general and the ideology du jour in specific which was often done by embellishing actual literary criticism with everything from polemics on current affairs to formulaic references to the writings of Lenin, Marx, Engels, or the general secretary of the Communist Party of the Soviet Union (especially if an opportune quotation or two on the subject of discussion could be found)...In tandem, all of these requirements lent an aura of social and political legitimacy to the work in question.[10]

Needless to say, these critical commentaries included a lot of chaff with the wheat, despite being written by prominent men of letters (and they were nearly all men; one rare exception was the literary scholar Raisa Orlova).[11] As Khmelnitsky points out, Soviet literary criticism necessarily combined "actual literary insights" with ideologically driven "pot-shots" at the West.[12] The paratexts were rarely convincing, and most readers probably skipped over them. However, the content of the critical essays and summaries accompanying Vonnegut in translation is important for understanding who Vonnegut was for the Soviet state. They crystallize how Vonnegut became a sanctioned and even desirable American writer.

Before opening the curtain onto the world of Soviet literary criticism vis-à-vis Vonnegut, I would like to take a short glimpse backstage. There we see Rita Rait, who Vonnegut once described as being "about as high as your coffee table," actively shooing away critics whose reviews might besmirch the reputation of "her" author, Kurt Vonnegut. Ever Vonnegut's champion, Rait intervened to protect Vonnegut from critics she disagreed with or did not like. Donald Fiene explained this to Vonnegut in 1978.

> Rita told me to tell you that she had succeeded in preventing the Soviet critic M.O. Mendelson from writing the foreword to the forthcoming volume of your collected works. He is first in status of all Soviet critics

[10] Khmelnitsky, "Sex, Lies, and Red Tape," 30–1.
[11] Best known as Hemingway's translator in the Soviet Union, Raisa Orlova, wife of Lev Kopelev, had her Soviet citizenship revoked in 1981 by a decree signed by Brezhnev. Orlova and Kopelev left the Soviet Union for the United States. See Raisa Orlova and Lev Kopelev, *My Zhili v Moskve* [We Lived in Moscow] (Ardis, 1988).
[12] Khmelnitsky, "Sex, Lies, and Red Tape," 57.

and has written endlessly about you. But he's an asshole, Rita says; doesn't understand a single thing you've written. (She's right. I've read the guy.)[13]

Conversely, Rait *did* like the literary critics Aleksei Zverev and Raisa Orlova. Rita claimed she got them gigs to write several paratextual entries alongside her Vonnegut translations.[14] Zverev's paratext defended Vonnegut from potential ideological critique. According to literature scholar Ilaria Sicari, Zverev distinguished "Vonnegut's [literary experimentation] from the experiments of the Nouveau roman and those of French structuralism, with the aim of 'exonerating' the author's poetics and guarding them against a harmful interpretation that would certainly compromise the work's publication in the USSR."[15]

Sicari calls Soviet literary critics' machinations "critical domestication" and "ideological education of the Soviet reader."[16] Both are apt descriptions. The writer Sergei Dovlatov, who was compelled to emigrate from the Soviet Union to the United States in 1979 due to his own problems with the Soviet government, summed up succinctly the approach Soviet literary critics took to Vonnegut's work. "Soviet literary criticism slyly interprets Vonnegut's books. His pessimistic rejection of reality, his apocalyptic thinking, is presented as a denial of the concrete bourgeois order. The universal sarcastic farce of his novels is interpreted as anti-bourgeois satire."[17] Indeed, Soviet critics could point to Vonnegut's startlingly unique style and voice as evidence of unrest in America and social change in the making. One critic, for instance, concluded his review of *Slaughterhouse-Five* with the argument that "Vonnegut's work is proof of what Updike wrote a few years ago, speaking directly to Russian readers: that changes in literature are obvious evidence of the inner turmoil of American society." With his "unsentimental dethroning of idols" and "sharp changes in style," argued critic Aleksandr Borshchagovskii, Vonnegut's prose expressed the overwhelming social anger in the United States.[18]

Generally speaking, Soviet reviewers and literary critics conveniently parlayed Vonnegut's critiques of American society and human nature to support the official Soviet line on the U.S. war in Vietnam (bad), the excesses

[13] DMF to KV, September 16, 1978, p. 14, FIEN, Folder 4, "1978."
[14] RRK to DMF, May 2, 1970, DMFC, Box 4, Folder 2, "Rait-Kovaleva, Rita. 1968–1978;" RRK to DMF, October 25, 1977, p. 2, DMFC, Box 4, Folder 5, "Rait-Kovaleva, Rita. 1976–1982." Raisa Orlova, "O romane Kurta Vonneguta" [On Kurt Vonnegut's novel], *Novyi Mir* 4 (1970): 179–80; Zverev, "Warning signal."
[15] Sicari, "Paratext as Weapon," 364.
[16] Sicari, "Paratext as Weapon," 354.
[17] Dovlatov, "Therefore there will be war."
[18] Aleksandr Borshchagovskii, "Takie dela" [So it goes], *Literaturnaia gazeta* 29 (July 15, 1970): 3.

of capitalism (many), the degraded state of American society and cultural values (irredeemable), the achievements of the Red Army (great), the virtues of the working class (obvious), and others. To curate this image of an idealized "comrade Vonnegut," these ideology brokers had to present a sanitized version of Vonnegut. This approach omitted his "real-life" commitments, statements, and speeches, especially those that were critical of Soviet political repression.

Vonnegut as an anti-American American

On a most basic level, Vonnegut served a useful role for the Soviets as an "anti-American American." Skorobogatov provides insights on this score.

> When *Novy Mir* [New World] published . . . *Slaughterhouse-Five*, in 1970, shifts in superpower politics were creating new demand for anti-capitalist, and especially anti-American, rhetoric at home. The best pieces of anti-American propaganda were those that were being produced by Americans themselves. For instance, since the beginning of the American civil rights movement, Kremlin officials went out of their way to feature stories of police dogs attacking protesters and students being blocked from entering desegregated schools in the pages of *Pravda* and *Izvestia* to shame the U.S. government for condoning discrimination against its own citizens. By the mid-1970s, prominent figures like Malcolm X, Angela Davis, and Muhammad Ali had become easily recognizable symbols of American injustice in Cold War Russia.[19]

Vonnegut's fundamental critiques of base cultural values were ripe for citation and elaboration by Soviet critics. He emphasized the greed and ignorance of the American middle class and the vast divide between rich and poor, a consequence of unfettered capitalism, with its built-in class inequality. He suggested that Americans fundamentally lacked "culture." It was easy for Soviet critics to identify in Vonnegut an obvious "contempt for specifically American values."[20] "Vonnegut's Soviet critics," Fiene noted, "are . . . united in recognizing the author's genuinely savage attack on Western capitalism and the American way of life."[21] M. O. Mendel'son, a highly respected critic

---

[19] Skorobogatov, "Kurt Vonnegut," 28.
[20] Fiene, "American Dissident," 264.
[21] Fiene, "American Dissident," 268.

who wrote extensively on Vonnegut (the very same Mendel'son whom Rita Rait called an "asshole"), was especially prone to quote at length Vonnegut's anti-American jibes. These included Vonnegut's critique of the perverted "American dream" that opens *God Bless You, Mr. Rosewater*, the contrast between the "fabulously well-to-do" in America and those who "couldn't get their hands on doodley-squat" in *Breakfast of Champions*, and so on.[22]

Critic Ia. El'sberg picked up on this theme of America's capitalism-induced social ruin. In an article entitled "In the Battle for Humankind," El'sberg compared Soviet writer Viktor Astaf'ev's book *The Shepherd and His Wife* (1972) with Vonnegut's *Slaughterhouse-Five*.[23] El'sberg noted that Vonnegut's novel "is full of critiques of the cruelty that characterizes everyday life in the United States, and which has rather linked the war-time and post-war periods: 'the second world war made everyone more cruel.'" If, argued El'sberg, "in Astaf'ev's writing the hero's strivings are backed by the spirituality and will of a great people, who created and continue to create a new life, behind Vonnegut's wandering hero we find only a cruel social order, overwhelming and perverting the greatest ideals of its people, of the whole human race." El'sberg continued, "Vonnegut ably depicted the melding of technological power and helplessness in his country, as well as the blindness to social problems . . ." For El'sberg, reading Vonnegut is a reminder of all that is wrong with the capitalist system and the warped forms of scientific-technical progress that system has engendered. "[Scientific-technical] progress under capitalism too often engenders in the 'regular person' anti-intellectualism, irrationality, and individualistic isolation . . . Let us recall Vonnegut." (The piece ran under a large historical photograph from 1934 with the footer "A Rare Photo." It depicted H. G. Wells with a group of Soviet writers at the dacha of Maksim Gorky.)

Vonnegut also served the Soviet establishment as a symbol—maybe a spokesperson—of America's disaffected youth and its burgeoning youth protest movements. This included but was not limited to students and other young people who had protested the Vietnam War. A 1973 newspaper article, "USA: Youth, Culture, Peace," described the newly invigorated youth movements in the United States. Author V. Vul'f quoted Vonnegut's introduction to "his collection of articles about 'youth protests.'" "Only peace in the country can overcome fear and dread, and for this, you have to poison

---

[22] M.O. Mendel'son, *Amerikanskaia satiricheskaia proza XX veka* [American satirical prose of the twentieth century] (Nauka, 1972); M.O. Mendel'son, "Amerikanskii roman posle Khemingueia, Folknera, Steinbeka" [The American novel after Hemingway, Faulkner, Steinbeck], *Novyi Mir* 8 (1975): 246–63.

[23] Ia. El'sberg, "V bitve za cheloveka" [In the battle for humankind], *Literaturnaia gazeta* 1 (January 1, 1971): 1.

people's minds, poison them, while they are still young."[24] Many other critics repeated this oft-cited quote of Vonnegut's, including Raisa Orlova. Reviews likewise dwelt on Vonnegut's popularity with teen and young adult readers, who absorbed his messages and his anti-Vietnam War stance. In this way, Vonnegut was harnessed as a conduit to reach America's youth with the (necessary) "poison" of reason.

Soviet critics also loved to quote Vonnegut's observations about Americans' supposed lack of culture. In *Literary Gazette*, the well-known literary critic A. Muliarchik surveyed recent American literature and lamented the end of the radical 1960s. He pointed to a crisis of culture in "bourgeois America." Muliarchik quoted Vonnegut from an uncited recent interview: "It is simply impossible to live without culture." Muliarchik explained, "According to Vonnegut . . . American life is generally unhappy, in part because it doesn't have enough culture."[25] (The article appeared adjacent to a poem entitled "Lenin," penned by a poet from India named R. V'ias.)

Fiene found Soviet critics unified in their emphasis on Vonnegut's humanity and his compassion for the insulted and wounded, those society had thrown away.

> On this point, too, virtually all of Vonnegut's Soviet critics are in agreement. Again and again they refer to his humanity, to his genuine compassion for the insulted and injured, the destitute, the ignorant, and the unemployed—for the unlovable and bewildered souls who can only cry out absurdly, "What are people for?"[26]

Indeed, Soviet critics often emphasized the contrast between Vonnegut's humanistic approach and sensibilities of the author, and the perverted technocratic society in which his characters struggled. But the reference to "humanism" was an ideological tactic, one derived from the Marxist-Leninist discursive toolkit Soviet critics had to work with. As Sicari explains, "Humanism—namely the tendency to place man at the center of society— became a key concept in the ideological domestication of foreign literature in the USSR."[27] "In this way," continues Sicari, "the theme of dehumanization, as a result of the capitalist system, was an ideological domestication that alluded

---

[24] V. Vul'f, "SShA: Molodezh', kul'tura, mir" [USA: Youth, culture, peace]. *Sovetskaia Kul'tura* 48, no. 4640 (June 15, 1973): 7.
[25] A. Muliarchik, "Maiatnik kachnulsia vnov': Po stranitsam amerikanskoi prozy i publitsistiki [The pendulum has swung again: Through the pages of American prose and publicism], *Literaturnaia gazeta* 36 (June 25, 1975): 15.
[26] Fiene, "American Dissident," 268.
[27] Sicari, "Paratext as Weapon," 368.

to Marxist historical materialism. Thus, referring to anti-humanism, Soviet critics were able to highlight the distortions and perversions of capitalism, namely as an economic and social system that exploited and transformed man into an automaton in the gears of a mechanized society."[28]

In other words, for Soviet literary critics, calling Kurt Vonnegut a "humanist" was code for "one of ours." A self-declared humanist who was elected the honorary president of the American Humanist Society in 1992, Vonnegut made this task exceedingly easy. Soviet critics underscored Vonnegut's humanistic "tone." "[Vonnegut] is humane, and soft in his own way . . . [he] never raises his voice, but his ideas and convictions are no weaker for that. He also understands that people want to live with dignity, and they have the right to do so."[29]

In Soviet criticism, Vonnegut's concern for the unfortunates contrasted with the callous *lack* of concern felt by most of (U.S.) society for the outcast and nonconformist. This point was crystallized in V. Simukhov's review of *The Wanderings of Billy Pilgrim* stage adaptation.[30] The review focused on Billy Pilgrim's suffering after surviving the firebombing of Dresden. Simukhov emphasized Billy's neglect by American society, which throws trauma victims into asylums and expects them to pull themselves up by their own bootstraps. In this context, Fiene reminds us that Soviet critics were "inclined to view the bulk of [Vonnegut's] social satire as applying especially to America."[31] At times this interpretation flowed from the translation itself, where key passages and critiques (e.g., of the Soviet Union, of communism, of totalitarianism) were left out or heavily modified (see Chapter 3). However, even if Soviet literary critics had access to Vonnegut in the original (and chances are they sometimes did), they stressed Vonnegut's critiques of *America*. They did not frame Vonnegut as critiquing society in general, and certainly not Soviet society. The concluding lines of Aleksei Zverev's review of *Slaughterhouse-Five* encapsulate this approach. "The hopelessness that pervades Slaughterhouse 5 is not invented. It is indicative of the spiritual climate of contemporary America, and of the mood that is so pervasive in that country now, 25 years after the war."[32]

Vonnegut was a generally convenient anti-American American. His critiques of the soulless, cultureless existence of the American middle class, and his excoriations of capitalism run amok made useful copy. What

[28] Sicari, "Paratext as Weapon," 365.
[29] Borshchagovskii, "So it goes," 13.
[30] Simukhov, "The Wanderings of Billy Pilgrim," 4.
[31] Fiene, "American Dissident," 268.
[32] Aleksei Zverev, "De profundis Kurt Vonneguta" [Kurt Vonnegut's de profundis], *Inostrannaia literatura* 8 (1970): 268.

additional uses did the Soviet literary establishment—and by extension, the Soviet state—find for Comrade Vonnegut? A 1977 article in *Literary Gazette* provides some clues. In "A View on Literature from the Brooklyn Bridge," G. Gerasimov, on assignment in New York City, quotes three major American writers: William Faulkner, Robert Penn Warren, and Kurt Vonnegut. All three writers lamented the American public's lack of interest in literature and the arts. In support of his argument that Americans are ill-read and devalue writers and literature, Gerasimov quotes Vonnegut: "National, state, and local administrations . . . simply do not notice our writers. And this has been the case for 200 years. . . . Nearly all our best-selling authors were against the war in Vietnam. They threw the moral equivalent of a nuclear bomb on our society." Gerasimov continues, "And with what result? The United States pulled out of Vietnam, but the indignation of writers and intellectuals played no major part in that decision." Gerasimov quotes Vonnegut again on the "harmlessness" of writers in America: "Writers are harmless . . . they can be given all the freedoms birds enjoy—to chirp when they like, to hop around and fly."[33] Here Gerasimov reveals two ways Vonnegut was useful for the Soviet government. First, as a critic of the anti-intellectualism and complacency engendered by American capitalism (and U.S. authorities' total disinterest in writers). And second, as a critic of the Vietnam war.

"Every day my Government gives me a count of corpses created by military science in Vietnam"[34]

Vonnegut's outspoken opposition to the U.S. war in Vietnam made him very useful for the Soviet government. The official Soviet line on Vonnegut was straightforward and effective. It lifted Vonnegut's condemnation of war from *Slaughterhouse-Five* and his other novels and published speeches and channeled it into a critique of the war in Vietnam. Critics of *Slaughterhouse-Five* almost always mentioned Vonnegut's "hatred of war." But the anti-war themes of *Happy Birthday, Wanda June* also received some play.[35] There was a lot of material to work with, and critics frequently melded Vonnegut's critiques of war—the literary ones and the "real life" ones.

---

[33] G. Gerasimov, "Vzgliad na literatury s bruklinskogo mosta" (A View on Literature from the Brooklyn bridge.) *Literaturnaia gazeta* (September 28, 1977): 14.
[34] Kurt Vonnegut, *Slaughterhouse-Five or The Children's Crusade: A Duty-Dance with Death* (Dial Press Trade Paperback, 2009), 268.
[35] Vul'f, "USA: Youth, Culture, Peace," 7.

Take, for instance, a key review of *Slaughterhouse-Five* by Borshchagovskii. Vonnegut's conversation with Mary O'Hare helped him crystallize his approach to describing the Dresden firestorm. According to Borshchagovskii,

> Mary O'Hare is just a tiny window into the world that Vonnegut himself inhabits in the novel 'Slaughterhouse Five.' He despises war and drops an accusation, so to speak: "Every day my Government gives me a count of corpses created by military science in Vietnam."[36] He says this to his own sons—in the novel, and, by the way, in real life—so they "would never, for any reason, take part in wars."

In the same review, Borshchagovskii lambasts Jack Richardson's dismissive—even contemptuous—review of *Slaughterhouse-Five* in *The New York Review*.[37] Fiene similarly reflects, "[Richardson's] almost willful indifference to the moral issues raised in the novel could well have seemed to the Soviet critic [Borshchagovskii] a perfect example of that American indifference to suffering that characterized the dogged pursuit of the war in Vietnam and has been the principal target of Vonnegut's satire as well."[38]

Additionally, Soviet critics—and many Soviet readers—tended to (and still do) refer to *Slaughterhouse-Five* with its extended title, "the Children's Crusade." This underscores Vonnegut's key point that wars are fought by naïve youths, who must die like grown-ups. This critique resonated with Soviet readers and critics. The devastation of the Second World War still resonated as a key historical and social touchpoint. Reference to "the children's crusade" was also an effective way to mesh critiques of the firebombing of Dresden and the war in Vietnam. To understand how war, warmongering, and the arms race melded together for Soviet critics, consider, for instance, V. Skorodenko's Afterword to *Cat's Cradle*. The critic made "thinly-veiled references to the links between the Third Reich and the American inventors of the atomic and hydrogen bombs."[39]

B. Ileshin wrote an *Izvestiia* article during a 1970 trip to New York. He draws direct parallels between the scenes described by Vonnegut in *Slaughterhouse-Five* and the "barbarian" conduct of the American commanding officers and soldiers in "the current war in Southeast Asia." Ileshin avers that although

---

[36] Borshchagovskii, "So it goes," 13. Borshchagovskii's rendering of this line from *Slaughterhouse-Five* translates as, "How many corpses were created in Vietnam thanks to military science."
[37] Jack Richardson, "Easy Writer, review of *Slaughterhouse-Five* by Kurt Vonnegut, Jr.," *The New York Review*, July 2, 1970.
[38] Fiene, "American Dissident," 265.
[39] Khmelnitsky, "Sex, Lies, and Red Tape," 50.

Slaughterhouse-Five is about the firebombing of Dresden, the novel is "also about the current American reality, with its lies, hypocrisy, and cruelty. Kurt Vonnegut, having himself experienced the horrors of war, having been an unwilling witness in Dresden of the perishing of tens of thousands of people, tries to articulate the lessons of the past, and speaks out against today's saber-rattlers."[40] Ileshin takes scenes and characters from *Mother Night* and *Slaughterhouse-Five* to illustrate "American reality" characterized by greed, lies, and hypocrisy. Examples are Howard Campbell, with his cynical views about poor people's "lack of self-love and love for others," and the greasy Paul Lazzaro, who would do anything to anybody for a few bucks.[41]

Ileshin uses these motifs to elaborate and analyze his experiences in New York City. He focuses on the extreme wealth and power differentials he observed when visiting Wall Street, Manhattan, Central Park, and Harlem. The critic notes that whereas (according to *The New York Times*) the U.S. government had spent $150 billion on the Vietnam War effort, official U.S. statistics indicated around 7 million people were going hungry. The author describes the racial tensions he witnessed and how he saw students burning their draft cards to protest the war in Vietnam. "That's the American reality. It is reflected, as if in a mirror, in the novel Slaughterhouse Five, whose author reminds us once more that the past is not in the past, and that across the ocean are forces ready to drown the world in blood."[42]

Another scathing article in *Izvestiia* cites Vonnegut at length. Author Stanislav Kondrashov lambasts the sham "homecoming" of American military pilots from Vietnam after the signing of the Paris Peace Accords on January 27, 1973. Kondrashov refers to Seymour Hersh's March 1973 article in *The New York Times*, "P.O.W.'s Planned Business Venture."[43] He describes returning pilots' plot to form a strategic "corporation" and make piles of money off their memoirs about being prisoners of war in Hanoi. Kondrashov ends the piece with a reference to Kurt Vonnegut.

> Not long before the signing of the Paris agreement . . . [Vonnegut] described a conversation with a friend of his who said she was unable to

---

[40] B. Ileshin, "Za politseiskimi bar'erami" [Beyond the police barriers], *Izvestiia* 282 (November 27, 1970): 4.

[41] Rita Rait's brilliant translation of Vonnegut's description of Lazzaro as a "rabid little American" is the delightful *amerikashka*. It's a clever wordplay that translates as "little American shit."

[42] Ileshin, "Beyond the Police Barriers."

[43] Seymour M. Hersh, "P.O.W.'s Planned Business Venture," *The New York Times* (March 6, 1973): 12. https://www.nytimes.com/1973/03/06/archives/pows-planned-business-venture-agreed-at-camps-to-set-up-unit-on.html

sympathize with American pilots who had bombed civilians and ended up captured by the enemy. "The War in Vietnam," observes Vonnegut, "has caused us to secretly and unjustifiably distain our soldiers, especially our pilots. As time goes on this disdain will become less and less secretive."[44]

Agreeing with Vonnegut, Kondrashov only wondered why Vonnegut found this disdain "unjustified."[45]

The arms race intensified the Soviet state's need for an anti-American American spokesperson, and Vonnegut continued to fit the bill quite nicely. Long after the Vietnam War had ended, Vonnegut was being cited in the Soviet Union as a critic of the U.S. war in Vietnam *and* as an anti-nuclear activist. In July 1982, *Literary Gazette* republished in abridged form a translation of Vonnegut's July 13 editorial in *The New York Times*, "Avoiding the Big Bang."[46] In his argument for world peace, Vonnegut pointed out how modern communications have broken down cultural barriers and exposed most humans on the planet (e.g., through television footage) to the fact that war is absolute horror. A short, unattributed introductory paragraph instructs Soviet readers on how to interpret Vonnegut's article.

> In the atmosphere of military psychosis and anticommunism that currently envelops the USA, more and more cultural figures in that country feel the urgent imperative to enlighten their irresponsible politicians. . . . [In this article] the writer [Kurt Vonnegut] is compelled to prove the obvious—that war is grotesque and senseless, and that no one, anywhere, wants to kill one another. That's precisely why he takes to the extreme today's bourgeois propaganda, which one way or another promotes the arms race. And it is no mistake that Kurt Vonnegut mentions the "great moralist," the American industrial magnate of the last century Jim Fisk—the dishonest thief unashamed to speak of honesty . . . are today's "moralists" in Washington speaking and acting any differently?[47]

---

[44] S. Kondrashov, "'Khoumkaming' i dollar" ["Homecoming" and the dollar] *Izvestiia* 58 (March 9, 1973): 3.
[45] Kondrashov, "Homecoming," 3.
[46] Kurt Vonnegut, "Avoiding the Big Bang," *The New York Times* (June 13, 1982, section 4): 23. https://www.nytimes.com/1982/06/13/opinion/avoiding-the-big-bang.html
[47] Kurt Vonnegut, "Mne snilis' nashi potomki. . ." [I dreamed about our progeny], transl. Sergei Tartakovskii, *Literaturnaia gazeta* 27 (July 7, 1982): 13.

At least two things are interesting about this reprint and prefatory commentary in *Literary Gazette*. First, the paratextual information emphasizes Vonnegut's critique of American foreign policy and American capitalist greed (Jim Fisk). In fact, his *Times* editorial had cast a broader net of blame for the nuclear arms race. Second, and not surprisingly, certain of Vonnegut's passages are omitted from the *Literary Gazette* translation/reprint. This sentence is missing: "Thanks to modern communications, the poor, unlucky young people from the Soviet Union, now killing and dying in Afghanistan, were dead sick of war before they ever got there." Here we can track how critics (and the state-run publications they wrote for) carefully sanitized and packaged Vonnegut for delivery to Soviet readers.

When U.S. troops finally pulled out of Vietnam, comrade Vonnegut morphed from being the Soviets' favorite anti-Vietnam War critic into one of America's staunchest "No Nukes!" spokespersons. In 1983, *Literary Gazette* published translations of several of Vonnegut's speeches and letters from the collection *Palm Sunday*. Vonnegut's anti-nukes speech, "I am Embarrassed," which he delivered at a rally in Washington, D.C., was published in its entirety. The speech was a scathing attack on the entire nuclear industry, especially, as Vonnegut put it, the "so-called 'profession' of public relations, an American invention, [which] stands thoroughly disgraced today."[48] *Literary Gazette* harnessed Vonnegut's speech to deliver a one-two punch to both the American nuclear arms industry and the sinister nuclear lobby.

Vonnegut's positive relationship with the Red Army was the flip side of his role as an anti-Vietnam, anti-nukes spokesperson. That Kurt Vonnegut was an American veteran whose life was saved during the Second World War by the Soviet Army was a terrific checkmark in his favor for the Soviet establishment. Significantly, Vonnegut was liberated by the Red (Soviet) Army from his captivity as a prisoner of war under the Germans in rather strange circumstances. He had barely survived the firebombing of Dresden by his "own side"—the American and English armed forces! This made for quite a story, one Vonnegut repeated often in his writing and public lectures (including at the House of Littérateurs in Moscow in 1974), and even in Soviet newspapers. For example, Vonnegut sent a congratulatory telegram to the Red Army that was published in the May 9, 1975 (Victory Day) edition of *Literary Gazette*. "Accept my heartiest congratulations on the anniversary of Victory Day. As I already said in Moscow, if not for the Red Army, I would not

---

[48] Kurt Vonnegut, "Istinnuiu bol' prichiniaiut lozh' i beschestnye postupki," (True pain comes from lies and dishonest deeds), passages from *Palm Sunday*, transl. Sergei Tartakovskii, *Literaturnaia gazeta* 10 (March 9, 1983): 11.

be alive today."⁴⁹ And as discussed in Chapter 7, in Vonnegut's 1974 telegram to theater director Mikhail Levitin, he said if he could enlist in the Red Army, he would.

In 1978, literary critic Professor Iasen Zasurskii visited Vonnegut's home in New York City for a conversation. The encounter coincided with a Soviet-American roundtable of writers in which both Vonnegut and Zasurskii participated. Zasurskii spent time with several of the American writers—Joyce Carol Oates, John Gardner, and Kurt Vonnegut, and included short profiles of them all in his article. The critic recounts Vonnegut's experiences being captured by the Nazis not far from Luxembourg, surviving the firebombing of Dresden, and "being freed from capture" thanks to the Soviet Army. "Our soldiers appeared. Vonnegut was spotted first by a Russian Major. They kissed one another joyfully. A photograph of this scene exists somewhere. Perhaps the Major is still alive and remembers this scene. . . ."⁵⁰ Zasurskii had asked Vonnegut to show him a photograph of the Soviet soldier who freed him from the concentration camp, but Vonnegut was unable to find it.

Another useful Soviet framing of Vonnegut is the "blue-collar writer." Soviet critics dwell on Vonnegut's indebtedness to Red Army soldiers, his own record of military service, and other "grassroots" elements of Vonnegut's biography. This includes work experience at General Electric and his previous job as a car salesman. Zasurskii, for instance, describes Vonnegut as a writer who was close to the "regular people," including blue-collar workers and soldiers. Zasurskii's Vonnegut is estranged from many other American writers, who are representatives of the intellectual class. Zasurskii quotes Vonnegut as saying, "The Vietnam War dealt a big blow to American literature . . . not wanting to serve in the army, a lot of would-be writers enrolled in universities, instead of going to work for newspapers or becoming sailors."⁵¹ Zasurskii continues,

> In this regard he [Vonnegut] prefers writers who lived through the war in Vietnam, such as Robert Stone, author of the novel, *Soldiers*. Vonnegut is frequently classified as a science fiction writer, to which he responds: "[This is a result of] the aristocratic sensibilities of critics who are highly suspicious of people who have a technical education; they think that no one who understands how his refrigerator works can be a true artist."⁵²

---

⁴⁹ Kurt Vonnegut, "Telegrama Kurta Vonneguta" [Telegram from Kurt Vonnegut], *Literaturnaia Gazeta* 19 (May 9, 1975): 14.
⁵⁰ Iasen Zasurskii, "V poiskakh pravdy" [In search of truth], *Literaturnaia Gazeta* 27 (July 5, 1978): 15.
⁵¹ Zasurskii, "In Search of Truth," 15.
⁵² Zasurskii, "In Search of Truth," 15.

The critic goes on to briefly describe the new book Vonnegut was working on. It was *Jailbird*, a novel about a 64-year-old man, a former trade union activist, who would revisit the 1920s and 1930s for a lesson in workers' rights movements. "In his prose today Vonnegut is addressing the history of the labor movement. This is wonderful. The author continues to search for complex and serious themes..."[53]

Kurt is *not* a black humorist! He's a satirist

Soviet literary critics, of course, were not only interested in Vonnegut's key themes and messages. They also attended to the underlying sensibilities, moral motivations, and existential commitments that animated his prose. American and Soviet debates over which literary bucket Vonnegut belonged in had similar contours rooted in like concerns. Critics in both countries pondered what was so fresh and edgy about Vonnegut's work, particularly his novels that did not feel like novels. They lined him up beside other exciting authors, tried to identify similarities and differences in the work, and proposed appropriate classifications.

A key concern for Soviet critics, much like their American counterparts, was to rescue Vonnegut from the purgatory of the "science fiction writer" label. This was usually accomplished in the first few sentences of the review. Nearly all of Vonnegut's Soviet critics pointed out with relish that he was decidedly *not* a science fiction writer. They delivered a sharp elbow to those misguided American readers and critics who, during his first years of fame, had labeled him a sci-fi author, ensuring his long-term neglect as a great writer.[54]

Vonnegut's humorous tone and style of writing always merited mention. Sometimes the Soviet "thick journals" published his short stories under a "Humor and Satire" rubric. One example is the February 2, 1972 issue of *Literary Gazette*, which featured Margarita Kovaleva's translation of Vonnegut's short story "Tom Edison's Shaggy Dog." The unattributed editorial introduction to the translation of "Shaggy Dog" offered the piece as "a story

---

[53] Zasurskii, "In Search of Truth," 15.
[54] Some literary critics writing relatively early in the Soviet love affair with Vonnegut did identify him as a science fiction writer. For example, writing in *Pravda* in 1970, Vl. Dmitrevskii included Vonnegut's name in his list of "leading masters of science fiction" in the West, along with Ray Bradbury, Robert Sheckley, and Paul Anderson. TASS correspondent M. Belov, writing about Americans' affinity for the works of Leo Tolstoy (an argument he supported with quotes from Vonnegut), called Vonnegut a "science fiction psychology" writer *(fantast-psikholog)*.

to acquaint the reader with Vonnegut-the-humorist." It described Vonnegut's short story collection *Welcome to the Monkey House* (where "Shaggy Dog" originally appeared) as a book of "original parables about human stupidity, written breezily, with light irony; fabrication and reality, fantasy and truth, are tightly interwoven."[55]

Soviet critics did not question whether Vonnegut was a humorist. Of course he was. The important question—and one that literary scholars across the world have debated in relation to Kurt Vonnegut—was whether Vonnegut was or was not a "black humorist." Soviet critics in the 1960s and 1970s shared this conundrum with their American counterparts. To oversimplify a complex debate, critics in both countries pondered whether Vonnegut was either a black humorist or a satirist. Some American critics stood firmly on the black humorist side. Others proved Vonnegut was a satirist. Still other scholars complained about the limits and misleading nature of labels. Once an author is dropped in a "bucket," it is hard to fish them back out.[56] Vonnegut himself objected to being tagged a black humorist, or anything at all. Of the black humorist label, he once reflected, "Bruce Friedman did that. He put the label on me. I don't know what he means. It's just a convenient tag for reviewers. Out I go into the ashcan with Terry Southern and Jack Barth."[57]

American literary critic Robert Scholes was an early proponent of Vonnegut as a black humorist. "The term black humorist is probably too clumsy to be of much use to criticism, but before discarding it we should do well to milk it of such value as it may have in helping us to understand this new fiction and to adjust to it."[58] Scholes identified some more-or-less agreed-upon techniques and motives of the black humorists. Other critics elaborated on these further. Scholes famously identified the characteristic difference between satire and black humor.

> [Black Humor] is generally more playfully and carefully constructed, it is more certain esthetically and less certain ethically than its ancestors .... The spirit of playfulness and the care for form characteristic of the best Black Humorists operate so as to turn the materials on satire into comedy .... These writers reflect quite properly their heritage from the esthetic movement of the nineteenth century and the ethical relativism of the twentieth. They have some faith in art but they reject all ethical

---

[55] Kurt Vonnegut, "Lokhmatyi pes Toma Edisona" [Tom Edison's shaggy dog], transl. Margarita Kovaleva, *Literaturnaia Gazeta* 5 (February 2, 1972): 16.
[56] John R. May, "Vonnegut's Humor and the Limits of Hope," *Twentieth Century Literature* 18 (1972): 25.
[57] Rollene W. Saal, "Pick of the Paperbacks," *Saturday Review* 53 (March 28, 1970): 34.
[58] Scholes, *The Fabulators*, 37.

absolutes. Especially they reject the traditional satirist's faith in the efficacy of satire as a reforming instrument. They have a more subtle faith in the humanizing value of laughter.[59]

Scholes further offered: "The Black Humorist is not concerned with what to do about life but with how to take it. In this respect, Black Humor has certain affinities with some existentialist attitudes, roughly distinguishable in terms of the difference between seeing the universe as absurd and seeing it as ridiculous—a joke."[60] This means that, as Stanley Schatt explained, ". . . black humorists usually view the world as so complex and so fragmented that any answers can only be tentative; and the best advice they can offer their readers is how to smile through their tears at the absurdities of the world . . . black humorist characters are fortunate merely to survive their ordeals."[61]

Some scholars make an important distinction between black humorists and satirists. Satirists, they say, employ the rhetoric of "moral certainty." Black humorists reject it.[62] Scholes argued that as a black humorist, "in Vonnegut, as in his contemporaries, we do not find the rhetoric of moral certainty, which has generally been a distinguishing characteristic of the satirical tradition."[63] For the Soviets, this was hard to swallow. To be acceptable and useful, Vonnegut had to be a satirist, not a black humorist. Why was that so?

An important ideological distinction drove the debate over whether Vonnegut was a satirist or a black humorist, a form of nihilist. Any sanctioned author in the Soviet Union was required to employ moral certainty. Vonnegut had to believe in a "way out," a solution to the problems his characters embodied. He had to leave open the possibility for a brighter future. Ideally, he would point readers toward it. Soviet critic O. Aliakrinskii published a long review article in *Problems of Literature* [*Voprosy literatury*] that made a case for Vonnegut's role as a satirist. The piece can be our guide through the reasons why, for a Soviet readership, a sanctioned American author-in-translation like Kurt Vonnegut absolutely could not be a black humorist.[64]

Aliakrinskii summarizes Western evaluations of Vonnegut and engages with Vonnegut Studies debates in the United States. He outlines the reasons

---

[59] Robert Scholes, "'Mithridates, He Died Old:' Black Humor and Kurt Vonnegut, Jr.," *The Hollins Critic* 3, no. 4 (October 1966). Gale Document Number: GALE|A133025607.
[60] Scholes, *The Fabulators*, 43.
[61] Stanley Schatt, *Kurt Vonnegut, Jr.* (Twayne Publishers, 1976), 55–6.
[62] James M. Mellard, "The Modes of Vonnegut's Fiction: Or, Player Piano Ousts Mechanical Bride and The Sirens of Titan Invade the Gutenberg Galaxy," in Klinkowitz and Somer, eds., *The Vonnegut Statement*, 200.
[63] Scholes, *The Fabulators*, 54.
[64] O Aliakrinskii, "Kurt Vonnegut: S raznykh tochek zreniia" [Kurt Vonnegut: From Different Points of View], *Voprosy literatury* 4 (April 1982): 236–47.

"formalist" or "neocritical formalist" interpretations of Vonnegut's prose (by P. Jones, by M. Dickstein) are inadequate and flawed. The critic argues for a more complex approach, one that captures the "variable-meaning" (*neodnozanchnost'*) nature of Vonnegut's ideological position. Vonnegut's prose is ironic and polyphonic, offers Aliakrinskii. His humor is "deceptive." That is why American critics have so often labeled him a "black humorist."[65]

Black humorists, Aliakrinskii reminds us, do not believe human nature can be changed. They see no way out. Black humorists point out problems, contradictions, and incongruities just to laugh at them. Aliakrinskii harnesses Friedman and Scholes's arguments that black humorists focus more on aesthetic problems than ethical ones. Black humorists, according to these authors, have retained an interest in the art of words but have rejected all ethical absolutes. They do not believe in the possibility of changing human nature. Aliakrinskii offers his own feature to this list. Black humorists think life itself is absurd at its very core.

In contrast, the critic argues, satirists poke at problems so they can be recognized, named, and addressed. A satirist holds out hope for change, for reform, for saving the human race. The door is still cracked. Vonnegut believes that society, and thus reality, can change. He is therefore a satirist, not a black humorist. Aliakrinskii quotes Conrad Festa: "Vonnegut's satires offer us hope, not despair—but not hope without action. They tell us simply that we are not necessarily bound to a determined future and that we are capable of making a better world if we will have the will and the courage."[66] Aliakrinskii adds that unlike black humorists, Vonnegut is not cynical, though he is skeptical. Further, black humor is written "for the sake of writing." An author like Vonnegut who writes to "change the world" cannot be a black humorist. The critic adds arguments by American critics such as Jerome Klinkowitz in support of his thesis: "Whereas Klinkowitz described Vonnegut as a black humorist in 1975, in his 1977 volume, he did not even mention the term."[67]

Aliakrinskii's review is a useful summary of critical assessments of Vonnegut by leading American critics. It also provides some useful original insights. Crucially, the review illustrates why Soviet critics needed Vonnegut to be "just" a satirist. They needed him to acknowledge at least *some* possibility that societies can change, that people can wake up, that doomsday can be avoided, or at least delayed. Vonnegut could be sanctioned reading for the

---

[65] Aliakrinskii, "Kurt Vonnegut," 240.
[66] Conrad Festa, "Vonnegut's Satire," in Klinkowitz and Lawler, eds., *Vonnegut in America*, 147. Quoted in Aliakrinskii, "Kurt Vonnegut," 244–5.
[67] Aliakrinskii, "Kurt Vonnegut," 243.

educated Soviet reading public only if the dystopian scenarios he imagined could be "fixed." Vonnegut wrote of global destruction caused by immoral scientific "advancements," crass Western consumer capitalism run amok, class inequalities of preposterous proportions, and human relationships rooted in greed, lust, and utilitarianism instead of feeling, compassion, and morality. For Soviet critics and the state they worked in, the only possible "fix," of course, was the application of socialist principles of rationality, equality, and the "struggle for peace" (discussed below). And Vonnegut could only offer such hope for the future if he was "just" a satirist, not a black humorist.[68]

In this context, a lot of Soviet literary criticism dwelt on Vonnegut's use of satire. According to Fiene, Soviet critics believed Vonnegut was the best contemporary writer of satire in America. Vonnegut's more conservative critics classified Vonnegut as a critical realist. They argued that Vonnegut's views about the possibility for a better future were influenced by socialist ideals and the principles of socialist realism. More liberal critics, Fiene asserted, "emphasize[d] the moral rather than the political basis for Vonnegut's satire."[69] Whatever the basis for his satire, for the Soviet literary establishment, Vonnegut *was*—and had to be—a satirist.

This vision of Vonnegut as a satirist who believed people and their circumstances could change ran directly counter to Fiene's own reading of Vonnegut. He explained this in a May 1970 letter to Rita Rait.

> Why is it that you like Vonnegut so much? I also think he is charming, a true humanist; he has a good sense of humor; he is my favorite American author, perhaps. But he is also a total pessimist about the human race—he knows that evil will always triumph over good in human affairs, and that the universe is absolutely indifferent to men, hence irrational—and there is nothing at all that men can do to improve their collective lot. He is uniformly disgusted with all governmental institutions; he sees no hope from them at all, nor from any of the world's religions. To be sure, he privately advocates, like Jesus, loving your fellow humans and not judging them (he knows we are all equally sinners). But he knows that 99 percent of men will not love their fellow men and there is no way to persuade them otherwise. I do not think he believes his novels will really

---

[68] There were exceptions. Raisa Orlova, for example, classified Vonnegut as a black humorist. She also labeled him a pacifist (a minority Soviet view), also for ideological reasons, as explored later in this chapter.

[69] Fiene, "American Dissident," 263.

make men behave better.... I know that his view of life is correct—but it makes me sad to perceive this truth.[70]

Fiene, albeit only in private letters to Rita Rait, thereby poked holes in the Soviet critics' framing of Vonnegut as an author who holds out hope for social and political reform.

Kurt is not a pacifist! He's a fighter in the struggle for peace (redux)

Records of the deliberations of the Foreign Commission and the Translators' Section of the Soviet Union of Writers are shot through with the discourse of "struggle for peace" (*borba za mir*). This narrative pillar of Soviet foreign policy during the Cold War reverberated through the sections' meetings in the 1950s. In fact, the *borba za mir* was at the center of the Foreign Commission's official mandate.

> [The Commission shall undertake] study of the contemporary state of foreign literature, the activities of writers' organizations and the social activities of writers in foreign countries; systematic selection of material for publication by Soviet writers and critics, unmasking "literature" inciting wars and popularizing the work of progressive *writers–fighters for peace* [emphasis added]; cooperation and assistance in the work of collectives of literary critics and literature scholars, who specialize in questions of foreign literature.[71]

Professional translators like Rita Rait had to prove that the authors sanctioned for translation in the Soviet Union were "fighters for peace," not pacifists. This was often a challenge. Described in Chapter 7, as a self-declared pacifist, Kurt Vonnegut sometimes posed a problem for his supporters in the USSR. Accusations that *Slaughterhouse-Five* was a pacifist work nearly derailed the stage adaptation of the novel in Moscow in 1975–6. Thankfully, although probably unwittingly, Vonnegut nevertheless did his part to perpetuate the "struggle for peace" discourse.

---

[70] DMF to RRK, May 18, 1970, p. 2, DMFC, Box 4, Folder 1, "Rait-Kovaleva, Rita. 1961–1989."
[71] RGALI 631/26/10.

In December 1976, the journal *Problems of Literature* released a special issue on "World writers on the struggle for peace." Along with reactions from prominent writers from the USSR, France, Cuba, Japan, Italy, Turkey, and many other countries, the journal published three American writers' responses to questions about literature and "the struggle for peace, defense of human values, and strengthening the friendship of peoples." The three American writers were Kurt Vonnegut, William Saroyan, and D. North. They were asked to describe the role literature played in the struggle for peace, the defense of human values, and strengthening the friendship of peoples. What creative and aesthetic challenges arose from this? What role did these issues play in each author's life and work? Vonnegut sent his answers.

> All I can say in response to the question is that any true writer, no matter where he is, is already, by virtue of his profession, a defender of peace, human values, and people's friendship. That must be the writer's primary goal already, and no prizes from an editorial board or other recognition are going to make the writer a better citizen of the world. As far as I can tell, artists of all stripes are already the most peaceful of earthlings. Inhabitants of other planets will have a hard time keeping up with them in this regard.[72]

Here Vonnegut emphasizes the mediating role a writer must play to foster peace and mutual understanding. He positions writers as citizens of the earth unfettered by (inter)national politics.

In June 1982, *Foreign Literature* published Vonnegut's response to a similar survey. Entitled "The Responsibility of Talent: A Word from World Writers," the survey posed two questions:

(1) How are the pressing problems of our time (*sovremennosti*) treated in your works (literally, your "schemes, intentions" (*zamysli*))? What are you currently working on?
(2) How can works of art and literature contribute to preserving world peace?[73]

Vonnegut answered these questions in less optimistic and jovial terms than he had in 1976. His response focuses on the threat that mass armament poses to humans' existence. "More than anything I fear another world war, which

---

[72] Kurt Vonnegut, "Response to survey of world authors," *Voprosy literatury* 12 (1976): 21.
[73] "Anketa Inostrannoi literatury" [Foreign literature's survey], *Innostrannaia literatura* 6 (June 1982): 188.

would, without question, destroy life on earth. That's why I continue to write short essays and argue for disarmament." Vonnegut describes the book he is working on—*Deadeye Dick*—the key idea of which is that "the very existence of weapons can turn us into unwilling killers" (like the book's twelve-year-old protagonist). But, Vonnegut continues, the chances that artists and writers, or even soldiers, can enact arms control are slim. "Therefore, all art can do is calm and entertain us, while people, like machines—with the help of machines, too—will decide what happens next. And something terrible is going to happen."[74]

As a "fighter in the struggle for peace," Vonnegut spoke into another important Soviet foreign policy discourse: the friendship of peoples, in particular friendly relations between the people of the U.S. and the USSR. As discussed above, Vonnegut seized every chance to praise the Red Army, which had liberated him from Nazi capture in the rubble of Dresden. He was likewise outspoken about the dangers of the arms race, especially its nuclearization. He constantly swore that average citizens of the U.S. and the USSR had nothing to fight over. These sentiments were crystallized in a published conversation between Vonnegut and Chinghiz Aitmatov, who at the time was editor-in-chief of *Literary Gazette*. They talked about the 1975 Apollo-Soyuz Project, the first joint US-Soviet space flight. Yana Skorobogatov deftly sums up the significance of this article.

> "I sit here and think: if there is no animosity in outer space, why must there be animosity here?" Aitmatov asked his peer. Vonnegut agreed, reassuring Aitmatov that "there's never any hostility among our citizens." He offered the following scenario: "If you stopped an average American walking on the street and asked him whether he hates Russians, he would be shocked: 'Why? Why should I hate Russians?'" The comment is quite telling. The conflict, from both Aitmatov and Vonnegut's points of view, existed in the minds of the statesmen who staked their countries and their reputation on its perpetuation. By the mid-1970s, the Cold War, in the eyes of American and Russian citizens, had lost its raison d'être and devolved into a grotesque status quo.[75]

Vonnegut goes on to praise the Soviet Union for getting back on its feet so quickly after the Second World War, especially in terms of its "excellent machinery" (*tekhnika*) and advancements in science. Vonnegut talks about

---

[74] Kurt Vonnegut, "Response to Foreign Literature's Survey," *Innostrannaia literatura* 6 (June 1982): 189.
[75] Skorobogatov, "Kurt Vonnegut," 36.

how standards of masculinity have changed in the United States since he was a boy in Indianapolis. Men are no longer expected to appear as a "threat" to other men and are even allowed to cry. He compares this change in standards and behavior to a similar change in U.S.-USSR relations. The United States no longer feels it needs to be a threat. Interestingly, when Vonnegut raises the prickly question of how to ensure that both the American and Soviet governments pay their fair share for joint space exploration, Aitmatov quickly intervenes. He takes over the conversation for the rest of the interview.[76]

Soviet translators, critics, and other culture brokers managed to push Vonnegut—an infamous pacifist—through official channels, even with all their tricky ideological control measures. They did this by framing him as a "fighter in the struggle for peace." He was a veteran of the Second World War, a hero of American youth (especially anti-Vietnam War protesters), a staunch critic of America's cultural degradation under the weight of bourgeois capitalism, and a master satirist of American life. In short, he was the perfect personification of a "fighter in the struggle for peace" between the nations. Vonnegut thus became an unwitting starting player in the Soviets' Peace Offensive.

Here the already confusing story of Vonnegut as a "fighter for peace" takes a plot twist. With Rita Rait's reluctant blessing, Orlova's Afterword to the Russian translation of *Slaughterhouse-Five* had firmly established Vonnegut's reputation as a pacifist back in 1970. Rita revealed this in a letter to Donald Fiene dated May 2, 1970.

> I am continuously running into people who don't always understand the meaning of the words "humanist" and "pacifist." I promote these words in their direct sense, without the adjectives "abstract humanist" or "rabid pacifist." I think it is important to understand that a humanist—loves people and DOES NOT LOVE NON-PEOPLE, and a pacifist does not love war.
>
> But, in light of the unclarity (*neiasnosti*) of these terms for some people, it was necessary to include an Afterword to Vonnegut's book, and it was written by my colleague, a rather dear and not-stupid [literary critic and translator, Raisa Orlova] ... And if EVERYTHING WILL GO O.K. then in the 3rd and 4th issues of "Novii Mir"—prepared long ago, under the old director [Tvardovsky]—my translation of "Slaughterhouse 5" will be published ...

---

[76] Aitmatov and Vonnegut, "Meeting above planet Earth," 2.

... Still, in the afterword you will read that Vonnegut—is a pacifist!!! But, don't let that surprise him: all of us are for the same thing (*za odno*), and just understand words differently . . . I myself hate war and all violence![77]

Here's what the renowned literary critic Raisa Orlova wrote about Vonnegut's "pacifism" in the obligatory paratext to *Slaughterhouse-Five*.

One could call Vonnegut a pacifist: he hates war, perceives it as a reflection of mystical-abstract global evil and therefore does not know, if war is preventable, and if so, how. In this he resembles many other Western writers, as varied as Remarque, Aldington, Lana, Böll. But the work of Vonnegut, even if he is a pacifist (*pust' on i patsifist*), today stands against the powers who are ready to conduct new wars, even more effectively perhaps than the anti-war novels of Remarque forty years ago.[78]

I interpret this fiasco over Vonnegut's "pacifism"—which became a SNAFU Rita Rait had to untangle to launch the *Billy Pilgrim* play—as follows. To get *Slaughterhouse-Five* published in 1970, Rait had to make a compromise. She agreed to a critique of Vonnegut in the Afterword that called him out as a "pacifist." This was a preemptive critique to dissuade Soviet readers from "appreciating" (i.e., sympathizing with) Vonnegut's "pacifist" stance. Readers were assured that even though the author is mistaken in his commitment to X (here, commitment to pacifism, and thus denial of any "just" conflicts), we can still read and appreciate his views on Y and Z. In her memoirs, Orlova outlined the compromises critics and translators had to make to get foreign literature published in the USSR. They highlighted "obvious limitations," "mistaken representations," and so on. These compromises eventually exacted a high price.[79] No one knew this better than Rita Rait, as illustrated by her later struggles in 1975–6 over the staging of *The Wanderings of Billy Pilgrim*.

---

[77] RRK to DMF, May 2, 1970, DMFC, Box 4, Folder 2, "Rait-Kovaleva, Rita. 1968–1978."
[78] Orlova, "On Kurt Vonnegut's novel," 179–80.
[79] Orlova and Kopelev, *We Lived in Moscow*, 132.

Kurt is a victim of book burning and censorship in the U.S. of A!

Another detail from Vonnegut's writerly scrapbook worked in his favor for the Soviets. He was a victim of censorship in the United States. Soviet critics harnessed the banning, and burning, of Vonnegut's books as evidence of repression of the printed word in America, that duplicitous beacon of free speech. Book bans telescoped the narrow-mindedness and provincialism of Americans writ large. One article in *Literary Gazette* by Genrikh Borovik illustrates how Soviet correspondents lassoed news of book bans to illustrate broad crises in American society and politics. Unsubtly titled "'Democracy' with a Police Cudgel: SOS Signal from the Statue of Liberty," Borovik's piece depicts the United States as a police state. Borovik describes various instances of police brutality he said he witnessed in New York, Washington, D.C., Los Angeles, and Chicago.[80] The author mentions Vonnegut after a paragraph on the recent Kent State trials, the ongoing trial of the peace activists the Berrigan brothers, and the impending trial of Angela Davis.

> The state of Michigan has banned the writer Kurt Vonnegut's antiwar book Slaughterhouse Five, or The Children's Crusade, about the American air force's senseless destruction of Dresden at the end of the war. But the book by Xaviera Hollander, madam of a New York brothel, circulates freely; just as freely the war criminal Wernher von Braun advertises his autobiography over the television.

Borovik goes on to describe the harsh sentences imposed on Vietnam War protesters and those protesting other injustices such as racism. Borovik's messages were clear.

(1) All kinds of freedoms in the "land of the free" are stomped on, and critique of U.S. domestic policy is not tolerated.
(2) Those who criticize the U.S. government face consequences, even great writers like Kurt Vonnegut.
(3) American readers are free to read trashy books written by prostitutes and war criminals, but not literature by great novelists like Kurt Vonnegut that critiques U.S. warmongering.

---

[80] Genrikh Borovik, "'Demokratia' politseiskoi dubinki: Signal SOS na statue svobody" ["Democracy" with a police cudgel: SOS signal from the Statue of Liberty], *Literaturnaia gazeta* 8 (February 23, 1972): 14.

(4) American readers have poor taste in literature.

Ten years later, in 1983, *Literary Gazette* featured translated excerpts of several of Vonnegut's essays and speeches from the recent *Palm Sunday* collection. This included portions of "Dear Mr. McCarthy," Vonnegut's letter to the head of a school committee in Drake, N.D., where his books were burned; "Un-American Nonsense," Vonnegut's essay in *The New York Times* about the banning of his books by the school committee of Island Trees, N.Y.; "Self-Interview," "How Jokes Work," and "I am Embarrassed," Vonnegut's anti-nuclear speech at a rally in Washington, D.C. Together, these translated excerpts emphasize Americans' lack of culture. They underline the provincialism and ignorance of the American masses. The reprints illustrate egregious instances of lack of freedoms of the press and free speech in the United States. The collection of *Palm Sunday* excerpts appears directly above a translated long-narrative article about child homelessness in the U.S. Southwest, with a photograph of "Child farm laborers coming home after a full day's work in the field" in Southern California.[81]

Of course, these articles contain grains of truth, but they omit important context and details of Vonnegut's public political commitments. They aptly focus on Vonnegut's strong position of support for freedom of speech and the First Amendment in the United States. But they neglect his outspoken criticism of lack of such freedoms in other countries, in particular those of the Soviet bloc.[82] Notably absent from the *Literary Gazette* sampling of *Palm Sunday*, is "Dear Felix," the letter that Vonnegut wrote to Felix Kuznetzov, "a distinguished critic and teacher, and an officer in the Union of Writers of the USSR." In the letter, Vonnegut protests the harassment of writers in the USSR (and, it should be noted, calls out harassment of writers in the United States as well).[83] These translated, selected reproductions of Vonnegut's work and reflections on his struggles as a "censored" author illustrate how Soviet outlets enlisted cherry-picked morsels from Vonnegut's writings and speeches to support their reporting on social, economic, and political chaos in the United States. However, and not surprisingly, they ignored the way Vonnegut overtly defended Soviet dissidents and exiled writers, even at the height of his popularity in the Soviet Union in the last half of the 1970s. (Chapter 10 describes these cautious engagements.)

---

[81] Vonnegut, "True Pain," 11.
[82] Richard R. Lingeman, "God Bless You, Mr. Mihajlov," *The New York Times Book Review* (July 2, 1978). https://www.nytimes.com/1978/07/02/archives/book-ends-god-bless-you-mr-mihajlov.html
[83] Kurt Vonnegut, *Palm Sunday: An Autobiographical Collage* (Delta Trade Paperbacks, 1981), 11.

Soviet critics had a strategy ready, should Vonnegut's (or any other translated author's) writing prove ideologically "inconvenient." They could hedge with a caveat that "even if the author does not realize it, their book is definitely a criticism of X." This was the technique Igor Bestuzhev-Lada employed. Vonnegut's earliest Soviet critic Bestuzhev-Lada wrote the Foreword for the 1967 publication of M. Brukhnov's mostly overlooked translation of *Player Piano* (titled *Utopia-14*).[84] Bestuzhev-Lada offered elaborate musings on how Vonnegut's book foretold the horrors of late-stage capitalism, with dominance of service industries and total dependence on computers, automobiles, and mechanized labor. Human labor was made superfluous.[85] Bestuzhev-Lada left open the possibility that the book's actual message and utility as an ideological weapon may not line up with the author's subjective views.[86] As Friedberg noted, Soviet criticism frequently took the tack that the "objective" political significance of a literary work may be divorced from the "subjective" views of its creator.[87]

It is ironic that the Soviet reading public and literary establishment was so in love with Kurt Vonnegut because Vonnegut certainly was not in love with the Soviet Union. In fact, he quite disliked it. In his private correspondence, Vonnegut said churlish things about the Soviet Union, particularly the limits on travel and other restrictions placed on people like Rita Rait. By way of example, consider the following excerpts from Vonnegut's letters to friends, family, colleagues, and critics.

Letter to William Styron, June 25, 1974

We [Jill and I] are going to Moscow in October, to see my translator, and perhaps yours, too—Rita Rait (Рита Раит). She is one of those who wants to stay there, and, with a little help from her friends, to make the Soviet Union more amusing and humane. Fat chance, I suppose.[88]

---

[84] Ihor Bestuzhev-Lada, "Kogda lishnim stanovitsia chelovechestvo" [When humankind becomes superfluous], Foreword to *Utopiia 14* [Utopia 14/Player Piano] by Kurt Vonnegut, transl. M. Brukhnov (Molodaia Gvardiia, 1967), 5–24.
[85] As described by Skorobogatov ("Kurt Vonnegut," 46), Bestuzhev-Lada proposed a colorful subtitle for *Player Piano*: "The Story of How automated and cybernetized production processes helped monopoly capitalism reach its logical conclusion and bring man to the point of extinction." Translation by Yana Skorobogatov.
[86] See Skorobogatov, "Kurt Vonnegut," 40–50; Sicari, "Paratext as Weapon," 363–4; and Friedburg, *Decade of Euphoria*, 293–4 for analyses of Bestuzhev-Lada's paratextual review of *Utopia-14 (Player Piano)*.
[87] Friedberg, *Decade of Euphoria*, 294.
[88] Wakefield, *Kurt Vonnegut—Letters*, 216–17.

Finding Comrade Vonnegut 215

Letter to Aaron Spiegel, July 29, 1974

> I have worked hard for peace all my adult life. I am going to the Soviet Union for the second time this fall. My books have all been published there, and I have several Russian friends. I will go over there with the same attitude I tried to express in my statement [which you misunderstood as being] about hating Russians. My exact meaning was this: I love the Russian people, but I think their leaders have often treated my fellow artists most swinishly, and it makes me mad. O.K.?[89]

Letter to Sam Lawrence, August 29, 1974

> As for when I go to the Soviet Union: the tentative date is October 7. I'm really not at all eager to go. The Russians, incidentally, won't let me pay any of my hotel bills in my own roubles. They want American cash in advance. The same goes for my ticket on Aeroflot. The more I think about it, the less I want to go. It always gives me the heebee-jeebies to visit a dictatorship.[90]

Letter to Mary Glossbrenner (a cousin), September 30, 1974

> Here I am warmed again [by your letter], a week before taking off for the fleshpots of Moscow. I'm going over there to see my seventy-six-year-old translator, a magnificent woman who took a doctor's degree under Pavlov. She has been allowed out of the worker's paradise only four times in her entire life. We got to know her during one of those times—in Paris. Now she will probably never be allowed out again. She has made friends with too many of the wrong people.[91]

Letter to Donald Fiene, October 25, 1974

> I behaved politely [in Moscow]. The theory is that my good behavior would do a lot to loosen up travel restrictions on Rita. That country sure is full of envy, by the way.[92]

---

[89] Wakefield, *Kurt Vonnegut—Letters*, 217–18.
[90] Wakefield, *Kurt Vonnegut—Letters*, 218.
[91] Wakefield, *Kurt Vonnegut—Letters*, 219.
[92] Wakefield, *Kurt Vonnegut—Letters*, 220.

Letter to Jane Vonnegut, October 30, 1974

> I'm fresh back from the Worker's Paradise. The elevators still don't work, and it's still perfect hell to be a Jew over there. Hi ho. I don't intend to write about it. I was sweet as pie, and didn't ask a single embarrassing question. And over here I never crack off in public about Solzhenitsyn or any of the hundreds of writers in jails and loony bins. There are plenty of others to do that.[93]

These sentences are cherry-picked extracts from letters Vonnegut wrote before and after a short trip to Moscow in 1974. They are decontextualized, much like Soviet correspondents and critics used decontextualized snippets from Vonnegut's oeuvre to shape him into an anti-American American fighter in the "struggle for peace." However, I believe these witty private letters do represent Vonnegut's sincere evaluation of the Soviet Union. He had nothing against Soviet citizens, but he renounced the totalitarian state they were forced to operate in. He was especially concerned for his fellow "cultural workers."

To the extent that Vonnegut was aware of how his popularity, and his image, was selectively wielded by the Soviet authorities, he went along with it. He did so first, out of concern for his friends in the Soviet Union in "various degrees of trouble," and, second, out of caution lest his books be rejected by Soviet authorities. Donald Fiene outlined Vonnegut's conundrum in a brief postscript to a letter to Professor Lauren Leighton in September 1978. "Vonnegut has constant battles with himself over when and whether or not to make public criticism of Soviet censorship and treatment of dissidents. Rita always tells him to say nothing, for fear that publication of his novels will be blocked. She takes the long-range cultured view of life. . ."[94]

Vonnegut was strategic in how he engaged—or did not engage—the Soviet authorities. He focused on making and sustaining connections with fellow writers, artists, and creative people in the Soviet Union. He sought to bypass as much as possible all official apparatuses. Vonnegut's several trips to the USSR were all under the auspices of personal tourism, even though it was the Union of Writers that probably provided his invitation for the 1974 Moscow trip. As much as cultural bureaucrats tried to enlist him for various "to-dos" and engagements, Vonnegut kept a low profile when traveling in the Soviet Union. Through the years, he turned down numerous invitations to

---

[93] Wakefield, *Kurt Vonnegut—Letters*, 221.
[94] DMF to LGL, September 26, 1978, p. 1, DMFC, Box 4, Folder 1, "Leighton, Lauren Gray. 1978–1979."

join official delegations of writers in US-Soviet exchange and dialogue. At the same time, as Chapter 10 explores, Vonnegut followed the fates of dissident writers in the Soviet Union closely. He leveraged his position as an author beloved by Soviet readers to publicly advocate for the release of at-risk and jailed writers in the USSR.

9

Interlude

No Free Breakfast in the Land of Lenin, 1977

In October 1977, Kurt Vonnegut and his American publisher Seymour (Sam) Lawrence undertook a European book promotion tour. They visited Vonnegut's publishers in Amsterdam, Munich, Copenhagen, Oslo, Stockholm, and Helsinki. Kurt and Sam traveled from Helsinki to Leningrad for a two-day visit.[1] Vonnegut wrote to Don Fiene, "We'll be staying at the Astoria, from which I was ejected many years ago, supposedly for being a suspected homosexual.... We will spend most of our time with Rita, I hope."[2] As in Moscow in 1974, Rita Rait did her utmost to spend time with Vonnegut one-on-one. She tried to protect his visit from intrusions. Rita wrote to the young literary scholar Konstantin Azadovsky, asking him to give her a ride to meet Vonnegut at the "Finland" train station in Leningrad, the station handling transport to Helsinki and other "westerly" destinations. Rita warned, "Don't tell ANYONE he's coming!"[3] Rita had sharp-elbowed Donald Fiene off the itinerary, even though Kurt had invited him along. Trying to "combine the meetings" would wear the nearly eighty-year-old Rita out.[4] Besides, Rita thought, Fiene's temperament was ill-suited to Rita and Kurt's goals to quietly discuss their artistic plans and talk about personal (i.e., family) matters.[5]

In the end, Kurt and Rita had little time to themselves. Despite Rita's best efforts to shield Kurt from obligations, he and Lawrence were roped into "all sorts of excursions with a guide." Rita and Kurt "were constantly bothered."[6]

---

[1] "Kurt Vonnegut itinerary," MSS 259 Seymour Lawrence Publishing, University of Delaware Library Special Collections, Folder 231.
[2] KV to DMF, September 15, 1977, FIEN, Folder 3, "1977."
[3] RRK to KMA, Letter #1, no date, KMAC.
[4] DMFC, Box 4, Folder 1, "Leighton, Lauren Gray. 1978–1979."
[5] DMF to LGL, December 21, 1978, p. 4, DMFC, Box 4, Folder 2, "Rait-Kovaleva, Rita. 1968–1978;" RRK to DMF, April 28, 1977, p. 1, DMFC, Box 4, Folder 5, "Rait-Kovaleva, Rita, 1976–1982."
[6] RRK to DMF, October 25, 1977, DMFC, Box 4, Folder 5, "Rait-Kovaleva, Rita, 1976–1982."

The tense and unpleasant task at the heart of each side's agenda shaded the reunion. They had to negotiate the terms of future publication of Vonnegut's work in the Soviet Union. Poor Rita Rait was stuck with the unfortunate mission of representing the Soviet side, a role she abhorred but was not in a position to decline. To make matters worse, Rita was rather disabled. She had terrible problems with her eyes, and she could no longer read without an enormous magnifying glass.[7] (Rita had a double lens replacement a year later.) Sam Lawrence made a poor impression on all who met him, further souring the situation. In all, Vonnegut's disappointing forty-eight hours in Leningrad in October 1977 shone a light on the economic and cultural divides that continued to separate the United States and the USSR. The tension drove something of a wedge between Kurt and Rita, too.

Before dwelling on the negatives, one should acknowledge the high points of the trip. It was in October 1977 that Kurt first met Rita's talented protégé Irina Grivnina, a computer programmer turned human rights defender. Vonnegut would be instrumental in helping Grivnina out of hot water, and out of the USSR, just a few years later. Little could Grivnina know that her pleasant outing with Vonnegut to the former headquarters of the Russian Imperial Navy, the Admiralty, would change the course of her life.

For Vonnegut, a major trip highlight was a new theatrical staging of Gogol's *Dead Souls* at the Pushkin Theater, where the play's director and cast threw a big reception in Kurt's honor.[8] Vonnegut, who frequently named Gogol as one of his favorite "Russian" authors, cherished the performance and commented on it frequently in interviews.[9] " . . . It was so brilliantly done that Sam and I almost got nosebleeds from laughing. We needed no interpreter."[10]

Spending time with Sam Lawrence was less pleasant. Rita later remarked on "fat Sam Lawrence," who she complained "got in the way" of Kurt's visit. "Mister Babbit was more pleasant! (I translated him.)"[11] (Rita was referring to Sinclair Lewis's infamous character, after whom the word "Babbit" entered the English language to mean "a person and especially a business or professional man who conforms unthinkingly to prevailing middle-class standards.")[12] For Rita, Lawrence was the embodiment of provincialism and petty bourgeois values, called *meshchanstvo* in earlier days. She wished Kurt

---

[7] KV to DMF, November 11, 1977, FIEN, Folder 3, "1977."
[8] Minchin, "Kurt Vonnegut," 58–9.
[9] Gogol was born in Poltava region, in what is now central Ukraine.
[10] KV to DMF, November 11, 1977, FIEN, Folder 3, "1977."
[11] RRK to LV, June 10, 1978, p. 2, BA-RRK.
[12] James M. Hutchisson, "All of Us at 46: The Making of Sinclair Lewis' Babbitt," *Journal of Modern Literature* 18, no. 1 (1992): 98.

had left him behind in Boston.[13] Vonnegut seemed similarly unimpressed by Lawrence. He wrote to Fiene after the trip, "Amazingly, as I discovered a week later, Sam had never read *Dead Souls*."[14]

To oversimplify matters and boil down to one word the nasty problem that inserted friction into Vonnegut and Rait's relationship, the issue was money. To be precise, the issue was Rita and Kurt's philosophical differences over the relationship of the arts to profit, and the calculus of intellectual, physical, and emotional labor to financial gains. Kurt, the author of books that had been translated into Russian and sold to Soviet readers (initially without his knowledge), wanted his due. He wanted Soviet publishing houses to keep their side of the UCC and pay appropriate royalties (what the Soviets called "honoraria") to foreign authors published in the Soviet Union. Vonnegut frequently called the Soviets "pirates," initially for publishing books in translation without authors' knowledge, and later, for paying authors in rubles that could only be spent in the USSR. For Vonnegut, the issue was not the money itself, but the principle. The Soviets had signed an agreement. They needed to join the rest of the civilized world, recognize copyright, and compensate authors for their intellectual property.

To Rita, this obsession with pecuniary rules and details, this constant focus on economic gain, was vulgar and unbecoming. Especially for someone who had plenty of money! She did not understand Kurt's preoccupation with the unseemly financial side of making art. She had introduced him to a voracious reading public who couldn't get their fill of his wonderful stories. Wasn't that enough?

Complicating matters was the fact of Kurt and Rita's vastly different financial realities. Even while criticizing Kurt for his over-focus on economic negotiations, Rita herself was by necessity keenly focused on money. She didn't have enough. Granted, the money she received from publishers to translate Vonnegut's work (and Faulkner's, and Salinger's and many others' besides) helped her make a modest living. She even saved up to help her daughter acquire a small apartment. But Rita constantly worried about money. She couldn't afford not to. These two professionals—one American, one Soviet—were meeting on a fundamentally unequal economic playing field. This inevitably introduced tension into their relationship. Rita called the question of money "ticklish," and it never seemed to leave her alone.

---

[13] Dan Wakefield recalled something Vonnegut told him about his 1977 Leningrad trip with Sam Lawrence. Out of the blue, while in Leningrad, Sam had turned to Kurt and said: "Kurt, you're programmed to be a writer. I'm programmed to be a publisher." Author's interview with Dan Wakefield, May 15, 2020, telephone.

[14] KV to DMF, November 11, 1977, FIEN, Folder 3, "1977."

These tensions came to a head during Kurt's brief trip to Leningrad in autumn 1977, but they did not begin there. Rita didn't translate Vonnegut just because she loved his writing and wanted to share it with the Soviet reading public. She needed the money. In a letter from 1969 or 1970 Rita lamented, "If I don't get it done, and can't finish what I've promised . . . I am never going to crawl out of this destitution that I fell into without noticing: the translation of Kafka's *Castle* hasn't moved in three years, and Vonnegut's *Slaughterhouse-Five* hasn't been published either . . ."[15] Rita similarly complained in a 1971 letter:

> Nobody has work right now: the editors and their friends are taking all the 'lucrative' work for themselves, and the rest of us have to wait, until we find something [to translate] OURSELVES . . . . Search [for something]! I translated two of Vonnegut's short stories—to help Margarita, since she translated two others—all for a hypothetical journal publication.[16]

Rita's friend the literary scholar Konstantin Azadovsky confirmed that Rita was not always a "favored" translator. "There were 'official' translators, but Rita—for a certain period of time—was not one of them. They 'gave' her work [as if it were a gift]."[17]

In this situation Rita and her daughter Margarita got entrepreneurial by necessity. They sometimes identified works that might appeal to a publisher, went ahead and translated them, and then pitched them for publication. As detailed in Chapter 3, this was not entirely unusual, but a safer bet post-UCC was to secure a contract first and only then translate the work. In late 1971 Rita detailed a few other strategies to bring in some cash flow. "I'm engaging in a little bit of '*sonechkomarmeladstvom*' ['prostitution']: I did a radio broadcast for a 20 [ruble note], sold one of Vonnegut's short stories to a local newspaper, and wrote something else for another radio editor. . . . After all I have to 'feed the family!'"[18] The next summer Rita checked in with a colleague who had loaned her some funds. She had translated two more of

---

[15] RRK to Lidia Chukovskaia, no date, RGALI 3401/1/584/2.
[16] RRK to KMA, November 8, 1971, pp. 3-4, KMAC.
[17] Author's interview with Konstantin Azadovsky, October 31, 2019, St. Petersburg.
[18] *Sonechkomarmeladstvom* was a reference to one of Dostoevsky's iconic characters, Sonya Marmalade, a prostitute. RRK to KMA, December 5, 1971, p. 2, KMAC. Proffer noted in the early 1970s that Soviet translators were well paid. This was true, and working translators could make a living solely by translating, unlike their American counterparts. However, they worked on contract, and no contracts (Rita's frequent situation) meant no salary. Proffer, "Introduction," xv-xvi.

Vonnegut's stories, probably "Miss Temptation" and "The Foster Portfolio," because she needed the money.[19]

Things had brightened for Rita when Vonnegut visited Moscow for five days in October 1974 (see Chapter 6). Presenting Vonnegut to the reading public and the Soviet publishing establishment bolstered Rita's already high stature in the literary world. It no doubt also sharpened others' jealousy of that high stature. What is more, Vonnegut deposited the 2,000 rubles (roughly equivalent to $2,000 at the time) the Young Guard publishing house paid him for *Cat's Cradle* into a bank account that he left in Rita's care. Rita noted triumphantly in a letter to friends in New York at the end of 1974 that *Foreign Literature* would pay her for translating *Breakfast of Champions*, due out in early 1975. "... The proofs of my translation of the new Vonnegut novel *Breakfast of Champions* have come, and there were discussions with Kurt's agent about payment—I'm going to get some money! ... I spoke with Kurt on the phone on his dime: he left me part of his honorarium when he left, and that is very nice."[20]

The 2,000 ruble windfall Kurt left her was both a source of relief for Rita and cause for anxiety. In April 1975 Rita told a friend that Kurt had "given her permission" to spend the rubles in his Soviet bank account. But the conditions of that arrangement were never made clear. Rita expressed relief that access to these funds would help her stay afloat until her daughter could move in with her and start contributing to the family budget. But she was unsure about Kurt's expectations and conditions. Could she do with the money as she liked? Did Kurt expect her to pay him back? Rita wasn't sure, and it made her very nervous.[21]

To make matters worse, when Vonnegut learned about the stage adaptation of *Slaughterhouse-Five* being planned for the Soviet Army Theater, he went around Rita. He wrote to an officer in the Union of Writers, David Nall, to inquire about his royalties. Kurt wondered if he would receive "the money he's owed for this production."[22] It frustrated Rita that in lieu of reaching out to her, "instead he wrote this cult[ural]-attache" from the Writers' Union, David Nall. Rita unleashed in a letter to an émigré friend in New York.

> [I explained to David] that the novel was translated BEFORE THE CONVENTION, and neither Kurt nor I will receive anything, and the director for that matter will only receive his regular salary . . . They

[19] RRK to A.V. Shchekin-Krotovaia ("Gelinka"), August 12, 1972, RGALI 3018/2/326.
[20] RRK to SG and Esia, December 23, 1974, BA-RRK.
[21] RRK to SG, April 6, 1975, p. 2, BA-RRK.
[22] RRK to SG, April 26, 1975, BA-RRK.

are using my translation of the text <u>word for word</u>, but I am not even considered one of the play's authors! It was the same with three of my other translations: Böll, Salinger and Graham Greene: The Theater produced three plays, and there's NOT A SINGLE WORD that wasn't taken from my translation—but NOT EVEN THE NAME of the translator is indicated! And of course no money either...

After all, they didn't pay Kurt anything for Slaughterhouse Five— "Novyi Mir" refused to. And the money he did receive [for Cat's Cradle]— Young Guard gave it to him just out of love for him—they could have refused, too, since before the convention we were "pirates," as Kurt said ... But the Soviet Army Theater wants to invite Kurt to the premier this autumn, and pay for his hotel and take him wherever he wants to go—in short, they'll will do everything they can for him.... And his plans to involve the Writers' Union in these matters is just a childish fantasy: this hasn't worked for anyone—BEFORE THE CONVENTION nobody paid anybody for anything.

I'm very disappointed that Kurt hasn't written me. Surely he doesn't think that all of us—his friends, his readers, and I—his faithful translator—have let him down somehow (*v chem to vinovaty*)? Then he hasn't understood anything... Explain to him that dearer than money is that love that ALL THE GOOD, intelligent readers feel for him. I get so many compliments for "Breakfast!" Readers love all his novels so! Two articles—both in serious journals—about him were just published.

Rita went on to emphasize how little money she was paid over the years for her translations of Vonnegut's work.

The praise is much dearer to me than the little bit of money I receive for the translation. You will laugh, but for No. 1 of Ino Lit [*Foreign Literature*, where *Breakfast of Champions* was published] after deducting the machinist's fee, the advance and so on, I got . . . THREE RUBLES 80 kopeks[,] and [then] 500 rubles for the second volume. THAT'S ALL. If it had been a book there would have been a print run—but for journal publications they pay very little. But I don't care—more important is the joy you feel when they love and praise you and your author.[23]

---

[23] RRK to SG, April 26, 1975, BA-RRK.

Though grateful for the money Kurt had left her, Rita was unsure if it was really "hers" to spend. And now Kurt, she felt, had betrayed her by naïvely demanding royalties from the Writers' Union for *The Wanderings of Billy Pilgrim*. It was embarrassing for her and insulting to boot. Was Kurt not satisfied with how ably Rita had rendered his oeuvre for the vast Russian-language readership? She certainly was not getting paid her just desserts, and she was doing all the hard work now. Why should Vonnegut concern himself with money, instead of appreciating the love and admiration of his Soviet readers? It is not clear whether Rita ever confronted Kurt directly about this slight, or if she only vented in letters to friends.

Despite Rita's complaints of poverty, in autumn 1975 she did manage to help her daughter Margarita acquire a "lovely" small Moscow apartment in the building just across from hers. The details of this substantial transaction are not clear. Since housing was provided by the Soviet state, Rita may have paid a "top up" to help Margarita jump the line, or land an apartment situated close to Rita's, or both. In any case, Rita exclaimed in October, "I reckon that Faulkner, Salinger, and Vonnegut gave her that apartment—the honoraria from their works (in my translation) covered the ENTIRE cost!!!"[24]

It seems Rita finally decided that Kurt's 2,000 rubles were hers to do with as she liked, so she put them toward an apartment for her daughter. But the constant worrying about money, and the stress of Kurt management, was taxing for Rita. All these frustrations set the stage for the financial negotiations during Vonnegut and Sam Lawrence's forty-eight hours in Leningrad in October 1977, an experience Rita found most unpleasant.

When Rita wrote to her protégé Konstantin Azadovsky asking for a ride to the Finland Station to meet Kurt and Sam Lawrence on October 10, she mentioned that Artistic Literature was planning a collection of four of Vonnegut's novels (all Rita's translations) in one volume. The publishers were hounding her to "get Kurt to sign an agreement." Rita warned Azadovsky that associate editor Teliatnikov would travel with her to the station. He wanted "to ask Kurt to sign a contract, since he (more precisely, his publisher) IS NEGOTIATING WITH US POOR PEOPLE. . . . I've had it up to here. . . The [four-book] collection might fall through."[25]

In the end, Teliatnikov begged off the adventure and the negotiating task was left to Rita. Rita later vented to Donald Fiene. "I had to take upon myself a ridiculous duty—to talk to Sam Lawrence about the contract. I DID NOT WANT TO DEAL WITH THIS STUPID PIECE OF PAPER, BUT THEY SIMPLY BEGGED ME TO DO IT . . . Now, it looks like the collection

---

[24] RRK to LV, October 1975 (no date), BA-RRK.
[25] RRK to KMA, no date, KMAC.

(*odnotomnik*) will come out early next year (more likely, in spring)—God willing!"²⁶ A month later, Vonnegut described in a letter to Don Fiene Rita's awkward situation as the publishing house's "sole negotiator."

> [Rita's] bosses, incidentally, sent contracts along with her, made her their sole negotiator, instructed her to tell us to accept their terms or go to hell, that they weren't all that interested in publishing me anyhow. Their offer was a generous one by Russian standards, but the shabbiness of making Rita close the deal was dishonorable in the extreme.²⁷

This is how Vonnegut remembered the transaction nearly a decade later in an interview.

> One thing I remember well: the Soviet Union had just signed on to the international convention for protecting authors' copyright; it was 1977. My book was the second one, after Alberto Moravia, that the Soviets bought. During that trip they negotiated the price with me—$1,500. Better than nothing... I didn't care about the money. Every writer wants more readers.²⁸

Indeed, for Vonnegut it was the principle of the thing—acknowledgement of copyright—that seemed to matter most. Presumably, the contract Kurt signed in October 1977 with Artistic Literature publishing house was an agreement to publish the four-book collected volume, which included *Slaughterhouse-Five*; *Cat's Cradle*; *God Bless You, Mr. Rosewater*; and *Breakfast of Champions*. *Slaughterhouse-Five* and *Cat's Cradle* already had been published (in Rita's translation) in the Soviet Union, but only *Breakfast* fell under the UCC. This was important for Kurt. He was finally getting paid for his intellectual property, even if the sum was not one he deemed significant ("better than nothing!"). It was also important for Rita. It meant, possibly thanks to Kurt's intervention and insistence, that she would get additional payment for translation work she had already done on *Breakfast* and the three other books in the collection.

Recall, in December 1974 Rita had written her friend Sara Ginsburg that she'd just received page proofs for *Breakfast*. "There were discussions with

---

²⁶ RRK to DMF, October 25, 1977, DMFC, Box 4, Folder 2, "Rait-Kovaleva, Rita. 1968–1978."
²⁷ KV to DMF, November 11, 1977, FIEN, Folder 3, "1977."
²⁸ Minchin, "Kurt Vonnegut," 58–9.

Kurt's agent about payment—I'm going to get some money!"[29] Evidence of how this shook out is in several documents from the Artistic Literature archives. There's a "Publisher's Agreement" with Rita Rait for her "translation from the English, for the collected volume, of Kurt Vonnegut," dated March 10, 1977.[30] There's also an "accounting receipt" for an author's agreement with Kurt Vonnegut for *Breakfast of Champions*, dated October 17, 1977.[31] For her work on the translated collected volume, Rita would receive between 2,550 and 2,900 rubles. As the foreign author of the work *Breakfast of Champions* (again, the only book in the collection beholden to the UCC), Vonnegut would receive approximately 2,400 rubles.

We cannot know for sure, but it may be thanks to Vonnegut's intervention (those "discussions with Kurt's agent about payment") that Artistic Literature paid Rita for the translated collected volume. After all, each of her translations had already been published, so she completed little if any new work for the collection. It is also likely that Vonnegut entrusted his "better than nothing" royalties from *Breakfast of Champions* to Rita, as he had done for *Cat's Cradle* in 1974.

As distasteful as it was for Rita to have to negotiate a contract with Kurt and Sam Lawrence for *Breakfast* and the four-volume anthology, it was to her ultimate benefit. She was paid a tidy sum for the 1978 collection, and she may have inherited Kurt's earnings, too. Rita's abhorrence of Vonnegut's laser-sharp focus on money matters may seem like a case of "the lady doth protest too much, methinks." Nevertheless, Rita was in a complicated position as both a supplicant and protector. In some ways she was indebted to Kurt, but Rita was also the reason he "made it" in the Soviet Union. The focus on agreements, contracts, and rubles left Rita sour after Kurt's brief visit in 1977. Still, he'd come bearing gifts, and useful ones, too: a gigantic magnifying glass to help Rita read, and a dictation machine to make her life easier.[32]

Konstantin Azadovsky, a professor of English, French, and German languages, was a key witness to Rita and Kurt's reunion at Leningrad's Finland

---

[29] RRK to SG and Esia, December 23, 1974, BA-RRK.
[30] RGALI 613/10/4859/7, 7ob.
[31] RGALI 613/10/4859/1, 1ob.
[32] RRK to DMF, October 25, 1977, DMFC, Box 4, Folder 2, "Rait-Kovaleva, Rita. 1968–1978."

Figure 9.1 Konstantin Azadovsky (far left, fur hat), Rita Rait-Kovaleva (center, white hat), Kurt Vonnegut (second from right), and unknown colleagues, Finland Station, Leningrad, 1977. Courtesy Konstantin Azadovsky.

Station in October 1977.[33] In 1969, when he was twenty-eight, Azadovsky, a native Leningrader, had lost his place as a graduate student at the Herzen Institute due to his behavior at the trial of his good friend Efim Slavinsky (1936–2019, London). Azadovsky had refused to confirm false accusations that he had engaged in marijuana use along with Slavinsky. He retreated to Petrozavodsk, the capital city of Karelia (north of Leningrad), traditionally a haven for persecuted members of the Leningrad intelligentsia.[34]

Azadovsky was able to complete his PhD degree on F. Grillparzer and the Austrian Theater in 1971, and by 1975 things had settled down enough for him to return to Leningrad. He took a post at what is now the St. Petersburg

---

[33] The "Finland Station" in Petrograd (later Leningrad, now St. Petersburg) is a major site of Soviet historical memory. Vladimir Lenin arrived there from Finland in April 1917 and launched the socialist revolution, a scene reproduced *ad nauseum* in socialist realist artworks. On the reverse side of the photograph in Figure 9.1, which Rita sent to Konstantin Azadovsky, she wrote, "at the Finland Station, but in a different context" (*v drugom kachestve*). Rita wittily underscored that she and Azadovsky had greeted a different figure of global importance who'd just arrived from Finland—not Vladimir Lenin, but Kurt Vonnegut.

[34] Petr A. Druzhinin, *Soviet Suppression of Academia: The Case of Konstantin Azadovsky* (Bloomsbury Academic, 2022), 12.

Art and Industry Academy as head of the Department of Foreign Languages. When he gave Rita a ride to the Finland Station in October 1977 to meet Kurt Vonnegut, Azadovsky's life seemed to be "normal." His papers on Rainer Maria Rilke, Thomas Mann, and Stefan Zweig had received high critical praise, as had his work on Russian Symbolism (Blok, Bryusov, Klyuev). He was an accomplished translator too, having been nudged in that direction by his mentor Rita Rait. Azadovsky received a respectable salary and was one of the few literary scholars in Leningrad to own a car.[35] Azadovsky was no fan of the Soviet government. He had seen his own father—Mark Azadovsky, also an accomplished academic—destroyed in the campaign against "rootless cosmopolitans" (Jews) in 1949.[36] Konstantin kept his own head down.

Nevertheless, in December 1980, Azadovsky was arrested. In a search of his apartment, the KGB supposedly found a small quantity of hashish (which Azadovsky vehemently denied) and a few contraband books from the American publisher Ardis. In early 1981, Azadovsky, one of the USSR's best scholars of comparative literature, was sentenced to two years of hard labor and transported to one of the notorious Kolyma labor camps. His case, and the preposterous incongruity between the minor drug possession charges and the harsh sentence, had a chilling effect on Soviet academia. Some believed he'd been nabbed because he intended to publish his sensational research on the unpublished correspondence between Boris Pasternak, Marina Tsvetaeva, and Rilke, with a Western publisher—that very same Ardis Publishers, located in Ann Arbor, Michigan. No matter that the publication had been officially approved by the Soviet authorities. Azadovsky, with his international scholarly contacts, had to be made an example of, and the KGB was more than willing to do it.[37]

The "Azadovsky affair" became a cause célèbre for Soviet dissidents and exiles, and Joseph Brodsky founded an Azadovsky Defense Committee. It drew the attention of the Soviet and Russian Studies establishment in the United States and eventually became a major case study for the "Soviet suppression of academia."[38] Still, Konstantin Azadovsky served his two years

---

[35] Druzhinin, *Soviet Suppression*, 12.
[36] Konstantin Azadovsky, *Zhizn' i trudy Marka Azadovskogo. Dokumental'naia biografia* [*The life and works of Mark Azadovsky*. Documentary biography] (NLO Press, 2025).
[37] Joseph Brodsky, "The Azadovsky Affair," *The New York Review* (October 8, 1981). https://www.nybooks.com/articles/1981/10/08/the-azadovsky-affair/
[38] Druzhinin, *Soviet Suppression*; Michael Scammell, "The Azadovsky Case," *The New York Review of Books* (April 15, 1982). https://www-nybooks-com.proxyiub.uits.iu.edu/articles/1982/04/15/the-azadovsky-case/

of hard labor and worked for at least a decade to reestablish his reputation after returning to Leningrad in 1983.

And so it was that both of the vibrant young scholar-creatives Vonnegut met during his forty-eight hours in Leningrad in 1977—Irina Grivnina and Konstantin Azadovsky—were viciously repressed by the Soviet state. Grivnina—for documenting abuses of political prisoners in psychiatric institutions. Azadovsky—for advancing a brilliant scholarly career in comparative literature with too much contact with the West. It is not clear whether Vonnegut knew of Azadovsky's situation. It is possible that he knew because he had contact with Sergei Dovlatov, author of a report about "Azadovsky's case" in the Russian émigré paper *New American* [*Novyi Amerikanets*]. (See Chapter 10.) Vonnegut stayed silent about Azadovsky, but he championed Grivnina's cause in the United States. Grivnina's arrest brought Soviet repression of its citizens' rights "home," so to speak. Now, it was personal. As we'll explore in the next chapter, Vonnegut was ready to protest. But in her precarious situation as a cultural mediator, all Rita Rait could do was quietly observe, as her protégés one by one fell under the weight of the Soviet state's heavy hand.

10

Vonnegut and the Dissidents

In late October 1974, Vonnegut wrote a letter to his first wife, Jane Vonnegut. He described his recent trip to Moscow.

> I'm fresh back from the Worker's Paradise. The elevators still don't work, and it's still perfect hell to be a Jew over there. Hi ho. I don't intend to write about it. I was sweet as pie, and didn't ask a single embarrassing question. And over here I never crack off in public about Solzhenitsyn or any of the hundreds of writers in jails and loony bins. There are plenty of others to do that. I am a vice president of American P.E.N., and I ask favors from the other side from time to time. And they may listen to me, since my public record is so uncontroversial. And maybe not. What the hell.[1]

Vonnegut made his Moscow trip to visit Rita Rait, not to perform outreach as an officer of American PEN. The visit was nevertheless an act of literary diplomacy. Vonnegut acknowledged as much in his letter to Jane Vonnegut. He noted that he "asked favors from the other side from time to time" and implied a hope that his journey to Moscow might grease those wheels, if only just a little.

This chapter explores one of the lesser-known aspects of Kurt Vonnegut's engagements with the Soviet Union during the 1970s and 1980s. In his role as both vice president of American PEN and as a prominent man of letters and voice for freedom of speech, Vonnegut championed dissident Soviet writers. As an American author sanctioned for consumption in the Soviet Union, Vonnegut could exert a measure of influence on domestic Soviet politics regarding the treatment of writers. At the same time, Vonnegut recognized the precarity of this influence. It required him to cultivate favorable relations with the Soviet establishment.

It was not exactly true that Vonnegut never "crack[ed] off in public" about dissident Soviet writers who had been arrested, jailed, sentenced to labor camps, or exiled from the Soviet Union. In late 1969, he added his name to a

---

[1] Wakefield, *Kurt Vonnegut—Letters*, 221.

letter of protest from prominent writers from around the world condemning the expulsion of Aleksandr Solzhenitsyn from the Soviet Writers' Union.[2] In 1970, Vonnegut remarked that he thought Aleksandr Solzhenitsyn was the greatest living writer.[3] As the vice president of American PEN, he had a mandate to speak out against the mistreatment of his fellow writers in the USSR. Vonnegut felt this moral obligation as both a writer and a human being. In making these public endorsements and pleas, Vonnegut risked losing permission for his own work to be translated and published in the Soviet Union. Other foreign writers previously published in translation had run afoul of the establishment and were banned from publication in the USSR, including Saul Bellow, Heinrich Böll, Graham Greene, Bernard Malamud, and Arthur Miller.

In the 1970s and 1980s, Vonnegut pursued a delicate strategy that I call "tolerant engagement." Tolerant engagement allowed Vonnegut to simultaneously remain in the good graces of Soviet authorities, protect the well-being of his friends in the Soviet Union, and make strategic and meaningful interventions into the international politics of writers' rights and freedom of speech and the press. Vonnegut was not the only American author to have relationships with Soviet bloc dissident writers, a phenomenon that has to date received little scholarly attention.[4] Exploring this aspect of Vonnegut's literary career sheds important light on a little-explored angle of US-Soviet relations during the Cold War.

It is well known that Vonnegut and Sergei Dovlatov—who emigrated to the United States in 1979—shared a certain affinity. Several stories about their friendship in New York after Dovlatov's emigration circulated in the popular press and imagination. Observers also tend to associate Vonnegut with Vladimir Voinovich (exiled from the USSR in 1980 but returned in 1990), probably due to certain similarities in style. Like Vonnegut, Voinovich was a humorist and satirist. He wrote of dystopian futures and authored a satirical novel set during the Second World War, *The Life and Extraordinary Adventures of Private Ivan Chonkin*. Interviewers frequently asked Vonnegut if he knew and admired the famous exiled writers Joseph Brodsky, Vladimir Nabokov, and Aleksandr Solzhenitsyn, all of them living in the United States.

---

[2] Shields, *So it Goes*, 265.
[3] Bruce Cook, "When Kurt Vonnegut Talks—And he Does—The Young All Tune In," *National Observer* (October 1970): 21.
[4] Harilaos Stecopoulos, *Telling America's Story to the World: Literature, Internationalism, Cultural Diplomacy* (Oxford University Press, 2022), chap 5, p. 3.

Vonnegut did admire these authors. He had met most of them and had done public outreach on their behalf.⁵ But the deeper story of Vonnegut's affinity for and defense of Soviet dissident writers—particularly those who were under arrest or threat of arrest and languishing in Soviet prisons and labor camps—is a story that has not yet been told. This chapter places Vonnegut's efforts to defend Soviet dissident writers in the broader context of his engagements in US-Soviet literary diplomacy. Vonnegut gave with one hand while applying pressure with the other. He maintained a balancing act between making friendly statements about the Soviet people and the society of letters in the USSR, while critiquing repression of freedom of speech and advocating for endangered dissident writers in the Soviet Union.

Donald Fiene wrote about this in 1977.

> In general, despite his knowledge of his popularity in the Soviet Union, he [Vonnegut] has continued to take a firm stand against Soviet treatment of dissident writers and other intellectuals. Both as a member of the international writers' society, P.E.N. (the American center of which he has been a vice-president since 1972), and as a private person, Vonnegut has sent a half dozen or more letters and cables to the Writers' Union in Moscow since 1970, protesting the harassment of Solzhenitsyn and other dissident writers.⁶

Additionally, Vonnegut pointed out in print the flaws in the Soviet system of literary publication, especially the failure to remunerate foreign authors for their translated works. In the November 1974 issue of the American *PENewsletter*, for instance, Vonnegut offered a gentle critique of the USSR's long-time incompliance with the UCC. He included some witty yet critical barbs about the Soviets' refusal to share information on which works by American authors had been published in translation.⁷ He poo-pooed the convoluted rubles-only compensation system for American writers. The system made it impossible for writers to spend their earnings anywhere except in the Soviet Union. In the same article, however, Vonnegut applauded

---

⁵ For instance, as Shields noted, in late 1969 Vonnegut "added his name to a letter of protest from PEN, the writers' organization, condemning the expulsion of Aleksandr I. Solzhenitsyn from the Soviet writers' union" (Shields, *And So it Goes*, 265). In 1966 Vonnegut had joined numerous American writers in signing an open letter in support of the Soviet dissidents Andrei Sinyavsky and Yuli Daniel, who had been accused and convicted of anti-Soviet propaganda for publishing work abroad and had received sentences of seven years' and five years' hard labor, respectively.

⁶ Fiene, "American Dissident," 266.

⁷ Vonnegut, "Writers, Vonnegut and the U.S.S.R.," 1–2.

the USSR for at least seeking to comply with the Convention. He proposed a "friendship of the peoples" type initiative that would allow all those unspendable rubles to be pooled as a scholarship fund for young American writers who wished to spend time in the Soviet Union. (The proposal went nowhere.)

This combination of gentle (and sometimes not so gentle) critique and constructive attempts at problem-solving was characteristic of Vonnegut's approach of "tolerant engagement." Even as he wired cables to the Soviet Writers' Union in defense of dissident writers (more on these engagements below), he offered strategic olive branches in the form of congratulatory telegrams to individuals and institutions (e.g., newspapers, editorial boards). Vonnegut did favorable interviews with major outlets like VOA and *Literary Gazette*. He participated in joint US-USSR events such as roundtables and telebridges.

Vonnegut was self-reflexive about this strategy to "behave himself" vis-à-vis the USSR. He wanted to remain in favor so that when he needed to issue a defense of a Soviet writer or dissident being persecuted, his intervention would be taken seriously, and hopefully have some impact. Vonnegut carefully weighed decisions about participating in these rights defense campaigns in the Soviet bloc. He knew that the wrong kind of intervention could make things worse for dissidents and their friends and families, including Rita Rait, who disapproved of such activities. Rita was concerned that criticizing the Soviet state would lose Vonnegut his favored status and make him an "untouchable" foreign writer. She was also worried about her own career. Political involvement and participation in campaigns to support outcast writers (like Daniel and Sinyavsky, or Solzhenitsyn), could lose writers and translators work, as happened to Lev Kopelev and many others.[8]

Vonnegut advocated for the rights of Soviet dissident writers both as a private citizen and as a member, board member, and elected official of PEN America. American PEN was and continues to be concerned with support of writers "at home," in the United States, in particular emerging and young writers. As a charter member of PEN International, PEN America has a broad international mandate. (PEN International, created in 1921, was described in its early days as "a league of nations for men and women of letters.")[9] Vonnegut envisioned PEN as an umbrella organization for writers worldwide to self-advocate for their rights to write and publish. This included

---

[8] Orlova and Kopelev, *We Lived in Moscow*, 186–7.
[9] PEN International, "Who We Are: History," https://pen-international.org/who-we-are/history See Stecopoulous, *Telling America's Story*, chap. 5, pp. 18–21 for an overview of PEN International's founding history.

writers with unpopular views on controversial topics. He once said, ". . . I think everybody ought to join this group. I don't care if the person is a fascist or a member of the Klan—if the person's a writer, he belongs in PEN."[10] In the 1960s through the mid-1980s, PEN claimed to have "nothing whatever to do with State or Party politics."[11] Vonnegut, too, consistently framed PEN and his PEN-associated activities as apolitical. But he ultimately found it impossible to divorce politics from discussions of literature, human rights, and freedom of speech.[12]

Vonnegut traveled globally for his leadership role in American PEN. He was an invited representative and sometimes keynote speaker at International PEN meetings, including in Stockholm (1973), Vienna (1975) and Tokyo (1984). Vonnegut did not limit his advocacy of repressed writers in the Soviet bloc to those in peril in the Soviet Union. Through American PEN, Vonnegut provided financial support in the mid-1970s for Czech dissident writers, who were "not allowed to publish at all, who can't even get jobs as janitors."[13] In March 1985 Vonnegut traveled with William and Rose Styron to Czechoslovakia, Poland, and East Berlin under the auspices of American PEN, to, as he put it, "find out how our fellow artists were."[14] He reported back to PEN on the treatment of fellow artists in those state socialist locales.[15] In an interview with *The New York Times*, Vonnegut expressed concern that the Polish government had disbanded the Polish PEN Club. He praised Solidarity and Lech Walesa, who he had met during the trip.[16]

PEN International might seem a curious vehicle for Vonnegut's advocacy efforts. After all, PEN International was revived in the mid-1960s in the wake of the exposure of the Congress for Cultural Freedom (CCF) as a CIA-

---

[10] William Rodney Allen and Paul Smith, "An Interview with Kurt Vonnegut," in *Conversations with Kurt Vonnegut*, ed. William Rodney Allen (University Press of Mississippi, 1988), 279.
[11] Stecopoulous, *Telling America's Story*, chap. 5, p. 18.
[12] Shields, *So it Goes*, 371–2.
[13] Wakefield, *Kurt Vonnegut—Letters*, 226. In July 1974, Vonnegut asked his agent and attorney Donald Farber to send $50 a month via the PEN American Center, to support the Czech Writers Fund, specifically Alexander Kliment, who as Vonnegut put it, was "being more or less starved to death by his government." The writer Philip Roth had alerted Vonnegut to Kliment's plight (KV to Donald Farber, July 17, 1974, KVM, Box 1, Folder 25, "1974, June-Sept."). In October 1984 Vonnegut received a letter from Harvard Professor Stanislav Baranczak, former member of the Polish Writers' Union, requesting that Vonnegut arrange to have any royalties he might have received in Poland, channeled into a fund through PEN America for beleaguered Polish writers. Vonnegut asked Donald Farber to look into it, but I have found no further record. Baranczak to KV, October 1974, KVM, Box 2, Folder 19, "1984, Mar.-Dec."
[14] Loree Rackstraw, *Love as always*, 115.
[15] Shields, *So it Goes*, 366.
[16] "Vonnegut, in Poland: 'Spirit of Solidarity Lives On,'" *The New York Times* (June 9, 1985).

funded propaganda initiative. It was "a vehicle for American government interests" with an expressly anti-communist orientation.[17] In other words, PEN, in its mid-1960s reincarnation from its 1921 origins as an apolitical "league of nations" for writers, was a new anti-communist baby, born of Cold Warriors. However, it had several things going for it. The new president of PEN International in 1966 was Arthur Miller, a playwright of famously leftist sensibilities who had visited the Soviet Union and was widely read and respected there. One of Miller's primary (if failed) mandates in the first years of his PEN presidency was to establish PEN Centers in the USSR, an effort that had to have appealed to Vonnegut.[18] (Instead, Miller himself was banned in the Soviet Union in 1970 after he published *In Russia*.)

The bulk of Vonnegut's tolerant engagements on behalf of Soviet writers took place against the backdrop of the 1975 Helsinki Accords, an agreement signed by thirty-five nations including the United States and the Soviet Union. An outcome of the Conference on Security and Cooperation in Europe, the Helsinki Agreement was an effort to soothe Cold War tensions by implementing formal shared guidelines about a host of economic, political, and military issues. The *Helsinki Final Act* required signatory states to guarantee human rights and freedoms. By signing the *Helsinki Final Act*, the USSR had committed itself to certain things on paper, and theoretically could now be held accountable. After 1975, human rights activists—including in the USSR—set up "Helsinki Groups" and other watchdog collectives to monitor compliance and document human rights violations. Letters of concern from foreign individuals and organizations about human rights abuses of writers in the Soviet Union were often couched in terms of the freedoms guaranteed Soviet citizens under the Helsinki Accords.

In the United States, Vonnegut was on the ground floor of the global human rights movement. He was one of the original members of the Fund for Free Expression (FFE). Started by Robert L. Bernstein, the president and CEO of Random House, the FFE brought together writers, editors, publishers, attorneys, and civic leaders concerned about human rights abuses. FFE was the parent organization of Helsinki Watch, created in 1978, and Americas

---

[17] Frances Stonor Saunders, *The Cultural Cold War: The CIA and the World of Arts and Letters* (The New Press, 2013), 362.

[18] Miller blamed the Soviet Writers' Union for the failure of this campaign. He said the "Soviet Writers Union could not accept the P.E.N. Constitution which pledges its members to fight censorship." Arthur Miller, "Banned in Russia," *The New York Times* (December 10, 1970): 47.

Watch, founded in 1981.[19] Both organizations became part of Human Rights Watch in 1988.

We can consider Vonnegut's role as a (usually unofficial) literary cultural diplomat and outspoken critic of Soviet policy toward dissident writers from at least two productive angles. One approach might center the delicate balancing act Vonnegut performed. On one hand he was a favorite American author of the Soviet reading public, an ambassador for American values of democracy and free speech. But he managed to publicly encourage the Soviet government to respect the human rights of dissidents. Another approach might consider American authors' critiques of communist censorship, alongside U.S. writers' engagements with Eastern bloc authors, as constituting "a response to a crisis in American literary culture."[20] As Stecopoulos notes, "increasingly aware that literature no longer commanded significant respect in the United States, many U.S. authors focused on their East European peers because totalitarian persecution, while horrible, testified to a social valuation of literature that had largely disappeared at home."[21] That is, in defending their comrade writers-turned-dissidents in Soviet bloc countries, American writers advanced a critique of the low status of writers and literature in the United States. Vonnegut famously noted that even if the Soviet Union repressed writers, at least writers in the Soviet Union were taken seriously.[22] Our inquiry here will privilege the first angle—we'll watch Vonnegut walking the literary diplomacy tightrope from Leningrad to Moscow to the labor camps of Siberia. But we shall keep angle number two—Vonnegut's coterminous critique of the low status of literature and writers in the United States—in the back of our minds.

Dovlatov

Kurt Vonnegut and Sergei Dovlatov are strongly associated in the popular imagination. This was true in the 1970s and 1980s, and it is true today. A group called "Sergei Dovlatov and Kurt Vonnegut" on "V Kontakte" (a popular Facebook-like social media site in Russia), "a group for fans of the

---

[19] See Human Rights Watch, "The Fund for Free Expression," https://www.hrw.org/reports/1990/WR90/MISC.BOU.htm#P8_0; and Caitlin Bertin-Mahieux, "The Reminiscences of Jeri Laber," Harriman Institute Oral History Project, 2016. https://api.harriman.maptian.com/sites/default/files/2018-04/LABER1-2.pdf
[20] Stecopoulous, *Telling America's Story*, chap. 5, p. 4.
[21] Stecopoulous, *Telling America's Story*, chap. 5, p. 4.
[22] Fiene, "American Dissident," 267.

works of S. Dovlatov and K. Vonnegut," had 389 followers as of March 2025.[23] A certain fascination about these writers' supposed affinity is a gorilla in the room of this chapter on Vonnegut and Soviet dissidents. Let's go ahead and sit this gorilla down for a talking to, so we can move on.

Who was Sergei Dovlatov? Born in 1941 in Ufa (the capital of Bashkortostan), Dovlatov moved to Leningrad in 1944. He failed to finish university and was called up for mandatory military service as a prison guard in high-security (GULAG) camps. A storyteller from a young age, Dovlatov had started writing as a school pupil. He continued writing during and after his military service.[24] In the 1960s, Dovlatov attended meetings of literary associations in Leningrad and consorted with a group of writers known as the "Urbanists" (*Gorozhane*). The Urbanists included Boris Vakhtin, Vladimir Maramzin, Vladimir Gubin, Igor Efimov, and eventually, Sergei Dovlatov himself.[25] They were part of the experimental "new prose" movement, as were Andrei Bitov and Vassily Aksyonov.[26] These writers insisted on personalistic and experimental writing. They refused to moralize or implement the party's priorities in their works. All this meant their prose circulated in only unofficial channels.[27]

Dovlatov continued to write fiction he could not get published. He worked mostly as a journalist, including in Tallinn, in the then-Estonian SSR. Life changed dramatically for Dovlatov in 1975 when one of his acquaintances was arrested, and some of Dovlatov's manuscripts were confiscated during the search of the arrestee's apartment. He was fired from his job at the newspaper *Soviet Estonia* and had to move back to Leningrad, where the situation for writers was increasingly difficult. As an untouchable with a rap sheet, Dovlatov could not find employment. Meanwhile, Dovlatov's works circulated in samizdat, and the KGB put pressure on his associates. He was arrested, imprisoned, and advised by the KGB to apply to leave the Soviet Union. He emigrated to New York in 1979, where he enjoyed success in translation until his death from heart failure in 1990, at the age of forty-eight.

The two writers—Dovlatov and Vonnegut—did indeed admire one another, and they corresponded. They met in person at least once in New York, in 1982 when Dovlatov interviewed Vonnegut for his Russian language magazine, *New American*. But Vonnegut had nothing to do with springing

---

[23] https://vk.com/club3971392
[24] Jane Bobko, "An Interview with Sergei Dovlatov," *The Threepenny Review* 20 (Winter 1985): 16.
[25] Young, *Sergei Dovlatov*, 13.
[26] Katerina Clark, *The Soviet Novel: History as Ritual* (Indiana University Press, 2000), 232–3.
[27] Young, *Sergei Dovlatov*, 3–35.

Dovlatov from the Soviet Union. He played no role in defending Dovlatov after his arrest in Leningrad. (NB: Dovlatov did not self-identify as a dissident. He said, "I wasn't a dissident, I didn't take part in any political struggle, all I did was write stories no one wanted to print. I left so that I could write without fearing for myself or my family.")[28]

There is something about Dovlatov's style that is reminiscent of Vonnegut. Both writers have been described as possessing a "laconic style" and a "light touch." Both writers were masters of humor and experimented with forms. Dovlatov was especially taken with the short story form. Dovlatov embraced the techniques of the youthful "new prose" movement in the USSR. He used colloquial speech and slang in his works, another similarity he shared with Vonnegut. Both authors inserted themselves as characters in their stories. (Dovlatov wrote of his story "Straight Ahead," published in the *New Yorker* (see below), ". . . the author takes part in the narration, as it were . . . Like Vonnegut in 'Slaughterhouse.'")[29] And Dovlatov admitted that growing up during Khrushchev's Thaw in the Soviet Union he was influenced by the translated works of Vonnegut and many other American writers. He valued American prose for its "aesthetic brilliance . . . genuine tragic note, attention to real human problems, and competent observation of life."[30]

The urban legend of the Vonnegut-Dovlatov bond revolves primarily around a sympathetic exchange they had that "went viral" (as much as anything could go viral in the days before social media). In a January 22, 1982 letter to Dovlatov, Vonnegut expressed his admiration and mild jealousy that Dovlatov had published three articles in the *New Yorker* magazine, an outlet Vonnegut never managed to conquer.[31] Vonnegut's generous letter included a pointed critique of the *New Yorker* and its "upper middle class" exclusivity.[32]

> Dear Sergey Dovlatov—I love you, too, but you have broken my heart. I was born in this country, and served it fearlessly in time of war, and yet I have never managed to sell a story to the New Yorker. Now you come over here, and bang! You sell a story right away. Something very fishy is going on, if you ask me.

[28] Bobko, "An Interview," 17–18.
[29] Young, *Sergei Dovlatov*, 57, quoting letter from Dovlatov to Efimov, January 21, 1982.
[30] Bobko, "An Interview," 17.
[31] Dovlatov went on to publish seven more stories in the *New Yorker*. It was Joseph Brodsky who recommended Dovlatov to the editors at the *New Yorker*, for which the latter was eternally grateful.
[32] Dovlatov's third *New Yorker* story, "Straight Ahead," a spoof set in a Russian prison camp, had just been published. The storyline revolves around booze and women.

In all seriousness, I congratulate you on a very fine story, and I congratulate the New Yorker for publishing a truly deep and universal story at last. As you have surely discovered for yourself by now, most of their stories deal with the joys and sorrows of the upper middle class. Until you came along, not much had been said in a New Yorker story about people who might not even be regular readers of the New Yorker.

I look forward to seeing a lot more of both you and your work. You have great gifts to give this crazy country. We are lucky to have you here.

Your colleague—Kurt Vonnegut[33]

Dovlatov likewise thought highly of Vonnegut. "Vonnegut is not just a black humorist, he is also a romantic, he professes complete skepticism, but in life he is an unbelievably kind person, he recently turned 60 and he looks like a terribly worn-out little boy."[34] We know that Dovlatov and Vonnegut met at least once in person. There is photographic and epistolic evidence to prove it. Dovlatov wrote to fellow émigré and literary giant Raisa Orlova to express his great admiration of American fiction. "When I met Vonnegut I quoted to him about 20 lines from his Slaughterhouse [Five] and Vonnegut got scared stiff, thinking he had a dangerous madman in front of him."[35]

Dovlatov also mentioned Vonnegut quite frequently in his letters to Igor Efimov. Yet, an early letter to Efimov (April 1982) did not put much stock in the two writers' friendship. "I am thought well of by [Harrison] Sailsbury, [Robert] Kaiser and Vonnegut (when they are able to recall who I am, that is) . . ."[36] In November 1983, Dovlatov's literary agent Andrew Wylie asked Vonnegut to review Dovlatov's recently published book *The Compromise*. Wylie feared the book "would simply get lost were it not soon reviewed in *The New York Review of Books*."[37] There is no indication that Vonnegut showed interest. *The Compromise*, which *The New York Times* reviewed in August 1983, was reviewed in *The New York Review of Books* only a year later, on November 22, 1984.[38] Vonnegut did not write the review.

[33] Vonnegut's congratulatory letter, which Dovlatov framed and hung in his home office, circulates widely online. Photographs of the letter are on these Dovlatov fan websites: https://samsebeskazal.livejournal.com/296494.html, https://jenya444.livejournal.com/432134.html.
[34] Dovlatov to T.N. Zubinovaia, December 27, 1982. https://jenya444.livejournal.com/432134.html.
[35] Dovlatov, unpublished letter to Raisa Orlova, February 4, 1988. Cited in Young, *Sergei Dovlatov*, 42.
[36] Dovlatov to Efimov, April 12, 1982. https://jenya444.livejournal.com/432134.html.
[37] Andrew Wylie to KV, November 15, 1983, KVM, Box 2, Folder 17, "1983, Nov.-Dec."
[38] The review considered Dovlatov's book alongside four other books by émigré Russian authors in translation: Yevtushenko's *Wild Berries*; *It's Me, Eddie: A Fictional Memoir*, by Limonov; and Aksyonov's *The Burn* and *The Island of Crimea*. The very long review devoted only a couple of sentences to Dovlatov's work. John Bayley, "Kitsch and the Novel," *The New York Review of Books*, November 22, 1984. https://www.nybooks.com/articles/1984/11/22/kitsch-and-the-novel/.

Vonnegut and the Dissidents   241

Figure 10.1 Writers Sergei Dovlatov and Kurt Vonnegut at Vonnegut's New York apartment, 1982. Photograph by Nina Alovert. Used with permission.

The Vonnegut-Dovlatov affinity is a nice story. No doubt, Vonnegut's widely reproduced letter praising Dovlatov positively impacted Dovlatov's reception in the United States. But Vonnegut pursued more interesting engagements with Soviet dissident and émigré writers. He advocated for arrested and jailed authors who faced long prison sentences in Soviet labor camps, many of whom sought permission to emigrate from the Soviet Union.

Maramzin and Slavinsky

In May 1974, Vonnegut was organizing his October visit to Moscow. He received a letter from Donald Fiene who asked for Vonnegut's intervention in defending a young Russian writer named Vladimir Maramzin, who Joseph Brodsky was "quite worried about."[39] (Maramzin was, incidentally, part of the Urbanists group in Leningrad that Dovlatov had joined.) Fiene noted that Vonnegut's "name was put forth as the best person to write to M., because M. quite obviously has a Vonnegut soul and is very likely in your personal karass." Fiene suggested Vonnegut write to Maramzin in triplicate, sending one letter to a personal address in Leningrad, one c/o the Writers' Union in

---

[39] DMF to KV, May 9, 1974, FIEN, Folder 1, "1972–1974."

Moscow, and one c/o the Writers' Union in Leningrad. Hopefully, a letter from someone with Vonnegut's stature would "oblige the KGB to hold back." Fiene expected at least one of the letters would get through. With any luck, the letter would be intercepted and read by the authorities. But as Fiene opined, "Even if the letter goes through unexamined, the guy could use the moral support that a letter from you would provide."

I have found no evidence that Vonnegut sent a letter to Maramzin, who was arrested on July 24, 1974, for his part in publishing a samizdat five-volume collection of Joseph Brodsky's poetry. Maramzin was sentenced to five years of suspended imprisonment and allowed to emigrate to Paris, where he died in 2021. At the February 1975 trial, Maramzin (surely, under duress) condemned the Western writers who had supported him. Presumably, Vonnegut was not among those named.[40]

Vonnegut seriously considered the pros and cons of speaking out in defense of repressed Soviet writers. As he continued preparations for his trip to Moscow in October 1974, the potential benefits and drawbacks of public advocacy were foremost in his mind. In late June, Professor Lauren Leighton of the Department of Slavic Languages and Literatures at the University of Illinois at Chicago Circle sent Vonnegut a letter. Leighton described the case of Efim Slavinsky. Slavinsky had been arrested on charges of speculation and spent two years in prison in Novosibirsk. He was unemployable and had been denied permission to emigrate twice. Leighton suggested several avenues for intervention. These included sending letters to Senators, Congresspersons, and newspaper editors, to be forwarded to the Soviet Embassy for official information. Leighton also suggested direct expressions of awareness to the Soviet Ambassador to the United States.

On June 25, Vonnegut responded to Professor Leighton. His heartfelt letter conveyed Vonnegut's worries about potential repercussions for other "friends in varying degrees of trouble" in the Soviet Union, were he to endorse targeted support for one or another at-risk writer or intellectual.

Dear Professor Leighton—

I thank you for your good letter about Efim Slavinsky, received this morning. I am saddened by the man's plight and thrilled by his bravery. I myself have friends in varying degrees of trouble over there, and as an officer of P.E.N., I find it my bureaucratic responsibility to worry about hundreds of strangers as well. And so we face the gruesome problem of

---

[40] Ivan Tolstoi, "V Parizhe umer pisatel' Vladimir Maramzin" [The writer Vladimir Maramzin has died in Paris], *Radio Svoboda*, April 26, 2021. https://www.svoboda.org/a/31223756.html

how best to exploit the limited sensibilities of the bosses of the Soviet Union. Do we spend the next six months attempting to spring Slavinsky, with all American artists and intellectuals aiming themselves like a laser beam at the Slavinsky case? This seems to be what you are asking, and it is a beautiful thing for you to ask. And it may be the [sic.] Slavinsky will become the symbol for hundreds in trouble. But the selection of such a symbol is bound to be random, since there are so many tragic candidates to choose from.

I am going to an executive meeting of P.E.N. this coming Thursday, and I will read your letter aloud. It will touch off a fundamentally heart-broken debate about what can be done for anybody over there. And many people will no doubt refer to Solzhenitsen's [sic.] remarks on television last night—having to do with America's concern with Soviet citizens who want out of the country, and its indifference to those who wish to remain in the country and improve the political system.

And so on.

I feel so wooden. I have to tell you that I am not going to mount a letter-writing campaign to the Times and [Soviet ambassador to the US Anatoly] Dobrynin and [Ambassador Jakob] Malik [of the Soviet Mission to the United Nations] and [Consul General Alexander] Zinchuk [of the Consulate of the USSR in San Francisco] and so on in order to rescue Slavinsky. I am going to have to think of a more generalized thing to do, which, in all probability, will only marginally help Slavinsky.

If this seems a wrong-headed letter to you, I beg you to tell me why it seems so. I would welcome your advice.

Yours truly,
Kurt Vonnegut, Jr.[41]

Leighton's thoughtful response revealed the professor's shared uncertainty about the best way for foreign colleagues to support Soviet dissident writers in their plight.

> Now, not more than a month. . .after we have secured the help of many wonderful people [in support of Slavinsky], we have begun to wonder, what about the poor schnooks who do not have friends abroad, or are not Jews, or do not have a political martyrdom to recommend them?

---

[41] KV to LGL, June 25, 1974, DMFC, Box 4, Folder 1, "Leighton, Lauren Gray. 1978–1979." It is unclear how the correspondence between Vonnegut and Leighton came into Fiene's possession.

Having got Slavinsky on Mr. Kissinger's list, whose name was taken off—at random—to make room for him? By helping Slavinsky, what are we doing to the parents he will leave behind? And what about all his friends and ours who can be made to bear the revenge of a spiteful state in his stead?[42]

Leighton thanked Vonnegut for his offer to read his letter about Slavinsky at the P.E.N. meeting. "... I know from many, many Russians that your works have already had a good effect there, and they are very much appreciated."[43]

A few months later in September, Leighton sent Vonnegut an exuberant letter. "Efim Slavinsky has left the Soviet Union and is safe in Rome . . . I cannot begin to tell you how much I appreciate your interest in our appeal ... I understand that Slavinsky intends to thank you personally as soon as he can make himself believe that, indeed, he is out of the Soviet Union."[44] Leighton recalled in a letter several years later to Donald Fiene that Vonnegut had assisted substantially with the Slavinsky case. "... He raised the question at a meeting of P.E.N . . . .and managed to get us a lot of help after all."[45] Despite his fear of doing more harm than good, whatever support Vonnegut had thrown behind Slavinsky had a positive effect. In 1976, Slavinsky moved from Rome to London, where he worked for many years in a prominent position for the BBC.[46]

Amalrik, Shcharansky, and Ginzburg

Back in the United States after his October 1974 Moscow trip, Vonnegut continued to issue letters in defense of at-risk Soviet writers in his capacity as American PEN's vice president. In 1975 Vonnegut sent a cable to the Union of Soviet Writers. He asked them "to do all they could to protect the rights of [Andrei] Amalrik," a writer who recently had been sentenced to hard labor.[47] Vonnegut explained his actions in a letter to Donald Fiene.

---

[42] LGL to KV, July 9, 1974, DMFC, Box 4, Folder 1, "Leighton, Lauren Gray. 1978–1979."
[43] LGL to KV, July 9, 1974, DMFC, Box 4, Folder 1, "Leighton, Lauren Gray. 1978–1979."
[44] LGL to KV, September 23, 1974, DMFC, Box 4, Folder 1, "Leighton, Lauren Gray. 1978–1979."
[45] LGL to DMF, October 9, 1978, DMFC, Box 4, Folder 1, "Leighton, Lauren Gray. 1978–1979."
[46] Peter Udell, "Brilliant Linguist" (obituary of Efim Slavinsky), *Prospero* 5 (October 19, 2019): 11. http://downloads.bbc.co.uk/mypension/en/prospero_october_2019.pdf
[47] Wakefield, *Kurt Vonnegut—Letters*, 225.

Rita, I know, feels that such cables should not be sent, since they cripple efforts to produce good American books and plays over there. P.E.N. knows this, but has decided to keep up its complaints about the mistreatment of writers anyway. It's a tough choice to have to make. I think we've made the right one. You might tell Rita that many writers (in Iran, Korea, Greece, Yugoslavia, and so on) have told P.E.N., after getting out of prison or whatever, that P.E.N.'s strident interest in them had a lot to do with their staying alive.[48]

Amalrik, one of the founders of the Moscow Helsinki Group, was exiled from the Soviet Union in 1976. He moved with his wife the artist Gyuzel Makudinova to the Netherlands, later to the United States, and finally, to France. He died in a car accident in 1980.

In 1978, Vonnegut participated in actions to defend Alexander Ginzburg and Antatoly Shcharansky (later Natan Sharansky), who on July 13 were sentenced to eight and thirteen years in prison, respectively. Vonnegut appeared at a July 11 march in New York with a placard containing Ginzburg's photograph and the missive, "Help Ginzburg." Also a founder of the Moscow Helsinki Group, Ginzburg administered a fund Solzhenitsyn had set up with royalties from his books to support political prisoners and their families. He also played a role in the samizdat human rights publication *Chronicle of Current Events*. Ginzburg was convicted in 1978 of "anti-Soviet agitation and propaganda." He had already served three previous sentences to labor camps for his samizdat activities. In 1979 Ginzburg was expelled to the United States in a prisoner exchange along with four other dissidents: Mark Dymshits, Valentin Moroz, Eduard Kuznetsov, and Georgy Vins. Shcharansky, a refusenik convicted of high treason, was not released from Soviet prison until a 1986 prisoner exchange, after which he emigrated to Israel.

In July 1979, Vonnegut received a letter of thanks from Alexander Ginzburg.

Dear Mr. Vonnegut,
    I thank you with all my heart for your help in defending me. Your words and deeds helped me to survive in very difficult moments, and I value this no less than the freedom I enjoy today.

---

[48] Wakefield, *Kurt Vonnegut—Letters*, 225–6.

> Your support has also had enormous significance for my friends who continue in my homeland the charitable work of the Russian Social Fund founded by Alexander Solzhenitsyn to help political prisoners.
> Not a single good deed passes without a trace, and your heartfelt participation will be remembered with gratitude by a future Russia.
> In our terrible time, the defense of those who are persecuted is the best contribution to tomorrow's world if we want to make it a good and happy place for people.
> Once again, *spasibo* [thank you]! Alexander Ginzburg[49]

Irina Grivnina

Donald Fiene wrote to Vonnegut in September 1978. "[Rita] still does not like it when you make public statements supporting Soviet dissidents. Irina [Grivnina], of course, thinks you are a saint for doing so."[50] Grivnina had every reason to think Vonnegut a saint. Just a few years later he would play a large role in the successful effort to spring Grivnina herself from "the Workers' Paradise" after her own arrest, imprisonment, and political exile.

Irina Grivnina was a Russian writer who originally trained as a computer programmer and engineer. Grivnina became Rita Rait's protégé, and Vonnegut met her during his short 1977 trip to Leningrad.[51] After that initial meeting, Vonnegut corresponded with Grivnina mostly through Donald Fiene. In spring 1979 Fiene couriered a gift from Irina in Moscow to Vonnegut in New York. Vonnegut sent Grivnina a thank-you letter in April of that year.

> Our friend Don Fiene delivered your handsome gift and sweet letter to me. They make me very cheerful. The cloth is in a place of honor in my library, along with gifts from Rita. Our meeting in Leningrad meant a lot to me, too. You were such a vivacious guide in what may be the most beautiful city in the world. I will never forget how you took us right down by the water, at the base of the old beacon to give us the most stunning and mystical view of all.[52]

---

[49] Alexander Ginzburg to KV, July 23, 1979, KVM, Box 1, Folder 4, "Vonnegut mss. Correspondence F-G."
[50] DFM to KV, September 16, 1978, pp. 10–11, FIEN, Folder 4, "1978."
[51] The Irina Grivnina papers are at the Hoover Institution Library and Archives, Collection No. 2018C13. I did not consult them for this project.
[52] Wakefield, *Kurt Vonnegut—Letters*, 263–4.

Figure 10.2 Kurt Vonnegut near the headquarters of the Soviet Mission to the United Nations in New York, protesting the trials of dissidents Anatoly Shcharansky and Alexander Ginzburg, July 11, 1978. Courtesy of Getty Images.

On September 16, 1980, Grivnina was arrested in Moscow for her membership in a group called the "Working Commission to Investigate the Use of Psychiatry for Political Purposes in the U.S.S.R." She was charged with slandering the Soviet state, including "dissemination of deliberately false fabrications, defamatory to the Soviet state and social system," according to Article 190-1 of the Criminal Code of the Russian SSR. Grivnina was accused of publicizing accounts of Soviet abuses of psychiatry for political ends and delivering "slanderous" (*kleventicheskaia*) information abroad via telephone.[53] She was detained in Butyrskaya ("Butyrka"), a KGB prison.

Rita Rait sent word to Vonnegut of Irina Grivnina's arrest in a letter to Don Fiene dated October 10, 1980. She wrote in code to describe Grivnina's plight.

> My Irishka was "isolated" due to the same illness that Yulika and Andriushka had. . .I'm very sad. . .but I try not to think about it and I hope she will get better soon. . .Write to Kurt, ask him to remember Irishka—but not officially!—she was with me in Leningrad and went with him to the theater.[54]

By "Yulika and Andriushka," Rita meant writers Yuli Daniel and Andrei Sinyavsky, who had served labor camp sentences for supposed "anti-Soviet agitation." By "isolated" she meant "detained/imprisoned." Vonnegut had already heard about Grivnina's situation and he was deeply concerned. He decided to respond "officially," despite Rita's protestations. Vonnegut published a letter to the editor in *The New York Times* on October 19, 1980, "Irina Grivnina's Crime Against the Soviet State."[55] The letter was carefully worded, and Vonnegut insisted that he had not known of Grivnina's alleged political activities.

> When I protested in the past about people I thought had been unjustly arrested in the Soviet Union, those people, most of them with large reputations in the learned professions or in the arts, were strangers to me.

---

[53] George James, "Soviet Dissident Told to Leave," *The New York Times*, October 19, 1985. https://www.nytimes.com/1985/10/19/world/soviet-dissident-told-to-leave.html

[54] RRK to DMF, October 10, 1980, DMFC, Box 4, Folder 5, "Rait-Kovaleva, Rita. 1976–1982."

[55] Kurt Vonnegut, "Irina Grivnina's Crimes against the Soviet State," *The New York Times*, October 19, 1980, 20. https://www.nytimes.com/1980/10/19/archives/letters-our-wrong-answer-to-street-crime-a-crucial-gap-in-the.html

But now a close friend, and merely a computer programmer, is in Butyrka Prison, arrested in Moscow on Sept. 16, evidently for her membership in an organization called the Working Commission to Investigate the Use of Psychiatry for Political Purposes in the U.S.S.R.

Her name is **Irina Grivnina**. We met through mutual friends, and she showed me around Leningrad. I have never sensed until now that she was in any way a dissident. Our conversations and letters have all had to do with friends and the arts. It is from others that I have learned that she forwarded food parcels to political prisoners and their families and traveled widely to give what help she could to such prisoners in psychiatric hospitals.

Her arrest is clearly unjust under the laws of the U.S.S.R., since that nation has affirmed the right to free speech contained in the Universal Declaration of Human Rights and the Helsinki accords. The accords specifically grant individuals the right to monitor their implementation, the nature of Mrs. Grivnina's crime.

I am deeply worried about what might become of her.

The VOA broadcast Vonnegut's editorial letter in the USSR, and Grivnina's friends and family later expressed thanks to Vonnegut for his intervention. Vonnegut further commented in a letter to Donald Fiene on December 20, 1980. "A lot of hell is being raised about Irina's arrest here and in Japan and Europe. This might help just a little bit."[56]

In a letter Vonnegut sent Fiene several years later, he revealed that he had made several additional interventions. Vonnegut had written frequently to the Soviet Ambassador to the United States, Dobrynin. His letters to Dobrynin expressed concern for Grivnina, and asked "his embassy to O.K. my invitations, all plastered with stamps and seals, for the whole family to come visit me."[57] In April 1981, Daniel Jaffe of the Harvard Jewish Law Students Association wrote a grateful update to Vonnegut about Grivnina's situation.

> Dear Mr. Vonnegut,
>
> Irina Grivnina's family and friends wish to offer you the most sincere thanks for your help.
>
> An émigré friend of Irina's just received a letter (sent by means other than the ordinary mails) from Irina's friends in Moscow. They explain that for a while after Irina's arrest, the authorities were threatening to

[56] Wakefield, *Kurt Vonnegut—Letters*, 278.
[57] Wakefield, *Kurt Vonnegut—Letters*, 309.

change the criminal charge against her from one with a maximum 3-year sentence to one with a maximum 12-year sentence. After your letter appeared in the New York Times and was broadcasted to the USSR over the Voice of America, these threats immediately stopped. It is the belief of Irina's friends in Moscow that your letter made the difference.[58]

Jaffe went on to explain that Grivnina's family and friends would like Vonnegut to write another letter to the Soviet authorities and to *The New York Times* about Grivnina's health. "She is now suffering from an untreated liver condition. The authorities of Lefortovo Prison will not allow medicine brought by her husband to be delivered to her . . . Her friends hope that publicity about her illness may lead to treatment of her condition."[59]

Vonnegut continued to write to Ambassador Dobrynin but published no further editorials regarding Grivnina in *The New York Times*. Grivnina was tried on July 14–15, 1981. She was sentenced to five years of internal exile in the Kazakh SSR.[60] (She served two years.) Vonnegut updated Donald Fiene on Grivnina's situation in January 1982. "Irina G is outside the slammer. Her arrest depressed me more than any other event in the past five years. I just didn't want to hear any more about life over there."[61] Grivnina may indeed have been "outside the slammer," but she was still in internal exile in the Kazakh SSR. She languished in a remote village called *Krasnyi Iar* (Red Ravine) until she was returned to Moscow on July 25, 1983. With her husband Vladimir Neplekhovich, Grivnina was stripped of her Soviet citizenship on October 2, 1984. The couple was forced to leave the USSR and emigrated with their young daughter to Amsterdam in late October 1985.

Vonnegut wrote to Fiene in mid-November.

Did you notice that Rita's friend Irina Grivnina was finally sprung from the Worker's Paradise, and has now taken up residence with her family in the Netherlands? I had a little do [sic] with that, I think, writing [Ambassador] Dobrynin frequently about my dear friend in Moscow . . . when they [Grivnina and family] finally got out, I sent him a copy of Galapagos, most respectfully and gratefully inscribed. He wrote back, thanking me for the book, and saying, as though an afterthought, that my dear friend had left his country.[62]

---

[58] Daniel Jaffe to KV, April 3, 1981, KVM, Box 2, Folder 4, "1981, Jan.-May."
[59] Daniel Jaffe to KV, April 3, 1981, KVM, Box 2, Folder 4, "1981, Jan.-May."
[60] "Soviet Tries Rights Activist," *The New York Times*, July 15, 1981, Section A, 6. https://www.nytimes.com/1981/07/15/world/soviet-tries-rights-activist.html
[61] KV to DMF, January 19, 1982, FIEN, Folder 6, "1981–1984."
[62] Wakefield, *Kurt Vonnegut—Letters*, 309.

Other tolerant engagements

Vonnegut made additional efforts in defense of Soviet writers. He sent cables and added his name to sign-on letters. In 1979 he joined an effort to support writers and editors who had come under attack at *Metropol* magazine, an almanac put together without permission from the Soviet censorship authorities. As Vonnegut described it, because of some mildly offensive content, "the Metropol people were denounced, and the magazine was suppressed, and ways were discussed for making life harder for anyone associated with it."[63] Along with Edward Albee, William Styron, and John Updike, Vonnegut sent a cable to the Writers' Union, "saying that we thought it was wrong to penalise writers for what they wrote, no matter what they wrote."[64]

Beyond these direct interventions to speak up for dissident writers at risk, Vonnegut performed other kinds of outreach. He sat for interviews with relevant news and entertainment outlets, and participated in high-profile roundtables for American and Soviet writers. Vonnegut agreed to an extended interview with the VOA that was broadcast in Russian in the Soviet Union in 1976. Vonnegut recounted his trips to the Soviet Union in 1967 and 1974 and discussed his happy working relationship with Rita Rait. When the question of dissident writers came up, Vonnegut carefully explained to Soviet listeners why the Soviet writers Americans were most familiar with, were dissidents. "After all, he said, the Soviet Union pays the most attention to our dissidents—among whom he was proud to number himself.... Anyway, he concluded, there's nothing strange in this phenomenon at all: Dissident writers are *always* more interesting."[65]

The VOA interview was a big success. Rita Rait informed Vonnegut that her friends across the USSR had listened to it and approved. (In correspondence with others Rita did call the woman who interpreted for Vonnegut on "the wretched Voice [of America]" an "idiot.")[66] Rita, who generally was uncomfortable with Vonnegut speaking about politics and literature, seemed satisfied that the VOA broadcast had a positive impact. She assured Fiene that "it was very very good for his friends here of which there are many."[67] But Vonnegut grew skeptical (or at least tired) of giving

---

[63] Vonnegut, *Palm Sunday*, 12.
[64] Vonnegut, *Palm Sunday*, 12.
[65] Fiene, "American Dissident," 266, emphasis in original.
[66] RRK to DMF, rec'd February 19, 1976, p. 2, DMFC, Box 4, Folder 5, "Rait-Kovaleva, Rita, 1976–1982."
[67] RRK to DMF, rec'd February 19, 1976, p. 2, DMFC, Box 4, Folder 5, "Rait-Kovaleva, Rita, 1976–1982."

interviews to Soviet outlets. In December 1978, Fiene wrote in a letter to Leighton: "He [Vonnegut] said TASS had asked him for an exclusive interview of some kind, but he turned them down, he said, 'Because the Russians always misquote me.'"[68]

In the interview he gave Sergei Dovlatov in New York in 1982, Vonnegut mentioned he had been at "four meetings of Russian and American writers."[69] It is not clear if he was counting any of the engagements he had with members of the Soviet Writers' Union during his Moscow trip in 1974. Other than those early encounters, all his official interactions with Soviet writers took place on American soil.

Vonnegut received numerous invitations during the 1970s and 1980s to travel to the Soviet Union as a guest of the Writers' Union and other official organizations. He declined them all. In 1977 Vonnegut was asked to go on a trip sponsored by the U.S. State Department. He demurred. As Donald Fiene wrote to Loree Rackstraw, "It would have been just the usual bullshit: propaganda meetings sponsored by both sides and no free time."[70]

Vonnegut did attend the 1978 iteration of the Soviet-American writers' roundtable meeting, which took place on his home turf in New York. The formal theme was "The Modern Soviet and American Novel: New Forms of Literary Connections." Prominent representatives of the Soviet literary establishment attended and reported on these meetings. Participants Nikolai Fedorenko (head editor of *Foreign Literature* and co-chair of the meetings) and literary critic Iasen Zasurskii both published articles in *Literary Gazette* in 1978. Zasurskii's article devoted an entire section to Kurt Vonnegut. (Other sections were devoted to Joyce Carol Oates and John Gardner.) During these meetings Vonnegut hosted both Felix Kuznetsov (an officer in the Soviet Writers' Union) and Zasurskii in his home in New York City for informal conversation. As mentioned in Chapter 8, in his report for *Literary Gazette* Zasurskii focused on Vonnegut's credentials as a blue-collar writer "of the people," his military service, his interest in labor issues, and Vonnegut's indebtedness to the Soviet Army. Fedorenko did not single Vonnegut out for attention, and mostly offered platitudes about the "progress" made in Soviet-American literary cooperation during the three-day meeting. He peppered his report with obligatory quotations from Brezhnev and Karl Marx.[71]

---

[68] DMF to LGL, December 21, 1978, DMFC, Box 4, Folder 1, "Leighton, Lauren Gray. 1978–1979."
[69] Dovlatov, "Therefore there will be War."
[70] DMF to Loree Rackstraw, August 7, 1977, DFMC, Box 5, "Rackstraw, Loree. 1979–1983."
[71] Nikolai Fedorenko, "Real'nost'" [Reality]. *Literaturnaia gazeta* 25 (June 12, 1978): 14.

Vonnegut had different takeaways from the three-day 1978 literary exchange. He described it as "an ecumenical meeting . . . sponsored by the Charles F. Kettering Foundation, of American and Soviet literary persons, about ten to a side."[72] Vonnegut noted that the American delegation included authors who were published and widely read in the Soviet Union. He named himself, Edward Albee, Norman Cousins, Arthur Miller, William Styron, and John Updike, but neglected to mention that Vera Dunham, Elizabeth Hardwick, Joyce Carol Oates, Harrison Salisbury, and William Jay Smith also participated. Yet, "few, if any, of the Soviet delegates had had anything published here, and so their work was unknown to us."[73] In other words, the Soviet side had sent functionaries, authors of little interest to American readers and writers. The Americans were much more interested in what dissident, or at least mildly controversial, writers in the USSR had to say. Vonnegut believed "that the USSR could easily have put together a delegation whose works were admired and published here—and that we could easily have put together a delegation so unfamiliar to them that its members could have been sewer commissioners from Fresno, as far as anybody in the Soviet Union knew."[74]

At this meeting of Soviet and American writers Kurt landed another blow in the service of promoting "problematic" figures in the literary world of the Soviet Union. Rita Rait had become such a figure. He told the Russian writers that whereas formerly he had always thought about his late sister while he wrote, now he wrote to Rita as his imagined audience. Whether or not this was true, it was a very generous and politic thing to say, and Rita Rait was very pleased when she heard it.[75]

Fiene opined to Lauren Leighton, "He [Vonnegut] really dislikes the Soviet Union and would not go there at all except to see Rita."[76] Indeed, during the mid- to late-1980s, Vonnegut turned down at least four serious invitations to visit the Soviet Union as a guest of the Writers' Union and related institutions. The Union of Soviet Writers invited him for a fourteen-day visit during December 1986-January 1987, for "trips to our national republics and meetings with Soviet writers." While asking Vonnegut to foot the bill for his own round-trip New York-Moscow flight, the Writers' Union

---

[72] Vonnegut, *Palm Sunday*, 10.
[73] Vonnegut, *Palm Sunday*, 11. In addition to Nikolai Fedorenko and Iasen Zasurskii, the Soviet delegation of writers included Felix Kuznetsov, V. Kataev, S. Zalygin, G. Baklanov, M. Slutskis, N. Dumbadze, I. Zooina, A. Kosorukov, and F. Lur'e (Fedorenko, "Reality," 14).
[74] Vonnegut, *Palm Sunday*, 12.
[75] DMF to KV, September 16, 1978, FIEN, Folder 4, "1978."
[76] DMF to LGL, December 21, 1978, DMFC, Box 4, Folder 1, "Leighton, Lauren Gray. 1978–1979."

assured him that "all expences [sic.] connected with your 14 days stay here [are] on us."[77]

At least three more invitations to visit the USSR followed in quick succession. The first arrived on December 12, 1986. A "Group of Soviet Men of Letters-Artists" telegrammed Vonnegut an invitation to a February 1987 "round table discussion ... in Moscow in order to exchange frank opinions on [the] current world situation." The roundtable would proceed in conjunction with a forum of "scientists, scholars, businessmen, [and] clergy who favour nuclear-free world and are concerned with safeguarding life and civilization on our planet." This time however, all Vonnegut's travel expenses—domestic and transatlantic—would be covered, as well as a "five days trip to one of our cultural centres after the meeting is over." The invitation was signed by Chinghiz Aitmatov, Andrey Voznesensky, and Sergey Zalygin. Vonnegut declined.[78]

About a month later Vonnegut received an invitation from the journal *Znamya* to participate in an "informal meeting" of "ten American and ten Soviet writers, World War II veterans." Editor-in-chief Grigorii Baklanov sent the invite. "This informal meeting would afford us an opportunity to have a free and frank exchange of opinions on bygone days and the present, on what bound and still binds our nations together, and on the kind of the [sic.] world we would like to leave to our children and grandchildren." Vonnegut did not make the trip, but his lawyer's notes indicate he at least considered applying for a Soviet visa.[79]

In the United States, throughout the 1980s Vonnegut occasionally took part in events in support of Soviet dissidents. This included a 1986 banquet in New York for Dr. Elena Bonner, the wife of Andrei Sakharov, the physicist, human rights activist and Nobel Peace Prize laureate who had been arrested in 1980 and was serving internal exile in Gorky. Vonnegut celebrated Bonner, and by extension Sakharov. He told an oft-repeated story of a delightful realization he'd had while traveling in Leningrad and Moscow. In the Soviet Union, scientists were regarded as artists because of their playful imaginations.[80]

Vonnegut was one of the American participants in the 1989 Soviet-US telebridge between Moscow State University (MGU) and Tufts University on the theme "Nuclear Century. Culture and the Bomb." The other American

---

[77] KVM, Box 2, Folder 25, "1986, Nov.-Dec."
[78] "Group of Soviet Men of Letters Artists" to KV, December 12, 1986, KVM, Box 2, Folder 25, "1986, Nov.-Dec."
[79] Don Farber's handwritten note on invitation from Baklanov (January 22, 1987), KVM, Box 2, Folder 26, "1987, Jan.-Mar."
[80] Rackstraw, *Love as Always*, 124.

participants included writer E. L. Doctorow, psychologist and writer Robert Lifton, and historian Martin Sherwin. Soviet participants were the philosopher Merab Mamardashvili, the actor Rolan Bykov, historian Roy Medvedev, and sociologist Yurii Levada. The audience, comprised largely of students from MGU and Tufts, greeted Vonnegut with thunderous applause. Characteristically for such occasions, Vonnegut began his remarks at the telebridge by thanking the Red Army soldiers who had saved his life in 1945.[81] Vonnegut did not speak much in the forum but when he did, his remarks focused on ethical issues vis-à-vis the creation and use of the nuclear bomb. He centered the terrifying fact that the professional identities of entire cadres of scientists in both the USSR and the United States hinged on the "success" of nuclear weapons.

But oh, for the philistines and bigots

Vonnegut's stature as a critic of American politics and culture, and his identity as a "repressed" and somewhat controversial writer at home, gave him an authoritative voice to speak up for "writers of the world." He carefully and measuredly used this voice to promote tolerant engagements in support of writers and other artists in trouble or at risk in the Soviet Union and socialist bloc countries. Vonnegut balanced his cables to the Soviet Writers' Union, his published Op-Eds, and other forms of advocacy, with patient endurance of interviews with Soviet literary newspapers and the VOA. He participated in meetings and summits, many of which he no doubt found tiresome. As we saw in his wrenching letter to Lauren Leighton regarding the Slavinsky affair, Vonnegut did not take the responsibility of protest lightly. He was aware that vociferous support for one dissident writer could have all kinds of negative repercussions for that writer, their family and friends, and other writers at risk.

Vonnegut took the view that writing is a fundamentally political act, and that writers should serve their society. In 1973 an interviewer asked Vonnegut, "Why do you write?" "My motives are political. I agree with Stalin and Hitler and Mussolini that the writer should serve his society. I differ with dictators as to *how* writers should serve. Mainly, I think they should be—and biologically *have* to be—agents of change. For the better, we hope."[82]

---

[81] A full video of the event (in Russian) is available at https://www.youtube.com/watch?v=Z9VfCeJ0YFc.
[82] Kurt Vonnegut, "Playboy Interview," 237.

Vonnegut abhorred the repression of dissident writers in the Soviet Union by their government. But he recognized that repression as a sign that writers were taken seriously in the USSR. He did not think this was true in the United States. At a PEN conference in Stockholm in 1973, Vonnegut remarked that in the United States, teachers and journalists may be jailed for their views, but never novelists. "Fiction is harmless in the U.S.," he gloomily averred.[83]

On the other hand, when explaining his concern about Soviet writers in peril and his and other American writers' interest in supporting their human rights, Vonnegut tried to depoliticize the situation. He detached the discourse from its Cold War ideological context. Vonnegut framed his interventions as a writer-to-writer endeavor; he was simply an author "expressing loyalty to the great and vulnerable family of writers throughout the world."[84] Vonnegut articulated this "apolitical" position clearly in his letter to Felix Kuznetsov. Kuznetsov was an officer of the Soviet Writers' Union. Vonnegut had met him several times and they exchanged letters about the persecuted writers and editors from *Metropol*. Vonnegut believed an attack on a writer anywhere, is an attack on writers everywhere. Vonnegut explained that he too had been condemned, mostly by parents and school boards, who had sued in the courts to have his books banned. He wanted Kuznetsov to understand, "that we [Americans who signed cables in support of the *Metropol* writers] are not nationalists, taking part in some cold-war enterprise. We simply care deeply about how things are going for writers here, there, and everywhere. Even when they are declared nonwriters, as we have been, we continue to care."[85]

Vonnegut's support for writers' rights went far beyond the Soviet bloc countries. In February 1986, for instance, Vonnegut spoke about writers' involvement in politics at the International PEN Congress in New York. The theme that year was "The Writer's Imagination and the Imagination of the State."[86] Vonnegut emphasized the writer's blanket responsibility to defend free speech, full stop. That August, as an executive board member of the PEN American Center, he spoke before a subcommittee of the Senate Foreign Relations Committee that was reviewing the McCarthy-era McCarran-Walter Act of 1952. Part of this Act excluded certain aliens from immigrating to the United States on ideological grounds. Vonnegut called the 1952 law (whose ideological clauses were subsequently stripped out) "embarrassing, foolish, mean-spirited and xenophobic ... The free exchange of ideas among

---

[83] Kurt Vonnegut, "Address to P.E.N. Conference in Stockholm, 1973," in *Wampeters, Foma & Granfalloons (Opinions)*, 227.
[84] Vonnegut, *Palm Sunday*, 13.
[85] Vonnegut, *Palm Sunday*, 14.
[86] Shields, *So it Goes*, 373.

nations and individuals does not endanger our security, but strengthens it, and the belief that, as citizens of the United States, all freedoms of expression are our rights."[87]

Vonnegut did not pretend that it was only the Soviet bloc that violated writers' rights to freedom of speech. He called out abuse of free speech all over the world—including in the United States—in his role as an officer in the American PEN, and as a concerned citizen. We know a lot about Vonnegut's struggles with U.S. public school boards and his advocacy for free speech and the First Amendment as an American writer. The National Coalition against Censorship was right to hail Vonnegut as a "hero of free speech."[88] But much less is known about Vonnegut's advocacy for the right to free speech of writers in the Soviet Union and socialist bloc countries like Czechoslovakia. He made these tolerant engagements as a favored American writer, an invested subject of the "world of letters" and, in some cases—like Irina Grivnina's—as a personal friend. Although they did not always agree on the correct means and approach, Kurt agreed wholeheartedly with Rita Rait that enlightened people everywhere must do everything possible to thwart "the philistines and bigots who do all they can to ruin the Brotherhood of art EVERYWHERE..."[89]

Vonnegut's tolerant engagements, incidentally, earned him an FBI file. A Letterhead Memorandum dated March 19, 1971 indicates that a "confidential source" (presumably, a Soviet citizen) approached and was interested in four specific things:

(1) The New York Committee to Free Angela Davis
(2) Advice about songs indicative of youth culture in the U.S.
(3) The chance to listen to church sermons of pastors passionate about politics
(4) Getting Kurt Vonnegut's phone number.[90]

The names of the "confidential source" and the SA (special agent) who conversed with them are blacked out. We may never know the identity of the presumably Soviet citizen who sought these cultural insights and wanted to telephone Kurt Vonnegut. One aspect of the FBI Memorandum would have

---

[87] Shields, *So it Goes*, 373.
[88] National Coalition against Censorship, "Kurt Vonnegut: Remembering a Hero of Free Speech," https://ncac.org/resource/kurt-vonnegut-remembering-a-hero-of-free-speech.
[89] RRK to DMF, rec'd February 19, 1976, p. 2, DMFC, Box 4, Folder 5, "Rait-Kovaleva, Rita. 1976-1982."
[90] Freedom of Information/Privacy Acts (FOIPA) Request No.: 1458339-000; Subject: VONNEGUT, KURT, JR., rec'd January 31, 2020.

thoroughly amused Kurt Vonnegut, who likely never saw his own FBI file. It was typed on a form with a standard letterhead, "United States Government: MEMORANDUM." But the memo featured a classically American footer: "Buy U.S. Savings Bonds Regularly on the Payroll Savings Plan." In the United States, even your FBI file is a capitalist advertisement.

11

Conclusion: Back to the Future

Rita Rait-Kovaleva did not live to see the fall of the Soviet government in 1991. Nor did she see the USSR separate into fifteen independent states, its international borders open, or the moves to usher in capitalism and democracy. Despite having met "her" author three times, Rita never met Vonnegut on American soil. When she died in 1989 at the age of ninety, Don Fiene wrote to her daughter, Margarita. "I heard recently that your mother had died. If so, I express my sympathy. I had not been in touch with her for several years." Then, understated in parentheses, he added, "(She was a difficult person, but a great translator.)"[1]

Several years after Rita's death, Nataliya Shulga, the Ukrainian superfan from Chapter 5 who illustrated scenes from Vonnegut's books in the 1970s, did meet her hero, and in the United States, too. Nataliya was now a renowned cell biologist specializing in molecular genetics. She had been recruited from newly independent Ukraine for a postdoctoral fellowship at the University of Rochester in 1992. When Vonnegut gave a lecture there in 1995, Nataliya approached him and told him about the drawings. Twenty years earlier her co-artist Oleksandr had a chivalrous idea to make identical originals, so both would have two full sets. He managed to complete one set, and when he started the second, Nataliya stopped him and suggested they scan the drawings and send them to Vonnegut. High-quality scanners were not yet available, but Nataliya believed they would be in the future. "One day technology will catch up, and he'll see the thirty-six colors we used." In 1995 her department at the University of Rochester received a new Xerox high-end laser multi-function machine for testing, and she made superior-quality prints for Vonnegut using the world's best printer, developed right there in Rochester. A coincidence like that, says Nataliya, was preordained. A Vonnegutian miracle.

Vonnegut sent Nataliya a thank you note via a mutual acquaintance. "Enclosed, find my reply to the astonishing package from Natalia Shulga.

---

[1] DMF to Margarita Kovaleva, October 23, 1989. DMFC, Box 4, "Rait-Kovaleva, Rita, 1961–1989."

Figure 11.1 Nataliya Shulga (left) and Eri Shulga (right) with Kurt Vonnegut, Rochester, NY, 1995. Courtesy of Nataliya Shulga.

What a stupid country this would be if it weren't for immigrants."[2] Nataliya Shulga stayed in the United States for ten more years, then returned to Ukraine to lead education and science reforms and teach university science courses. She had all her science students read Vonnegut's novel *Cat's Cradle*. Nataliya continues to promote global science diplomacy as Senior Manager of Global Science at The Aspen Institute in Washington, D.C.

Donald M. Fiene, the Slavicist and bibliographer extraordinaire who first introduced Vonnegut's novels to Rita Rait, died in 2013. I never met Don, but he made this book possible. I like to think he'd be pleased with the result. Fiene and Vonnegut last corresponded in 2005, before Vonnegut's death in 2007.

Coincidentally (or not), I read Vonnegut for the first time in 2007. I remember because I was pregnant with my second child. I read his first novel, *Player Piano*, a book some critics find overwritten, but which is still my favorite. I got a second big dose of Vonnegut in 2017 when I joined an Indiana University Bloomington Public Humanities Project, "Salo University," that convened faculty members from the disciplines of anthropology, history, religious studies, English, physics, and others to read Vonnegut's first five

---

[2] KV to Susan Feinstein, November 22, 1995. Shared with author by Nataliya Shulga. At the time she contacted Vonnegut, she spelled her name "Natalia."

novels and collectively consider his continued relevance in contemporary society and politics.³

In summer 2017, I was writing a blog post about *Mother Night* when I ran across a 1977 *New York Times* article by Donald M. Fiene about Vonnegut's popularity in the USSR. I happened to be in Ukraine, a country I have visited a dozen times for research since 1995. The Russian Federation had invaded and annexed parts of Ukrainian territory (Donbas and Crimea) in 2014, so my travels were restricted to central Ukraine. In Kyiv, I stayed with my friend Natalka, a former librarian who worked at the U.S. Embassy at the time. I asked Natalka's teenage daughter Sasha what she was reading. She showed me the book, *Boinia nomer p'iat'*, *Slaughterhouse-Five* in Ukrainian translation.⁴ *Slaughterhouse-Five* was first published in Ukrainian in 1976, but translation aficionados considered it a sketchy re-translation of Rita Rait-Kovaleva's Russian version.⁵ It wasn't "real" Ukrainian. A new *bona fide* Ukrainian version had just hit the shelves, and Sasha said all her high school friends were reading it. "Our country is at war. We're all reading war novels, and we love Kurt Vonnegut."

Kurt Vonnegut brought relevance to the war in eastern Ukraine when the renowned Viktor Marushchenko School of Photography published a collection of war photographs by Ukrainian and Russian photographers in 2015. The Russians, who worked for Western media, often had better access to the Russian-occupied conflict zone because of their Russian passports. The project's goal was to "approach the war through photographs, circumventing both politics and propaganda. We hope that this issue can convey the absurd ugliness of the events, and present a persuasive case against the war."⁶ The color photographs, all taken with cell phone cameras, are shocking. They show corpses, some just after torture, towns leveled by shelling, children toting machine guns, and badly battered civilians.

The portfolio's sparse softback cover is crimson red, with only the words "Poo-tee-weet?" in white lettering in the upper left corner. Poo-tee-weet, of course, is the famous phrase that ends Vonnegut's *Slaughterhouse-Five*, after Billy Pilgrim has witnessed the massacre at Dresden and stumbled through

---

³ In Vonnegut's novel *Sirens of Titan*, Salo is an eleven-million-year-old mechanical messenger from the planet Tralfamadore.
⁴ Kurt Vonnegut, *Boinia nomer p'iat', abo Dytiachyi khrestovyi pokhid* [Slaughterhouse-Five, or the Children's Crusade], trans. Volodymyr Dibrov and Lidiia Dibrov (Vydavnytstvo Staroho Leva, 2017).
⁵ Kurt Vonnegut, *Boinia nomer p'iat', abo Khrestoviy pokhid ditei* [Slaughterhouse-Five, or the Children's Crusade], trans. Petro Sokolovs'kyi (Dnipro, 1976).
⁶ Viktor Marushchenko and Olga Kostyrko, "Introduction," in *Poo-tee-weet?* (Osnovy Publishing, 2015), 1.

Figure 11.2 Sasha with the new Ukrainian translation of *Slaughterhouse-Five*, Kyiv, 2017. Photograph by Sarah D. Phillips.

"hundreds of corpse mines," unable to keep up with the impossible number of decaying corpses, former human beings. The editors explained their choice of title: "The war in Eastern Ukraine has many names: information warfare, hybrid war, civil war, cognitive war. But wars are irrational by their very nature. We don't have a name for it, nor do we have a title for this edition. We just had the epigraph to *Slaughterhouse-Five, or The Children's Crusade* by Kurt Vonnegut, and that's what we've put on the cover."[7] They go on to quote a passage in *Slaughterhouse-Five*. "Everything is supposed to be very quiet after a massacre, and it always is, except for the birds. And what do the birds say? All there is to say about a massacre, things like 'Poo-tee-weet?'"[8]

Relations between Russia and Ukraine deteriorated steeply during the years I researched this book. After its long-time occupation of parts of eastern Ukraine and Crimea, in February 2022 the Russian Federation launched a brutal full-scale invasion. Under President Biden, the United States government condemned the imperialist actions and associated human rights abuses and war crimes committed by the Russian state. The United

---

[7] Marushchenko and Kostyrko, "Introduction."
[8] Kurt Vonnegut, *Slaughterhouse-Five*, 24.

States provided weapons and other support to Ukraine and joined other countries and alliances to impose sanctions and embargoes on Russian elites and Russia's industrial base, financial institutions, and technology suppliers. The Ukrainian people continue to suffer catastrophic losses, with massive death and disablement of troops, a shattered economy, and brain drain as people flee the country. Russian bombs have reduced entire cities and towns to rubble. Evidence of the indiscriminate killing and torture of civilians proliferates in what many consider a genocide.

Sasha, the teenage reader of *Slaughterhouse-Five* in 2017, earned degrees in marketing and anti-corruption from Ukraine's top university. Since the beginning of Russia's full-scale invasion, Sasha has volunteered to help support the Ukrainian Armed Forces and people displaced by war. She works for Reporters Without Borders, assisting journalists from all over the world who come to report on Ukraine. She helps them reach the front lines (but does not accompany them directly) by aiding with logistics, contacts, and protective equipment such as helmets and body armor. She demonstrates basic first aid such as applying bandages and medical tourniquets. In her spare time, she raises funds to support her friends currently engaged on the front lines. Fortunately, her close friends in active combat are all alive, but some of her classmates from her elementary school days have been killed. A young man she worked with lost his legs, and some classmates have fled to other parts of Europe. But Sasha stays put, and like many people who grew up in Russian-speaking families in Kyiv and other Ukrainian cities, Sasha now never speaks Russian, the "language of the enemy."

Today, the questions Vonnegut poses seem more important than ever, whether one is standing in Washington, D.C., Kyiv, Beijing, Moscow, or Tralfamadore. How does one remain human in inhumane conditions? Who or what controls the universe, and what is our purpose here? In an unethical, brutal world, can simple decency and compassion exist, and even prevail? After witnessing unspeakable violence, after experiencing with all one's senses the awful, visceral, rotting carnage of the senseless war dead, how does one go on? Vonnegut asks this question, Billy Pilgrim asks this question, and Sasha and millions of people in Ukraine continue to ask this question.

At the time of this writing, the United States and other allies continue to support Ukraine in its fight to survive Vladimir Putin's violent imperial mission to obliterate the Ukrainian people, their language, their culture, and their history. US-Russia relations in 2025 have deep parallels with US-Soviet tensions during the Cold War. Cultural relations have been severely affected, as official routes for cultural exchange are on hiatus, and many U.S. cultural and educational institutions have suspended relations with any entities connected to the Russian state. Broadly speaking, the United States and

Russia are in a new Cold War, one that arguably holds even less room for cultural exchange than détente did in the 1970s. It is sobering that the acts of literary diplomacy Vonnegut performed at the height of the Cold War, including his three trips to Soviet Russia where he met with writers, translators, artists, theater directors, and other cultural figures, would likely be impossible today. Here's hard evidence: In June 2025, the Russian State Archive of Literature and Art denied my request for digital scans of newly available materials about Vonnegut's visits to the USSR. "Your request has been deemed inappropriate due to your anti-Russian statements." All hail the wooden vocabulary of authoritarian officialese. All hail the little green men scouring scholars' social media. I can hear Kurt laughing from here.

In 2022, just after Russia's full-scale invasion of Ukraine, a post on the social media platform Reddit went viral. "Dmitry Reznikov simply held up a sign with asterisks in Moscow. A court convicted him of 'discrediting Russia's armed forces' and fined him 50,000 rubles ($480)." In the accompanying photo, a male university-age student with dark hair wearing a long black parka stands near Red Square. He holds a sign with "asterisks" arranged in two rows, three + five, which could be interpreted as code for the phrase "*Nyet voine*," or "No war" in Russian. Protesting with this essentially blank sign got Reznikov arrested and fined.

However, friends, those were no asterisks Reznikov was wielding. They were eight replications of Vonnegut's famous stylized drawing of an "asshole" (*Breakfast of Champions*). In response to the Reddit post, a knowing user commented, "Your Honor, this is a row of three assholes on top and five on the bottom. Not one asterisk on this paper. I'm innocent of all asterisk charges . . . or would you like me to draw one more asshole?"[9] I don't know what has happened to the protester, Dmitry Reznikov, but I think Kurt would approve of his assholic war protest near Red Square.

In this book, I have used the tools of anthropology and literary and cultural history to explore Kurt Vonnegut's influence in the Soviet Union during the Cold War. He was a humorous, satirical writer with technical and practical smarts who thought deeply about ethics, religion, language, technology, and science. He was a champion of free speech and a veteran who hated war. Vonnegut's moral and ethical system was rooted in postmodern humanism.[10] He eschewed all grand narratives and the illusion that there

---

[9] https://www.reddit.com/r/Vonnegut/comments/tk3i90/dmitry_reznikov_simply_held_up_a_sign_with/.

[10] Todd Davis, *Kurt Vonnegut's Crusade, Or, How a Postmodern Harlequin Preached a New Kind of Humanism* (State University of New York Press, 2006).

Figure 11.3 Anti-war protester near Red Square, Moscow, March 13, 2022. Courtesy of Sota Vision.

are "essential truths." Vonnegut rejected all "isms," whether communism, socialism, capitalism, corporatism, or whataboutism.

In the 1970s and 1980s, Vonnegut's clear moral voice helped Soviet readers, especially the youth, laugh at themselves and the system they lived in. Vonnegut offered visions of a different reality, both in the present and the future. Vonnegut decentered the individual and centered all of humanity and encouraged others to do the same. It is no coincidence that people living in war-torn Ukraine, especially the youth, find solace and inspiration in Vonnegut's books. They want to live decently in an indecent world. They want to imagine a different reality in the present and the future.

Babylon Library Press in Ivano-Frankivsk, Ukraine, has published new Ukrainian translations of *Breakfast of Champions*, *Sirens of Titan*, *Bluebeard*, *God Bless You, Mr. Rosewater*, *Galapagos*, and *Slapstick*. The press, founded in 2013, also collaborated with L'viv publishing house *Vydavnytstvo Staroho Leva* (Old Lion Publishers) on the new Ukrainian translation of *Slaughterhouse-Five* in 2017. Vonnegut is Babylon's best-selling author and their social media posts about him go viral. The press's founder, Roman Malynovsky, told me in 2020 that when he promotes the Vonnegut translations to audiences at book fairs and presentations, he quotes from Vonnegut's 1975 telegram to theater director Mikhail Levitin: "Nothing has made me so happy and proud. Place a chair in the wings for my soul on opening night—my body must remain here." He then places an empty chair on the stage or at the book table.

I don't know whether "Vonnegut writes better in Russian," as many fans in Eastern Europe are wont to declare (see Chapter 3). But I do know that through his prose he speaks to us in Russian, Ukrainian, Spanish, Japanese, Persian, Greek, Arabic, and dozens of other languages. And what he says is, "We are here to help each other get through this thing, whatever it is."[11]

If in this book's pages the reader has been inspired by Kurt Vonnegut, Rita Rait, Don Fiene, Nataliya Shulga, Sasha, and others to search for our shared humanity, to practice compassion and decency above all, I will have achieved one of my major goals. Lovers of humanity, those who hate wars, those who see good in themselves and in one another, take heart. Vonnegut is with us. Put out a chair for him. There is still hope.

---

[11] Kurt Vonnegut, *A Man Without a Country* (Random House Trade Paperbacks, 2007), 66.

Bibliography

Archives:

Personal archives of Konstantin Markovich Azadovsky, Correspondence (KMAC).
Donald M. Fiene Archive (Correspondence), University of Louisville (DMFC).
Donald M. Fiene Manuscripts, Lilly Library, Indiana University, Bloomington, Indiana (FIEN).
Kurt Vonnegut Manuscripts, Lilly Library, Indiana University, Bloomington, Indiana (KVM).
MSS 259 Seymour Lawrence Publishing, University of Delaware Library Special Collection.
Rita Rait-Kovaleva Correspondence, Bakhmeteff Archive, Rare Book and Manuscript Library, Columbia University Library (BA-RRK).
Russian State Archive of Literature and Art (RGALI).

Secondary Sources:

Agamben, Giorgio. "What is the Contemporary?" In *What is an Apparatus? And other Essays.* Stanford University Press, 2009.
Aitmatov, Chinghiz, and Kurt Vonnegut. "Vstrecha nad planetoi zemlia: Dialog sovetskogo i amerikanskogo pisatelei" [Meeting over planet earth: Dialog between soviet and American writers]. *Literaturnaia gazeta* 30 (July 23, 1975): 2.
Aksyonov, Vassily. *In Search of Melancholy Baby.* Vintage Books, 1989.
Alekseeva, Liudmila. *Soviet Dissent: Contemporary Movements for National, Religious, and Human Rights.* Translated by Carol Pearce and John Glad. Wesleyan University Press, 1985.
Aliakrinskii, O. "Kurt Vonnegut: S raznykh tochek zreniia" [Kurt Vonnegut: From different points of view]. *Voprosy literatury* 4 (April 1982): 236–47.
Allen, William Rodney, and Paul Smith. "An Interview with Kurt Vonnegut." In *Conversations with Kurt Vonnegut*, edited by William Rodney Allen. University Press of Mississippi, 1988.
Amalrik, Andrei. *Will the Soviet Union survive until 1984?* Harper and Row, 1981.
Andrews, James T., and Asif A. Siddiqi, eds. *Into the Cosmos: Space Exploration and Soviet Culture.* Pittsburgh University Press, 2011.

"Anketa Inostrannoi literatury" [Foreign literature's survey]. *Innostrannaia literatura* 6 (June 1982): 188–91.

Azadovsky, Konstantin. *Zhizn' i trudy Marka Azadovskogo. Dokumental'naia biografia* [*The Life and Works of Mark Azadovsky*. Documentary biography]. NLO Press, 2025.

Baer, Brian James. *Translation and the Making of Modern Russian Literature*. Bloomsbury Academic, 2016.

Ballinger Fletcher, Zita. "Our Review of Putin's Recommended Book: The Living and the Dead." *HistoryNet*, April 15, 2020. https://www.historynet.com/our-review-of-putins-recommended-book-the-living-and-the-dead/.

Bayley, John. "Kitsch and the Novel." (Review of Yevgeny Yevtushenko, *Wild Berries*; Sergei Dovlatov, *The Compromise*; Edward Limonov, *It's Me, Eddie: A Fictional Memoir*; Vassily Aksyonov, *The Burn*; and Vassily Aksyonov, *The Island of Crimea*) *The New York Review of Books*, November 22, 1984. https://www.nybooks.com/articles/1984/11/22/kitsch-and-the-novel/.

Bertin-Mahieux, Caitlin. "The Reminiscences of Jeri Laber." Harriman Institute Oral History Project, 2016. https://api.harriman.maptian.com/sites/default/files/2018-04/LABER1-2.pdf.

Bestuzhev-Lada, Igor. "Kogda lishnim stanovitsia chelovechestvo" [When Mankind Becomes Superfluous]. Foreword to *Utopiia 14* [Utopia 14 (Player Piano)], by Kurt Vonnegut. Translated by M. Brukhnov. Molodaia Gvardiia, 1967.

Bobko, Jane. "An Interview with Sergei Dovlatov." *The Threepenny Review* 20 (Winter 1985): 16–18.

Borovik, Genrikh. "'Demokratia' politseiskoi dubinki: Signal SOS na statue svobody" ["Democracy" with a police cudgel: SOS signal from the Statue of Liberty]. *Literaturnaia gazeta* 8 (February 23, 1972): 14.

Borshchagovskii, Aleksandr. "Takie dela" [So it goes]. *Literaturnaia gazeta* 19 (July 15, 1970): 3.

"Bowdlerize." Oxford English Dictionary (online). Accessed May 28, 2020. https://www.oed.com/viewdictionaryentry/Entry/22199.

Boyer, Paul. *By the Bomb's Early Light: American Thought and Culture at the Dawn of the Atomic Age*. University of North Carolina Press, 1985.

Brodsky, Joseph. "The Azadovsky Affair." *The New York Review*, October 8, 1981. https:/www.nybooks.com/articles/1981/10/08/the-azadovsky-affair/.

Brown, Deming. *Soviet Attitudes Toward American Writing*. Princeton University Press, 1962.

Burak, Alexander. *"The Other" in Translation: A Case for Comparative Translation Studies*. Slavica, 2013.

Burns, Robert. *Robert Burns in the translations of S. Marshak*. Pravda, 1979.

Chernetsky, Vitaly. "Nation and Translation: Literary Translation and the Shaping of Modern Ukraine." In *Contexts, Subtexts and Pretexts: Literary Translation in Eastern Europe and Russia*, edited by Brian James Baer. John Benjamins Publishing Company, 2011.

Choldin, Marianna Tax. *A Fence Around an Empire: Russian Censorship of Western Ideas under the Tsars*. Duke University Press, 1985.

Choldin, Marianna Tax. *Garden of Broken Statues: Exploring Censorship in Russia*. Academic Studies Press, 2016.

"Christopher Bigsby in conversation with Kurt Vonnegut." Kaleidoscope broadcast. Interviewer Christopher Bigsby, program producer Carroll Moore (September 20, 1984). Kurt Vonnegut Manuscripts, Lilly Library, Indiana University, Bloomington, Indiana. Box 2, Folder 19.

Chukovsky, Kornei. *Vysokoe iskusstvo: o printsipakh khudozhestvennogo perevoda* [A high art: on principles of artistic translation]. Iskusstvo, 1964.

Chukovsky, Kornei, and Andrei Fedorov. *Iskusstvo perevoda* [The art of translation]. Academia, 1930.

Clark, Katerina. *The Soviet Novel: History as Ritual*. Indiana University Press, 2000.

Cook, Bruce. "When Kurt Vonnegut Talks—And he Does—The Young All Tune In." *National Observer*, October 12, 1970, 21.

Davis, Todd. *Kurt Vonnegut's Crusade, Or, How a Postmodern Harlequin Preached a New Kind of Humanism*. State University of New York Press, 2006.

Dobrzhanskaia, Liubov'. Interview by A. Smolianskii and L. Levikova, *Sovetskaia kul'tura* 82, no. 4882 (October 10, 1975): 3.

Dovlatov, Sergei. "…Poetomu budet voina: Beseda s Kurtom Vonnegutom" [Therefore there will be war: Conversation with Kurt Vonnegut]. *Novyi Amerikanets* 101 (January 15–21, 1982): 24–5. Article is reproduced at https://dzen.ru/media/azibuli/dovlatov-beseduet-s-vonnegutom-5d81a73 0027a1500ad140c3b.

Dovlatov, Sergei. *Solo on Underwood: Notebooks*. Tret'ia volna, 1980. Accessed May 22, 2020. http://lib.ru/DOWLATOW/dowlatow.txt.

Druzhinin, Petr A. *Soviet Suppression of Academia: The Case of Konstantin Azadovsky*. Bloomsbury Academic, 2022.

Edelman, Robert, and Christopher Young, eds. *The Whole World Was Watching: Sport in the Cold War*. Stanford University Press, 2019.

El'sberg, Ia. "V bitve za cheloveka" [In the battle for humankind]. *Literaturnaia gazeta* 1 (January 1, 1971): 1.

Enzensberger, Hans Magnus. "On Leaving America." *The New York Review of Books*, February 29, 1968. https://www.nybooks.com/articles/1968/02/29/on-leaving-america/.

Ermolaev, Herman. *Censorship in Soviet Literature, 1917-1991*. Rowman and Littlefield, 1997.

Etkind, Efim. "Introduction." In *Mastera russkogo stikhotovornogo perevoda* [Masters of Russian Literary Translation], edited by Efim Etkind. Sovetskii pisatel', 1968.

Fainberg, Dina. "Radio Moscow, Decolonization, and the Cold War." Discussant comments presented at the 53rd convention of the Association for Slavic, East European and Eurasian Studies (virtual), December 2, 2021.

Fedorenko, Nikolai. "Real'nost'" [Reality]. *Literaturnaia gazeta* 25 (June 21, 1978): 14.

Festa, Conrad. "Vonnegut's Satire." In *Vonnegut in America: An Introduction to the Life and Work of Kurt Vonnegut*, edited by Jerome Klinkowitz and Donald L. Lawler. Delacorte Press/Seymour Lawrence, 1977.

Field, Douglas, ed. *American Cold War Culture*. Edinburgh University Press, 2005.

Fiene, Donald M. "First Meeting." In *Happy Birthday, Kurt Vonnegut: A Festschrift for Kurt Vonnegut on His Sixtieth Birthday*, compiled and edited by Jill Krementz. Delacorte Press, 1982.

Fiene, Donald M. "J.D. Salinger: A Bibliography." *Wisconsin Studies in Contemporary Literature* 4, no. 1 (Winter 1963): 109–49.

Fiene, Donald M. "J.D. Salinger in the Soviet Union—A Brief Report." Unpublished manuscript. Donald M. Fiene Correspondence, University of Louisville, Box 4, "Rait-Kovaleva, Rita, 1963-1976."

Fiene, Donald M. "Kurt Vonnegut as an American Dissident: His Popularity in the Soviet Union and His Affinities with Russian Literature." In *Vonnegut in America: An Introduction to the Life and Work of Kurt Vonnegut*, edited by Jerome Klinkowitz and Donald L. Lawler. Delacorte Press/Seymour Lawrence, 1977.

Fiene, Donald M. "Kurt Vonnegut in the USSR: A Bibliography." *Bulletin of Bibliography* 45, no. 4 (1988): 223–32.

Fiene, Donald M. "Vonnegut—Big in Russia." *The New York Times Book Review*, April 3, 1977. https://www.nytimes.com/1977/04/03/archives/vonnegut-big-in-russia-vonnegut-in-russia.html.

Fiene, Donald M. "Vonnegut Staged in Moscow." Unpublished article dated December 29, 1975. Donald M. Fiene Correspondence, University of Louisville, Box 4, Folder 2.

Fish, Stanley. *Is There a Text in This Class? The Authority of Interpretive Communities*. Harvard University Press, 1980.

Fosler-Lussier, Danielle. *Music in America's Cold War Diplomacy*. University of California Press, 2015.

Freedom of Information/Privacy Acts (FOIPA) Request No.: 1458339-000; Subject: VONNEGUT, KURT, JR., rec'd January 31, 2020.

Friedberg, Maurice. *A Decade of Euphoria: Western Literature in Post-Stalin Russia, 1954-64*. Indiana University Press, 1977.

Friedberg, Maurice. *Literary Translation in Russia: A Cultural History*. The Pennsylvania State University Press, 1997.

Fürst, Juliane. *Stalin's Last Generation: Soviet Post-War Youth and the Emergence of Mature Socialism*. Oxford University Press, 2010.

Fürst, Juliane, and Josie McLellan, eds. *Dropping Out of Socialism: The Creation of Alternate Spheres in the Soviet Bloc*. Lexington Books, 2017.

Galmarini, Maria Cristina. *Ambassadors of Social Progress: A History of International Blind Activism in the Cold War*. Northern Illinois University Press, 2024.

Gerasimov, G. "Vzgliad na literatury s bruklinskogo mosta" [A view on literature from the Brooklyn bridge]. *Literaturnaia gazeta* 39 (September 28, 1977): 14.

Gilburd, Eleonory. *To See Paris and Die: The Soviet Lives of Western Culture*. The Belknap Press of Harvard University Press, 2018.

Giustino, Cathleen M., Catherine J. Plum, and Alexander Vari, eds. *Socialist Escapes: Breaking Away from Ideology and Everyday Routine in Eastern Europe, 1945–1989*. Berghahn, 2013.

Goriaeva, T.M. *Politicheskaia tsenzura v SSSR 1917-1991* [Political censorship in the USSR 1917-1991]. ROSSPEN, 2022.

Haslam, Jonathan. *Russia's Cold War: From the October Revolution to the Fall of the Wall*. Yale University Press, 2011.

Hassan, Ihab Habib. *Contemporary American Literature, 1945-1972: An Introduction*. Ungar, 1973.

Heldt, Barbara. "Motherhood in a Cold Climate: The Poetry and Career of Mariia Shkapskaia." *The Russian Review* 51, no. 2 (April 1992): 160–71.

Hersh, Seymour M. "P.O.W.'s Planned Business Venture." *The New York Times*, March 6, 1973, 12. https://www.nytimes.com/1973/03/06/archives/pows-planned-business-venture-agreed-at-camps-to-set-up-unit-on.html.

Human Rights Watch. "The Fund for Free Expression." https://www.hrw.org/reports/1990/WR90/MISC.BOU.htm#P8_0.

Hutchisson, James M. "All of Us at 46: The Making of Sinclair Lewis' Babbitt." *Journal of Modern Literature* 18, no. 1 (1992): 95–114.

Ileshin, B. "Za politseiskimi bar'erami" [Beyond the police barriers]. *Izvestiia* 282 (November 27, 1970): 4.

Ilnytzkyj, Oleh S. *Nikolai Gogol: Ukrainian Writer in the Empire: A Study in Identity*. De Gruyter, 2024.

James, George. "Soviet Dissident Told to Leave." (Article about Irina Grivnina.) *The New York Times*, October 19, 1985. https://www.nytimes.com/1985/10/19/world/soviet-dissident-told-to-leave.html.

Kachan, Liubov. "Ee velichestvo perevodchik! Rita Rait" [Her majesty the translator! Rita Rait]. Accessed November 22, 2023. https://www.proza.ru/2012/02/29/434.

Kamovnikova, Natalia. *Made Under Pressure: Literary Translation in the Soviet Union, 1960-1991*. University of Massachusetts Press, 2019.

Kashkin, Ivan. *Dlia chitatelia-sovremennika: Stat'i i materialy* [For the modern reader: Articles and materials]. Sovetskii pisatel', 1968.

Katanyan, Vasily. *Khronika zhizni i deiatel'nosti Maiakovskogo 1919* [Chronicle of the life and works of Mayakovsky 1919]. Accessed June 3, 2020. http://mayakovskiy.lit-info.ru/mayakovskiy/bio/katyanyan-hronika/1919.htm.

Khmelnitsky, Michael. "Sex, Lies, and Red Tape: Ideological and Political Barriers in Soviet Translation of Cold War American Satire, 1964-1988." PhD diss., University of Calgary, 2015. https://doi.org/10.11575/PRISM/27766.

Kim, Iulii. "Kak ia stal dramaturgom" [How I became a dramatist]. In *Mozaika zhizni* [Mosaic of life]. Eksmo-Press, 1999.

Komaromi, Ann. "The Material Existence of Soviet Samizdat." *Slavic Review* 63, no. 3 (2004): 597–618.

Kondrashov, S. "'Khoumkaming' i dollar" [Homecoming and the dollar]. *Izvestiia* 58 (March 9, 1973): 3.

Kozlov, Denis. *The Readers of Novyi Mir: Coming to Terms with the Stalinist Past*. Harvard University Press, 2013.

Kuhn, Annette. *Cinema, Censorship and Sexuality, 1909–1925*. Routledge, 1988.

Kutuzov, Andrey. "Change of Word Types to Word Tokens Ratio in the Course of Translation (Based on Russian Translation of K. Vonnegut's Novels)." *Tyumen State University*, 2010. Accessed April 2, 2020. https://arxiv.org/ftp/arxiv/papers/1003/1003.0337.pdf.

Lange, Anne, Daniele Monticelli, and Christopher Rundle. "Translation and the History of European Communism." In *Translation Under Communism*, edited by Christopher Rundle, Anne Lange, and Daniele Monticelli. Routledge, 2022.

Ledeneva, Alena. *Russia's Economy of Favours: Blat, Networking and Informal Exchange*. Cambridge University Press, 1998.

Leeds, Marc. *The Vonnegut Encyclopedia: An Authorized Compendium*. Greenwood Press, 1995.

Leighton, Lauren G. "Rita Rajt-Kovaleva's Vonnegut: A Review Article." *Slavic and East European Journal* 24, no. 4 (1980): 412–19.

Leighton, Lauren G. *Two Worlds, One Art: Literary Translation in Russia and America*. Northern Illinois University Press, 1991.

Levitin, Mikhail. *Posle liubvi: Roman o professii* [After love: A book about a profession]. AST, 2019.

Lingeman, Richard R. "God Bless You, Mr. Mihajlov." *The New York Times Book Review*, July 2, 1978. Accessed February 14, 2025. https://www.nytimes.com/1978/07/02/archives/book-ends-god-bless-you-mr-mihajlov.html.

Lipsitz, George. *Class and Culture in Cold War America: Rainbow at Midnight*. Praeger Scientific, 1981.

Locmele, Gunta, and Andrejs Veisbergs. "The Other Polysystem: The Impact of Translation on Language Norms and Conventions in Latvia." In *Contexts, Subtexts and Pretexts: Literary Translation in Eastern Europe and Russia*, edited by Brian James Baer. John Benjamins Publishing Company, 2011.

Markish, Shimon. "O perevode" [On translation]. *Ierusalimskii zhurnal* 18 (2004). Antho.net.

Marsh, Rosalind J. *Soviet Science Fiction Since Stalin: Science, Politics and Literature*. Barnes and Noble Books, 1986.

Marushchenko Viktor, and Olga Kostyrko. "Introduction." In *Poo-tee-weet?* Osnovy Publishing, 2015.

May, John R. "Vonnegut's Humor and the Limits of Hope." *Twentieth Century Literature* 18 (1972): 25–36.

May, Lary. *Recasting America: Culture and Politics in the Age of Cold War*. University of Chicago Press, 1988.

Mehnert, Klaus. *The Russians and Their Favorite Books*. Hoover Institution and Stanford University Press, 1983.

Mellard, James M. "The Modes of Vonnegut's Fiction: Or, Player Piano Ousts Mechanical Bride and The Sirens of Titan Invade the Gutenberg Galaxy." In *The Vonnegut Statement*, edited by Jerome Klinkowitz and John Somer. Delacorte Press/Seymour Lawrence, 1973.

Mendel'son, M.O. *Amerikanskaia Satiricheskaia Proza XX Veka* [American Satirical Prose of the 20th Century]. Nauka, 1972.

Mendel'son, M.O. "Amerikanskii roman posle Khemingueia, Folknera, Steinbeka" [The American novel after Hemingway, Faulkner, Steinbeck]. *Novyi Mir* 8 (1975): 246–63.

Mikhailin, Vadim. 2002. "Perevdei menia zherez made in: neslol'ko zamechanii o khudozhestvennom perevode i o poiskakh kanonov" [Translate me through made in: a few remarks on artistic translation and on searching for canons]. *Novoe literaturnoe obozrenie* 1 (January 1, 2002): 319–39.

Miller, Arthur. "Banned in Russia." *The New York Times*, December 10, 1970, 47. Accessed February 14, 2025. https://www.nytimes.com/1985/06/09/opinion/vonnegut-in-poland-spirit-of-solidarity-lives-on.html.

Minchin, Aleksandr. "Kurt Vonnegut." In *21 Interviews*. Prometei, 2013.

Mirchev, A. "Inter'viu s Kurtom Vonnegutom" [Interview with Kurt Vonnegut]. *Kontinent* 51 (1987): 437–46.

Morse, Donald E. *The Novels of Kurt Vonnegut: Imagining Being an American*. Praeger, 2003.

Muliarchik, A. "Maiatnik kachnulsia vnov': Po stranitsam amerikanskoi prozy i publitsistiki" [The pendulum has swung again: Through the pages of American prose and publicism]. *Literaturnaia gazeta* 36 (June 25, 1975): 15.

National Coalition against Censorship. "Kurt Vonnegut: Remembering a Hero of Free Speech." Accessed February 14, 2025. https://ncac.org/resource/kurt-vonnegut-remembering-a-hero-of-free-speech.

Nudelman, Rafail. "Soviet Science Fiction and the Ideology of Soviet Society." *Science-Fiction Studies* 16, no. 1 (1989): 38–66.

Oldenziel, Ruth, and Karin Zachmann. *Cold War Kitchen: Americanization, Technology, and European Users*. MIT Press, 2009.

Orlova, Raisa. "Istoriia odnogo poslesloviia" [History of one afterword]. In *SSSR: Vnutrennie protivorechiia* [USSR: Inner contradictions] 13, edited by Valery Chalidze. Chalidze Publications, 1985. Accessed February 13, 2025. https://vtoraya-literatura.com/pdf/sssr_vnutrennie_protivorechiya_13_1985__ocr.pdf.

Orlova, Raisa. "O romane Kurta Vonneguta" [On Kurt Vonnegut's novel]. *Novyi Mir* 4 (1970): 179–80.

Orlova, Raisa, and Lev Kopelev. *My Zhili v Moskve* [We Lived in Moscow]. Ardis, 1988.

PEN America, "About Us." Accessed February 14, 2025. https://pen.org/about-us/.

PEN International. "Who We Are: History." Accessed February 14, 2025. https://pen-international.org/who-we-are/history.

Proffer, Carl R. "Introduction: American Literature in the Soviet Union." In *Soviet Criticism of American Literature in the Sixties: An Anthology*, edited and translated by Carl R. Proffer. Ardis, 1972.

"Protokol No. 9 Zasedaniia Sekretariata Leningradskoi pisatel'skoi organizatsii 25 aprelia 1974 goda" [Protocol No. 9 of the Meeting of the Board of the Leningrad writers' organization April 25, 1974]. *Revue des etudes slaves* 70, no. 3 (1998): 719–23.

Rabotnov, Nikolai. Diary entry for June 11, 1982. Accessed February 14, 2025. https://corpus.prozhito.org/note/19055.

Rackstraw, Loree. *Love as Always, Kurt: Vonnegut as I Knew Him*. Da Capo Press, 2009.

"Raisa Iakovlevna Rait." Archival inquiry (Spravka) No. 655/5-4. Provided to the author by the Russian State Archive of Literature and Art (September 25, 2019).

Rait, Rita. "Reflections on Kurt Vonnegut." In *Happy Birthday, Kurt Vonnegut: A Festschrift for Kurt Vonnegut on His Sixtieth Birthday*, compiled and edited by Jill Krementz. Delacorte Press, 1982.

Rait, Rita. *Robert Burns*. Molodaia Gvardia, 1959.

Rait-Kovaleva, Rita. *Chelovek iz muzeia cheloveka: povest' o Boris Vil'de* [Man from the Museum of Man: The Story of Boris Vil'de]. Sovetskii pisatel', 1982.

Rait-Kovaleva, Rita. "Kanareika v shakhte" [Canary in a coal mine.] *Rovesnik* 1 (1974): 16–19.

Rait-Kovaleva. Rita. "Kanareika v shakhte, ili moi drug Kurt Vonnegut" [Canary in a coal mine, or my friend Kurt Vonnegut]. In *Slaughterhouse five, or the Children's Crusade; Cat's Cradle; God Bless You, Mr. Rosewater, or Pearls before Swine; Stories*, by Kurt Vonnegut. Translated by Rita Rait-Kovaleva. Literatura artistike, 1981.

Rait-Kovaleva, Rita. "Nadpisi na knigakh" [Book inscriptions]. In *Ia dumal, chuvstvoval, ia zhil: vospominaniia o S.Ia. Marshake* [I thought, I felt, I lived: remembrances of S. Ia. Marshak], edited by B.E. Galanov, I.S. Marshak, and Z.S. Papernyi. Sovetskii pisatel', 1971.

Rait-Kovaleva, Rita. "Nit' Ariadny" [Ariadna's Thread]. In *Redaktor i perevod* [Editor and translation], edited by E.B. Kuz'mina. Kniga, 1965.

Rait-Kovaleva, Rita. "Tol'ko vospominaniia" [Just remembrances]. In *Vladimir Mayakovsky: V vospominaniiakh sovremennikov* [Vladimir Mayakovsky: In the recollections of his contemporaries], edited by A. Kozlovskii. GIXL, 1963.

Rait-Kovaleva, Rita. "Upushchennaia Liubov" [Missed Love]. Unpublished memoir dedicated to the memory of Kornei Chukovsky, Russian State Archive of Literature and Art 3401/1/630/3-4. (No date, 1970s.)

Rait-Kovaleva, Rita. "Vse luchshie vospominaniia..." [All the best memories....]. In *Trudy po russkoi i slavianskoi filologii IX: Literaturovedenie* [Works in

Russian and Slavic Philology IX: Literary Studies], edited by B.F. Egorov, Iu.M. Lotman, and V.T. Adams. Tartu State University, 1966.

Rait-Kovaleva, Rita. "Vstrechi s Akhmatovoi" [Meetings with Akhmatova]. *Literaturnaia Armeniia* [Literary Armenia] 10 (1966): 54–62.

Raleigh, Donald. *Soviet Baby Boomers: An Oral History of Russia's Cold War Generation*. Oxford University Press, 2011.

Richardson, Jack. "Easy Writer." (Review of *Slaughterhouse-Five* by Kurt Vonnegut, Jr.) *The New York Review*, July 2, 1970.

Richmond, Yale. *Cultural Exchange and the Cold War: Raising the Iron Curtain*. The Pennsylvania State University Press, 2004.

Ritter, Jess. "Teaching Vonnegut on the Firing Line." In *The Vonnegut Statement*, edited by Jerome Klinkowitz and John Somer. Delacorte Press/Seymour Lawrence, 1973.

Royce, Anya Peterson. *Anthropology of the Performing Arts: Artistry, Virtuosity, and Interpretation in a Cross-Cultural Perspective*. AltaMira Press, 2004.

Ryan-Hayes, Karen L. *Contemporary Russian Satire: A Genre Study*. Cambridge University Press, 2006.

Saal, Rollene W. "Pick of the Paperbacks." *Saturday Review* 53 (March 28, 1970): 34–6.

Safiullina, Nailya, and Rachel Platonov. "Literary Translation and Soviet Cultural Politics in the 1930s: The Role of the Journal Internacional'naja Literatura." *Russian Literature* 72 (2012): 239–69. https://doi.org/10.1016/j.ruslit.2012.08.005.

Saunders, Frances Stonor. *The Cultural Cold War: The CIA and the World of Arts and Letters*. The New Press, 2013.

Scammell, Michael. "The Azadovsky Case." *The New York Review of Books*, April 15, 1982. Accessed February 14, 2025. https://www.nybooks.com/articles/1982/04/15/the-azadovsky-case/.

Schatt, Stanley. *Kurt Vonnegut, Jr.* Twayne Publishers, 1976.

Schneider, Cynthia P. "Cultural Diplomacy: Hard to Define, but You'd Know It If You Saw It." *The Brown Journal of World Affairs* 13, no. 1 (2006): 191–203.

Scholes, Robert. *The Fabulators*. Oxford University Press, 1967.

Scholes, Robert. "'Mithridates, He Died Old:' Black Humor and Kurt Vonnegut, Jr." *The Hollins Critic* 3, no. 4 (October 1966). Gale Document Number: GALE|A133025607.

Sherry, Samantha. "Better Something than Nothing: The Editors and Translators of Inostrannaia literatura as Censorial Agents." *Slavonic and East European Review* 91, no. 4 (2013): 731–58.

Shields, Charles J. *And So it Goes. Kurt Vonnegut: A Life*. St. Martin's Griffin, 2011.

Shipler, David K. "Vonnegut's 'Slaughterhouse-Five' Staged in Moscow." *The New York Times*, January 13, 1976.

Shkapskaia, Maria. *Stikhi* [Poems]. Overseas Publications Interchange Limited, 1979.

Sicari, Ilaria. "Paratext as Weapon: The Role of Soviet Criticism in the Cultural Cold War." *Translation and Interpreting Studies* 15, no. 3 (2020): 354–79. https://doi.org/10.1075/tis.20081.sic.

Simukhov, V. "Stranstviia Billi Pilgrima" [The Wanderings of Billy Pilgrim]. *Trud*, March 10, 1976, 58.

Skorobogatov, Yana. "Kurt Vonnegut in the U.S.S.R." MA thesis, University of Texas at Austin, 2012. https://repositories.lib.utexas.edu/handle/2152/19910.

Skorodenko, V. "O bezumnom mire i pozitsii khudozhnika (Roman K. Vonnegata [sic.] Kolybel' dlia Koshki)" [On the absurd world and the position of the artist (K. Vonnegat's [sic.] novel Cat's Cradle)]. Afterword to *Kolybel' dlia Koshki* [Cat's Cradle], by Kurt Vonnegut. Translated by Raisa Rait-Kovaleva. Molodaia Gvardia, 1970.

Smith, Hedrick. "A Soviet Artist Displaying his Work at the 'second fall outdoor art show' near Izmailovo Park in Moscow." *The New York Times*, September 30, 1974, 73. Accessed November 22, 2023. https://www.nytimes.com/1974/09/30/archives/excited-russians-crowd-modern-art-show-russians-some-excited-others.html.

Snow, Charles P. *The Two Cultures and the Scientific Revolution (The Rede Lecture, 1959)*. Cambridge University Press, 1961.

"Soviet Tries Rights Activist." *The New York Times*, July 15, 1981, Section A, 6. Accessed February 14, 2025. https://www.nytimes.com/1981/07/15/world/soviet-tries-rights-activist.html.

Spechler, Dina. *Permitted Dissent in the USSR: Novy Mir and the Soviet Regime*. Praeger, 1982.

Stecopoulos, Harilaos. *Telling America's Story to the World: Literature, Internationalism, Cultural Diplomacy*. Oxford University Press, 2022.

"Telemost 'Moskva – Boston.' Iadernyi vek – kultura i bomba (1989.)" [Telebridge "Moscow – Boston." The nuclear age - culture and the bomb (1989.)] YouTube recording (68 min.). Accessed February 14, 2025. https://www.youtube.com/watch?v=Z9VfCeJ0YFc.

Tolstoi, Ivan. "V Parizhe umer pisatel' Vladimir Maramzin" [The writer Vladimir Maramzin has died in Paris]. *Radio Svoboda*, April 26, 2021. Accessed February 14, 2025. https://www.svoboda.org/a/31223756.html.

Turovsky, V. "Liudi I teni" [People and shadows]. (Review of "The Wanderings of Billy Pilgrim" at Soviet Army Theater) *Komsomol'skaia Pravda*, February 6, 1976.

Udell, Peter. "Brilliant Linguist." (Obituary of Efim Slavinsky) *Prospero* 5 (October 19, 2019): 11. Accessed February 14, 2025. http://downloads.bbc.co.uk/mypension/en/prospero_october_2019.pdf.

Vaingurt, Julia. *Soft Matter: The Poetics of Weakness in Late Soviet Socialism*. Northwestern University Press, 2025.

Vari, Alexander. "Introduction: Escaping the Monotony of Everyday Life under Socialism." In *Socialist Escapes: Breaking Away from ideology and Everyday*

Routine in Eastern Europe, 1945-1989, edited by Cathleen M. Giustino, Catherine J. Plum, and Alexander Vari. Berghahn Books, 2013.

Varshavskii, Viktor Il'ich. "Potok soznaniia" [Stream of consciousness]. Accessed May 21, 2020. http://is.ifmo.ru/important/_potok.pdf.

Verdery, Katherine. *What Was Socialism, and What Comes Next?* Princeton University Press, 1996.

Vinograde, Ann C. "A Soviet Translation of Slaughterhouse-Five." *Russian Language Journal* 26, no. 93 (1972): 14–18.

Vishnevetskaia, Iuliia, Ol'ga Andreeva, Vladimir Shpak, Iuliia Idlis, Vitalii Leibin, Konstantin Mil'chin, and Grigorii Tarasevich. "Genom russkoi dushi" [Genome of the Russian soul]. *Russkii reporter* [Russian reporter] 5, no. 283 (February 7, 2013). Accessed February 14, 2025.

Vishnevsky, S. "Kogda real'nost' absurdna..." [When Reality is Absurd...]. *Inostrannaia literatura* 2 (1975): 209–13.

Vladimirov, Leonid. "Soviet Censorship: A View from the Inside." In *The Red Pencil: Artists, Scholars, and Censors in the USSR*, edited by Marianna Tax Choldin and Maurice Friedburg. Unwin Hyman, 1989.

Vonnegut, Kurt. "Address to P.E.N. Conference in Stockholm, 1973." In *Wampeters, Foma & Granfalloons (Opinions)*. Delta Trade Paperbacks, 1999.

Vonnegut, Kurt. "Avoiding the Big Bang." *The New York Times*, June 13, 1982, section 4, 23. Accessed February 14, 2025. https://www.nytimes.com/1982/06/13/opinion/avoiding-the-big-bang.html.

Vonnegut, Kurt. *Boinia nomer p'iat', abo Dytiachyi khrestovyi pokhid* [Slaughterhouse-Five, or the Children's Crusade]. Translated by Volodymyr Dibrov and Lidiia Dibrov. Vydavnytstvo Staroho Leva, 2017.

Vonnegut, Kurt. *Boinia nomer p'iat', abo Khrestoviy pokhid ditei* [Slaughterhouse-Five, or the Children's Crusade]. Translated by Petro Sokolovs'kyi. Dnipro, 1976.

Vonnegut, Kurt. *Breakfast of Champions*. Dial Press Trade Paperbacks, 2006.

Vonnegut, Kurt. *Cat's Cradle*. Dial Press Trade Paperbacks, 2010.

Vonnegut, Kurt. "Irina Grivnina's Crimes against the Soviet State." *The New York Times*, October 19, 1980, Section 4, 20. Accessed February 14, 2025. https://www.nytimes.com/1980/10/19/archives/letters-our-wrong-answer-to-street-crime-a-crucial-gap-in-the.html?searchResultPosition=10.

Vonnegut, Kurt. "Istinnuiu bol' prichiniaiut lozh' i beschestnye postupki" [True pain comes from lies and dishonest deeds]. Passages from *Palm Sunday*, translated by Sergei Tartakovskii. *Literaturnaia gazeta* 10 (March 9, 1983): 11.

Vonnegut, Kurt. *Kolybel' dlia koshkyi, roman* [Cat's cradle, a novel]. Translated by A. Nemirova. Book Club "Klub Simeinoho Dozvillia," 2016.

Vonnegut, Kurt. "Lokhmatyi pes Toma Edisona" [Tom Edison's Shaggy dog]. Translated by Margarita Kovaleva. *Literaturnaia gazeta* 5 (February 2, 1972): 16.

Vonnegut, Kurt. *A Man Without a Country*. Random House Trade Paperbacks, 2007.

Vonnegut, Kurt. "Mne snilis' nashi potomki..." [I dreamed about our progeny...]. Translated by Sergei Tartakovskii. *Literaturnaia gazeta* 27 (July 7, 1982): 13.

Vonnegut, Kurt. *Palm Sunday: An Autobiographical Collage*. Delta Trade Paperbacks, 1981.

Vonnegut, Kurt. "Playboy Interview." In *Wampeters, Foma & Granfalloons (Opinions)*. Delta Publishing Co., 1974.

Vonnegut, Kurt. "Response to Foreign Literature's survey." *Innostrannaia literatura* 6 (June 1982): 189.

Vonnegut, Kurt. "Response to survey of world authors." *Voprosy literatury* 12 (1976): 21.

Vonnegut, Kurt. *Slaughterhouse-Five or the Children's Crusade, a Duty-Dance with Death*. Dial Press Trade Paperbacks, 2009.

Vonnegut, Kurt. "Telegrama Kurta Vonneguta" [Telegram from Kurt Vonnegut]. *Literaturnaia gazeta* 19 (May 9, 1975): 14.

Vonnegut, Kurt. "Writers, Vonnegut, and the USSR." *American PENewsletter* 17 (November 1974): 1–2.

Vonnegut, Kurt. *Zavtrak dlia chempionov* [Breakfast of champions]. Translated by Rita Rait-Kovaleva. AST, 2018.

"Vonnegut, in Poland: 'Spirit of Solidarity Lives On.'" *The New York Times*, June 9, 1985. Accessed February 14, 2025. https://www.nytimes.com/1985/06/09/opinion/vonnegut-in-poland-spirit-of-solidarity-lives-on.html.

"Vonnegut to Russia." *American PENewsletter* 16, October, 1974.

Vowinckel, Annette, Marcus M. Payk, and Thomas Lindenberger, eds. *Cold War Cultures: Perspectives on Eastern and Western European Societies*. Berghahn Books, 2012.

Vul'f, V. "SShA: Molodezh', kul'tura, mir" [USA: Youth, culture, peace]. *Sovetskaia Kul'tura* 48, no. 4640 (June 15, 1973): 7.

Wakefield, Dan, ed. *Kurt Vonnegut—Letters*. Dial Press Trade Paperbacks, 2014.

Walker, Gregory. *Soviet Book Publishing Policy*. Cambridge University Press, 1978.

Whitfield, Stephen J. *The Culture of the Cold War*. 2nd ed. Johns Hopkins University Press, 1996.

Young, Jekaterina. *Sergei Dovlatov and His Narrative Masks*. Northwestern University Press, 2009.

Yurchak, Alexei. *Everything Was Forever, Until it Was No More: The Last Soviet Generation*. Princeton University Press, 2005.

Zasurskii, Iasen. "V poiskakh pravdy" [In search of truth]. *Literaturnaia gazeta* 27 (July 5, 1978): 15.

"Zolushka v lagere dlia voiennoplennykh. Chast' 1, 2" [Cinderella in the concentration camp. Part 1, 2]. (Script of the "Cinderella" libretto from *The*

Wanderings of Billy Pilgrim.) Accessed February 14, 2025. http://www.bards.ru/archives/part.php?id=47773.

Zverev, Alexei. "De profundis Kurt Vonneguta" [Kurt Vonnegut's de profundis]. *Inostrannaia literatura* 8 (1970): 265–8.

Zverev, Alexei. "Signal prodesterezheniia" [Warning signal]. In *Boinia nomer piat', ili Krestovyi pokhod detei, i drugie romany* [Slaughterhouse-Five, or the Children's crusade, and other novels], by Kurt Vonnegut. Khudozhestvennaia literatura, 1978.

Index

Note: Page numbers followed by 'n' denotes note numbers

Aitmatov, Chingiz 169, 209–10, 254
Akhmatova, Anna 12, 40, 43
Aksyonov, Vassily 110, 238
Aliakrinskii, O. 204–5
Amalrik, Andrei 98, 128, 171, 244–5
arms race 197, 199–200, 209
Azadovsky, Konstantin 14, 129, 219, 225
   friendship with Rita Rait 65, 222
   imprisonment 229–30
   role in Vonnegut's visits to the USSR 225, 227–8

Bestuzhev-Lada, Igor 31, 214
black humor 62, 107, 112, 115, 122, 240
   Vonnegut as "black humorist" 202–6
Bokonon 15, 57, 137–8, 142
   Bokononism 34 n.30, 102 n.3
Böll, Heinrich 99, 110, 211, 232
   Rita Rait's translations 33, 45, 160–1, 224
borba za mir 16, 166, 168, 207
Borshchagovskii, Aleksandr 191, 197
Breakfast of Champions 85, 104, 129–30, 138, 141–2, 149, 193, 264–5
   censorship in the Soviet translation 76–83
   Rita Rait's translation 27, 31, 57, 139, 148, 223–4, 226–7

Brezhnev, Leonid 6, 113, 118, 190 n.11, 252
Brik, Lili 41, 55, 62–3, 95 n.20, 98, 170 n.26
   friend of Rita Rait 37, 39
Bryusov, Valery 38, 46, 48, 122, 229
Bulgakov, Mikhail 12, 22, 122, 124, 138
   comparisons with Vonnegut 2, 107, 126, 141
   in samizdat 7
Burns, Robert 43, 50–1, 54

capitalism 26, 44, 116, 129, 142, 166, 259
   critique in Vonnegut's work 66, 73, 128, 192–3, 195–6, 206, 210, 214, 265
Cat's Cradle 1, 11, 25, 31, 33, 86, 105, 189, 197, 223–4, 227, 260
censorship 7, 30, 169, 171–2, 189, 212, 216, 237, 251, 257
   "naturalism" 75
   Rita Rait's translation 22, 27, 57–8, 62, 67–9, 71, 79, 81, 85, 91, 130, 139, 226
   Soviet reader impressions 114–16, 129–30, 133–4
   Soviet practices 45, 71–6
   translations 11, 15, 48
   translations of Vonnegut 12, 31, 76–86
Chernomordik, Raisa. *See* Rait, Rita
Chronicle of Current Events 7, 110, 245

Chukovsky, Kornei 34, 46–9, 51–2, 63
Cold War 2–3, 9, 13, 43, 67, 94, 96, 101, 117, 142, 166, 178, 192, 207, 209, 232, 236, 256, 263–4
 culture 3–4, 11, 30, 61, 177
 cultural diplomacy 17, 43, 94, 177
 Vonnegut's role in 2, 9–14, 16, 142, 237

Daniel, Yuli 65, 233 n.5, 234, 248
Dashkevich, Vladimir 150–1, 161, 167, 175
Deadeye Dick 115–16, 209
détente 5, 17, 43, 105, 264
dissidents 1–2, 6, 9, 15–16, 86, 110, 127, 161, 182, 229
 Rita Rait's support 64–5
 Vonnegut's advocacy for 14, 99, 128, 213, 216–17, 231–3
Dobrynin, Anatoly 243, 249–50
Dostoyevsky, Fyodor 25, 117, 124, 140–1, 187 n.1
Dovlatov, Sergei 2
 contacts with Vonnegut 16, 230, 232–41, 252
 on Vonnegut 58–9, 191

El'sberg, Ia. 187, 193

Faulkner, William 4, 6, 22, 108, 111–12, 117, 196
 Rita Rait's translations 1, 44–6, 58, 225
Fiene, Donald M. 10–11, 14, 29–32, 35–6, 57, 64, 67, 75, 86–7, 92–3, 97, 101, 117–18, 138, 140–1, 150, 164, 173–4, 178–9, 184–5, 192, 194–5, 197, 216, 233, 252–3, 259–61, 266
 background and education 25, 27
 correspondence with Rita Rait 22, 25–8, 33–4, 52, 54, 56–8, 63, 67, 69–71, 74, 80–1, 89, 96, 98–9, 103–4, 129–30, 157, 177, 179–80, 186–7, 206–7, 210, 225, 251
 correspondence with Vonnegut 1, 22–3, 61, 74, 83, 85, 89–90, 156, 158, 171, 190, 215, 219, 221, 226, 241–2, 244–6, 249–50
 political views 26
 visits to the Soviet Union 27, 173, 177, 185–6, 188, 246
Foreign Literature (*Inostrannaia literatura*) 6, 65, 143–5, 150, 252
 editorial practices 74–5
 publication of foreign authors 25–6, 43–4
 publishing Vonnegut 115, 208
 readership 109, 111, 131–2
 Rita Rait's work with 57, 63, 80, 223–4

Gapova, Elena 107, 109
Gilburd, Eleonory 4, 6, 111
Ginzburg, Alexander 99, 128, 244–7
Glavlit 7–8, 73–4, 76, 85
God Bless You, Mr. Rosewater 85, 193, 226, 265
 Soviet translations 27, 31, 61, 81, 130
Gogol, Nikolai 141, 220
Great Terror 5–6, 43–4
Grivnina, Irina 220, 229–30, 246–50, 257

Happy Birthday, Wanda June 27, 196
Hemingway, Ernest 4, 6, 11–12, 22, 44–5, 48
 impact on Soviet readers 4, 8–9, 108–10, 112

humanism 36, 108, 168, 181, 210
  in Vonnegut's work 116–18,
    127, 141, 176, 182, 194–5, 206,
    264

Jailbird 81, 113, 202

karass 34, 57, 101–2, 133, 137,
    241
Kashkin, Ivan 46, 48–9, 60
Khmelnitsky, Michael 12, 85, 131,
    189–90
  analyzing Rita Rait's translations
    of Vonnegut 61, 76–8, 81,
    83–4
Khrushchev, Nikita 4–6, 9, 11, 43,
    65, 239. *See also* Thaw
Kim, Yulii 14–15, 150–1, 161,
    164–5, 171, 174
Kovaleva, Margarita (daughter of
    Rita Rait) 39–41, 56, 150–1,
    170, 225, 259
  translating Vonnegut 71, 85,
    115, 123, 187, 202, 222
Krementz, Jill 58, 90–1, 93–4,
    183
  travels to the Soviet Union 57,
    143–4, 146–7, 150–1, 155
Kudriavtseva, T. 143–6, 150, 154
Kyiv 8, 15, 86, 147, 261, 263
  informant experiences in 8, 103,
    108, 124, 132, 136

Lawrence, Seymour (Sam) 14, 149,
    215, 219–21, 225, 227
Leighton, Lauren G. 150, 179, 216,
    252–3, 255
  involvement in Efim Slavinsky's
    case 242–4
  on Rita Rait's translations of
    Vonnegut 28, 56, 60–1, 81,
    84, 138–9
  writings on translations in the
    USSR 11, 72–3

Leningrad 9, 39–41, 49, 103, 115,
    119, 137, 147, 161, 174, 228,
    237–9
  literary center 241–2
  Soviet publishing center 7, 85–6
  Vonnegut's trips to 19–23, 28,
    219–20, 222, 225, 229, 246,
    248–9, 254
Levitin, Mikhail 70, 157, 201, 266
  friendship with Rita Rait 59, 63,
    65, 161
  meeting Vonnegut 150–1
  staging *The Wanderings of Billy
    Pilgrim* 14–15, 117, 161–5,
    167, 169–75, 177–8, 180,
    182–5
literalism 47–9
Literary Gazette (*Literaturnaia
    gazeta*) 7, 66, 131, 167, 209,
    234, 252
  on Vonnegut 194, 196, 212
  Vonnegut's work published 189,
    199–200, 202, 213
Lozinsky, Mikhail 46–7

Maramzin, Vladimir 238, 241–2
Marshak, Samuil 46, 49–51
Marxism-Leninism 75, 140, 194–5
Mayakovsky, Vladimir 33, 35–40,
    50, 122, 162
Mendel'son, M. O. 190, 193
Meyerhold, Vsevolod 162, 172,
    179, 184
Miller, Arthur 44, 158, 232, 236,
    253
Moscow 1, 4, 11, 14, 22, 33, 37–9,
    41, 51, 54, 89, 101, 237, 263–5
  informant experiences in 9, 15,
    21, 109, 121, 132
  publishing center 7, 85–6
  Vonnegut's visits 28, 57, 64,
    82–3, 96, 143–58, 165, 167,
    200, 214–16, 219, 223, 231,
    241–2, 244, 252, 254

Index

Moscow Helsinki Group 236, 245
Mother Night 70–1, 172, 198, 261

Nabokov, Vladimir 29–30, 40, 232
New World (*Novyi Mir*) 7, 46, 62, 66, 131, 167
  publishing Vonnegut 68–9, 84–5, 192
Nixon, Richard 4, 11, 22–3, 89

O'Hare, Bernard 19, 21–3
ostranenie 138–40

pacifism 16, 65–9, 180–1, 207–11. *See also* Borba za mir
Pasternak, Boris 37, 39, 43, 46, 229
PEN (literary associations) 98–9, 145, 149, 231–6, 244, 256–7
Player Piano 140, 260
  Soviet translation 31, 68, 85, 123, 214
Prague Spring 2, 6, 8–9, 85, 127, 137

Rait, Rita
  approach to translation 12, 15, 28, 31–3, 46, 49–62, 75, 78–84, 102–5
  correspondence with Donald Fiene 25–8, 33–4, 52, 54, 56–8, 63, 67, 69–71, 74, 80–1, 89, 96, 98–9, 103–4, 129–30, 157, 172, 177, 179–81, 186–7, 206–7, 210, 225, 251
  correspondence with Vonnegut 98–9, 169–70, 251
  "domesticating" Vonnegut 12, 76, 78, 139, 142, 248
  during World War II 40–1
  family and background 34–41
  friendship with Vladimir Mayakovsky 36–9
  meetings with Vonnegut 28, 89, 91–4, 96, 144, 146–56, 214–15, 219–20, 222–3, 225, 227–8, 231
  political positions 64–5
  role in staging *The Wanderings of Billy Pilgrim* 159–61, 165–9, 172–4, 177, 181, 183, 211

Salinger, Jerome David 6, 22, 44, 110. *See also* The Catcher in the Rye
Rita Rait's translations 1, 12, 25–7, 45, 49, 51, 56, 58, 61, 221, 224–5
samizdat 2, 15, 245
  fiction 7, 110, 126, 238, 242
  "Book of Bokonon" 15, 137–8
Sarraute, Nathalie 45, 49, 54, 63, 89, 93–4
satire 36–7, 58, 61, 137, 184, 232
  Vonnegut as satirist 101, 122, 124–5, 191, 195, 197, 202–6, 210, 264
science fiction 9, 31
  elements in Vonnegut's work 62, 101, 103, 106–8, 115, 122–8, 201–2
Shcharansky, Natan 244–5, 247
shortages 128–32, 149
Shulga, Nataliya 103, 112, 114–15, 119, 132, 134, 259–60, 266
Simonov, Konstantin 120–1
  meetings with Vonnegut 144, 147, 151, 154–5
  role in staging *The Wanderings of Billy Pilgrim* 167–9, 171–2
Sinyavsky, Andrei 65, 233 n.5, 234, 248
Slapsticki 55, 69–70, 85–6, 265
Slaughterhouse-Five 14–15, 19, 105, 117, 129, 141, 168–9, 180, 191, 207, 212, 223–4, 239–40, 261–3, 265. *See also* The Wanderings of Billy Pilgrim
  censorship in translation 83–5

Rita Rait's translation 22, 25, 27, 57, 62, 69, 71, 76, 79, 91, 119, 210
Soviet publications 11, 22, 31, 68, 85–7, 130, 192, 222, 226
Soviet reviews 193, 195–8, 207, 211
Soviet readers 111, 119–21
Slavinsky, Efim 98, 228, 241–4, 255
Snezhana (informant) 125–6, 133–4
socialism 9, 70, 73, 75, 116, 122, 125–6, 128–9, 133, 136, 265
socialist realism 48, 206, 228 n.33
Solzhenitsyn, Alexander 2, 128, 141, 216, 243
  legal troubles and exile 231–4
  publications in the Soviet Union 84
  support of political prisoners 245–6
  works in samizdat 7, 110, 126
Stagnation (Soviet Union) 1–2, 5–8, 12, 110, 142
  Soviet citizens' experience 15, 101–2, 125–6, 137
  Soviet publishing 8, 72, 76, 86, 123
  stereotype 8
Stalin, Joseph 5–6, 43, 119, 122, 255
  Stalinism 47–8, 66, 86
strange making. *See* Ostranenie
Styron, William 64, 214, 235, 251, 253

technical intelligentsia 9, 15, 32, 106–7, 111, 122
Thaw (1953–1964) 86, 171, 239
  effects on Soviet culture 5–6, 9, 43–4, 111
The Catcher in the Rye 6, 8, 25–6, 45, 51–3, 109. *See also* Salinger, Jerome David

The Wanderings of Billy Pilgrim 15, 27, 104, 150, 211, 225
  "Cinderella" operetta 162–5, 175–9, 181–2
  reviews 177–82, 195
"thick journals" 2, 7, 45, 122, 129, 131, 202. *See also* Novyi Mir, Foreign Literature
Tolstoy, Leo 124, 139–40, 181
translation 2, 5–9, 15, 28, 45, 71–6, 80, 156, 190, 207, 221
  fallback for Soviet writers 12
  importance for Soviet culture 11, 13, 42–3, 111–12, 125–6, 142
  in non-Russian Soviet republics 85–7
  re-authoring 12
  Soviet schools 46–52
Tsvetaeva, Marina 43, 63, 229

Ukraine 15, 35–6, 86, 103, 114–15, 121, 132, 134, 259–65
Ukrainian language 14, 56, 71, 86, 140, 188, 265–6
Ukrainian SSR. *See* Ukraine
Uniform Copyright Convention (UCC) 68–9, 87, 149, 221–2, 226–7, 233
Updike, John 33, 158, 191, 251, 253

Vietnam War 2, 63–4, 135, 178, 180, 191, 193, 212
  Vonnegut's opposition to 66–7, 194, 196–201, 210
Vilde, Boris 30, 43, 54, 89, 93–4, 194
Voice of America (VOA) 2, 109, 174, 234, 249–51, 255
West 13, 43–4, 55, 71, 101–2, 117, 142, 157, 230
  role of concept in Soviet culture 4–9, 108, 110, 136, 142
  Soviet criticism 2, 12, 166, 190

World War II   3, 40, 43, 65, 89, 151,
    167-8, 179, 197, 209, 232
    impact on Soviet art and public
        life   4, 6, 16, 55, 118-19,
        121
    Vonnegut's experience   19, 55,
        66, 169, 200, 210, 254
Writer's Union (USSR)   41, 67,
    73-4, 89, 143, 151, 224, 241-2

role in Rita Rait's travel
    restrictions   17, 156-8
Translator's Section   63, 66
Vonnegut's interactions with   17,
    145-6, 148, 223, 225, 232-4,
    251-3, 255-6

Zverev, Aleksei   106, 187-8, 191,
    195